Fun Places to Go

with *Children* in

New England

4TH EDITION

Over 500 Listings, Completely Revised & Updated

By Diane Bair and Pamela Wright

CHRONICLE BOOKS

SAN FRANCISCO

For Charlotte, Connor, Sadie, and Jared

Library of Congress Cataloging-in-Publication Data available.
ISBN: 0-8118-3598-7

Manufactured in the United States of America
Cover design by Aya Akazawa
Maps by Ellen McElhinny
Illustrations by Willow Cook
Typesetting by Jack Lanning

Distributed in Canada by Raincoast Books
9050 Shaughnessy Street
Vancouver, British Columbia V6P 6E5

10 9 8 7 6 5 4 3 2 1

Chronicle Books LLC
85 Second Street
San Francisco, California 94105

www.chroniclebooks.com

Contents

Introduction

WE RECENTLY OVERHEARD a mature woman on a plane sniff, "Look at all these babies! In my day, we didn't travel with our children until they were at least three years old." Well, times have changed.

With an ever-expanding universe of fun places to go with kids, why stay home? *Fun Places to Go with Children in New England* is full of places we think—and our "test kids" think—are really neat, places you're likely to remember long after you've returned home. We've focused on attractions that are uniquely New England, such as boat cruises where kids can play "lobster-man for a day," a schooner cruise where you haul in and identify creatures of the deep, medieval castles to play "knight in shining armor," aerial train rides to mountain summits, and farms where you cannot only pet the animals, but help milk cows and shear sheep. The emphasis is on interactive fun, places where kids can get involved in the action, not just watch. And we looked for places where grown-ups will enjoy themselves. After all, it's your precious leisure time, too.

We admit a personal bias toward nature activities and outdoors pursuits. In this edition of *Fun Places,* we continue to expand our coverage of New England's outdoors and how to enjoy it. You'll find lots of places to view wildlife, go hiking, paddle a canoe or kayak, and tour on a bicycle. As mountain biking, kayaking, and snowboarding have become hot activities for kids, we've added lots of places where you can enjoy these sports. You'll also find our picks for best family beaches, "don't miss" attractions, and advice as varied as "Do you need a car on Block Island?" and what to pack for an incredible sunset picnic (including cheap transportation) on Nantucket Island. For convenience, we've updated prices (but be sure to check yourself as these change frequently) and added websites. As you navigate the book, please note that we have grouped the attractions according to neighborhood, rather than alphabetically. That way, you'll discover things to see and do within each area as you read. For example, the Boston Common Frog Pond and Freedom Trail are just a few steps apart, so we've included them in that order.

We invite you to get into the spirit of it all and enjoy. Rediscover the fun-loving kid inside you, connect with your own children, and have a great time discovering an incredible place for everyone—New England.

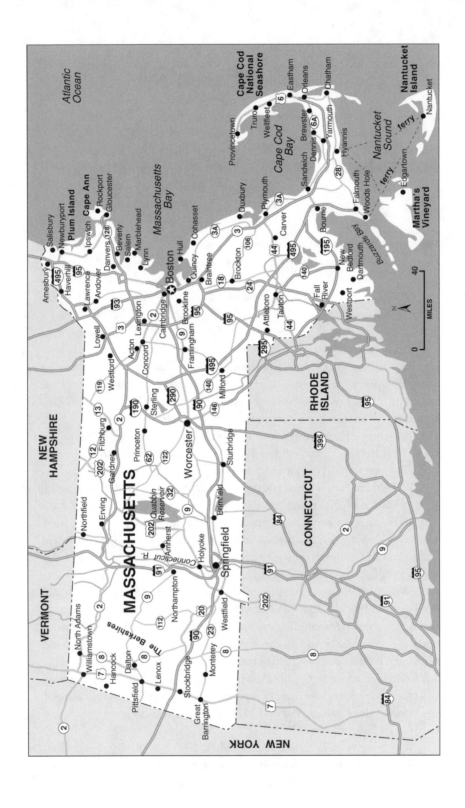

Massachusetts

■ Boston

Boston loves kids. It's colorful, it's walkable, and it's chock-a-block with appealing attractions and museums, some with tours designed expressly for small fry. Venerable institutions, such as the Museum of Fine Arts (opened in 1870), offer activities tailor-made for families. But Boston's history isn't confined to museums, it's everywhere you look. The site of the Boston Massacre, for example, is marked by a plaque in the street, while Mother Goose, everybody's favorite storyteller, is buried in a downtown cemetery. Year-round, the heart of the city is abustle with families: The Public Garden is filled with kids ice skating on Frog Pond in winter and gliding along Lagoon Pond in a swan boat in summer. Boston hotels are more child-friendly than they once were, and most offer special packages for families, including "kids stay free" offers, milk and cookies at night, and more. Once comfortably ensconced in your hotel or bed-and-breakfast inn, get ready to discover why Boston is one of the most popular tourist destinations in the world.

You've heard the phrase, "Pahk yah cah in Hahvahd yahd?" Forget about it. Boston's maze of narrow, one-way streets is best navigated by foot, trolley, or subway, not by car, since parking spaces are scarce. Don your most comfortable shoes (forget fashion; given Boston's climate and cobblestones, comfort and protection beats style every time), and start walking. When little feet get tired, board the "T." Boston's subway system is (relatively) clean and modern and will get you to all major points of interest in the city. Or board a trolley (most will let you hop off and on as much as you like for one fare) and pick up a few factoids about the city as you cruise. (An example of trolley driver humor: "Paul Revere had 16 kids. Guess that's why they called him a minute man.")

Before you visit, consider sending for the "Kids Love Boston" kit ($3.25), a packet that includes a city map and family discount offers, as well as a rundown of hotel packages for visitors traveling en famille. Contact the Greater Boston Convention and Visitors Bureau at 1-888-SEE-BOSTON or visit www.BostonUSA.com.

DOWNTOWN

● Museum of Science
Science Park, (617) 723-2500, www.mos.org. Daily, 9–5; Fri., 9–9. Exhibit halls: adults, $11; 3–11, $8. Planetarium, laser show, or Mugar Omni Theater: adults, $7.50; 3–14, $5.50. Omni Theater: adults, $7.50; 3–11, $5.50. **All ages.**

You won't want to miss this world-renowned museum, which has more than 600 participatory exhibits. The Computer Museum merged with this museum in 1999, providing a high-tech edge. (Example: Check out the virtual fish tank, where visitors can build and release an artificial fish into a giant simulated aquarium and then watch the surprising result.) Walk beside a humongous *Tyrannosaurus rex, see* live animal and physical science demonstrations, or test your wits in the computer center. Watch light bounce, bend, and beam in "The Light House." Don't miss the lightning show in the Theater of Electricity. The Mugar Omni Theater boasts the world's largest projection system and a four-story domed screen. It's the perfect venue for multi-image presentations such as "Bears" and "Shackleton's Antarctic Adventure." Even Hayden Planetarium is interactive; visitors don't just watch but actually design a celestial adventure. Nighttime laser shows, set to the music of rock bands, are a great hit with the preteen and older set.

● Museum of Fine Arts

465 Huntington Ave., (617) 267-9300, www.mfa.org. Mon. and Tues., 10–4:45; Wed.–Fri., 10–9:45; Thurs. and Fri., (West Wing only) 5–9:45. Sat. and Sun., 10-5:45. Adults, $14; 17 and under, free except during school hours. All fees Thurs. and Fri. after 5 P.M., $2 discount. Free to all (voluntary contributions accepted), Wed., 4–9:45. All general admission tickets include a repeat visit within 30 days. **Ages 6 and up.**

You'll probably be attracted to the Fine Arts for its terrific collections of Chinese, Japanese, Indian, Egyptian, Greek, Roman, European, and American art; happily, the kids can get a lot out of this wonderful museum as well. In the Children's Room, geared to ages 6 to 12, drop-in workshops highlight the museum's collections through dramatics, art projects, poetry, and music. (It's kids only here; you can tour the museum while they're busy with projects.) In the Family Place you can all get into the act by setting out on a museum scavenger hunt, for example. You'll meet at the Family Place, then explore the museum together. There's also a self-guided tour for families; you can pick up a booklet about this tour at the Information Desk.

Special note: May is Museum-Goers' Month in Boston. More than 40 area museums participate, with special events and exhibits, free days, and more, a real bonus for museum hoppers.

● Faneuil Hall Marketplace

Merchants Row, (617) 242-5642, www.faneuilhallmarketplace.com. **All ages.**

Amazing to think that Quincy Market, the centerpiece of this shopping and dining complex, was built as a trading center for produce and livestock. These days, herds of people (more than 10 million tourists a year) amble through the cafés and clothing stores and past pushcarts laden with all sorts of kid-tempting fare. Face it: If you visit Boston, you'll end up here at some point—it's practically the law. There are street performers galore, and they're good (they have to be—they audition for this plum position). Among their ranks: clowns and mimes, harpists, guitarists, and jugglers. This colorful, festive area has become a model for the restoration and conversion of older urban areas into shopping, dining, and entertainment centers. Little kids will want to check out the huge Disney store; older ones will have a grand time picking out the coolest souvenir T-shirt from among hundreds of possibilities. And once they discover there's a whole hall filled with nothing but delectable edibles— look out. Tip: While at Faneuil Hall, stop by the Bostix Booth to see what's happening in the arts around town; buy half-price, day-of-performance tickets here. They also serve as a full-service Ticketmaster outlet. Also located at Copley Square; call (617) 482-BTIX (recorded info) or visit www.bostix.org.

● Boston Duck Tours

Tours leave from Prudential Center on Huntington Ave., (617) 723-3825, www.ducktours.com. Daily, early Apr.–Nov. Tickets available 48 hours in advance, although they do save a block of tickets for same-day sales. Hotel concierges also have reservation privileges. Adults, $23; kids 12 and under, $13; 3 and under, $.25. **Ages 3–12.**

This is one tour of Boston that really makes a splash. The "ducks" in question are authentic WWII amphibious vehicles that take in most of the major tourist sites in town, then splash down into the Charles River for a brief cruise. The "conducktors" have no shame; they make goofy jokes, play kazoos, and honk at passersby. The coolest part (and a good photo op for families): Kids get to drive the half-boat, half-truck hybrid once it's in the water. This 80-minute tour doesn't take in all the must-sees, but it's great fun.

● Boston Common Frog Pond

Bounded by Beacon, Charles, Boylston, Tremont, and Park Sts., (617) 635-2120. Daily, 10–6 in July and Aug. for wading. Free. Open Mon., 10–5; Tues.–Thurs. and Sun., 10–9; Fri. and Sat., 10–10; from Nov. to mid-Mar. for ice skating. Adults, $2; 13 and under, free. **All ages.**

Every visiting family should make time to check out Boston Common, the oldest public park in the United States, located in the heart of the city. In colonial days the 48-acre space was pastureland for animals and training ground for the militia. Today you're likely to find street musicians, art exhibits, and plenty of local color. A highlight for families is a visit to Frog Pond. In summer, cool off tired tourist tootsies in the pond's 440-foot-long spray pool. The shallow water (just 6 to 18 inches deep) is a super wading spot for tykes. Swim diapers are required for toddlers (available at the concession stand). More family-friendly features: Lifeguards are on duty, treats are available, and the picnic tables have umbrellas. This is also the starting point for Boston's Freedom Trail. Pick up maps and information at the Visitors Information Center located on the hilly east side. In winter, enjoy a Boston tradition: ice skating on Frog Pond. Bring your skates (or rent a pair for $5) and warm up with cocoa in the Pond Cottage.

● Freedom Trail

Boston Common to Charlestown, (617) 227-8800, www.thefreedomtrail.org.
All ages.

If you really want to see downtown Boston, put on some sensible shoes and follow the red-brick road. Boston's Freedom Trail is a self-guided, 2.5-mile walking tour of 16 historic sites. A bold red stripe on the sidewalk, beginning at the Boston Common Visitors Information Center, leads visitors through the downtown financial and shopping district to Faneuil Hall, through the North End, and into Charlestown. Depending on how fast you walk, how many sites you see, and how long you stay at each site, the trail can take anywhere from two hours to a full day to complete. Pick up maps at Visitors Information Centers located throughout the city. Freedom Trail sites include: the State House, Park Street Church, Granary Burying Ground, King's Chapel, Ben Franklin's statue and site of the first public school, Old Corner Bookstore, Old South Meeting House, Old State House, site of the Boston Massacre, Faneuil Hall, Paul Revere House, Old North Church, Copp's Hill Burial Ground, the USS *Constitution,* and Bunker Hill Monument. You might want to pick and choose sites along the tour that best match your family's interests.

● Boston-By-Little-Feet

Starts at the statue of Samuel Adams in front of Faneuil Hall (Congress St. side) on Sat. and Mon. at 10 A.M. and Sun. at 2 P.M. throughout the summer, rain or shine, (617) 367-2345, www.bostonbyfoot.com. Per person, $6. Children must be accompanied by an adult. **Ages 6–12.**

This is a nifty idea, and we highly recommend it—it's an hour-long guided tour designed for children ages 6 through 12. It covers a major portion of the Freedom Trail and introduces kids to Boston history and architecture in a fun, participatory style. Kids get a special Explorer's Map with footprints leading to each location. This is a great way to introduce kids to the city of Boston.

● Public Garden

Bounded by Beacon, Charles, Arlington, and Boylston Sts., (617) 635-4505, www.cityofboston.com/parks. Swan boats: mid-Apr.–mid-Sept. Adults, $2; ages 2–15, $1. **All ages.**

An oasis of tranquility in the middle of a bustling city, the Public Garden is a wonderful place to relax and catch your breath before the next stop on your agenda. Sure to grab your attention, if you visit in season, are the swan boats, an enduring symbol of Boston. The swan boats have been delighting children since 1877. Do take a 12-minute ride and enjoy. This is the venue for Robert

McCloskey's *Make Way for Ducklings,* the classic children's story of a mallard family looking for a home. (The kids can even pose for a picture with bronze replicas of the story's characters.)

● Wheelock Family Theater

200 The Riverway, (617) 734-4760, www.wheelock.edu/wft.htm. Late Oct.–May. Performances Fri., 7:30 P.M.; matinees Sat. and Sun., 3 P.M. Tickets, $10–$17. **Ages 3–12.**

This is a 650-seat professional equity theater whose actors are members of the Boston theater community. The three main stage productions per year typically include a family musical, a children's play, and an adult drama or comedy. Multicultural, intergenerational casts add to the magic. Recent productions have included *Rebecca of Sunnybrook Farm* and *Trumpet of the Swan.*

● Boston Children's Theatre

Performances at C. Walsh Theatre, Suffolk University, 55 Temple St., (617) 424-6634, www.bostonchildrenstheatre.org. Performances Dec., Feb., Apr., and summer (outdoors). Matinees Sat., Sun., and Boston school vacations, 2 P.M. Tickets, $13–$17; summer performances free. **Ages 3–12.**

This is live theater, for children and performed by children. Local young actors star in three main stage productions a year, such as *Honk!,* the award-winning British musical based on Hans Christian Andersen's tale, "The Ugly Duckling."

● Jillian's

145 Ipswich St. (near Fenway Park), (617) 437-0300, www.jilliansofboston.com. Daily, til 7 P.M., for kids under 18. Prices are per game. **Ages 7 and up.**

By night, this is a billiards parlor that draws 20-something singles; by day, kids rule the high-tech fantasyland of virtual reality games, rides, darts, Pong-Pong, video games, and more.

WATERFRONT

● Children's Museum of Boston

Museum Wharf, 300 Congress St., (617) 426-8855 (info line), www.bostonkids.org. Daily, 10–5; Fri., 10–9. Adults, $7; 2–15, $6; 1-year-olds, $2; under 1, free. Fri., 5–9 P.M., $1 for everyone. **Ages 1–10.**

This multilevel space is fairly bursting with wonderful things to do; if the world were designed by kids, it would probably look a lot like the Children's Museum. Want to climb a rock gym, visit the home of *Arthur* the aardvark, appear on your own TV show, make giant bubbles, or put bones together to make a skeleton? It all happens here, and that's just a sampling.

Traveling exhibits and special events are always part of the fun, too. Many events are tied in with holidays and celebrate cultural diversity. At the Smith Family Playspace, set aside for kids ages three and under and their caretakers, tots can climb, play, and put together puzzles without the distraction of big kids.

Tip: The recycling center has lots of neat stuff (cheap) that's great for at-home craft projects.

● Boston Fire Museum

344 Congress St., (617) 482-1344. Open Sat., noon to 4. Free, donations accepted. **All ages.**

This former fire station features vintage apparatus and memorabilia.

● New England Aquarium

Central Wharf, (617) 973-5200, www.neaq.org. Mon.–Fri., 9–5; Sat., Sun., and holidays, 9–6. Adults, $13; 3–11, $7; under 3, free. IMAX movie ticket: 12–59, $7.50; 3–11 and seniors, $5.50; double feature, $12.50/ $9.50. Aquarium/IMAX combination ticket: $17.50/$11. **All ages.**

Appropriately set on the Boston waterfront, this attraction just gets bigger and better. The most striking feature here is the world's largest circular, glass-enclosed tank. At four stories high, with 187,000 gallons of water, this mega-tank houses its own coral reef, bringing sharks, rays, turtles, and hundreds of underwater creatures within inches of your face. At feeding time, five times a day, divers jump into the tank to feed the fish. Kids adore hand-dunking for crabs, shells, and starfish at the Tidal Pool. In the harbor, see harbor seals cavort. Dolphin and sea lion shows are included in the price of admission; someone is always chosen from the audience to get a sloppy sea lion kiss. The recently opened Simons IMAX 3-D theater is a whopping six stories high, measuring 65 by 85 feet. Look for science- and conservation-themed flicks like *Lost Worlds* and *Into the Deep,* the world's first giant-screen underwater film.

● HarborWalk

15 State St., (617) 242-5642. Daily. **All ages.**

Get in touch with Boston's shoreline on this two-mile, self-guided tour. Visit the National Park Service Visitors Center at 15 State Street for a map and brochure that includes tidbits on Boston's maritime history. Sites along the way include the New England Aquarium and the Children's Museum. Are you ready, Nikes? Start walkin'. . . .

● Boston Harbor Islands

Managed by National Park Service, (617) 223-8666, www.nps.gov/boha.

Tired of city sounds and sights? Consider a short ferry trip to one or more of the islands that make up the Boston Harbor Islands National Recreation

Area. There are more than 30 islands altogether; at this writing, 6 are reachable by public ferry. (Slated to open next: Spectacle Island.) Spend a day exploring an old fort, swimming in an ocean cove, hiking along wooded trails, and berry picking; each island has its own unique character. Several cruise companies will take you by ferry from Boston's waterfront piers to George's Island, home to an old fort. (See Boat and Whale-Watching Cruises.) Ferries also run from Salem and Hingham. From there, take a free water taxi to the other islands.

BACK BAY

● Skywalk

Prudential Center, 50th floor, 800 Boylston St., (617) 859-0648, www.prudentialcenter.com/tourist. Mon.–Sat., 10–10; Sun., 12–10. Adults, $4; 5–15, $3. **Ages 3 and up.**

Get a 360-degree view of Boston and beyond from the 50th floor of this 52-story building. Interactive exhibits feature Boston history; signs on the wall indicate points of interest.

● Where's Boston?

Copley Place, 100 Huntington Ave., (617) 267-4949. Mon.–Sat., shows on the hour, 10–5. Adults, $3.50; under 12, $2. **All ages.**

This multimedia show gives a quick, all-around introduction to the city's sights, sounds, and people.

● Mapparium

175 Huntington Ave., (617) 450-2000, www.tfccs.com. Tues.–Sat., 9:30–4; Sun. and holidays, 1–5. Free. **Ages 5 and up.**

Inside the headquarters of the First Church of Christ, Scientist, you'll find a 30-foot, walk-through stained-glass globe, an intriguing sight for adults as well as kids. Constructed between 1933 and 1935, the globe—the only one of its kind in the world—is made of 608 stained-glass panels.

BEACON HILL

● State House

Beacon St., Mon.–Fri., 10–4. Free. **Ages 6 and up.**

Samuel Adams laid the cornerstone for this gold-domed Boston landmark. Sitting atop Beacon Hill, the State House is now the seat of Massachusetts government. Two tours are offered; older children might enjoy the Legislative Process Tour that covers how laws are made; a historical/architectural tour features the Hall of Flags and House and Senate rooms. Be sure to pick up the special booklet for children at the tour desk.

● Museum of Afro-American History

8 Smith Ct., (617) 725-0022, www.aftromuseum.org. Mon.–Sat., 10–4,
Memorial Day–Labor Day; after Labor Day, daily, 10–4. Free. **All ages.**

Set in the African Meeting House, the oldest standing African-American church in the United States, this museum explores the abolitionist movement in Massachusetts. Exhibits feature the text of speeches by Frederick Douglass and other black leaders, the Underground Railroad, and Black America's fight for equality. Also look for contemporary exhibits of African-American art (recently, "Jubilation Quilts") and family events, such as Kwanzaa workshops.

● Granary Burying Ground

Tremont St., next to Park Street Church, (617) 542-3071. Daily, 8–4. Free.
All ages.

Step back into history and recall the lives and times of several American heroes. This is the final resting place of John Hancock, Samuel Adams, Robert Paine, and the parents of Ben Franklin and Paul Revere. Some say the grave of Mother Goose is also here.

● Black Heritage Trail

Guided tours (2 hours long) meet at Shaw Memorial, across from the State House.
Tours, Mon.–Fri. at 10, 12, and 2, Memorial Day–Labor Day. Donation
suggested. Also self-guided tours. (617) 742–5415, www.afroamuseum.org.
All ages.

This walking tour, covering about a mile and a half, commemorates the history of Boston's 19th-century black community, which settled in this part of Beacon Hill. The trail begins at the African Meeting House (8 Smith Center), the oldest black church building still standing in the United States, and continues through Beacon Hill. It stops at the Smith Court Residences, Abiel Smith School, George Middleton House, Robert Gould Shaw and the 54th Regiment Memorial, Phillips School, the home of John J. Smith, Charles Street Meeting Houses, Lewis and Harriet Hayden House, and Coburn's Gaming House. Pick up maps and information at Visitor's Information Centers throughout the city.

NORTH END

● Paul Revere House

19 North Sq., (617) 523-2338, www.paulreverehouse.org. Daily, 9:30–5:15,
mid-Apr.–Oct.31; 9:30–4:15, Nov. 1–Apr. 14; closed Mon., Jan.–Mar.
Adults, $2.50; 5–17, $1. **Ages 6 and up**.

Visit Boston without stopping by the Paul Revere House? Unthinkable. The famous patriot was living in this very house when he took his famous ride, shouting, "The British are coming!" This house is the oldest building in

Boston (built around 1680) and contains many original furnishings. Most visitors spend a half hour to 45 minutes here; with kids, you'll spend about half that time, we're guessing!

● Haymarket Square

Haymarket St., adjacent to Quincy Market, behind the Bostonian Hotel. Fri. and Sat., dawn–dusk. **All ages.**

If you're near Boston's North End on Friday or Saturday, you won't be able to miss this open-air farmers market. Push your way through the crowds and hear the staccato sales pitches of the vendors, amid the color and aroma of fresh produce, fish, and flowers. Bargains abound, especially at the end of the day. You might find fresh oysters on the half shell for a quarter apiece, or succulent peaches for a buck a bag. Yes, this can be a wild scene for kids, but it's pure Boston.

● Feasts and Festivals

North End (Hanover, Salem, and Prince Sts.), weekends throughout the summer. For schedule, call 888-SEE–Boston or visit www.bostonusa.com. **All ages.**

The narrow streets of the North End, Boston's "Little Italy," come alive with celebration, in honor of the saints. The statues are decorated, and the streets are blocked off to make way for pushcarts laden with pizza, sausages, pastries, Italian ices, and other treats. Add parades, music, and song and you have a colorful and lively outdoor festival. Walk over and join the fun. (See Annual Events for more information.)

● Scenic Strolls

Newbury St. and Beacon Hill. **All ages.**

Boston is a walker's paradise. You've probably visited several of the city's attractions on foot, or plan to; the following are suggestions for rambling along, with no particular itinerary in mind. After spending some time in Boston, you'll no doubt discover your own favorite spots to sit back and savor the city. Newbury Street, from Arlington Avenue to Massachusetts Avenue, is lined with antique shops, boutiques, unique stores of every kind (some not so unique), and restaurants. Sit at an outdoor cafe, visit an art gallery (if your kids are school-aged or are able to look but not touch!), window-shop, and people-watch. If you have time, meander down Marlborough Street (our pick as the most beautiful street in Boston); stroll down Commonwealth Avenue, a tree-lined promenade of parks; or walk over to Copley Square, where you'll see the impressive Trinity Church and the Copley Square fountain.

There's no other place in the country quite like Beacon Hill. The very first Bostonians resided here, and it's still regarded as a highly desirable residential location. This is a neighborhood of charm and antiquity, full of

18th- and 19th-century townhouses, cobblestone streets, courtyard gardens, brick walkways, and gas-lit lanterns. The best way to see it all is to wear comfortable shoes (most of the area is steep), start at Charles and Beacon Streets, and meander.

● Charles River Esplanade and Hatch Shell

Located off Storrow Drive, the Esplanade is a hub of activity when good weather beckons Bostonians outdoors. Join them and you'll see why this stretch along the river is perfect for walking or in-line skating, bicycling (along the Paul Dudley White bike trail), or simply grabbing a picnic and a park bench and watching the sailboats and sculls zigzag up the Charles. On summer evenings, the action centers at the Hatch Shell, where there's often an outdoor concert or (on Friday night) a free movie screening under the stars. This is also the site of Boston's giant July 4th fireworks gala, with dazzling pyrotechnics set to music by the Boston Pops. Tip: If you're visiting the city and plan to take in the fireworks, be warned: Local folk stake out their little plot of ground in the wee, wee hours, and make a day of it, playing Frisbee, picnicking, and so on. The crowd swells to half a million or so, which can get pretty crazy when everybody tries to leave at the same time. So, if you're doing this with small fry, plan to bug out a few minutes early to beat the rush (you'll still hear the 1812 Overture and see the 'works!).

● Sports Museum of New England, Boston

Fleet Center, Causeway St., (617) 624-1234, www.sportsmuseum.org.
Tues.–Sat., 11–5; Sun., 12–5. Adults, $5; 6–17, $4; 6 and under, free.
Ages 6 and up.

Pay homage to local boy/baseball legend Ted Williams and other New England sports heroes at this exhibition space in Fleet Center. You'll relive some of the greatest moments in New England sports history here, featuring all-star names like Bobby Orr, Larry Bird, and Carl Yastrzemski. Sections are devoted to hockey, basketball, baseball, and football; there's also space for temporary exhibits and bronze sculptures of sports heroes. Check out what's in the gym lockers of Pedro Martinez, Nomar Garciaparra, and Mo Vaughn.

● Boat and Whale-Watching Cruises

Discover a humpback whale playground, visit the Boston Harbor Islands, or board a ship that will take you to the tip of Cape Cod and back again. A number of cruise companies offer several options for folks who want a view of Boston from the water. All depart from points along Boston's waterfront piers; call ahead for schedules and rates. A good option for families: the 55-minute, narrated cruise of Boston's inner harbor offered by **Bay State Cruise Co.** Departing from Long Wharf, it's just the right length for kids.

Call (617) 748-1428; www.baystatecruisecompany.com. Other good trips are offered by **A.C. Cruise Line,** (800) 422-8419, www.a.c.cruiseline.com; **Boston Harbor Cruises,** (617) 227-4321, www.bostonharborcruises.com (no charge for kids under 12 on some of their tours); and **New England Aquarium Whale Watch & Harbor Cruises,** (617) 973-5281, www.neaq.org. If this is your first whale-watch trip, be prepared; it's colder out there than you'd expect, so bring extra layers. The trip to Jeffrey's Ledge or Stellwagen Bank (the whales' favorite local feeding grounds) can be a bit roll-y, so seasickness is common. If you or yours are prone to this malady, take precautions, because the boat won't turn around even if you turn green.

● Sailing

Community Boating, 21 David Mugar Way, Boston, (617) 523-1038, www.community-boating.org. Mid-June through third week in Aug., weekdays, 1–sunset; weekends and holidays, 9–sunset. **Ages 10–18.**

If you're a sailing family, you've probably spotted the Tech dinghies and other craft dotting the Charles River. With Boston on one side and Cambridge on the other, sailors enjoy wonderful views from port and starboard. You can join 'em. **Community Boating,** off Storrow Drive on the Esplanade in Boston, offers two-day visitor memberships for $100, allowing you the use of a 16-foot Mercury sailboat. Community Boating is a nonprofit organization dedicated to teaching local youngsters (ages 10-18) to sail or row for just $1 per 10-week summer season. Instructors are certified sailing teachers and also certified in First Aid and CPR. Students (with parental permission) get lessons and use of boats from 9 A.M. to 3 P.M., Monday through Friday. A 75-yard swim test is required.

● Boston Sports

While other cities have built mega-stadiums, Bostonians revere tiny, classic Fenway Park, home of the Red Sox, as an enduring symbol of the city. This intimate setting, with its in-your-face action, is perfect for kids. Want to get behind the scenes and learn the secrets of the Green Monster? Go on a behind-the-scenes tour and visit places normally off-limits to the public, such as the dugout, the press box, and private suites—perfect for the young BoSox fanatic. Tours run weekdays at 9, 10, 11, 12, and 1 (also 2 P.M. on nongame days). No tours are scheduled when there is an afternoon game or on weekends and holidays. Call (617) 236-6666.

Would you rather see the Celts or the "Broons"? Perhaps the "Pats"? Or maybe the Boston Breakers, Boston's hot new professional women's soccer team? The Celtics and Bruins play in the Fleet Center, while the New England Patriots do their thing in the new CMGI Stadium, about 24 miles south of Boston. The Boston Breakers play at Boston University's Nickerson Field, easily reachable via the MBTA's green line. Just pick your favorite spectator sport—Beantown is well known for its championship teams (not to mention enthusiastic fans). For tickets and information, call the following numbers: **Boston Red Sox,** (617) 482-4SOX, www.redsox.com; **Boston Celtics,** (617) 624-1000, www.nba.com/celtics; **Boston Bruins,** (617) 624-1000, www.bostonbruins.com; **New England Patriots,** (508) 543-1776, www.patriots.com; **Boston Breakers,** (781) 292-1017, www.bostonbreakers.com.

JUST OUTSIDE BOSTON

● Franklin Park Zoo

Franklin Park, off Blue Hill Ave., Dorchester, (617) 541-LION, www.zoonewengland.com. Mon.–Fri., 10–5; Sat., Sun. and holidays, 10–6. May close during winter due to funding cutbacks; call first to inquire. Adults, $7; 2–15, $4; under 2, free. **All ages.**

Just outside the city, this state-of-the-art zoo is something special. The centerpiece is a dazzling three-acre African Tropical Rainforest pavilion. The setting is so authentic that it has 60 to 70 percent humidity and occasional rainstorms! Other features include an aviary, a children's zoo with New England farm animals, and a waterfowl pond. Residents include a pair of African warthogs named Elvis and Priscilla. Special events include the annual Zoo Bash, when *Sesame Street* characters join the fun with songs, shows, and lots of photo opportunities. Ride the Zoo Mobile from Faneuil Hall Marketplace or Copley Square; call the zoo for details.

● Harvard's Museum of Natural History

26 Oxford St., Harvard University, Cambridge; (617) 495-3045, www.hmnh.harvard.edu. Mon.–Sat., 9–5; Sun., 1–5. Adults, $6.50; students, $5; 3–13, $4; free Sat., 9–12, Wed., 3–5, and Sun., 9–12 from Sept.–May. **Ages 3 and up.**

If you're visiting Harvard, don't miss this four-museum complex. The site encompasses the Museum of Comparative Zoology, the Botanical Museum, the Mineralogical-Geological Museum, and the Peabody Museum of Archaeology and Ethnology (across the street). Most fun for kids: the four large rooms full of bones, skeletons, and trilobites at the zoology museum. (Lots of mounted specimens, too, ewwww!) Junior rock hounds will be wowed by the massive specimens of gemstones and crystals (including diamonds in the rough) in the Mineralogical-Geological Museum. Look for temporary installations, as well. The Peabody is a good bet for school-aged kids, offering intriguing exhibits like the recent "Bushmen of the Kalahari."

● MIT Museum

265 Massachusetts Ave., Cambridge, (617) 253-4444, www.mit.edu/ museum. Tues.–Fri., 10–5; Sat. and Sun., 12–5. Closed major holidays. Adults, $5; students/under 18, $1. **Ages 6 and up.**

Never let it be said that nerds lack a sense of humor. This rather quirky museum features the "MIT Hall of Hacks," celebrating great Techie "hacks" (pranks) such as putting a police car atop the Massachusetts Institute of Technology's Great Dome. Other ongoing exhibits include a holographic rainforest installation, "Math in 3-D" geometric sculptures, and "Robots and Beyond." For more, head to 55 Massachusetts Ave., home to MIT's Hart Nautical Gallery, featuring rare ship models, and a peek at ocean engineering at MIT.

● Bunker Hill Monument and Museum

Monument Ave., Charlestown, (617) 242-5641. Daily, 9–5. Free. **Ages 6 and up.**

This towering obelisk marks the site of the first major battle of the American Revolution. Poised on the summit of Breed's Hill, this 220-foot monument was built to honor those who died on June 17, 1775. Older children will love climbing the 294 steps to the top; join them and you'll be rewarded with a great view of Boston, not to mention a good workout.

● USS *Constitution* and Museum

Charlestown Navy Yard, Boston National Historical Park, Charlestown, (617) 426-1812, www.ussconstitutionmuseum.org. Open summer, daily, 9–6, rest of year, 10–5. Free. **Ages 6 and up.**

A visit to *Old Ironsides* can be an intriguing experience for families. The ship, originally launched in Boston in 1797, is the oldest commissioned warship afloat in the world. Climb aboard for a tour, guided by one of the ship's active-duty sailors, and you'll learn all about life at sea. Kids love peeking into the nooks and crannies and climbing the ladderlike steps. Even better, at the Constitution Museum children can play sailor-for-a-day. Several interactive exhibits and even a computer simulator allow you to be ship's captain.

● Bunker Hill Pavilion

55 Constitution Rd., Charlestown, (617) 241-7575. Daily, Apr.–May, 9:30–4; June–Aug., 9:30–5; Sept.–Oct., 9:30–4. Adults, $3; under 16, $1.50. Family rate (2 adults, up to 4 children ages 16 and under), $8. **Ages 6 and up.**

During your visit to the USS *Constitution* stop by the Bunker Hill Pavilion. Catch "The Whites of Their Eyes," one of the liveliest half-hour history lessons you're likely to encounter. This multimedia presentation on the Battle of

Bunker Hill is both entertaining and informative. You'll find yourself rooting for the badly outnumbered colonists who fought bravely until their ammunition was gone—an example of stubborn Yankee pride in action.

● Museum of Transportation and Larz Anderson Park

15 Newton St., Brookline, (617) 522-6547, www.mot.org. Park: year-round, daily. Museum: Tues.–Sun., 10–5. Adults, $5; 5–16, $3; under 5 free.
All ages.

Larz Anderson Park, located about 15 minutes west of Boston, is a lovely urban oasis where you'll always find children somersaulting on the vast lawn or skipping rocks on the pond. In winter, the rolling hills are a favorite sledding spot for local kids, and you'll get a great view of the Boston skyline in the distance. Don't leave without a visit to the Transportation Museum, also on the grounds. Rare and unique automobiles are housed in an 1888 carriage house. Kids can climb on cars and motorcycles, test their wits on the scavenger hunt auto quiz, or try out an antique bicycle. Special events might include a Model T Convention or Ferrari Fun Day; special exhibits feature subjects such as "Wild in the Streets," a celebration of "muscle" cars enhanced with Beach Boys music and surfing videos.

● Puppet Showplace

32 Station St., Brookline, (617) 731-6400. Sept.–June, Sat. and Sun., 1 and 3 P.M.; July and Aug., performances also on Wed. and Thurs. at 1 P.M. Additional shows scheduled during school vacation weeks. Tickets, $8.
Ages 5 and up.

Fairies, folk tales, fun, and fantasy all await you at Puppet Showplace in Brookline (a short "T" ride from Boston). Recent productions, featuring marionettes and puppets, have included Jabberwocky, Jack and the Beanstalk, Puss in Boots, and Snow White. Shows are designed for children ages five and up.

● Blue Hills State Reservation and Trailside Museum

1904 Canton Rd., Rte. 138, 10 mi. south of Boston, Milton, (617) 698-1802, (617) 333-0690, ext. 223. Reservation open daily, dawn–dusk. Museum: Wed.–Sun., 10–5. Adults, $3; 3–15, $1.50; under 3, free.
Ages 3 and up.

Just south of Boston, this unique area boasts a series of massive granite domes (monadnocks) rising more than 635 feet. The 7,000-acre reservation offers 150 miles of hiking, riding, and biking paths. A network of trails leads to a panoramic overlook on Great Blue Hill. Some of these trails are rugged; if your group includes young children or inexperienced hikers, stick to the lowlands of this vast area. Houghton's Pond is a popular swimming spot, while Ponkapoag Pond is best for fishing. A trailside museum operated by the

Massachusetts Audubon Society features the natural history of the Blue Hills, including native animals, a Native American wigwam, a crawl-through log, and more. Cross-country skiing in winter.

● Stone Zoo

149 Pond St., exits 34N and 35S off I–93, Stoneham, (781) 438-5100, www.stonezoo.com. Apr.–Sept. Weekdays, 10–5; weekends and holidays, 10–6. Adults, $6; children, $4; under 3, free. **All ages.**

Located a short hop north of Boston on I-93, this zoo boasts a tropical rainforest exhibit with a huge aviary and a South American Grasslands exhibit featuring lovable llamas. Wolves, snow leopards, flamingoes, and reindeer are among the residents here. Kids adore the new Touchable Barnyard area. Everybody loves their Halloween party, Boo at the Zoo, featuring creepy crafts and a howling contest.

 RESTAURANTS

● Joe & Nemo's

138 Cambridge St., (617) 720-4342. Daily, 9 A.M.–11 P.M.; Sat. and Sun., 11–11.

Sink your teeth into "one dog all around" (a hot dog with onions, mustard, relish, and horseradish) at this seven-seat Boston landmark. Back in 1928, this dog cost just a nickel; today, Joe & Nemo's wieners start at 89 cents (the original will set you back $1.65). The place closed in 1961; now, happily, it's back. They also sell sandwiches, clam chowder, and baked beans. Look for another Joe & Nemo's stand at Downtown Crossing.

● Quincy Market

Faneuil Hall Marketplace, Merchants Row, (617) 242-5642, www.faneuilhallmarketplace.com.

Between the numerous food stalls and pushcart vendors you can find every imaginable foodstuff here. Baked beans, brownies, bagels, big bowls of chowda, and that's just the "b" category. Some of it's great, some of it is just okay, but it all makes great grazing. Stay away if you hate crowds. Grab a table in the center courtyard or sit outside on benches. Now, if you're looking for a real sit-down restaurant at Faneuil Hall, consider . . .

● Durgin Park

Faneuil Hall Marketplace, (617) 227-2038, www.durginpark.com. Daily, 11:30–10; Fri. and Sat., 11:30–10:30; Sun., 11:30–9.

Touristy as all hell? You bet. But this has been a Boston landmark since 1827. You'll get real Yankee cooking here—pot roast, succotash, Indian pudding—all served family style. Not for shy types; you'll be seated at long tables next to other diners, and the waitstaff will give you a hard time if you don't finish your vegetables. At one time, the servers were as crusty as the bread, which some patrons adored and others apparently didn't. These days, Durgin Park is trying a more friendly approach.

● Barking Crab

88 Sleeper St., (617) 426-7222. Sun.–Tues., 11:30 A.M.–9:30 P.M.; Thurs.–Sat., 11:30–10.

This super-casual seafood shack sits on Fort Point Channel on Boston's waterfront. Sit at picnic tables, dig into fishy things, steamed, baked, and fried. Their outdoor tables are *the* place to be on a sultry summer night.

● Chau Chow City

83 Essex St., (617) 338-8158. Daily, 9–2 A.M.

For children who love to eat with their fingers, we've got just the place. This bustling, three-floor restaurant in the heart of Chinatown is known for its dim sum. Choose whatever looks good, say, shrimp and pork dumplings, then nibble happily til the next tempting steam-table cart rolls by. You'll be charged per serving. Even the pickiest eaters should find something appealing.

● Pizzeria Regina

11½ Thatcher St., (617) 227-0765. Daily, lunch and dinner; Sun., 2–11.

Not just a pizza place but a Boston landmark. Families have been coming here for more than 40 years to enjoy the thin-crust pizza and soft drinks by the pitcher. It's rustic as can be, so if someone knocks over an orange soda, no big deal. Another great place for pizza is Santarpio's, at 111 Chelsea St., near Logan Airport in East Boston. Not the easiest place to find, but the pizza is out of this world. Call (617) 567-9468 for directions.

■ Lexington and Concord Area

Prepare to soak up some 1775 spirit, and lots of history, when you retrace Paul Revere's famous ride. This is where the American Revolution began. As you stand on North Bridge, it seems you can still hear that first "shot heard 'round the world," and as you walk past Battle Creek, you just might feel the presence of patriots long gone.

The historical landmarks are the big attractions in this area. But when children tire of history lessons, there are plenty of other things to do. Visit the top-notch Children's Discovery Museums in nearby Acton, hike to Henry David Thoreau's cabin on lovely Walden Pond, or surround yourself with gossamer-winged swallowtails at The Butterfly Place. A visit to this area is a popular day trip from Boston, but if you come from that direction try to avoid morning and evening rush-hour traffic, which can be horrendous. In fact, locals joke that if Paul Revere were to make the ride today, he'd probably be delayed and opt to call John Hancock and Samuel Adams from his cell phone. ("Sam? Hi, it's me, Paul. I'm stuck in traffic. The British are coming!") Or maybe he'd just e-mail.

● Minute Man Statue and Battle Green

This is the spot where dramatic events began in the early morning of April 19, 1775. The mounting tension between the British occupiers and the independence-seeking rebels finally erupted at a place now known as Battle Green. Leading the Minutemen onto the green was Captain John Parker, immortalized by the Minute Man Statue. Captain Parker's rallying cry: "Stand your ground, don't fire unless fired upon; but if they mean to have a war, let it begin here!"

● Minute Man National Historical Park

Off Rte. 2A, (978) 369-6993, www.nps.gov/mima. Apr.–Dec., daily. Free.
Ages 6 and up.

This 750-acre park spans three towns: Lexington, Lincoln, and Concord. Stop wherever you like; there are several visitors centers in the park, each with maps and helpful staff to guide you. A good place to start is Minute Man Visitor Center, off Battle Road, run by the National Park Service. Catch the "Road to Revolution" multimedia presentation and exhibits featuring the events leading up to that fateful day in 1775. Several times a day, rangers give programs on Concord's two revolutions, the 18th-century political rebellion and the 19th-century literary renaissance. Be sure to visit the reconstructed North Bridge, where the shot heard 'round the world was fired. Rangers give chats at the bridge daily, from June to October.

● Longfellow's Wayside Inn

455 Lexington Rd., Concord, (978) 369-6975, www.wayside.org. Daily, except Wed., 9:30–5:30. Adults, $1; 6 and under, free. **Ages 8 and up.**

Follow Battle Road (Route 2A) into Concord, and you'll see a number of historic houses. This inn/restaurant/museum was immortalized in 1863 by Longfellow in "Tales of a Wayside Inn." The property features three period-style museum rooms filled with 18th- and 19th-century objects in colonial settings. In nearby Orchard House, Louisa May Alcott wrote *Little Women*.

● Sleepy Hollow Cemetery

Rte. 62, Bedford St., Concord. **Ages 6 and up.**

Visit the grave sites of famous people. Some heavy hitters are buried along Author's Ridge, including Thoreau, Emerson, Hawthorne, and the Alcotts.

● Walden Pond State Reservation

915 Walden St., Rte. 126, Concord, (978) 369-3254. Daily, 8–7. Parking fee, $2. Donations accepted. **All ages.**

Round out your trip to the Lexington and Concord area with a stop at Walden Pond, and you'll see why Henry David Thoreau (along with Don Henley, the singer who led a battle to save it) was so moved by its beauty. This freshwater kettle pond has been around a long time, dug out of the landscape by an Ice Age glacier. At the north end of the pond, you'll find a wooded walking path leading you to the site where Thoreau's cabin was located. This is where he lived and wrote from 1845 to 1847. The cabin is long gone, but look for a replica at the parking lot. Pack a lunch and bring your swimsuits— across the pond, in the 150-acre Walden Pond State Reservation, is a large picnic area and swimming beach.

● Minuteman Commuter Bikeway

Park at public lot in Lexington Center; look for bike path signs. (781) 316-3090; www.massbike.org. **All ages.**

This 11.2-mile multiuse path runs from Cambridge to Bedford. Gets busy on weekends in summer and fall, but it's a pleasant pedal on weekdays, especially through Lexington to Bedford (head left out of the parking lot) and back.

● Drumlin Farm Wildlife Sanctuary

South Great Rd., off Rte. 117, Lincoln, (781) 259-9807. Grounds open Tues.–Sun., 9–5; closed Mon., except major holidays. Hayrides, weather permitting, Sun. 1–3, $1. Weekend demonstrations, 11 A.M. and 2 P.M. Adults, $6; children, 3–16, $4. **All ages.**

Drumlin Farm, owned by the Massachusetts Audubon Society, is a great back-to-nature escape. The 180-acre property is made up of pastures, fields, ponds, and woodlands. The best part is that farm animals live here in several barns, as do wild animals native to the region. Programs on nature, farming, and ecology are free with admission. Hayrides are a special treat. Special events include Harvest Days, Bird Seed Day, and school vacation week activities. The Audubon Shop has lots of neat and also environmentally correct stuff, like binoculars, bird feeders, games, and books.

● DeCordova Museum and Sculpture Park

51 Sandy Pond Rd., Lincoln, (781) 259-8355. Open year-round, Tues.–Sun., 11–5. Sculpture park: free; museum: adults, $6; 6–12, $4; 5 and under free. **All ages.**

Indoors, there's contemporary art, mostly by New England artists. For kids, the best stuff is outdoors, though, in the ever-changing gallery of 70 contemporary sculptures. Wander through 35 acres of landscape and ogle a giant fiberglass chicken with a "human" head and other interesting installations. Some of the sculptures are musical. This pastoral spot is also the setting for outdoor concerts and other events; call to request a schedule.

● Canoeing

Henry David Thoreau paddled the waters of the Concord River; why not give it a go yourself? Rent a vessel at **Concord Canoe Rentals** at South Bridge Boat House, Rte. 62, (978-369-9438) or put in yourself at the boat ramp off Lowell Road, then meander the flat waters. In minutes, you'll slip under the Old North Bridge at Minute Man National Historical Park. Keep paddling, and you'll soon see signs for **Great Meadows National Wildlife Refuge,** (978-443-4661). Since both of these sites are accessible along the river, this is an awesome way to sightsee. Look for places along the riverbank to pull out, stretch your legs, and explore. Back on the water, look for turtles basking on logs and the occasional great blue heron.

● Discovery Museums

177 Main St., Rte. 27, Acton, (978) 264-4200. During school year: Tues., Thurs., and Fri., 1–4:30; Sat. and Sun., 9–4:30. Children's Discovery Museum open Wed., 9–4:30; Science Discovery Museum open Wed., 1–6. Summer hours: Tues.–Sun., 9–4:30. Per person, $7; both museums, same day, $10; under 1, free. **Ages 1–8.**

What a find: two wonderful hands-on museums, right next door to each other in the town of Acton. This is no secret to local children, though. They love the cozy Children's Discovery Museum, housed in a 100-year-old Victorian. Best enjoyed by kids ages one to eight, it is full of delightful things to explore. The train room boasts an old-fashioned ticket counter, costumes, bells, and whistles. Tots will like climbing aboard the Discovery Ship, constructing wondrous structures in the Lego room, setting off a roomful of chain reactions, and listening to the sounds of a humpback whale. There are 10 exhibit areas in all, an afternoon's worth of fun and learning.

Located behind the Children's Discovery Museum is the architecturally unique Science Discovery Museum for kids ages six and up. The spacious, colorful building is full of interactive science exhibits. Build dams and waterfalls in the Water Discovery Room, make patterns with sound waves, shout in the echo tube. There are hundreds of things to discover. Kids have so much fun they don't realize how much they're learning about science and technology.

● Lowell Heritage State Park and National Historical Park

Market Mills, 246 Market St., Lowell, (978) 970-5000. Mon.–Sat., 9–5; Sun. 10–5. Canal boat tours: adults, $3; 6–16, $1. **Ages 8 and up.**

Travel a maze of canalways on river barges or hop an antique trolley to the 19th-century mill complexes as you learn about life during the American Industrial Revolution. As you tour the restored textile mills, you'll meet the mill girls and canal workers who first set the revolution in motion. The American Industrial Revolution began when Francis Cabot Lowell brought the power loom design to the United States from England. Situated on the Merrimack River at Pawtucket Falls, the town of Lowell had enough waterpower to create a cloth manufacturing industry. Walk the Esplanade along the river, stop by Market Mills with its changing displays and shops, or attend one of the special family programs held throughout the summer.

● Sports Museum of New England, Lowell
25 Shattuck St., Lowell, (978) 452-6775. Tues.–Sat., 10–5; Sun., 12–5. Adults, $3; 6–17, $2; under 6, free. **Ages 6 and up.**

Worth a stop if your kids are really into sports, this museum features exhibits saluting women in sports, the baseball cartoons of Gene Mack, baseball photos by Bill Chapman, and more.

● The Butterfly Place
120 Tyngsboro Rd., Westford, (978) 392-0955. Mid-Apr.–early Oct., daily, 10–4. Adults, $7; 3–12, $5. **All ages.**

Your kids will be awestruck by nature's beauty here, surrounded by hundreds of colorful butterflies. This 3,100-square-foot atrium is a living museum of North American species. Watch them in action here, where you'll see the most activity on sunny days, when butterflies are busiest.

● Nashoba Valley Ski Area
Powers Rd., Westford, (978) 692-3033, www.skinashoba.com. Open Nov.– Mar., 9 A.M.–10 P.M. Sat. and Sun. at 8:30 A.M. Lift tickets: adults, $30; children, $22. **Ages 3 and up.**

With 9 lifts and 13 ski trails (when fully open), Nashoba Valley is an attractive option for skiing families. Snowboarders have their own terrain park with a half pipe. Night skiing is offered, too. Lessons and rental equipment are available; facilities include a lodge, restaurant, and bar.

 RESTAURANTS

● Michael's
208 Fitchburg Tpke., Concord, (978) 371-1114. Daily, 11:30–10.

This small, busy Italian place serves lotsa pasta (try the chicken-broccoli ziti) along with steaks, chicken, and salads. It's friendly and reliable, and the portions are large enough for sharing.

● Brewhouse Café and Grill

Brewery Exchange, 201 Cabot St., Lowell, (978) 937-2690. Mon.–Sat., 11:30–3 and 5–10; Sun., 11–10.

This fun, casual eatery offers a full menu of steaks, seafood, sandwiches, and great homemade desserts.

● Old Worthen House

141 Worthen St., Lowell, (978) 459-0300. Daily, 9 A.M.–2 A.M.

Set in an 1830s building, complete with original woodwork and pressed tin ceilings, this is Lowell's oldest tavern and restaurant. All meals are under six bucks; try their award-winning chowder.

■ North Shore and North of Boston

Beautiful beaches, picturesque seaside towns, a colorful history—these elements make the North Shore a popular destination for families. Located just 20-plus miles from Boston, it's an easy day trip. Without wheels? These communities are reachable by the MBTA's commuter rail, running from Boston's North Station all the way to Newburyport.

Many visitors are attracted by oh-so-bewitching Salem. If you're among them, you won't have to look hard to find traces of Salem's grim past. (Even its high school athletic teams are called the Salem Witches.) Salem has numerous attractions and museums that recount the events of the witch hysteria of 1692 in vivid detail. The city would like you to know that it offers more than witches, though. Salem has a rich maritime history and a great museum (the Peabody Essex) where you can learn all about it.

Venture beyond Salem and you'll find nautical Marblehead, which calls itself the Yachting Capital of America and boasts a beautiful harbor; artistic Bearskin Neck in Rockport, home of the most-painted motif in America; two very different castles; and some of the best beaches in New England. (Expect to pay dearly for parking; $15 on weekends in season, at this writing. Once you're on that lovely swath of sand, gazing into the Atlantic, you'll probably decide you got a bargain.) You'll also find plenty of magic.

For information, contact the North of Boston Convention & Visitors Bureau, (800) 742-5306 or (978) 977-7760, www.northofboston.org.

● Le Grand David and His Own Spectacular Magic Company

Cabot Street Cinema Theater, 286 Cabot St., Beverly, (978) 927-3677. Year-round, shows every Sun. at 3 P.M. (doors open at 2:15). Adults, $15; 11 and under, $10. **Ages 6 and up.**

Enter the beautifully restored Cabot Street Cinema Theater and leave reality behind. Le Grand David and his troupe of 30 performers will delight you with comedy, pageantry, and fast-paced fun. The 2.5-hour show will be a bit long for the very young, but school-aged children will enjoy this delightfully retro magical extravaganza. Sit up front if you can. More nice surprises are a hand-painted puppet theater with performing puppets, magicians' props on display, and clowns bearing goodies.

● North Shore Music Theatre

Dunham Rd., Beverly, (978) 922-8500, www.nsmt.org. Call box office or check website for schedule of children's performances and matinees. Ticket prices vary. **Ages 3–12.**

This not-for-profit theater is a venue for musicals and celebrity concerts. It is also home to the Theater for Young Audiences program, committed to bringing theater to children. Annual productions include a full-scale Shakespearean play, student matinees of musicals, and a children's musical/concert series. It's a theater in the round, so almost every seat is a good one.

● Lynch Park

55 Ober St., Beverly, (978) 922-0720. Memorial Day–Labor Day. Parking fee. **All ages.**

This waterfront park has it all: a small beach, two wooden playscapes (one for toddlers), picnic tables, a big grassy field for kite flying and Frisbee tossing, and a snack bar. (It features Dick & June's ice cream, the local favorite.) Family concerts are held here most summer weekends in front of the band shell. Take a minute to meander and admire the beautiful rose garden.

● Peabody Essex Museum

East India Sq., Salem, (978) 745-9500, (800) 745-4054, www.pem.org. Tues.–Sat., 10–5; Sun., 12–5. Adults, $10; 16 and under, free. Includes historic house tour. House tour only (Apr.–Oct.): Adults, $6; 16 and under, free. **Ages 5 and up.**

World-renowned collections of maritime art and history and of Asian and Pacific art and artifacts are housed here, making the Peabody Museum an interesting place to visit. Children will most enjoy the special events and programs geared toward them. Past programs have included a maritime music festival, Morris dancing and sea shanty performances, sailor's knot-tying demonstrations, kite making, and a Doll's Day event, based on the annual Japanese holiday. The museum is currently undergoing a massive renovation, with plans to add new exhibits and programs. Call or check their website for a schedule of events.

● Salem Whale Watch

*57 Wharf St. (Pickering Wharf), Salem, (978) 741-0434,
www.salemwhalewatch.com. May–Oct. Adults, $29; under 16, $19; under
3, free with purchase of adult ticket.* **All ages.**

Watch the whales frolic from the decks of 110-foot-long *Super Ranger*.
Trips are about three hours long, heading out to Stellwagen Bank or Jeffrey's
Ledge (wherever the whales are eating!). From early May to mid-June, trips
are on weekends only; in midsummer through September, trips run daily,
with two daily trips (9 A.M. and 2 P.M.) offered on weekends. During October,
when the whales start their migration south, trips are offered daily at 11 A.M.
Dress warmly and don't forget the seasick prevention medication, just in case!
(See also Whale -Watching Cruises, in Gloucester).

● Salem Witch Museum

*Washington Sq., off Washington St., Salem, (978) 744-1692,
www.salemwitchmuseum.com. Sept.–June, daily, 10–5; July and Aug., 10–
7. Adults, $6; 6–14, $4.* **Ages 8 and up.**

The tour buses parked out front will clue you in. This is one busy place—
the most-visited museum in Salem. Probably one of the oddest "museums"
you'll ever visit, this multisensory presentation re-creates the witch hysteria
of 1692 with 13 stage sets, life-size figurines, eerie music, and voice-overs.
It draws no conclusions about the chilling events but asks visitors to "be the
judge." Outside the museum, you'll notice a large statue of a figure that looks
like a witch. It's not; it's Roger Conant, one of the first settlers of Salem,
garbed in a flowing cape. Nonetheless, most kids prefer to think of him as a
witch and willingly pose for pictures beside him. How can you not like a place
that implores you to "Stop in for a spell"?

● Witch Dungeon Museum

*16 Lynde St., Salem, (978) 744-9812, www.witchdungeon.com. Apr.–Nov.,
daily, 10–5. Extended hours during Salem's Haunted Happenings (Halloween).
Adults, $6; 4–13, $4. Combination ticket with New England Pirate Museum
and Witch History Museum: adults, $15; 4–13, $9.* **Ages 8 and up.**

Featured here is a live reenactment of a witch trial, based on actual
transcripts, and a guided tour of a re-created dungeon (and you thought the
Witch Museum sounded creepy).

● Salem Wax Museum of Witches and Seafarers

*288 Derby St., Salem, (978) 740-2929, (800) 298-2WAX,
www.salemwaxmuseum.com. July–Aug., daily, 10–10; Sept., 10–6; Oct.,
extended hours; Nov.–Mar., 11–4. Adults, $5.50; under 14, $3; 5 and
under, free.* **Ages 3 and up.**

In this era of virtual reality "this" and computer-generated "that," it's somehow comforting to know that kids still appreciate the humble wax museum. This attraction explores the city's colorful past with 50 lifelike wax figures. Startlingly well made, they're set in 13 tableaux, enhanced by music, sound, and lighting effects. There's also an interactive area where kids can learn how wax figures are made, make a gravestone rubbing from headstone replicas, try out a 17th-century jail cell, and learn to tie nautical knots.

● New England Pirate Museum

274 Derby St., Salem, (978) 741-2800, www.piratemuseum.com. Daily, May–Oct., 10–5; weekends only in Nov. Adults, $6; 4–13, $4. Combination ticket with Witch Dungeon Museum and Witch History Museum: adults, $15; 4–13, $9. **All ages.**

Did you know that pirates lurked off the Massachusetts coast in 1692? Some (gasp!) are still here, cavorting among the exhibits of high-seas plunder and shipwreck artifacts at the Pirate Museum. A highlight: an 80-foot-long pirate's cave, with a surprise at the end.

● Salem's Museum of Myths and Monsters

59 Wharf St. (Pickering Wharf), Salem, (978) 745-8383. Open May– Dec., Mon.–Fri., 12–4; Sat. and Sun., 11–5. Adults, $5; children, $3.50. **Ages 8 and up.**

What does this attraction have to do with Salem's history? Absolutely nothing; it does not even pretend to be educational. But for kids who have graduated from *Goosebumps* books to more bloodcurdling fare, these werewolves and vampires have squeal appeal. Walk through a "haunted maze," where detailed scenes feature animated monsters. It's creepy, but not truly scary—nothing reaches out and grabs you. In October, this place is transformed into a full-fledged haunted house.

● House of Seven Gables

54 Turner St., Salem, (978) 744-0991, www.7gables.org. Year-round, except first three weeks of Jan. Apr.–June, daily, 10–5; July–Oct., daily, 10–7; Nov.–Dec., daily, 10–5; Jan.–Apr., Mon.–Sat., 10–5; Sun., 12–5. Adults (13 and up), $8; 5–12, $6; under 5, free. Combination ticket with Pioneer Village: adults, $14; 5–12, $10. **Ages 8 and up.**

Of interest to older children and adults who have enjoyed Nathaniel Hawthorne's classic novel, this tour includes several houses: the Gables (1668), Hawthorne's birthplace (1750), Hathaway House (1682), Retire Beckett House (1655), and period gardens. A museum shop and coffee shop are also on the grounds. The site is not stroller accessible; bring a backpack for baby.

● Salem Willows

173 Fort Ave., Salem, (978) 745-0251. Apr.–Sept., Mon.–Sat., 10–9; Sun., 11–9. Free. **All ages.**

It may be a little scruffy around the edges these days, but how can you not appreciate a place that claims to be the original home of saltwater taffy? This seaside park, shaded with willow trees, has a carnival-type charm all its own. Play skee-ball, have your fortune told by a mechanical gypsy in the old-fashioned arcade, or take a ferry ride around Salem Harbor. There are kiddie rides for small fry, including tiny tugboats and a 1920s carousel. And then there's the food. You could bring your own healthful picnic, but why miss an excuse to dig into fried clams, cotton candy, or—for the truly adventurous— a chop suey sandwich. Or stake out a picnic table and indulge in some classic New England cuisine: a lobster roll and onion rings, washed down with a raspberry-lime rickey.

● Pioneer Village

Forest River Park, West St., Salem, (978) 745-0525, www.7gables.org. Late Apr.–Nov., Mon.–Sat., 10–5; Sun., 12–5. Adults, $7; 5–12, $5. Combination tickets available at House of Seven Gables. **Ages 6 and up.**

Living-history museums are all the rage these days, and this is America's oldest. It's an authentic re-creation of Salem in 1630 when Salem was a Puritan fishing village, some 60 years before the witchcraft hysteria. Early buildings, gardens, and animals create the feel of life in the 17th century; you'll be guided by costumed interpreters and see demonstrations of crafts and day-to-day activities of the time. Special events are held throughout the summer. Combine your visit with some outdoor fun (swimming, picnicking) at Forest River Park, adjacent to Pioneer Village.

● Salem Trolley

Essex St. at National Park Service Visitors Center, (978) 744-5469, www.salemtrolley.com. Apr.–Oct., 10–5; weekends only, Mar. and Nov. All-day pass: adults (13 and up), $10; 5–12, $5; under 5, free. Family rate (2 adults, 2 kids), $25. **All ages.**

Hop the trolley for a one-hour tour of the city's attractions. Salem Trolley makes 13 stops, where you can disembark and visit museums and attractions such as the House of Seven Gables, Salem Willows, and Pickering Wharf. Get on and off as often as you like.

● Endicott Park

57 Forest St., Danvers, (978) 774-6518. Year-round, 7 A.M.–9 P.M. Parking fee on weekends. **All ages.**

This former estate property, now owned by the town of Danvers, is another great place to play. The 164-acre recreation area was the site of a working farm during the early 20th century. The original buildings are still there, but the attraction for kids is a large, inviting playscape. Wander over to the children's barnyard and meet horses, sheep, turkeys, and more. You'll also find walking trails and a pond, with a path leading to the Glen Magna estate. Rest rooms are located in the carriage house across from the barn.

● Myopia Polo

Rte. 1A, exit 20N off Rte. 128, Hamilton, (978) 356-468-POLO. Late May–mid-Oct., Sat. and Sun., 3 P.M. (grounds open at 1:30 for picnickers). Adults, $10; 12 and under, free. **Ages 5 and up.**

Bring the kids to a polo match? Are we joking? Not at all. While polo's image is genteel, the sport itself is a rough-and-tumble competition in which bumping is allowed and players traverse the field atop 1,000-pound horses traveling at 30 miles an hour. There's plenty of action, and the horses (called ponies) are beautiful. To get into the spirit, bring along a gourmet picnic (this isn't the place for fast-food cartons) and cheer the Myopia team from the grassy sidelines. At half time, go out on the field and help tromp down the divots of turf kicked up by the horses (kids love to do this). A different, and pleasant, way to spend a Sunday afternoon.

● Wenham Museum

132 Main St., Rte. 1A, Wenham, (978) 468-2377, www.wenhammuseum.org. Tues.–Sun., 10–4. Adults, $5; 2 and up, $3. **All ages.**

This gem of a museum invites visitors to explore "how we have lived, dressed, worked, and played from the 17th century to today." The centerpiece is the historic Claflin-Richards House (circa 1690) portion of the museum, one of the oldest dwellings on the North Shore. Exhibits include a world-famous doll collection (more than 1,000 dolls, dating from 1500 B.C. through the present), incredibly intricate dollhouses, toy soldiers, and a room devoted to model trains. The Play & Learn Room is a hands-on children's space featuring a child-size replica of a 17th-century saltbox home, Brio trains, and a puppet theater. Special events and exhibits have included a teddy bear parade, a hands-on blocks exhibit, a kite exhibit, and a demonstration of how to turn "junk" into sculpture. Call ahead for current information. Have lunch or tea across the street at the Wenham Tea House and make it a really special day.

● Crane Beach

Argilla Rd,. off Rte. 1A, Ipswich, (978) 356-4354. Parking fee charged for nonresidents. **All ages.**

With 1,400 acres and five miles of white sand, Crane Beach is considered by many to be the North Shore's best. It is certainly the most picturesque, with swaying sea oats along the boardwalk, graceful dunes, and sailboats bobbing in the distance. Although the water never seems to get warm, children (and warm-blooded adults) don't seem to mind. But you will mind the dreaded greenhead, a pesky fly that often infests the area in—wouldn't you know it?—midsummer. The Crane Reservation Staff posts a greenhead warning at the gate if the flies are bad, so once you pay the nonrefundable (and stiff) parking fee, you take your chances. Bathhouses, a snack bar, and lifeguards are on the premises.

Up on the hill you'll see Castle Hill, a 59-room English Stuart-style mansion built for plumbing magnate Richard T. Crane in 1927. The property is now open as a bed-and-breakfast inn.

● Russell Orchards

Argilla Rd., off Rte. 1A, Ipswich, (978) 356-5366. Mid-May–Dec., daily, 9–6. Open Sat. and Sun. in Apr. **All ages.**

Cap off a trip to Crane Beach with a visit to Russell's. Besides selling one of the world's best treats (a fresh cider doughnut with a cup of just-pressed cider), Russell Orchards offers pick-your-own produce. Pick your own strawberries from mid-June through July. Raspberries are ready to be picked in July, and blueberries are ripe from mid-July through mid-August. (Dates vary due to weather and crop conditions.) In the fall, pick a peck of apples and select a potential jack-o'-lantern from the piles of pumpkins. You can also watch cider being pressed or take a horse-drawn hayride (extra charge applies) through the orchard. Kids love meeting the farm animals, including horses, goats, turkeys, and Vietnamese potbellied piglets. Check out the goodies in the barn store, featuring farm-grown produce, cider, preserves, cheese, and delicious fresh-baked pies.

● Ipswich River Wildlife Sanctuary

87 Perkins Row, Topsfield, (978) 887-9264, www.massaudubon.org. Trails open Tues.–Sat., dawn–dusk. Nature Center open May–Oct., Tues.–Fri., 9–4; weekends and Mon. holidays, 4–5; Nov.–Apr., open Tues.–Fri., 9–4; weekends and Mon. holidays, 10–4. Fee charged for nonmembers: adults, $3; 3–12, $2; extra charge for special programs. **All ages.**

This site is the Massachusetts Audubon Society's largest sanctuary, covering about 2,000 acres of meadow, swamp, islands, ponds, and part of the Ipswich River, along with an observation tower. More than 10 miles of interconnecting trails wind through forests, meadows, and wetlands. Favorites include the Rockery, with huge boulder formations (no climbing, please), while the boardwalk takes you past a beaver lodge. The sanctuary offers a great selection of family programs; a recent spring lineup included "Nature Detectives" for kids ages six to eight; "Sense of Wonder Walks" for tots and their families, a bat-house-building workshop, and a maple-sugaring tour. All programs are held at the Ipswich River Sanctuary Barn. Pre-registration is required; call for information and fees. (See Canoeing.)

● Canoeing

The Ipswich River's serpentine twists offer delightful canoeing, through wooded swampland and open marshland that's home to a variety of birds. The Massachusetts Audubon Society's **Ipswich River Wildlife Sanctuary** runs a number of guided family paddle trips, complete with storytelling around a campfire. Call the sanctuary for a schedule of events. To paddle on your own: From May to October, the sanctuary rents canoes to Massachusetts Audubon members on a first-come, first-served basis. Canoes go out between 9 A.M. and 3 P.M., and must be in by 4:30. Call ahead to confirm availability. Massachusetts Audubon members can also canoe-camp overnight on Perkins Island, a 40-acre, pine-covered river island owned by the sanctuary. Call (978) 887-9264 for details. Canoe rentals are also available from **Foote Brothers,** 230 Topsfield Rd., Ipswich, (978) 356-9771.

● North American Wolf Foundation

Wolf Hollow, Rte. 133, Ipswich, (978) 356-0216, www.wolfhollowipswich.com. Sat. and Sun, 1–5; presentations at 1:30 and 3:30, Mar.–Nov. Adults, $4.50; 17 and under, $3. **Ages 3 and up.**

Did the wolf get a bad rap in "Little Red Riding Hood"? Those who study them think wolves are generally misunderstood; here's a chance to learn about gray wolves and their habits in their natural environment. This nonprofit educational facility is committed to the preservation of the gray wolf.

● Willowdale State Forest

Linebrook Rd., Ipswich, (978) 887-5931, www.state.ma.us/dem. Parking fee in season. **All ages.**

This 2,400-acre forest has hiking trails, both marked and unmarked, and canoeing on the Ipswich River. Canoes can be rented from Foote Brothers, 230 Topsfield Rd., Ipswich, (978) 356-9771.

● Bradley Palmer State Park

Rte. 1 to Ipswich Rd., Topsfield, (978) 887-5931, www.state.ma.us/dem. Parking fee in season. **All ages.**

Take a respite from the summer heat at this pleasant, relatively undeveloped state park. Hike along woodsy trails (the park has 20 miles of them marked) and enjoy a picnic among the pines. The trails double as bridle paths. Follow the path that loops around park headquarters and you'll see an old stone mansion. Mountain bikers test their quads on the roadway. In summer, a giant fountain pool provides a place for kids to splash and play. Adults watch the action from a grassy slope nearby. This is a popular and very beautiful site for cross-country skiing in winter. Separate trails are designated for snowmobiles.

● Singing Beach

Beach St., Manchester-by-the-Sea. Year-round, dawn–dusk. Beachside parking restricted to residents from Memorial Day to Labor Day; use paid parking lot off Beach St. Also reachable via commuter rail (MBTA) from Boston; beach is about 1 mi. from train depot. **All ages.**

It may take some effort to get here, but this delicious crescent of sand is well worth it. They call it Singing Beach because of the delightful squeaky sound the sand makes when you walk on it (or so goes one theory!). Even on the hottest days, this beach is usually uncrowded. Plus, Manchester-by-the-Sea is fun to wander, with a good ice cream shop a short stroll from the beach, a couple of casual eateries, and a grocery store for picking up last-minute picnic supplies and sunscreen.

● Wingaersheek Beach

Exit 13 off Rte. 128, Gloucester, (978) 283-1601. Memorial Day–Labor Day. Parking fee. **All ages.**

Looking for a perfect family beach? Wingaersheek has sand bars and warm, shallow inlets. Small children will be content to plop right down in the warm water, while older ones will enjoy rock climbing and swimming in the calm waters. Arrive early (by 9 on summer weekends) to secure a parking space. Eats are available at the snack bar. Other beaches to try in Gloucester: **Good Harbor Beach** and **Stage Fort Park.** The latter has a beach that's small but offers a playground area.

● Hammond Castle Museum

80 Hesperus Ave., off Rte. 127, Gloucester, (978) 283-7673, www.hammondcastle.org. Memorial Day–Labor Day, daily, 10–3; rest of year, weekends only, 10–3. (Call first; special events may affect hours.) Adults, $6.50; 4–12, $4.50. **Ages 3 and up.**

Like a fairy-tale setting come to life, Hammond Castle has a moat and drawbridge, parapets and turrets, even an indoor reflecting pool. This re-created version was built in the years between 1926 and 1929 as the home of inventor John Hayes Hammond Jr. and houses his unique collection of Roman, medieval, and Renaissance art—not to mention a huge, working, 8,200-pipe organ. This inventive guy produced ideas for more than 800 inventions. His development of remote control via radio waves earned him the title "Father of Remote Control." Take a self-guided tour of the castle's eight rooms. Children especially enjoy the child-size suits of armor (man-size, in their time) and the winding passageways. (The castle is not stroller accessible, so bring a backpack for baby.) Visit on a rainy day for an added element of spookiness, or during Halloween week when the castle becomes a truly awesome haunted house.

● Moby Duck Amphibious Sightseeing Tour

Rogers St., Harbor Loop, Gloucester, (978) 281-DUCK, www.mobyduck.com. Tours daily, Memorial Day–Labor Day; weekends only, Sept. Adults, $14; 12 and under, $8. No credit cards. Hourly departures, 10–4. Tickets go on sale at 9:30 A.M. *each day.* **All ages.**

This 55-minute, narrated land and sea tour takes you past Gloucester landmarks, then plops into the harbor with a splash. The water tour includes Gloucester's inner harbor and takes in Gloucester's fishing fleet and the famous "Man at the Wheel" statue. (Also look for the new Fishermen's Wives statue, dedicated to local women who lost sons and husbands at sea.)

● Whale Watching

Gloucester is a great place to get out on the water and learn about the gentle giants. Typically, whale-watch cruises go to Stellwagen Bank or Jeffrey's Ledge, favorite local feeding grounds (lots of krill) for humpbacks and minke whales. Although the whales don't always cooperate, local cruise companies claim sighting records of higher than 90 percent, and some guarantee you'll see whales—that's how confident they are. Onboard naturalists provide narration. Children—always the first to spot a whale's tail in the distance—squeal with delight as playful humpbacks leap into the air or pass near the boat. Bring a pair of binoculars, warmer clothes than you think will be necessary (it's always cool out there), and rubber-soled shoes. The trip out to Jeffrey's can be rough, so consider taking precautions if seasickness is a problem for you or yours. Cruises leave daily from Gloucester's waterfront. Companies to call: **Cape Ann Whale Watch,** Rose's Wharf, 415 Main St., (978) 283-5110; **Captain Bill's Whale Watch,** Captain Carlos Restaurant, 33 Harbor Loop, (978) 283-6995; **Seven Seas Whale Watch,** Seven Seas Wharf, Rte. 127, (978) 283-1776; and **Yankee Whale Watch,** 75 Essex Ave., 1-800-WHALING.

● The Paper House

52 Pigeon Hill St. (look for the sign on Rte. 127), Pigeon Cove, Rockport, (978) 546-2629. Apr.–Oct., daily, 10–5. Admission by donation. **All ages.**

Kids are really into recycling these days, and this 1922 house is a recycler's dream home. The entire cottage—even the furniture—is made from old newspapers, rolled and varnished. A half hour spent at this odd abode should inspire some interesting projects at home.

● Halibut State Park

Gott Ave., off Rte. 127, Rockport, (978) 546-2997, www.state.ma.us/dem. Daily, May–Oct., sunrise–sunset. Parking fee. **All ages.**

Pack a picnic basket, don your sneakers, and enjoy this beautiful spot overlooking Ipswich Bay. Once a granite quarry, this is now a prime spot for tide pooling and blueberry picking. Brochures will direct you on a self-guided walking tour.

● Maudslay State Park

Curzon's Mill Rd., Newburyport, (978) 465-7223, www.state.ma.us/dem. Year-round. **All ages.**

Once a private estate, this 450-acre park features 16 miles of hiking and nature trails. After a major snowfall, it's a mecca for cross-country skiers and it's great for sledding, offering hills both steep and gentle. In summer, the Children's Theater-in-Residence performs outdoors here. Watch for the summer arts festival, with plays, music, face painting, hayrides, and such regional big-name troupes as Vermont's Bread & Circus Puppets. Call (978) 465-2572 for a schedule of events.

● Parker River National Wildlife Refuge

Plum Island (take Water St. to Plum Island Tpke., then turn right to Sunset Blvd.), Newburyport, (978) 465-5753, www.northeast.fws.gov/ma/pkr.htm. Year-round, daily, one-half hour before sunrise to one-half hour after sunset. Parking fee, $5; $1 for visitors walking or biking. **All ages.**

Birders flock to this tranquil spot, where more than 300 species have been sighted. (Peak migration is from March to early June.) To help you identify what you see, you might want to visit one of the local shops catering to bird-watchers, such as **Birdwatcher of Newburyport,** 50 Water St. The refuge also offers miles of sandy beach that's great for strolling, though a bit rough for swimming, and nature trails. The two-mile Hellcat Swamp trail is a standout; a boardwalk takes you past habitats of birds and other wildlife. Branch off from the trail to an observation tower where an easy climb will reward you with sweeping vistas of the marsh, and a nice vantage point to look for beavers near the beaver lodge.

Special note: The beaches-and-dunes area here is sometimes closed, to allow piping plovers and least terns to nest in peace. The trails will still be open.

● Amesbury Sports Park

12 Hunt Rd., exit 54 off Rt. 495, Amesbury, (978) 388-5788, www.goslide.com. Open seasonally; snow-tubing in winter (when it's cold enough for snowmaking). Mon.–Thurs., 3–9:30 P.M.; weekends, holidays, and school vacations, 9 A.M.–10 P.M. Call before going to verify that park is open.

Weekdays, $15; weekends/holidays/school vacations, all-day pass, $28. 3-hr. pass: $20. Helmets (free) mandatory, ages 4–6. **Ages 4 and up; no toddlers.**

Totally tubular—that's the best way to describe New England's only snow-tubing facility. They even have snowmaking coverage. Rope tows haul you up the 10-story-high hill; oversize rubber doughnuts carry you down a choice of slopes, some steep, some bumpy. Tubes have attached loops, so you can all tie up together and make like a giant rubber roller coaster. Summer activities include a driving range, miniature golf, bumper boats (outfitted with squirt guns), sand volleyball courts, and go-karts.

● Salisbury Beach

Rte. 1A, exit 58 off I-95, Salisbury. Rides open Memorial Day–Labor Day, 12–10; arcades and shops open Memorial Day–Labor Day, 10 A.M.– midnight, and Labor Day–Dec. with reduced hours. **All ages.**

Since the 1800s, this little strip of beach has attracted fun seekers and, more recently, folks en route to Maine looking for a break from the car. One of the last of the seaside amusement parks, and suffering from a seedy reputation for a few years, Salisbury Beach is now a family-friendly destination, complete with a beach, kiddie rides, arcade games, and, thrilling for tots, a giant inflatable clown you can bounce on. (Find him at Pirate Fun Park, one of the family-run businesses that predominate here.) To go along with these pursuits, of course, the right treats are essential, like fried dough, homemade fudge, fried clams, and ice cream. Wednesday is Kiddie's Day, when children-only discounts are offered; on Friday nights, there are fireworks, and on Sundays, you're likely to see strolling musicians, a puppet show, or a petting zoo.

● Salisbury Beach State Reservation

Beach Rd. off Rte. 1A, (978) 462-4481, www.state.ma.us/dem. Year-round; parking fee. **All ages.**

Boasting some of the most beautiful views around, this 520-acre park is set on the Atlantic Ocean and the mouth of the Merrimack River. The sandy beach is great for swimming (lifeguards during summer season); it's also a great place to surf-cast. There's even a bait shop on the premises, with fishing gear for rent. It's a peachy spot for waterfront camping; book far in advance for a summer stay.

● Ski Bradford

South Cross Rd., Haverhill, (978) 373-0071; (866)644-SNOW, www.skibradford.com. Open Mon.–Fri., 8:30–6; Sat.–Sun., 8:30–4:30. Night skiing: Mon.–Sat., 6–10 P.M. Lift tickets: adults and juniors, $28 weekends, $20 weekdays; under 5, $15. Private and group lessons available for skiers and snowboarders. **Ages 4 and up.**

Family-friendly Bradford offers 13 trails and slopes on 48 acres. Just the right size for families with tiny skiers in tow; no worries about getting lost in the lift line! Bradford boasts snowmaking over 100 percent of the mountain, plus night skiing and a new terrain park for snowboarding enthusiasts. Little-B ski classes are offered for kids from 4 to 7. For ages 16 and up, Bradford offers a "Learn to Ski in 90 Minutes" deal; get down the mountain successfully after your first lesson, or the next lesson is free. Lifts include two triple chairs, two T-bars, and four rope tows.

● Harold Parker State Forest

1951 Turnpike St., Rte. 114, N. Andover, (978) 686-3391, www.state.ma.us/dem. Open daily, sunrise–sunset. Nature walks, mid-Apr.– mid-Oct., 9 A.M. Nature center open mid-Apr.–Oct. Berry Pond day use area, open daily, Memorial Day–Labor Day. Parking fee. **All ages.**

Straddling the towns of Andover, North Andover, North Reading, and Middleton, this 3,000-acre forest is a peaceful oasis of hardwoods, hemlock, and white pine, studded with 11 ponds. Thirty-five miles of logging roads and trails attract hikers, mountain bikers, and equestrians. There's a nature center located just inside the campground on Jenkins Road, open from April to October. Berry Pond is a fun summer escape for families, offering picnic areas, swimming, and a sandy beach.

● Scenic Strolls—Marblehead Harbor and Bearskin Neck

Marblehead's scenic harbor is a sightseer's delight. Park your car in the waterfront lot on Front Street and explore the winding streets of quaint Old Town. Crocker Park, off Front Street, offers a great view of Marblehead Harbor. On weekends, watch sailing regattas from Castle Rock.

Rockport was a sleepy fishing village until artists discovered it after the Civil War. Today, Rockport's Bearskin Neck is a thriving arts center. Even if you've never visited Bearskin Neck before, chances are it will look familiar: The fisherman's shanty overlooking Rockport Harbor, called Motif #1, has been depicted by artists more often than any other building in the United States. Plan to eat in one of the casual-but-good seafood restaurants overlooking the harbor.

 RESTAURANTS

● The Rockmore Floating Restaurant

Salem Harbor, Salem, (978) 740-1001, www.rockmoreco.com. Launch leaves from Pickering Wharf, Salem, and Village Street Pier, Marblehead. Memorial Day–Labor Day, Mon.–Fri., 11–9; Sat. and Sun., 11–10. (Last launch leaves prior to stated closing times.)

You've heard of waterfront dining. The Rockmore takes the concept one step further. To get to this restaurant (actually, a tricked-out 110-foot barge, anchored in Salem Harbor), you scoot over by water in a bright red launch boat. For kids, the food is secondary to the motorboat trip. This is a fun way to go on a steamy summer night, so expect to wait a bit for the launch to pick you up. But once you get to the Rockmore, it's a festive scene. Eats consist of burgers, fish sandwiches, and seafood. Cute touch: Kids' meals are served in little boats. If the weather's not right for al fresco dining, try the **Rockmore Drydock** restaurant (at Pickering Wharf) where kids can watch Disney flicks in the living room while parents relax, postmeal. (Can you tell the owners are parents themselves?) The Rockmore Drydock is open daily, year-round, 11–10.

● Clam Shacks

Most New Englanders consider it a rite of summer: a trip to a clam shack for a mess of fried clams. None of those wimpy clam strips for us; these are plump, juicy, and golden-crisp, with their briny bellies intact. Spend the rest of the week eating unadorned veggies, if you must, but don't miss a trip to one of the North Shore's best bets for fried clams. After much research, here are our picks. You can't miss **The Clam Box,** on Rte. 1A at Mile Rd. in Ipswich; it's shaped like a box of clams. *Yankee Magazine* once named them "the world's best fried clam"—we agree. Kids won't eat clams, not even clam strips? Get 'em a box of chicken fingers, or a burger. Downside: It's a tiny place, so expect a wait. Upside: (besides the food) picnic tables outdoors. Open Mar.–Nov., Sun.–Thurs., 11–8; Fri. and Sat., 11–8:30, (978) 356-9797. Another perennial favorite is **Woodman's,** 121 Main St., Rte. 133, Essex, (978) 768-6451. Just as much as Filene's Basement is famous for shopping, Woodman's is famous for clams. Billing itself as the birthplace of the fried clam, Woodman's also offers steamers, lobster-in-the-rough, chowder, and other (mostly fried) seafood. Noisy, rustic, and self-serve, this is the place to go for that quintessential taste of summer. Enjoy without guilt. Open daily, year-round.

● Prince Restaurant

517 Broadway, Rte. 1, Saugus, (617) 233-9950,
www.princerestaurant.com. Sun.–Thurs., 11–11; Sat., 11–midnight.

Located on Route 1 north of Boston, the Prince is hard to miss—its facade features a giant leaning tower. (Route 1 is not known for understatement, by the way.) Inside, the place is massive; so are the servings of pasta and made-to-order pizzas.

■ South Shore and South of Boston

Why stop when you're halfway to Cape Cod from Boston? For most families, the answer is Plymouth Rock. Sooner or later, nearly every child is carted to the spot where, in the autumn of 1620, the pilgrims first set foot in the New World.

Unfortunately, not much remains of this rock that looms giant-size in the minds of schoolchildren. Indeed, it once was giant—more than 3,000 pounds of Plymouth Rock have been chipped away by tourists. Today the rock is protected, and much of it remains underground.

Happily, there's more to Plymouth than a mostly buried rock. Plimoth Plantation is a favorite destination, and the *Mayflower II* awaits. Set aside time to hit the beaches, too. No matter what the season, they are wonderful. We'll even direct you to a place where you can camp right on the beach.

Before you go, call 1-800-USA-1620 or visit www.visit-plymouth.com to get maps and information, or stop by the visitors center at 170 Water Street.

● Plimoth Plantation

Rte. 3A, Plymouth, (508) 746-1622, www.plimoth.org. Pilgrim Village: Apr.–Nov., daily, 9–5. Hobbamock's Homesite: Apr.–Nov., daily, 9–5. Plantation only: adults (13 and up), $20; 6–12, $12. Combination ticket (includes Plimoth Plantation, Hobbamock's Homesite, Craft Center, and Mayflower II): *adults (13 and up), $22; 6–12, $14; under 5, free.* **All ages.**

If you jumped into a time machine and set the dial to "Plymouth Colony, 17th Century," you'd be zapped to a place like this. Plimoth Plantation's 1627 Pilgrim Village is a living museum, peopled by folks posing as real Pilgrims to re-create life in the Plymouth Colony. Portraying characters based on actual Pilgrims, each carefully researched by the plantation, the Pilgrims here perform the chores of everyday life in 1627. As in real life, chores change with the seasons. Busy as they are, the Pilgrims take time to chat with visitors. They're really good at staying in character, too; if your child asks them about Playstation or even Barbie dolls, they'll act totally clueless. Of course, kids love this.

Also on the grounds is Hobbamock's Homesite, where you'll see Indians (portrayed by Native Americans) engaged in their daily tasks in a re-created campsite. Seeing these two very different cultures presented side by side provides a history lesson your children won't forget. The Craft Center features demonstrations of pottery making, furniture building, basket weaving, or cloth weaving. Don't miss the museum shop, with its good selection of children's books, craft kits, and Pilgrim-themed paraphernalia.

● *Mayflower II*

State Pier, Plymouth Harbor, (508) 746-1622. Apr.–Nov., daily, 9–5;
July and Aug., 9–7. Mayflower II *only: adults, $8; 6–12, $6.* **All ages.**

Berthed at the State Pier in Plymouth, the *Mayflower II* is Plimoth Plantation's full-scale reproduction of the ship that carried the Pilgrims in 1620. Climb aboard the gangway and you'll meet *Mayflower* passengers, realistically portrayed by Plimoth Plantation staffers. The stories they tell about the hardships of the voyage will capture your attention and make an impression on your kids that no textbook can match.

● Pilgrim Hall Museum

75 Court St., Plymouth, (508) 746-1620, www.pilgrimhall.org. Daily, 9:30–4:30. Closed Christmas Day and month of Jan. Adults, $5; 5–17, $3; family rate (two adults, up to four children), $14. **Ages 3 and up.**

Did you know that the Pilgrims didn't really wear tall hats with buckles? Learn the facts about our famous forebears here, home of a premier collection of original Pilgrim artifacts. Take a look at a 10,000-year-old Native American arrowhead, the sword of Captain Miles Standish, a suit of armor worn by a Pilgrim, a cannon, and much more. The museum also houses artifacts from subsequent generations. Activities geared toward kids, from tots to teens, include "treasure hunts" for intriguing artifacts and "picture yourself as a Pilgrim" in a predrawn frame. Temporary exhibits cover topics such as "Popular Pilgrims," a look at how the Pilgrims have been depicted in the movies and other media.

● Plymouth National Wax Museum

16 Carver St., Plymouth (across the street from Plymouth Rock), (508) 746-6468. Mar.–Nov., daily, 9–5; June, Sept., and Oct., 9–7; July and Aug., 9–9. Adults, $6; 5–12, $3. **Ages 3 and up.**

Wax museums tend to be a little creepy, maybe because of the deathly pallor of the characters' faces, and this one is no exception. But it is educational (sort of) depicting the Pilgrim story through 26 lifelike scenes with 180 life-size characters. Special lighting, sound effects, and animation add to the experience; this is a good rainy-day activity.

● Cranberry World Visitors Center

158 Water St., Plymouth, (508) 747-2350. May–Nov., daily, 9:30–5. Free. **Ages 3 and up.**

If your kids are world-class juice drinkers, they probably help keep this place in business. Sponsored by Ocean Spray Cranberries, Inc., Cranberry World is filled with exhibits tracing the history and development of the cranberry industry. (If you visit from mid-September through early November, you may have noticed some scarlet fields—those are cranberry bogs.) You'll see antique and modern harvesting tools and machinery and learn everything you ever wanted to know (and probably more) about this native American fruit. Children will enjoy sampling the numerous cranberry beverage combinations.

● Plymouth Beach

Rte. 3, Plymouth. **All ages.**

Right on the open ocean, this 3.5-mile sandy beach offers views of Saquish Neck to the northeast and Manomet Bluffs to the southeast. Plymouth Beach has lifeguards, concessions, and a bathhouse.

● Duxbury Beach

Rte. 3A to Rte. 139N., Canal St., Duxbury, (781) 837-3112. Memorial Day–Labor Day, 8–8. **All ages.**

Probably the nicest beach in the area, this five-mile stretch of sand is privately owned but leased to the town. It's clean, well maintained, and alcohol free. Lifeguards are posted; bathhouses, a concession stand, and a luncheonette are on the grounds.

● Duck Tours

Splashdown Amphibious Tours, Harbor Place, Plymouth, (508) 747-7658, (800) 225-4000, www.ducktoursplymouth.com. Runs Apr.–Nov.; Adults, $17; under 12, $10; under 3, $3. **All ages.**

These amphibious land-and-sea tours, all the rage in Boston, are available in Plymouth, too. The one-hour cruises depart from Harbor Place (next to the Governor Bradford Motor Inn) and Village Landing (near the Sheraton hotel). The tour takes in the town's historic waterfront district, then splashes down into Plymouth Harbor, for a mariner's view of the *Mayflower II.*

● Colonial Lantern Tour

Purchase tickets at 5 North St., by phone, or at area hotels. Meets at the Governor Bradford Motor Inn, Plymouth. Call (508) 747-4161 or (800) 698-5636 for information. Nightly, 7:30 P.M., late Mar.–late Nov. Ghost tour, nightly, 9 P.M. Adults, $10; 6–17, $8. **Ages 6 and up.**

Now this is an appropriate way to explore an oh-so-historic town: on a candlelit walking tour. This 90-minute, mile-long tour (too long for the very young or easily bored) covers sites including the waterfront, the original Plimoth Plantation site, and other landmarks. They also offer a ghost tour, called Legends & Lore, beginning at 9 P.M. Departing from the John Carver Inn at 25 Summer St., this one highlights the more macabre side of

Plymouth's past. The sites are the same as the Colonial Lantern tour, but the narrative focuses on mysterious events in Plymouth's past. Special seasonal tours are offered for Halloween, Thanksgiving, and Christmas.

● Children's Museum of Plymouth

46–48 Main St., Plymouth, (508) 747-1234. Year-round, Mon.–Sat., 10–6; Sun., 12–6. $4 per person. **Ages 2–10.**

This interactive discovery museum caters to kids from two to 10. The 40-plus exhibits focus on the sciences and the humanities but, mostly, they're about fun. Want to go on a simulated whale watch, play on a fire engine, sink putts on a kid-size golf course, climb a giant tree fort, or be mayor (or whatever role you choose) of Tiny Town, USA? You can here.

● Super Sport Family Fun Park

108 N. Main St., Rtes. 44 and 58, Carver, (508) 866-8000. Year-round, daily, 10–9; Memorial Day–Labor Day, 10–11. Prices vary, depending on activity. Combination passes available. **Ages 3 and up.**

Feel like riding a bobsled, skiing down double black diamonds, or racing a motorcycle? You can do it all here, sort of. The Venturer motion simulator ride offers seven types of adrenaline rush. No chance of breaking a bone, unless you fall out of your seat. And that's just one of the fun options here. Others are a golf driving range, miniature golf, a bumper boat pool with waterfalls and geysers (you must be 38 inches tall to ride alone), batting cages, and a go-cart track (kids 58 inches tall can ride by themselves). A video arcade and an ice cream shop are on the premises, too, in case you want to part with more cash.

● South Shore Music Circus

130 Sohier St., Cohasset, (781) 383-1400. Children's performances, Thurs., 10:30 A.M. and 2 P.M. Ticket prices vary; typically $6–$12. **Ages 3 and up.**

Kids love live theater, and what could be a better introduction to the stage than a performance of one of their favorite fairy tales? *Hansel and Gretel, Alice in Wonderland,* and other well-loved stories are presented in the children's series here. Recently, Franklin the Turtle starred in *Franklin's Magic Fiddle.* (This is the same lineup, different day, offered at Cape Cod Melody Tent. See listing.)

● Nantasket Beach

Nantasket Ave., Rte. 228 exit off Rte. 2, Hull, (781) 925-4905. Year-round. **All ages.**

This three-mile stretch of fine, hard-packed sand draws crowds from all over the Boston area and the South Shore. Swimmers, sun worshipers, surfers (there's often a pounding surf), joggers, shell seekers, and, of course, beach-loving families congregate here. Bathhouses and refreshments are available, and lifeguards are posted. At the mainland end of the beach is the Paragon Carousel.

● Paragon Carousel

George Washington Blvd., Nantasket Beach, Hull, (781) 925-0472.
Memorial Day–Labor Day, daily, 10–10; May–Memorial Day and Labor Day–Columbus Day, Sat. and Sun., 12–6. Per ride, $2. **All ages.**

Paragon Park, Hull's landmark amusement park, is long gone. But, happily, its 1928 carousel remains, with 66 hand-carved, hand-painted horses, two Roman chariots, and a Wurlitzer band organ. Enjoy.

● Hull Lifesaving Museum

1117 Nantasket Ave., Hull, (781) 925-LIFE. Open Wed.–Sun., 10–4.
Adults, $2; children free. Fridays, free to all. **Ages 5 and up.**

Quick, put on a Coast Guard uniform and hop in the dinghy to rescue your friends. At this 19th-century U.S. lifesaving station, kids learn what rescuers did when ships and boats were in trouble off the shores of Hull (at one time, the only entrance to Boston Harbor). Children can climb to the loft and talk to each other using telegraph keys in the radio room, maneuver boats and blocks over a floor map of Boston Harbor, or make signal code flags out of construction paper. Throughout the year special demonstrations are held—children might be asked to go for a mock rescue ride or to pull the ropes in on a safety buoy.

● Myles Standish State Forest

Rtes. 3, 44, and 58, S. Carver, (508) 866-2526, www.state.ma.us/dem.
Daily, dawn–dusk. **All ages.**

This 15,000-acre preserve is a beautiful spot for communing with the great outdoors. Swimming (in College and Fearing Ponds), fishing, canoeing, trails for hiking, bike paths, snowmobiling, cross-country skiing, camping—these options make this park a favorite with active families.

● Wompatuck State Reservation

Rte. 228, Hingham, (781) 749-7160, www.state.ma.us/dem. Daily,
dawn–dusk. Parking fee. **All ages.**

This 3,500-acre state park offers hiking, biking, fishing, and camping. Don't be surprised if you share the trails with horses—this is a popular place for trail riding. World's End Reservation, located at the tip of the park and designed by Frederick Law Olmsted, offers great views of the Boston skyline.

● South Shore Natural Science Center

Jacob's Lane, Norwell, (781) 659-2559, www.ssnc.org. Mon.–Sat., 9:30–4:30. Free. Fee charged for nonmembers and for some activities. **Ages 3 and up.**

Children's programs, animal exhibits, and nature trails are offered here, including an interpretive trail for the visually impaired. Programs include winter walks and snowshoe hikes, evening crafts, birding walks, and a maple-sugaring festival. Recent additions to the resident animal population are Hegwig the owl and two ferrets (the lineup changes as some animals are adopted).

● Children's Museum in Easton

Old Fire Station, 9 Sullivan Ave., N. Easton, (508) 230-3789. Mon.–Sat., 10–5; Sun., 12–5. All, $4.50; under 1, free. **Ages 1–8.**

Small fry will be delighted with the hands-on options here, including a giant kaleidoscope, dinosaur table, and a kiddie medical clinic. Art and science classes are offered, too.

● Boat Cruises

Catch a codfish, spot a whale, or help trap a lobster aboard one of the excursion boats that cruise out of Plymouth Harbor. Or cruise from historic Plymouth to funky P-Town (Provincetown). For information, call these companies: **Captain John Boats** (deep-sea fishing, whale watching), departing from Town Wharf, Plymouth, (508) 746-2643 or (800) 242-2469; **Lobster Tales** (lobstering cruises), (508) 746-5342, www.lobstertalesinc.com. *Pilgrim Belle* (Plymouth Harbor cruises, sunset cruises), a paddle-wheeler, departs from Plymouth's State Pier, (508) 747-2400, www.plymouthharborcruises.com. **The Provincetown Ferry** makes daily departures, in late May through September, from Plymouth's State Pier to Provincetown, on the tip of Cape Cod, (508) 747-2400. **Captain Tim Brady & Sons** (508) 746-4809; www.fishchart.com. offers whale watching, fishing, and harbor cruises.

● Kendall Whaling Museum

27 Everett St., Sharon, (781) 784-5642. Tues.–Sat. and Mon. holidays, 10–5; Sun., 1–5. Adults, $4; students, $3; children, $2.50; family rate, $10. **Ages 5 and up.**

Inspired by your whale-watch trip? Here you'll find 10 galleries of maritime art and artifacts, scrimshaw, ship models, and an authentic whaleboat. Cool figureheads and real whaling gear, too. A recent family film series (free with admission) featured a nature documentary on whale song and an animated children's film about whales.

RESTAURANTS

● Lobster Hut

Town Wharf, Plymouth, (508) 746-2270. Year-round. Open daily, 11–9, Memorial Day–Labor Day; otherwise, 11–7.

Enjoy seafood in the rough at this hopping waterfront eatery. The extensive, wallet-friendly menu features everything from stuffed quahogs (clams) and broiled swordfish to chicken tenders and filet o' fish.

● Iguana's

170 Water St., Plymouth, (508) 747-4000. 11 A.M.–midnight.

Get your enchiladas, taco platters, and Texas chili here; ask for a seat on the deck in warm weather. The grilled chicken fajita salad is a happy choice; let the kids create their own taco/burrito/enchilada combo. (Three enchiladas for just $11 when we visited.)

● The Clam Box

789 Quincy Shore Dr., Quincy, (617) 773-6677. Daily, Mar.–Nov., 11–midnight.

This glorified clam shack is a local institution. It draws throngs of beachgoers from Wollaston Beach across the street, and regulars who've been coming here for a clam fix for more than 20 years. Forget the umbrellaed tables outside—too noisy—and head in to the atrium-style dining area to indulge in tasty fried clams, lobster rolls, shish kabobs, Greek salads, even fried oysters and (gasp!) fried lobster. Order ice cream and fried dough, too, if you really want to send that cholesterol count through the roof. (At least they use vegetable oil in the Fryolators.)

■ New Bedford and Fall River Area

About an hour south of Boston, this region has a colorful past. New Bedford was once the whaling capital of the world, and its revitalized waterfront offers plenty of evidence—from sea captains' homes to Seaman's Bethel, the mariner's chapel described in Herman Melville's *Moby Dick*. New Bedford's entire downtown and waterfront was recently designated as a National Historic Site. Melville described the city as home to "patrician-like" houses and "opulent" parks and gardens. "All these brave houses and flowery gardens came up from the Atlantic, Pacific, and Indian Oceans," he wrote. "One and all they were harpooned and dragged up hither from the bottom of the sea." Although the idea of killing whales is repugnant today, the whaling industry made New Bedford quite prosperous in the 19th century. Now, the city is a major commercial fishing port, but making one's fortune as a fisherman is a lot tougher. The Whaling Museum is the town's most popular attraction, and many visitors find that New Bedford's revitalized downtown is a nice place to knock around.

Fall River, on the Rhode Island border, was once a mill town, made famous by the Lizzie Borden ax-murder case. (The Victorian house where Abby and Andrew Borden were hacked to death is now a bed-and-breakfast inn, believe it or not.) Today, factory-outlet stores are the big draw—along with the World War II navy ships at Battleship Cove. Whatever you discover here, you'll most likely be surprised at how much this "un-touristy" area offers to those who seek it out.

● New Bedford Whaling Museum

18 Johnny Cake Hill, New Bedford, (508) 997-0046, www.whalingmuseum.org. Daily, 9–5; until 9 P.M. second Thurs. of every month. Adults, $6; 6–14, $4. **Ages 3 and up.**

New Bedford's intriguing past is revealed at this museum. Children love climbing aboard the *Lagoda,* a half-scale replica of a square-rigged whaling ship. (At 89 feet long, it's the largest ship model in the world.) You'll ooh and aah at the 66-foot skeleton of a blue whale and wonder how whalers ever managed to lift the enormous harpoons. The museum also has an impressive collection of scrimshaw. You'll marvel at the intricate detail of these designs, engraved on the teeth of sperm whales or on pieces of whalebone. Whale men usually whittled these as gifts for their mothers, wives, or sweethearts.

● New Bedford Fire Museum

51 Bedford St., New Bedford, (508) 992-2162. June–Aug., daily, 9–4. Admission: $2. **Ages 3 and up.**

Set in old Fire Station No. 4 (circa 1867), this fire museum is even more child-friendly than most. Slide down a real firefighter's pole, try on firefighters' helmets, boots, and coats, ring the bell, and (with parental supervision) climb aboard genuine fire trucks. Memorabilia dates back to the early 1900s.

● Battleship *Massachusetts*

Exit 5 off I–95, Battleship Cove, Fall River, (508) 678-1905, www.battleshipcove.com. Year-round, daily, 9–5; Sat. and Sun., 10–5. Adults, $10; 6–14, $5, under 6, free. Free to those wearing a military uniform. **Ages 6 and up.**

Six U.S. Navy warships from the World War II era are currently berthed at Battleship Cove. Climb aboard World War II warships and PT boats, and tour massive vessels from the Korean and Vietnam Wars and Operation Desert Storm. Check out the submarine USS *Lionfish*. Try on a Navy bunk for size or man the guns. The battleship *Massachusetts* is a permanent memorial to the 19,000 men and women from Massachusetts who gave up their lives in service. There's a collection of World War II–related memorabilia, too, as well as a gift shop and snack bar.

● Fall River Carousel

Two Central St., Battleship Cove, Fall River, (508) 324-4300. Open year-round; hours vary. (It's best to call first.) Per ride, $1; companion rider, $1.50. **All ages.**

Pick your favorite steed and take a whirl on this restored 1920s carousel.

● Marine Museum at Fall River

70 Water St., Battleship Cove, Fall River, (508) 674-3533. Mon.–Fri., 9–5; Sat., 12–5; Sun. and holidays, 12–4. Adults, $4; 5–12, $3. **Ages 3 and up.**

Young seafarers will get a kick out of this, as will anyone who's ever tried to put together a model ship (and how do they get them inside those glass bottles, anyway?). More than 150 ship models are on display here; the centerpiece is the 28-foot-long *Titanic* replica. Exhibits include model steamships, yachts, sailboats, and the world's largest collection of HMS *Titanic* artifacts. Listen to a *Titanic* survivor's recorded account of the disaster.

● Horseneck Beach State Reservation

John Reed Rd., Rte. 88 off I-95, Westport Point, (508) 636-8816, www.state.ma.us/dem. Parking fee. **All ages.**

Horseneck State Beach, overlooking Rhode Island Sound, is one of the state's most popular—and most stunning—beach destinations. Here you'll find more than 500 acres on the water's edge, with a three-mile-long stretch of sand, bathhouses, and a snack bar. The camping area (just south of the day-use beach entrance) offers primitive camping on the waterfront and less-windswept sites behind sand dunes. Reserve in advance; this is the most popular state park camping area in Massachusetts.

● Capron Park & Zoo

Rte. 123, County St., Attleboro; (508) 222-3047, www.capronparkzoo.com. Year-round, 9:30–5. Adults, $3; 3–12, $2; 2 and under, free. **All ages.**

Here's a find within a find: Inside this 63-acre park is a six-acre zoo housing everything from mice to sloth bears, llamas to snow leopards, about 90 specimens in all. Exhibits have a pro-conservation message. A picnic area, snack bar, gift shop, and playground are on the grounds, too.

● Demarest Lloyd State Park

Barney's Joy Rd., S. Dartmouth; (508) 636-3298, www.state.ma.us/dem. Parking fee. **All ages.**

Hiking trails, picnic areas, and a calm, sandy beach are the attractions here. Arrive early on weekends; the gates close when the parking lot is full.

● Lloyd Center for Environmental Studies

430 Potomska Rd., S. Dartmouth, (508) 990-0505. Visitors Center: Mon.– Fri., 8–4; Sat. and Sun., 11–4. Grounds open daily, dawn–dusk. Free. **Ages 5 and up.**

Exhibits and a touch tank highlight the sea life of Massachusetts; outdoors, nature trails meander past wetlands and salt marsh. They also offer guided nature walks and canoe and kayak trips.

 RESTAURANTS

● Freestone's City Grill

41 Williams St., New Bedford, (508) 993-7477. Daily, 11–11.

This is a rare find—a sophisticated little restaurant that welcomes kids. While the older kids and adults in your party are enjoying the contemporary artwork displayed, the little ones will be busy playing connect-the-dots on their menus; small fry receive a mug of crayons and a take-home kids' menu as soon as you're seated. The children's menu features the usual nonthreatening lineup, and a terrific option to soda pop: fresh-fruit smoothies.

● Newport Creamery

Area locations include 1670 President Ave., Fall River, (508) 678-6346; 1071 Kempton St., New Bedford, (508) 997-8383; and 950 Kings Hwy., New Bedford, (508) 998-5323; www.newportcreamery.com. Call for hours.

A step up from the fast-food chains, Newport Creamery is beloved by kids for its awesome ice cream treats (free cones with kids' meals), but the food is surprisingly pleasing. Think soups, sandwiches, burgers, and patty melts (what's not to like about turkey and Swiss on rye, grilled to gooey perfection?). The Lil Skipper menu features the usual suspects, but—surprise!— kids can get broccoli, mashed potatoes, or a veggie medley as a side, instead of fries (yeah, right!).

■ Central Massachusetts and the Pioneer Valley

This region may lack ocean views and salt air, but visiting families don't seem to care. They're too busy enjoying the museums, parks, and attractions here. Take Springfield, for example: Where else can you spend one day at a musket shoot and the next practicing your jump shot at the Basketball Hall of Fame? If there's a dinophile in your group, you'll want to put both the Springfield Science Museum and Dinosaur Land in South Hadley on your list of must-sees. Springfield's Quadrangle, a four-museum complex, is a great place to hang; don't miss the six bronzes that pay tribute to a famous local, Dr. Seuss. (Serious Seuss fans should visit in early March, for the Dr. Seuss Birthday bash.)

Worcester, the second-largest city in Massachusetts, boasts two destinations kids can't resist: Higgins Armory Museum and EcoTarium. And, if you're willing to roam a bit, there's plenty more to see and do, from state-of-the-art roller coasters to a centuries-old kid-size cave. Beyond the big cities, you'll find rural towns dotted with farms and antique shops.

● Springfield Science Museum

State and Chestnut Sts., Springfield, (413) 263-6800, (800) 625-7738, www.quadrangle.org. Wed.–Fri., 12–5; Sat. and Sun., 11–4. Planetarium shows: Wed.–Fri., 2:45; Sat. and Sun., 1:30 and 2:30 (2:30 feature is Magic Sky Show, best for young children). Admission (includes all four museums in the complex: Science Museum, Connecticut Valley Historical Museum, George Walter Vincent Smith Art Museum, and the Springfield Museum of Fine Arts): adults, $6; 6–18, $2; under 6, free. Planetarium: $1 per person. Free on Fri. to Springfield residents with current library card. **All ages.**

Put this one in the "don't miss" category. Part of a quadrangle of museums, Springfield's lively Science Museum was designed with families in mind. At the hands-on Exploration Center, for example, kids can listen to Native American folk tales in a real wigwam and visit a turtle pond, where turtles "talk" to you (on audiotape) as you look through eye-level portholes and watch them swim. Other areas include Dinosaur Hall (where you'll see a full-size replica of a *Tyrannosaurus rex* and can walk inside a giant dinosaur footprint), African Hall, with a huge African elephant, and a planetarium. The Monsanto Eco-Center features an aquarium and live animals, with re-created examples of a mangrove swamp, a coral reef, the New England coast, and the Amazon rainforest. Is there a fan of Springfield native Theodor Geisel (Dr. Seuss) in your bunch? Stop by the Connecticut Valley Historical Museum and take a peek at the Seuss exhibit.

● Dr. Seuss National Memorial

State and Chestnut Sts., the Quadrangle, Springfield, (413) 263-6800, ext. 312, www.catinthehat.org. **All ages.**

The newest addition to Springfield's Quadrangle, the Seuss memorial features five bronze sculptures of beloved Seuss characters. They range in size from a four-foot-tall Lorax to a life-size elephant (Horton, who else?). The

statues were designed by sculptor Lark Grey Dimond-Cates, stepdaughter of
Dr. Seuss. Theodor Seuss Geisel (Dr. Seuss's full name) was born in Springfield in 1904. He wrote and illustrated 44 children's books during his career,
which have sold more than 100 million copies in more than a dozen
languages.

● Basketball Hall of Fame

*1150 W. Columbus Ave., adjacent to I-91, Springfield, (877)-4HOOPLA,
www.hoophall.com. Daily, 10–5. Adults, $10; 7–15, $6; under 7, free.*
Ages 5 and up.

Don't expect hushed voices and "do not touch" signs at this Hall of Fame.
When you enter the door, you join the great American game of basketball,
which was invented in Springfield in 1891 by Dr. James Naismith. Participa-
tion is the key to this fun-filled sports museum. Shoot baskets, play virtual
reality games, and watch basketball's greatest moments (and funniest bloopers)
in the Converse Theater. Recently renovated, the Hall of Fame offers all-new
features and activities, including a scavenger hunt throughout the museum.

● Forest Park and Zoo

*Sumner Ave., Springfield, (413) 787-6434 (park), (413) 733–2251 (zoo),
www.forestparkzoo.com. Park: daily til dusk. Zoo: daily, mid-Apr.–Labor
Day., 10–5; Labor Day–mid-Nov., Mon.– Sat., 10–4; Sun. and holidays,
10–5; mid-Nov.–mid-Apr., Sat., Sun., holidays, and school vacations, 10–3.
Adults, $3.50; 5–12, $2.50; 2–4, $1; 1 and under, free. Train rides,
$1.25.* **All ages.**

This delightful city park boasts several fun features. You can rent
paddleboats and pedal your way around Porter Lake, duckling style; then pay
a visit to the Children's Zoo in the middle of the park to see wild and domestic
animals from New England's woods and farmyards. The zoo is also home to
exotic species such as a South American capabara, emus, and wallabies.
There's also a petting area with goats and sheep. If you want more action take
a trail ride on horseback or a pony ride at Forest Park Stable. Other options
include swimming, tennis, hiking, and picnicking.

● A Lark in the Park

*Holyoke Heritage State Park, 221 Appleton St., Holyoke, (413) 534-
1723,www.state.ma.us/dem/parks.* **All ages.**

A Lark in the Park is a collaborative effort of the Children's Museum at
Holyoke, the Merry Go Round, Volleyball Hall of Fame, and the Visitors
Center at Holyoke Heritage State Park. Working together, they offer
performances, programs, and activities for families. The Visitors Center has
all the details; it's a dandy place to begin your Holyoke adventure.

● Holyoke Children's Museum

444 Dwight St., Holyoke, (413) 536-KIDS, www.virtualvalley.com. Tues.–Sat., 10–4:30; Sun., 12–5. Admission $4; under 1, free. **Ages 1–8.**

This engaging museum houses three permanent exhibits that win rave reviews from small fry. At Paperworks, kids can create handmade paper out of recycled paper pulp (which is especially appropriate here, since Holyoke was once a leading paper producer). Cityscape is a child-size Main Street, with a half-dozen or so businesses to try out including a TV studio, health center, architect's office, and bodega (Latin market). Kids love The Scientific Company exhibit, offering exciting ways to explore scientific principles with bubbles, shadows, and objects in motion. If there's a toddler in your group, you'll appreciate the Tot Lot, where little ones can play without encountering rambunctious older kids. There's also a picnic area (and some indoor tables) in the complex.

● Holyoke Merry Go Round

Holyoke Heritage State Park, Holyoke, (413) 538-9838. Year-round, Sat. and Sun., 12–4 and during school vacations. $1 per ride. **All ages.**

Built in 1929, this antique carousel features 48 horses and two Roman chariots. Who can resist?

● Volleyball Hall of Fame

444 Dwight St. (at Heritage State Park), Holyoke, (413) 536-0926, www.volleyhall.org. Sat. and Sun., 12–4:30. Adults, $3.50; students and seniors, $2.50. **Ages 6 and up.**

Volleyball was invented right here in Holyoke, by William G. Morgan at the Holyoke YMCA in 1895. (Not on the beach by a bunch of Californians, as one might have expected!) This museum celebrates the game, with interactive video games and displays, a hitting machine, and more. Several big-time volleyball tournaments are played here each year. A proposed expansion will feature several interactive exhibits; call before you go to check progress and to confirm rates.

● Robert Barrett Fishway

Holyoke Dam, Holyoke, (413) 659-3714. Mid-May–June, Wed.–Sun., 9–5. **All ages.**

Watch migrating salmon and shad on two fish elevators—that's what they call 'em, all right—at Holyoke Dam on the Connecticut River. Peep through the viewing windows or view from the observation platform overlooking the dam.

● Mount Tom State Reservation

I–91N to exit 17W, then Rte. 141 to W. Holyoke, (413) 527-4805, www.state.ma.us/dem. Reservation: open year-round. Museum: open Memorial

Day–Labor Day; Sept.–Oct., Fri.–Sun. Parking fee charged from Memorial Day–Labor Day, and weekends in Sept. and Oct. **All ages.**

Just minutes from downtown Holyoke, this lovely natural area provides a scenic backdrop to the Connecticut River. You'll find more than 30 miles of hiking trails, many offering beautiful views of the Pioneer Valley. The Reservation Headquarters has trail maps. There's also a small nature museum, with collections of rocks, insects, butterflies, and birds, and a playground. In autumn, this is one of the best areas in the state for hawk watching. Cross-country ski and ice skate on Lake Bray in winter.

● Old Sturbridge Village

Rte. 20W, near exit 9 off Mass. Pike and exit 2 off Rte. 84, Sturbridge, (508) 347-3362, (800) SEE-1830, www.osv.org. Open Jan.–mid-Feb., weekends only plus Presidents' Day, 10–4; mid-Feb.–Mar., Tues.–Sun., 10–4; Apr. to June, Mon.–Fri., 10–5; Sat. and Sun., 10–6; July–Sept. 2, daily, 10–6; Sept. 3–late Oct., Mon.–Fri., 10–5; Sat. and Sun., 10–6; late Oct.–Dec., daily, 10–4; Dec. 2–Jan. 1, Tues.–Sun., 10–4. Adults, $20; 6–15, $10; under 6, free. (Tickets good for two consecutive days.) **All ages.**

What was it like to be a child growing up in rural New England more than 150 years ago? Children will have a good time finding out at Old Sturbridge Village, a living-history museum that re-creates life in a rural New England town, circa 1830s. The village includes residences, craft shops, meeting houses, mills, a school, and a working farm. Everywhere you look, you'll see costumed interpreters busily engaged in early-19th-century chores and pursuits. You'll see a printer, blacksmith, tinsmith, and others plying their trades in authentically restored buildings (transported to the village from throughout New England). Visit Freeman Farm, where you'll discover how much work, especially teamwork, was involved in raising crops and livestock, and in simply preparing meals for the family. One of the newest features at OSV is a pontoon boat ride on the Quinebaug River. In winter, horse-drawn sleigh rides are offered. Recently opened, the Tavern at Old Sturbridge Village (open for lunch and dinner) features a cast of New England characters. Emily Dickinson and Nathaniel Hawthorne might show up for a visit, along with strolling musicians and magicians.

Since this is a rural community, many of the daily activities will change with the seasons. Spring brings sheep shearing, for example, and autumn means a turkey shoot and an early-19th-century Thanksgiving dinner. Best time to visit: during OSV's Family Fun Days, scheduled throughout the year, mostly during school vacation weeks and holiday weekends. Activities might include toy hot-air balloon flights, 19th-century games on the Common, music, storytelling, puppets, and other amusements for families.

● Brimfield State Forest

Rte. 20, Brimfield, (413) 245-9966, www.state.ma.us/dem. Parking fee.
All ages.

This hilly forest is a favorite destination among hikers, with lovely views from several points along Mount Waddaquadduck. Cool off with a dip in the pond or fish for trout in fast-flowing streams. Cross-country skiing in winter.

● Look Memorial Park

300 N. Main St., Florence, (413) 584-5457. Dawn–dusk. Parking fee. Extra fees for some activities. **All ages.**

This 150-acre conservation area boasts a slew of activities, including swimming, paddleboats, and minigolf. Biking and hiking trails are open for snowshoeing and cross-country skiing in winter.

● Norwottuck Bike Path

Connects Northampton, Hadley, Amherst, and Belchertown. Access points include Elwell Recreation Area on Warren Wright Rd., on the Amherst/ Belchertown town line. For a trail map, call Connecticut River Greenway State Park, (413) 586-8706. **All ages.**

This 10-mile paved, multiuse path was once the B&M (Boston and Maine) Railroad rail bed. The trail passes through residential areas, forests, pasture, and a pond. Look for signs directing you to the path. The eight-foot-wide path is perfect for biking, in-line skating, walking, running, and cross-country skiing.

● Dinosaur Land

Amherst Rd., off Rte. 116, S. Hadley, (413) 467-9566. Year-round, daily, weather permitting, 9–5. Admission, $2. **Ages 3 and up.**

Also known as "Nash Dino Land," this attraction is named after the late Carlton Nash, who unearthed and sold dinosaur tracks here beginning in 1939. More than 5,000 footprints have been quarried here, created by prehistoric animals who once roamed these riverbanks and cliffs north of Springfield. The oldest item is a 500-million-year-old trilobite fossil. *Jurassic Park* this is not. Exhibits are fairly sparse, and, while the dinosaur prints are discernable, the harsh Massachusetts weather has taken its toll. An indoor museum features a collection of fossils, footprints, and related artifacts. Check out the gift shop for fossils, footprints, and dinosaur bones (all real) and dinosaur models. Dinosaur tracks range in price from $50 to $900.

● McCray's Farm & Country Creamery

55 Alvord St., S. Hadley, (413) 533-3714. Farm open year-round, daily, during daylight hours. Free. Ice cream shop open mid-Feb.–mid-Nov., 9 A.M.– dark (closing time varies with season). **All ages.**

This working farm is the home of two child-pleasing features: a petting zoo and an ice cream shop. Meet horses, goats, calves, sheep, ducklings, rabbits, pigs, peacocks, donkeys, chickens, and a llama. Take a 20-minute hayride around the grounds to work up an appetite. Then sit at a picnic table and enjoy a homemade double-dip ice cream cone (there are inside tables, too). Aah, simple pleasures.

● *Quinnetukut II* Boat Cruises

Rte. 63, Northfield, (800) 859-2960, www.nu.com/northfield. Mid-June–mid-Oct., Wed.–Sun. Cruises offered daily at 11, 1:15, and 3 P.M. Call ahead to reserve. Adults, $9; under 14, $5. **All ages.**

This 90-minute cruise takes passengers on a 12-mile ride on the Connecticut River between Gill and Northfield, through the French King Gorge and historic Barton Cove (look for nesting bald eagles). Narration covers the nature history and geology of the river environment.

● Barton Cove

Rte. 2, Gill, (413) 863-9300, www.nu.com/northfield. Memorial Day–Columbus Day. Canoe, kayak, and rowboat rentals: $10 per hour, $25 per day. **Ages 5 and up.**

Operated by the Northfield Mountain Recreation and Environmental Center (hydroelectric power station property), Barton Cove has a boat livery with canoes, kayaks, and rowboats for rent and an on-site campground. They can even shuttle you upriver (you paddle back downriver) for a real Connecticut River adventure.

● Erving State Forest

Off Rte. 2, Erving, (508) 544-3939, www.state.ma.us/dem. Parking fee. **All ages.**

Swim in pretty Laurel Lake or fish for trout in the lake or streams. There's also a two-mile hiking trail and a half-mile nature walk, both marked. Cross-country skiing in winter.

● Six Flags New England

Rte. 159, 1623 Main St., Agawam, (877) 4-SIX FLAGS, www.sixflags.com. Mid-Apr.–Oct., hours vary according to season. Call ahead to confirm hours of operation and currently operating rides, as some rides are occasionally closed for routine maintenance. Admission: over 54 in. tall, $39.99; junior (37–53 in. tall), $24.99; children under 36 in. tall, free. After 4 P.M., admission is $23.99. **All ages.**

Wow. New England's largest theme and water park offers 130 acres of rides, shows, and attractions. Bugs Bunny and his Looney Tunes pals appeal to small fry, as do junior-size counterparts to big-kid rides and roller coasters. Poison Ivy's Tangled Train, a steel coaster (parents and older sibs can ride, too), offers big thrills for little ones. Six Flags also offers family favorites like the spinning tea cups and antique cars. But don't kid yourself: This park is really known for its high-intensity thrill rides. A big draw is "hyper-coaster" Superman, Ride of Steel, a harrowing mile-long track of twists and turns that's scary just to *watch*. Rated one of the top coasters in the country, Superman climbs 20 stories high and reaches speeds in excess of 70 mph. Riders experience 10 seconds of weightlessness. One ticket gets you into the theme park and the water park, Island Kingdom, although the water park operates on a different (shorter) schedule. Look for a wave pool, a river ride, and lots of water slides. As you'd expect, this place gets very crowded in summer, and the numbers build at the water park as the day goes by. Head there first, if it's a must-do for your bunch, then take on the rides. Another crowd-beating tip: Arrive 30 minutes before the park opens, to get in line. Then, go to Guest Services to make a reservation; these are available for the park's most popular rides. The least-crowded days here are Monday and Tuesday, they tell us. Big benefit if you're night owls: The crowds thin out big-time after 6 P.M. Still, we'd leave an hour before closing time to avoid traffic.

● Children's Museum at Indian House Memorial

Main St., Deerfield, (413) 774-3768, www.deerfield–ma.org. Family program: July and Aug., daily, 11–4:30; weekends only, Sept. and Oct. Fees vary. **Ages 3 and up.**

Located in Old Deerfield, the children's museum offers hands-on history experiences during the summer. Weekly themes might include Wooden Toys & Games (play them, make one), Farm Activities (try tools, churn butter, grind and sift corn), and 18th Century Crafts (weaving, embroidery, drawing and calligraphy with quill pens). This is also the site of a "Turn-of-the-Century Ice Cream Social" on July 4th, featuring period games and other family activities.

● Candlemaking Museum at Yankee Candle Co.

Rte. 5, S. Deerfield, (413) 665-2929, (877) 636-7707, www.yankeecandle.com. Daily, 9:30–6. Free. **All ages.**

Watch candle makers dip beeswax and bayberry candles using centuries-old techniques. Of course, Yankee Candle Co. hopes you'll be enticed to buy oodles of their sweet-smelling product; there's also a Bavarian Christmas Village, a toy factory, and a car museum (extra charge applies) at the complex.

● Magic Wings Butterfly Conservatory & Gardens

281 Greenfield Rd., S. Deerfield, (413) 665-2805, www.magicwings.net. Open daily, year-round except Christmas Day and Thanksgiving; fall and *winter, 9–5; spring and summer, 9–6. Adults, $7; children, $4.50; under 3, free.* **Ages 3 and up.**

This indoor conservatory is filled with live native and tropical butterflies and plants. Butterflies are especially active on sunny days.

● Higgins Armory Museum

100 Barber Ave., Rte. 12N off I–90, exit 1, Worcester, (508) 853-6015, www.higgins.org. Year-round, Tues.–Sat., 10–4; Sun., 12–4. Closed Mon. and legal holidays. Adults, $6.75; 6–16, $5.75; under 6, free. **Ages 3 and up.**

This may be the only place in the country where your dream of being a knight in shining armor can come true. At this wonderfully unique museum, kids (adults, too!) can try on an authentic suit of armor in the Participatory Gallery. There's even armor for dogs. The action includes demonstrations of arms and armor, games, crafts, and special events. Knightly culture is presented in a sound and light show. Special kids' programs feature gargoyles, beastly dragons, and marionettes. The collections of medieval and Renaissance armor and related artifacts are fascinating.

● EcoTarium

222 Harrington Way, off Rte. 9, Worcester, (508) 929-2700, www.ecotarium.org. Year-round, Mon.–Sat., 10–5; Sun., 12–5. Adults, $7; 3–16, $5, free first Sun. of the month, 1:30–5. Walkway programs: $10, reservations recommended. **All ages.**

Exploration is the name of the game here. Set on 60 acres of woodlands, this three-story nature park celebrates the environment and all its creatures. Fun for kids and adults, the EcoTarium offers hands-on science exhibits, a planetarium and observatory, a nature trail, a narrow gauge railroad, and indoor and outdoor wildlife habitats for 200 animals. Brave and nimble souls can discover the 40-foot-high Tree Canopy Walkway. Visitors don helmets and harnesses, then explore the treetops on a network of swinging bridges and suspended platforms. (Open weather permitting.) Touch the insides of a giant clam shell, look inside microscopes to see cool, gross things like stink-bugs, magnified 20 times. Drawers are full of interesting things to touch. They also offer live animal demonstrations, since the EcoTarium is a refuge for injured animals and other creatures who could not survive in the wild.

● Wachusett Mountain

Rte. 140, Mountain Rd., Princeton, 1-800-SKI-1234, www.wachusett.com. Lift tickets: adults, $42 (weekends and holidays); children, $32. Call for snow condition updates. **Ages 3 and up.**

Location, location, location. That's the best thing about Wachusett Mountain. Ski here, an hour or so from Boston, and you avoid the often-brutal traffic heading to points north. Obviously snowmaking is important here, and they've got it, 100 percent from top to bottom. Features include night skiing (add $5 to the cost of your lift ticket and ski until 10 P.M.), NASTAR racing, a nursery, and the acclaimed SKIwee teaching program for kids ages three to 12. Children will have fun learning to navigate the Bamboo Bridge and Hoola Hoops in the Polar Playground; new-to-the-sport adults will feel comfortable in the beginners area. Those features make Wachusett Mountain—with 18 trails and 6 lifts—a great place to learn to ski.

● Davis' Farmland and Mega Maze

Redstone Hall Rd., off Rte. 62, Sterling, (978) 422-8888, www.davismegamaze.com. Petting farm open Memorial Day–Oct., Thurs.–Sun., 10–5, weather permitting. Adults, $3; 12 and under, $2. Mega Maze open daily, mid-July–early Sept., then weekends only through late Oct. Call ahead to confirm. Adults, $9.95; 4–14, $7.95; under 4 free. **All ages.**

Not your garden-variety petting zoo, this one has potbellied pigs, llamas, Scotch Highland cattle, and more than 100 more animals to pet and feed. Go on a hayride or a pony ride, and be sure to bring a picnic lunch; you can eat alongside the animals. When the corn gets tall, head across the street for Davis' Mega Maze. This all-natural adventure was crafted in England by master maze designer Adrian Fisher; some of his designs hold *Guinness Book* world records. Davis farmers actually create the maze, crafting it from eight acres of corn and sorghum. The maze design changes each year; the most recent creation featured a dinosaur theme and could be solved at least six different ways. Kids are amazingly good at this; grown-ups tend to think too much!

● Southwick's Zoo

Off Rte. 16, Mendon, (508) 883-9182, (800) 258-9182, www.southwickszoo.com. May–Oct., daily, 10–5. Limited operations in Apr. and Oct. Adults (13 and up), $13.50; 3–12, $9.50; under 3, free. **All ages.**

Dedicated to the preservation of rare and endangered species, this farm houses the largest collection of wild animals in New England. Meet lions, tigers, and bears (oh, my), plus a baby giraffe, ostriches, and several varieties of birds. Make new friends among the goats, sheep, and llamas at the petting area, ride a pony, and learn about them through exhibits and live animal presentations. The grounds also include a 35-acre deer forest that's home to 300 free-roaming European fallow deer. The playground is something to see—it's made of recycled materials, including 14, 944 soda cans!

● Turner Falls Fish Viewing Facility

Fish Ave., Turner Falls, (413) 659-3714. Mid-May–June, Wed.–Sun., 9–5. **All ages.**

The name says it all . . . watch the annual migration of salmon and shad through underground viewing windows. The staff and informational exhibits will fill you in on all the facts.

● Maple Sugaring

Sweeten up your winter with a visit to a sugarhouse. Massachusetts has more than 100 (several in this area), open for demonstrations from February through early April. They give samples, too. Call the Massachusetts Maple Producers at (413) 628-3912 for a free directory. A recorded message gives updates daily in season.

● Hiking

If you guessed this region offers some great hiking, you're right, and it's especially rewarding during fall foliage season. Places to go include **Chesterfield Gorge,** off Rte. 153, Chesterfield (a 30-foot gorge near the headwaters of Westfield River); **Laughing Brook Education Center and Wildlife Sanctuary,** 789 Main St., Hampden (nature and walking trails and an animal exhibit); and **Northfield Mountain Recreation and Environmental Center,** Rte. 2A, Northfield (a mile-long nature trail ringing Northfield Mountain).

● Douglas State Forest

Wallum Lake Rd., Douglas, (508) 476-7872, www.state.ma.us/dem. Daily, dawn–dusk; facilities open Memorial Day–Labor Day. Parking fee. **All ages.**

This 5,000-acre state forest offers outdoor fun aplenty. Lake swimming is the biggest attraction; lifeguards are posted in summer months. The park also offers multiuse trails in summer and winter.

● Purgatory Chasm State Park

Purgatory Rd., Sutton, (508) 234-3733. Daily, dawn–dusk, except during snow and ice conditions (usually, Jan.–Feb.). Guided tours Memorial Day– Columbus Day, Sat. at noon and 4 P.M., and Sun. at 4 P.M. **Ages 4 and up.**

This 1,200-acre state reservation is a boulder-strewn maze designed by Mother Nature. The chasm itself is an 80-foot-deep hole in the ground, with granite walls as high as 70 feet. This is a very cool place for a family adventure, but do keep in mind that the ledges of the chasm are wide open; nothing is closed off or roped off. We wouldn't recommend this for toddlers, as it takes surefootedness to climb the mossy boulders, but well-supervised kids will have a grand time crawling into "The Coffin" (a small cave), and shimmying their way through "Fat Man's Misery," a foot-wide, 10-foot-long space between two huge boulders. Even Moms and Dads can squeeze through "Devil's Corn Crib," although it may involve sucking in that tummy. Five trails have been carved through, and around, the chasm. So where did this family-friendly quirk of nature come from? There have been many theories over the years, but modern geologists believe that an enormous glacial lake melted nearby and Purgatory Chasm was carved by ice-fed torrents. Constant freezing and thawing results in natural sculpting, making the chasm a work in progress. On a hot summer day, this is a cool oasis. Bring some eats; there are picnic tables and (usually) an ice cream truck passes through the park.

● Dunn Pond State Park
Rte. 101, Gardner, (978) 632-7897. Year-round, dawn–dusk. Parking fee.
All ages.

This 119-acre park features walking trails, picnic tables, a playground area, and swimming on a 20-acre pond. Bring your own canoe or kayak, or rent a paddleboat from the vendor here. Naturalist-guided interpretive programs are offered throughout the summer; one popular program is an evening campfire with Native American storytelling. Call for a schedule. Dunn Pond is a favorite venue for ice skating in winter.

 RESTAURANTS

● Gus & Paul's
1500 Main St., Tower Sq., Springfield, (413) 781-2253. Mon.–Wed., 6 A.M.–6 P.M.; Thurs.–Sat., 6 A.M.–10 P.M.

No whining allowed; this casual eatery has something for everybody, even the pickiest palate. Open for breakfast, lunch, and dinner, they offer deli sandwiches, hot entrees, fresh bagels, desserts, and more. The patio is the place to be in summer.

● Spoleto
50 Main St., Northampton, (413) 586-6313. Open nightly for dinner; reservations suggested Sun.–Thurs.

The neo-Italian food wins raves from *Gourmet, Bon Appetit,* and *Yankee* magazines, but this restaurant is decidedly unstuffy. Kids love the simple pasta presentations; adults can sample more sophisticated fare.

● Weintraub's Restaurant & Delicatessen
126 Water St., Worcester, (508) 756-7870. Mon., 10 A.M.–4 P.M.; Tues.– Sun., 9 a.m– 8 P.M.

Voted best deli in New England by *Yankee Magazine*—need we say more? With so many possible choices and combinations, even the finicky will join the Clean Plate Club.

● Worcester Diners
True, diners are fairly small, and the sounds of one whiny child can really resonate, but if you're willing to take that chance and you love classic

diners, Worcester's got 'em. Dining cars were once manufactured here, and there are still more than a dozen functioning as diners to choose from. These include Mac's, Parkway, Miss Worcester, the Kenmore, Emerald Isle, and Boulevard. We haven't tried them all, so we can't vouch for their quality, but would they have lasted so long if they didn't send out some mean Blue Plate Specials?

■ Mohawk Trail and the Berkshires

The western region of Massachusetts, called the Berkshires (short for Berkshire Hills), is an area as graceful as its name implies. Blessed with beautiful countryside and charming Main Streets, the area offers a wealth of cultural and recreational activity. Plan to take it slow and savor the pleasures of the Berkshires. Enjoy a picnic on the lawn of Tanglewood as the Boston Symphony Orchestra (BSO) performs under a starlit sky. Visit a magnificent natural marble bridge with graffiti dating back to 1740. Or ride horseback through a forest of brilliant fall foliage. Even if you take a wrong turn along the way (and you probably will—it's easy to be distracted by the view), so what? You're bound to discover something special around the next curve in the road.

Speaking of that roadway, the Mohawk Trail (Rte. 2) is the road many travelers take to the Berkshires. Running nearly 100 miles, from Orange to Williamstown, the Mohawk Trail began as a Native American path. Early European settlers widened it, then the road was developed as America's first scenic auto route. Linking pastoral villages, picturesque bridges, and winding past rivers, the Mohawk Trail is especially dazzling in fall, when the surrounding hillsides are awash in brilliant hues. (Plan on plenty of traffic then; this is a much-publicized fall color route!) For information on the Berkshires, call the Berkshires Visitors Bureau at (800) 237-5747 or visit www.berkshires.org. For information about the Mohawk Trail region, call the Mohawk Trail Association at (413) 743-8127 or visit www.mohawktrail.com.

● Hancock Shaker Village

Rte. 20, Pittsfield, (413) 443-0188, www.hancockshakervillage.org. Year-round: open daily, May–Oct., for self-guided tours, 9:30–5. Adults, $13.50; 6–17, $5.50. Family rate: $33 for two adults and all accompanying children under 18. Nov.–Apr., open for guided tours only, $10 per person; under 18 free.
Ages 3 and up.

Hancock was one of 18 communities founded by the Shaker sect in the 18th century. Although the last of the Hancock Shakers left the church family in 1960, this museum is a permanent memorial to the Shaker way of life. Twenty buildings have been restored on the site, including an unusual (but amazingly practical) round stone barn. You'll see farm animals, herb gardens, and craft demonstrations. In the Family Discovery Room, kids can try on bonnets and shoes, write with a quill pen, and get a taste of a child's life in an 18th-century Shaker community. You might be treated to a Shaker music program, where everyone joins in. Guided tours are scheduled daily; plan to spend about two hours here, depending on the ages and attention spans of your kids. Light meals and snacks are available.

● Berkshire Museum

39 South St., Rte. 7, Pittsfield, (413) 443-7171. Sept.–June., Tues.–Sat., 10–5; Sun., 1–5. July and Aug., daily, 10–5; Sun., 1–5. Adults, $6; 3–18, $4; under 3, free. Free to all Wed. and Sat., 10–12. **Ages 3 and up.**

If Alexandra likes science museums but Christopher prefers art while Mom and Dad are history buffs, you've found the perfect museum. This one has something for everybody and a hands-on aquarium to boot. Young children will be absorbed by the Animals of the World in Miniature exhibit and the Egyptian mummy. We love the "Refrigerator Art Gallery," where children's work is displayed on 13 refurbished refrigerator doors. The Festival of Trees, in December, is a must-see, featuring unusually decorated Christmas trees. Special tours are offered for children. They also offer films and theater performances.

● Pittsfield Mets Baseball

Wahconah Park, 105 Wahconah St., Pittsfield, (413) 499-METS, www.pittsfield.com. Late June–Labor Day. Starting times: Mon.–Sat., 7 P.M. (Labor Day, 1 P.M.); Sun., 6 P.M. Tickets, $2–$7. Call for a schedule of home games. **All ages.**

Hey, battuh, battuh! Catch the Pittsfield Mets, a Class A affiliate of the National League's New York Mets, throwing the heat at historic Wahconah Park. You never know when you might discover the next headed-to-the-big-leagues superstar.

● Pittsfield State Forest

Cascade St., Pittsfield, (413) 442-8992, www.state.ma.us/dem. Parking fee. **All ages.**

This mountainous area offers plenty to see and explore, including caves, waterfalls, and cascades. Many species of mammals live here, and occasionally even a black bear or coyote is spotted. There are 30 miles of hiking trails, including several short ones. Drop a line in Berry Pond (which is stocked) or swim in the stream at Lulu Pond picnic area. Ten miles of cross-country ski trails are maintained in winter.

● Berkshire Scenic Railway Museum

Housatonic St. and Willow Creek Rd., Lenox, (413) 637-2210. Memorial Day–Oct. Train rides: weekends and holidays, on the half hour. **All ages.**

Don that conductor's cap and take a ride on a vintage railroad car. The little museum at restored Lenox Station offers interactive exhibits, model trains, a caboose, and lots of railroadiana.

● Berkshire Theatre Festival

Main St., Stockbridge, (413) 298-5576, www.berkshiretheatrefestival.com. July and Aug., Wed.–Sat., 12 noon. Tickets: adults, $7.50; children, $5. **Ages 8 and up.**

For nearly a century, this historic playhouse has showcased luminaries such as Joanne Woodward on its boards in plays written by the likes of Noel Coward and George Bernard Shaw. The company's Theatre for Young Audiences features plays performed by, and for, young people (recently showing: *The Odyssey*). During July and August, up-and-coming talents in grades four to six dazzle audiences in the festival's Children's Theatre under the tent. These Berkshire County youngsters, part of the Young American Playwrights Program, work side by side with theater professionals to polish, cast, direct, and produce their plays. The one-act plays are performed—for appreciative audiences—in July and August.

● Sterling and Francine Clark Art Institute

225 South St., Williamstown, (413) 458-9545. Year-round, Tues.–Sun., 10–5; also Mon., July–Aug. Free. **Ages 5 and up.**

This renowned museum offers a time-honored way to get youngsters involved in its galleries: a treasure hunt. Kids follow clues that direct them to specific paintings. If you can hold them back for a moment to savor the canvas before they sprint off to find the next one, so much the better! Collections feature important 19th-century paintings by Renoir, Degas, Monet, Toulouse-Lautrec, Homer, and many old masters, and sculptures by Degas and Remington, among others.

● Natural Bridge State Park

Rte. 8 (.5 miles from town center), North Adams, (413) 663-6392, www. state.ma.us/dem. May–Oct., daily, 10–8; Sat. and Sun., 10–6. **All ages.**

The highlight of this tiny state park is a natural marble bridge, the only one of its kind in the United States. The bridge extends across a gorge 60 feet aboveground. It was formed when flowing water and ice gradually eroded the many layers of rock covering the marble, at the rate of one foot every 2,500 years. (Obviously, someone was keeping track.) Now, deep chasms are sculpted into the rock. Some of the walls of the chasms sport graffiti dating back to 1740. Picnic tables and rest rooms are available.

● MassMOCA (Museum of Contemporary Art)

87 Marshall St., N. Adams; (413) 664-4481, www.massmoca.org. Adults, $6; 6–16, $2; under 6, free. **Ages 5 and up.**

The country's largest contemporary arts center is housed in a renovated 19th century factory. MassMOCA's sheer size means it can house some huge installations. All are loaned, not owned, by the museum, so visitors can count on always-changing, often fascinating, exhibits. Seen recently at MassMOCA: "Maya," featuring thousands of action figures, carefully arranged in a giant pyramid. The center is also the scene of live music performances, dance parties, and children's activities; contact MassMOCA for a performing arts schedule. Don't miss the museum shop, just inside the entrance, for lots of intriguing trinkets. Our kids loved the industrial-looking rest rooms, of all things. There's also a snack bar.

● Western Gateway Heritage State Park

B&M Freightyard, Rte. 8, North Adams, (413) 663-8059. Daily, 10–4:30. Free; donations appreciated. **All ages.**

This collection of historical attractions, specialty shops, and restaurants is located in a restored railroad freightyard. Admittedly it's a pleasant place to stroll around in, but we're including it in this book for a more specific reason: The Tunnel Experience. This intriguing display, located inside a set of railroad boxcars, has lots of kid appeal. Through sight-and-sound effects, visitors learn what it was like to dig the Hoosac Tunnel during the mid-1800s. Explosions, dripping water, and the rapping of pickaxes against stone all re-create the drama of this undertaking. Nearly 200 workers died while digging the tunnel, which eventually linked the East, the Great Lakes, and the West. Tales of train wrecks and ghosts add to the experience. Junior conductors will enjoy taking a ride through the park on the Tot Train.

● Mount Greylock

Access road (Notch Rd.) off Rte. 2 between N. Adams and Williamstown, North Adams, (413) 743-1591. Road to the summit is closed in winter (Dec.–early Apr.). **All ages.**

The pinnacle of Massachusetts, Mount Greylock (3,491 feet), can be reached by car. The nine-mile drive takes about a half hour and rewards you with a five-state view. If you're visiting the Berkshires during fall foliage season, you won't want to miss it. Check out the War Memorial Tower, which resembles a giant lighthouse (and was designed to be just that, in fact). Park interpreters are typically on duty here and can answer any questions. There are also several walking trails that connect with the parking lot at the summit, including a section of the Appalachian Trail. You can spend the night at Bascom Lodge, run by the Appalachian Mountain Club (AMC), from mid-May through mid-October. Reserve in advance, as this rustic, dormitory-style 1930s lodge is very popular. Meals and snacks are available here. The AMC runs guided hikes and nature walks, campfire programs, and other activities out of Bascom Lodge.

● Tanglewood Music Festival

Rte. 183, West St., Lenox, (413) 637-5165, (617) 266-1492. June–Sept. Call in advance for ticket information. **Ages 5 and up.**

This 210-acre estate is world famous as the summer home of the Boston Symphony Orchestra. Bring a picnic and spread out on a blanket to enjoy classical music under a star-filled sky. Or go earlier in the day and catch the BSO's rehearsal—a good option for families with young children and the least costly way to go.

● Pleasant Valley Wildlife Sanctuary

472 W. Mountain Rd., Lenox, (413) 637-0320, (800) AUDUBON, www.massaudubon.org. Nature Center: open Tues.–Sat., 9–5; Sun. and Mon. holidays, 10–4; open Mon. from end of June–Labor Day, 9–4. Nature trails: open same days as Nature Center, dawn–dusk. Nonmember adults, $3; nonmembers, 3–12, $2; members of the Massachusetts Audubon Society, free. **All ages.**

Hike along the nature trails here and you'll see beaver ponds and lodges, with muskrats sometimes sharing the living quarters. Visit the Trailside Museum and encounter live and stuffed animals, as well as electronic nature games—a fun way for kids to learn about the environment. Seven miles of hiking trails wind through hardwood forests, meadows, wetlands, and along the slopes of Lenox Mountain. Traverse them on cross-country skis in winter. Guided canoe trips are offered in summer.

● Jiminy Peak Ski Area

Rte. 7, Hancock, (413) 738-5500, (888) 4-JIMINY, www.jiminypeak.com. Open Nov.–Mar. (approx.), weekends and holidays, 8:30–10:30; midweek, 9–10:30. Adult lift ticket, weekends/holidays, $48; junior (12 and under), $35; toddlers (6 and under), $15. SKIwee/Explorers program, ages 4–12, weekends/holidays, $73, rentals additional. **Ages 6 mos. and up.**

This Berkshires-area resort is coming on strong as a family favorite, thanks to these appealing features: on-mountain lodgings; super snowmaking; a snowboard park with a quarter pipe; night skiing; kids' programs (including SKIwee) for youngsters from 4 to 17, offered seven days a week; and child care for tots as young as 6 months. If your bunch isn't the first to make tracks in fresh powder (and what family manages to be up, ready, and on the slopes at 8 A.M.?), you can still get your money's worth at Jiminy

Peak—day lift tickets are good til 6 P.M. Need a break from the slopes? Jiminy Peak offers free ice skating. If your kids are quickly leaving you in the dust, ski-wise, sharpen your skills with a Perfect Turn ski clinic. The stats: Jiminy Peak has a vertical descent of 1,140 feet, with 20 groomed trails and two glades, serviced by eight lifts. For hotshots, it offers double-black-diamond Jericho and Whitetail, one of New England's steepest, longest night runs.

In summer and fall, you can ride up the chairlift for panoramic views of the Berkshires. Even better, the alpine slide will zip you down again. An hour or so of this, and your children will be blissfully exhausted. Call for current schedule and rates.

● Norman Rockwell Museum

Rte. 183, Stockbridge, (800) 742-9450, (413) 298-4100, www.nrm.org. Open daily, Nov.–Apr., 10–4; weekends and holidays, 10–5; May–Oct., daily, 10–5. Adults, $10; 18 and under, free (limit 4 children per adult).
Ages 5 and up.

If you're a fan of Rockwell's work, take a look at the originals on display here. During summer, you can also peek at the actual studio where he worked. On Family Days (once a month), special tours and activities are planned, and parents' admission is halfprice. Look for interesting temporary exhibits, too; a recent show featured Charles Schulz's Snoopy. Call for information.

● Bartholomew's Cobble

Off Rte. 7A, Ashley Falls, (413) 229-8600. Mid-Apr.–mid-Oct., daily, 9–5. Museum open Wed.–Sun., 9–5. Adults, $3; 6–12, $1. **All ages.**

Let's keep this pretty spot a secret. Junior gardeners will be inspired by the rock garden, with 700 species of plants; the natural history museum has a neat collection of mounted birds, a bobcat, butterflies, arrowheads, and Mohegan Indian artifacts. Also head up to Hurlburt's Hill (the map at the entrance will direct you), a high pasture that's perfect for kite flying. (Fly before May, please, or you'll disturb nesting birds.) Round out your visit with an easy hike along Ledge's Trail or, beside the river, Bailey's Trail. Interpretive programs geared to kids are run several times a year. Call for a schedule.

● Beartown State Forest

Blue Hill Rd., 5 mi. east on Rte. 23, Monterey, (413) 528-0904, www.state.ma.us/dem. Parking fee. **All ages.**

Beartown Mountain is the major feature among a group of wooded peaks. Follow the signs to Laura Tower or the Alcott Trail lookout for scenic views. Hike along the Appalachian Trail, fish for bass, or swim in Benedict Pond. In winter, cross-country ski along 10 miles of marked trails.

 **RESTAURANTS**

● Dakota

Pittsfield-Lenox Line, Rte. 7, Pittsfield, (413) 499-7000,
www.dakotarestaurant.com. Open Mon.–Thurs., 5–10 P.M.; Fri., 5–11;
Sat., 4–11; Sun. brunch, 10 A.M.–2 P.M.

Everybody loves Dakota, where, they say, they serve "smiles" along with the steak and seafood. The Sunday brunch is an eye-popper; nightly, there's a killer salad bar and all the American standards. Kids' menu, too.

● Miss Adams Diner

Rte. 8, N. Adams, (413) 743-5300, www.missadamsdiner@aol.com.
Tues.–Sat., 6:30–3; Sun., 7-1. Closed Mon.

This downtown landmark is a restored, 1949 Worcester Lunch Car. If you've always wanted to take your kids to a diner but figured they'd balk at the Meat Loaf Special, this might be the ticket. There's meat loaf, all right, but there's also good homemade chili, pastrami sandwiches, and really tasty muffins in fun combinations like pineapple-corn and cranberry-pecan. Breakfast is available all day. Other treats include malted milkshakes (much better than fast-food shakes) and the Mount Greylock Sundae, a triumph of coffee ice cream, hot fudge, peanut butter chips, blueberries, walnuts, and whipped cream. Wow!

● Main Street Café

16 Water St., Williamstown, (413) 458-3210,
www.mainstcf@berkshire.net. Daily, 11:30 A.M.–2:30 P.M., then 5–10 P.M.

If you're looking for something more special than a sandwich, this casual, upscale eatery is a great option. The menu leans toward Italian, so the kids are sure to be happy.

● Pappa Charlie's Deli Sandwich

28 Spring St., Williamstown, (413) 458-5969. Daily, 9–9.

Care for a Bebe Rebozo? How about a Gwyneth Paltrow? This cheap, friendly eatery draws throngs of students from Williams College to feast on giant deli sandwiches, eggplant parm, and other stick-to-the-ribs fare. You'll sit in booths, overhear kids kvetching about bio exams, and try to pick out someone the kids have heard of in the black-and-white glossy photos of theater folk that serve as decor.

■ Cape Cod

More than four million people visit Cape Cod and the two tiny sister islands, Nantucket and Martha's Vineyard, each year. It is said that there are more people on this small elbow of sand on a summer day than there are in the entire city of Boston. Good news for Cape-bound travelers: new "Smart" traffic signs along Route 6 and Route 28. While they won't make the cars disappear, they'll help you avoid the trouble spots, providing information on traffic conditions, where to park for island ferries, which beach parking lots are full, and so on.

Why do vacationers continue to flock to the Cape? Why do they endure the legendary Cape Cod bottleneck, waiting sometimes nearly three hours to cross the Sagamore Bridge? Despite the summertime crunch, Cape Cod has an allure that few can resist. Vacationers put up with the traffic and summer crowds because they know what awaits them: miles of sandy, white beaches, wide-open salt marshes and clam flats, scenic harbors, lighthouses, and picturesque, historic sea captains' homes and cedar-shaked beach cottages.

Families enjoy the casual seaside atmosphere, where lobster-in-the-rough and steamers fresh from local shellfish beds are daily fare. For fun, there's hiking, sailing, windsurfing, fishing, swimming, sightseeing, and any amusement your family desires. Think petting zoos, water slides, video arcades, boat trips, train rides, museums, and more.

If your kids like lots of action, you won't be disappointed. The bustling resort towns of Hyannis and Provincetown sizzle with energy during the summer months. If you prefer more peaceful pleasures, they're here as well, tucked down the back roads of Falmouth, atop one of the striking cliffs in Truro, on a hike along spectacular beaches at Cape Cod National Seashore, or while digging for clams in Wellfleet. (Please check with local authorities before you dig, in case of "red tide" alert.) Nearly everywhere, despite the summer rush, it is possible to get away from the crush to enjoy the Cape's beauty. A local's best advice is to "get lost" (said with a bit of tongue in cheek!); meander the back roads and discover the lovely, hidden spots on the Cape. There, "Old Cape Cod" can still be found, far away from the shopping malls and fast-food eateries. But first you have to get there. Some words of advice:

1. Consider visiting Cape Cod off-season, if you can, during spring or fall. After Labor Day, the crowds diminish but the weather is still balmy—and most attractions stay open through September or October. Also, lodging prices drop dramatically after Labor Day. Personally, we think the Cape and islands are at their best in autumn. Springtime is a bit dicier, weather-wise, and many attractions don't open until Memorial Day. Still, if you're looking for a real escape, and if you're not yet tied to school vacation schedules, think about an early visit. Early June is also a good

time to visit, since many New England schools are in session until late in the month.

2. Avoid the weekend rush hours; don't try to get to the Cape on Fridays between four and nine, or leave on Sundays between noon and nine (unless sitting in a virtual parking lot is your idea of a fine time).

3. If you find yourself trapped in the infamous Cape Cod congestion, don't despair. In just a few hours you'll be eating some of the best, freshest seafood in the world on some of the most spectacular beaches in the country. Pack car toys for the kids and an ocean-wave relaxation tape to achieve serenity of spirit, and try to make the best of it. For information, call the Cape Cod Chamber of Commerce at (888) 33-CAPECOD (ask for a copy of the *Official Guide to Cape Cod*) or visit www.capecodchamber.org.

■ Upper Cape
(Includes Sandwich, Falmouth, Bourne)

● Water Wizz
Rtes. 6 and 28, Wareham, (508) 295-3255, www.waterwizz.com. Open daily, mid-June–mid-Aug., 10–6:30; mid-Aug.–Labor Day, 10–6. Adults, $26; under 48 in. tall and seniors, $11; after 4 P.M., $18/$10; after 5 P.M., $10 per person. **All ages.**

Located in the town known as the "gateway to Cape Cod," just eight minutes from the Bourne Bridge, Water Wizz is the only water park in southern New England. Water slides and pools are geared to all ages; check out the cool new wave pool and new kiddie attractions.

● Thermometer Museum
49 Zarahemla Rd., Onset, (508) 295-5504. Open daily. Free. **All ages.**

Is it hot? Is it cool? You be the judge. Either way, this museum, located in the home of collector Richard Porter, is one of the most unique you'll ever see. Porter, a retired science teacher, has collected more than 3,400 thermometers, on display in his basement. The collection includes some rarities, like a thermometer that traveled to the moon in 1969. The museum's motto: "Always open and always free, with over 3,000 to see!"

● Heritage Plantation
Rte. 6A at Grove and Pine Sts., Sandwich, (508) 888-3300. Mid-May–Oct., daily, 10–5. Adults, $9; 6–18, $5; 5 and under, free. **Ages 3 and up.**

A mixed bag of Americana spread throughout a beautifully landscaped 76-acre site, Heritage Plantation has something for everyone. Best for kids: "Clue Tours," where kids follow a trail of footsteps and decipher clues.

"Family Fun Packs" (backpacks) are available, offering interactive activities related to buildings on the grounds. Heritage Plantation is particularly enjoyable on a warm, sunny day when kids can skip along any of a dozen nature trails past flower beds, wood groves, and the shore of Upper Shawme Lake. A Shaker-designed round barn houses an impressive collection of antique cars, including one the kids can climb on. Other buildings house collections of Native American artifacts, antique military miniatures, firearms, early tools, and folk art. Don't miss the working (circa 1912) antique carousel. A children's program called "Sizzling Summer Step Outs" is offered on Thursdays in July and August.

● Thornton W. Burgess Museum

Rte. 130, on edge of Shawme Pond, Sandwich, (508) 888-6870, www.thorntonburgess.org. Apr.–Dec., daily, 10–4; Sun., 1–4. Winter hours vary. Story Hour, June–Aug., Mon., Wed., and Sat., 10:30, $1 per person. Not held on rainy days. Admission by donation. **All ages.**

The word "charming" springs to mind when you discover this place, a favorite of Cape Cod families. The museum is a memorial to author/naturalist Burgess, author of more than 15,000 children's stories, including "Peter Rabbit & the Briar Patch." It was established in 1976 to inspire reverence in children for wildlife and the environment—long before such concerns were common. On sunny summer afternoons, join the parents and children who gather under a tree for Story Hour, often "illustrated" with live animals. The small museum houses Burgess memorabilia and an interactive exhibit tied to Cape Cod natural history themes. The Burgess Society sponsors several delightful children's events and activities during the summer. Call for a schedule.

● Green Briar Nature Center and Jam Kitchen

6 Discovery Hill Rd., off Rte. 6A, E. Sandwich, (508) 888-6870. Apr.–Dec., daily, 10–4; Sun., 1–4. Admission by donation. **All ages.**

Here's one of those things you'd only consider doing while on vacation: watching jams and jellies being made in an old-fashioned kitchen. This is no factory tour; they use turn-of-the-century cooking methods. Take home some beach-plum jelly. Visit the award-winning wildflower garden and take the mile-long hike down historic Old Briar Patch trail. (Shorter walks are offered, too.) Before you leave, be sure to check out the natural history exhibits and say hello to Peter Rabbit, who resides here in his bunny hutch. The center is operated by the Thornton W. Burgess Society.

● Sandwich Glass Museum

120 Main St., Sandwich, (508) 888-0241, www.sandwichglassmuseum.org. Apr.–Dec., daily, 9:30–5; Feb.–Mar., 9:30–4. Adults, $3.50; 6–12, $1. **Ages 8 and up.**

We've hesitated to include this attraction in past editions, for the obvious reason: There's lots of breakable stuff here! We've discovered, though, that this museum is appropriate for older, artsy kids, who especially like the glass-bead-making demonstrations and activities geared to them. The museum displays more than 5,000 pieces of glass, produced at the Boston & Sandwich Glass Company from 1825 to 1888. This little seaside town became famous for its high-quality glass—blown, pressed, cut, and decorated.

● Yesteryears Doll Museum

Old Main St. at River St., Sandwich, (508) 888-1711. June–mid-Sept., Tues.–Sat., 10–4. Adults, $3; 2–17, $2; under 2, free. **Ages 3 and up.**

Hello, dollies. If you like dolls, you'll adore this international collection of antique dolls, housed in the First Parish Meetinghouse (circa 1638). Many of the dolls here are rare finds; some will look very familiar (vintage Barbie dolls and dolls that Mom and Grandma may have played with). The collection includes antique dollhouses, toys, and miniatures. Got an injured doll around the house? Bring her/him along; this is the best doll hospital around.

● Aptucxet Trading Post Museum

24 Aptucxet Rd., Bourne, (508) 759-5990. May–Columbus Day, Tues.– Sat., 10–4; Sun., 2–5. Open Mon., July, Aug., and Mon. holidays. Adults, $3; children, grades 1–12, $2. **Ages 6 and up.**

Sure it's touristy, but this attraction has some redeeming historical value. Established as a trading post by Pilgrims in 1627, it's billed as the first-known commercial enterprise in English-speaking North America. Today, this replica of a Pilgrim-Dutch trading post is filled with Native American artifacts. The site includes a windmill, a Victorian railroad station (built for the exclusive use of President Grover Cleveland, who owned a summer home in Bourne), and herb and wildflower gardens. A picnic area overlooks the Cape Cod Canal.

● National Marine Fisheries Aquarium

Corner of Water and Albatross Sts., Woods Hole, (508) 548-7684. Mid-June–mid-Sept., daily, 10–4. Off–season, Mon.–Fri., 9–4. Free. **All ages.**

This little gem—the oldest research aquarium in the United States—is a great place to get in touch with Cape sea life. Touch tanks house starfish, banded lobsters, horseshoe crabs, whelks, and snails. Watch the harbor seal feedings at 11 A.M. and 4 P.M. during summer months.

● National Marine Life Center

120 Main St., Buzzards Bay, (508) 759-8722, www.nmlc.org. Open Memorial Day–Labor Day, Mon.–Sat., 11–6; Sun., 12–6. Free. **All ages.**

This center for stranded marine animals is a great place to learn about whales, dolphins, seals, and sea turtles.

● Cape Cod Children's Museum

577 Great Neck Rd., Mashpee, (508) 539-8788. Mon.–Sat., 10–5; Sun., 12–5. Admission: 1–4 and seniors, $2.50; 5–59, $3.50. **Ages 1–10.**

Outdoor plans rained out? Kids ages 1 to 10 won't balk at a trip to the Children's Museum, featuring a pirate ship, indoor planetarium, a puppet theater, a toddler area, and more.

● Beaches

Upper Cape beaches include **Scusset Beach** (Scusset Beach Rd., near the Sagamore Rotary in Sandwich), a nice state-run beach on Cape Cod Canal. **Town Neck Beach** (on the bay side, off Rte. 6A and Tupper Rd., Sandwich) has pretty views and good swimming. It's a favorite spot of local photographers and artists. There's a nice hike along the boardwalk across Mill Creek. **Bourne Scenic Park** (Rte. 6, Buzzard's Bay on Cape Cod Canal, Sandwich) has 70 acres of hiking, fishing, swimming, and playgrounds. Take a dip in the unique sea-level pool—it changes with the tide. Other fine beaches include **Surf Drive Beach** (on Vineyard Sound, off Surf Dr., Falmouth); **Old Silver Beach** (on Buzzard's Bay, off Bay Shore Dr., N. Falmouth); and **Menauhant Beach** (on Vineyard Sound, off Menauhant Rd., E. Falmouth).

● Kettle Ponds

If you like gazing at the ocean but would rather dive into something, well, cozier, how about one of Cape Cod's little fishing holes, a kettle pond? Tucked behind the ocean beaches, these ponds were dug out of the landscape by Ice Age glaciers. They're round, deep (in the middle), clear, and warm. In short, they're perfect natural freshwater pools, great for swimming. Locally, check out **Long Pond** in Harwich (covering more than 700 acres, it's a biggie) and **Wakeby** and **Mashpee Ponds,** both in Mashpee. Pack a picnic and enjoy.

● Hiking

The Briar Patch in E. Sandwich is a 57-acre conservation area crisscrossed with marked woodland trails. Don't be surprised if you see a bunny or two; this is the area that inspired author and conservationist Thornton Burgess to write about Peter Rabbit and friends. Another nice place to ramble is the boardwalk at Town Neck Beach. The walkway spans the marshland and offers water views at high tide. Ashumet Holly Wildlife Sanctuary, run by the Massachusetts Audubon Society, offers eight self-guided trails, lots of holly trees, and more than 130 species of birds on 40 acres. The sanctuary is located on Ashumet Rd., off Rte. 151 in E. Falmouth. On a hot day, there's nothing more refreshing than a walk through the woods at Shawme-Crowell State

Forest, off Rte. 130 in Sandwich. (This 742-acre forest is also a great place to camp.)

● Bicycling

The **Shining Sea Bikeway** is a 3.6-mile trail running from Falmouth Center to Woods Hole along the shoreline. Stop, take a break, and watch the activity at busy marinas along the way. Pick up the path on Locust Street in Falmouth; you'll end up at the Steamship Authority dock in Woods Hole.

 RESTAURANTS

● The Lobster Trap

290 Shore Rd., Bourne, (508) 759-7600. Daily, in season, 11:30–8:30. Spring and fall, Sat. and Sun. only.

So, you've just hit the Cape and can't wait another nanosecond for a taste of fresh seafood? This is the place. Located right off the Bourne Bridge (take an immediate right as you exit the bridge), it's ultracasual and on the water (well, on the river). More important, the food is great and the prices are low. Try the Bourne scallops, lobster, fried clams, or, a good bet for kids, the expertly made lobster rolls, which are heavy on the lobster meat, light on the mayo. Already, the wretched ride is but a memory. . . .

● The Wharf

Grand Ave., Falmouth Heights, (508) 548-2772. Apr.–Dec., daily, 11:30– 10. Early-bird special: 4–6 P.M., $6.95 (includes entree, coffee, and dessert).

This is no family restaurant; it's more of a beachfront hangout. Part of a ramshackle structure that includes a dairy bar, T-shirt shop, and casino, The Wharf has lots to look at, making it the perfect place for kids. (We'd still avoid the peak dinner hour on Friday and Saturday nights; it's just too smoky and noisy.) Inside, it's like a TGI Friday's run amok—absolutely stuffed with junk like moose mounts, anchors, and buoys. Outside, there's the gorgeous sweep of Vineyard Sound and, in the distance, Martha's Vineyard. The best views, naturally, are from the deck. And the eats are great; blackboard specials usually feature fresh fish (often caught by the restaurant's owner) priced to move, German fare (the chef is from Germany), and steak, chicken, pasta, and prime rib.

● Hearth 'N Kettle

874 Main St., Falmouth, (508) 548-6111. (Other locations in Hyannis, Yarmouth, and Orleans.) Daily, 7 A.M.–9 P.M.; Fri. and Sat., 7 A.M.– 10 P.M.; stays open an hour later from Memorial Day–Labor Day.

This local chain offers friendly family dining at great prices; nothing fancy, but reliably good. The Falmouth outpost was the first in the chain and has survived on the Cape for more than 25 years, as trendier places have come and gone. You can get anything from a hearty breakfast to grilled salmon fillet, served by chipper waitpeople. More reasons to give the H 'n K a try: lots of low-fat options, a good kids' menu (the cod nuggets 'n fries win rave reviews), and early-bird specials served til 6 P.M.

■ Mid-Cape
(Includes Hyannis, Barnstable, Yarmouth, Dennis)

● Cape Cod Central Railroad
252 Main St., Hyannis, (508) 771-3800 or (888) 797-RAIL, www.capetrain.com. June–Oct., Tues.–Sun., departures at 10, 12:30, and 3. Scenic train rides: adults, $13; 3–11, $9. Family Supper Train: adults, $32.95; under 12, $24.95. **Ages 3 and up.**

Board a refurbished 1920s parlor car and take a scenic tour of undiscovered Cape Cod. You'll see Cape Cod Bay, historic villages, salt marsh, cranberry bogs, and more, with stops at Sandwich and the Cape Cod Canal. The trip takes two hours, departing from the station in downtown Hyannis. They also offer a Family Supper Train ride, Tuesday evenings from late June through August. Call for reservations.

● Cape Cod Potato Chip Tour
Breed's Hill in Independence Park (near Cape Cod Mall), Hyannis, (508) 775-7253. Mon.–Fri., 9–5. Free. **All ages.**

Looking for an unusual rainy-day activity? Head to the potato chip factory, and watch them hand-cook these tasty chips in giant kettles. Tours are self-guided. Even if you've sworn off chips forever, you won't be able to resist a sample.

● Cape Cod Melody Tent
West Main St., Hyannis, (508) 775-9100, www.melodytent.com. Children's performances, Wed., 11 A.M. Tickets, $6. **Ages 3 and up.**

Put a little culture into your Cape escape with a show at the Melody Tent. Productions feature all the kids' classics, like *Goldilocks and the Three Bears, The Velveteen Rabbit, Alice in Wonderland,* and *Hansel and Gretel.* (See South Shore Music Circus.)

● Cape Cod Duckmobile
Departs from 437 Main St., Hyannis, (508) 362-1117 or (888) 225-DUCK, www.duckmobile.com. Reservations required; call for current operating schedule. Adults, $14; kids/students/seniors, $11; under 5, $5; babies, free. **All ages.**

Take a narrated tour of local landmarks in a renovated U.S. military amphibious vehicle, then splash down into the harbor.

● ZooQuarium

674 Rte. 28, W. Yarmouth, (508) 775-8883, www.zooquar@capecod.net. July and Aug., daily, 9:30–6; mid-Feb.–June and Sept.–late Nov., daily, 9:30–5. Shows at 11, 1, 2:30, and 4. Adults, $8; 2–9, $5; under 2, free. **All ages.**

Many a road-weary family, trapped in traffic along Route 28, has sought refuge here. Features include seals and sea lion shows, pony rides, and a petting zoo. The animals who live here are native to Cape Cod and New England. You'll encounter deer, sheep, goats, pigs, bobcats, and porcupines—enough diversion, in short, to chase away the worst case of kiddie car crabbiness.

● Crab Creek

Public dock, N. Dennis Rd., Yarmouth. **Ages 3 and up.**

This is considered the best spot on the Cape for blue crabbing. No fancy equipment needed, just some leftover, cooked chicken (for bait) and a four-foot piece of string. Crash-course in crabbing: Stand on the dock, tie some string around a piece of chicken, lower string into the water, and wait for some action.

● Josiah Dennis Manse and Old West Schoolhouse

77 Nobscusset Rd. and Whig St., Dennis, (508) 385-3528. July and Aug., Tues., 10–12 and Thurs., 2–4 P.M. Donations appreciated. **Ages 3 and up.**

This saltbox house was the home of Reverend Dennis, for whom the town was named. The site features a 1770 schoolhouse, Indian and marine artifacts, and a Children's Room. See spinning and weaving demonstrations in the attic workroom. Costumed interpreters offer commentary.

● Cape Playhouse Children's Theatre

820 Rte. 6A, Dennis, (508) 385-3911 or (877) 385-3911, www.capeplayhouse.com. Performances June–Aug., Fri. at 9:30 and 11:30 A.M. Tickets, $6. **Ages 3 and up.**

Marionettes, puppets, teddy bears . . . kids' favorite stories come to life on stage at the Cape Playhouse, America's oldest professional summer theater (they say). Touring companies and local performers delight small fry with shows like *Beauty and the Beast,* presented by the National Marionette Theatre, Gary Rosen's *Teddy Bear Jamboree,* and more.

Tip: Also look for lively stage offerings at smaller venues on the Cape, such as Chatham High School, Barnstable High School, and Wellfleet Methodist Church. Magicians, storytellers, and family musicals appear on local stages all summer long. Typical ticket charge is around $8 to $10. Check the calendar section of the *Cape Cod Times* or a free publication called *Kids on the Cape* for prices and show times.

● Bicycling—Cape Cod Rail Trail

Trail begins in S. Dennis off Rte. 134 to LeCount Hollow in Wellfleet. Bike rentals available. **All ages.**

Formerly the Penn-Central Railroad right-of-way, this 26-mile-long, eight-foot-wide tarred trail runs from Dennis to Wellfleet. This popular path winds through forests, fields, marshes, and cranberry bogs. Try to stay on the right (fast riders can approach suddenly from behind) and remember that state law requires children ages 12 and under to wear helmets. Parking areas are located in Nickerson State Park on Rte. 6A in Brewster, Rte. 124 in Harwich, and at the Salt Pond Visitor Center off Rte. 6 in Eastham.

● Cape Cod Storyland

70 Center St., Hyannis, (508) 778-4339. Late June–Labor Day, daily, 10–9. **Ages 4 and up.**

It's New England's largest minigolf course—and as if that weren't enough, they've got bumper boats! It's clean, well-run, and pure retro fun.

● Sea View Playland

Lower County Rd., Dennisport, (508) 398-9084. Late June–Labor Day, daily, 10–10. **All ages.**

This is pure honky-tonk fun. Skee-ball, miniature golf, pitch and putt, and an old barn filled with nearly 100 different arcade games. Hey, you're on vacation—if not now, when? You'll find the newest and oldest coin-operated games. Ask anyone in the area for directions to the Barn of Fun; they'll be able to tell you.

● Boat Cruises

The mid-Cape area offers a couple of very cool ocean cruises. Be a pirate-for-a-day with **Pirate Adventures.** Departing from Ocean St. docks in Hyannis (and Town Cove in Orleans) in a sea-faring shanty boat, little mates will get their faces painted, use water cannons to keep the enemy at bay, even pull up sunken treasure from the deep. Trips run from late June through Labor Day; reserve in advance at (508) 430-0202, www.pirateadventurescapecod.com. Or get acquainted with the gentle giants of the sea on a whale-watch trip. Onboard naturalists provide commentary; whale sightings are guaranteed. Reserve a trip with **Hyannis Whale Watcher Cruises** at (508) 362-6088 or (888) 942-5392, www.whales.net. Trips depart from Barnstable Harbor. (Tip: Look for discount coupons for whale-watch trips in *Kids on the Cape* and other tourist-geared publications.)

● Beaches

Sandy Neck Beach, on Sandy Neck Rd. (off Rte. 6A) in Barnstable, is considered one of the best public beaches on the Cape. It's easy to hang around here for an entire day, sunning, swimming, and exploring the surrounding dunes and marshlands. For a spectacular view of the unspoiled Cape, take one of the many trails along Sandy Neck. Walk quietly, and you're likely to spot rare birds and wildlife; you can also search for relics in the dunes along the way and wade in the water along this magnificent stretch of beach. Be sure to return to the main entrance before dusk, where a wonderful surprise awaits: musicians, storytellers, and mimes performing around a campfire. **Sea Gull Beach,** off South Sea Ave. in Yarmouth, is another winner; on Nantucket Sound, it's calm, sandy, and considered the best beach for swimming in the Yarmouth area. It has a snack bar and picnic area. Teens or preteens in your group? They'll insist on making the scene at popular **Craigville Beach.** It boasts fine sand, gentle surf, and warm water. (An MTV beach party segment was shot here; enough said.)

 RESTAURANTS

● Baxter's Fish 'N Chips

117 Pleasant St. Wharf, Hyannis, (508) 775-4490. Apr.–Oct., Mon.–Sat., 11:30–10; Sun., 11:30–9; off-season, Thurs.–Sun., 11:30–10.

Boatless in Hyannis? Perish the thought! However, a meal at Baxter's is the next best thing. The outdoor deck of this classic fish house juts out into the harbor amid fishing boats and pleasure cruisers. Sometimes sea planes land alongside the restaurant, causing drinks to slosh. (Kids find this a hoot.) But don't get too distracted, or a seagull will make off with your entree. Lotsa luck getting it back. The menu features the usual fried seafood plates and fresh fish, grilled or broiled.

● Swan River Seafood Restaurant

5 Lower Country Rd., Dennisport, (508) 394-4466. Open late May–mid-Sept. Lunch, 12–3:30; dinner, 5–9.

Good, fresh seafood and breathtaking views of Nantucket Sound make this one hard to beat. Try the steamers, seafood pasta salad, or Cape-caught boiled lobsters. Not into fish? The menu includes paw as well as claw. There's a kids' menu, too.

● Barby Ann's

120 Airport Rd., Hyannis, (508) 775-9795. Daily, 11:30–11; Sun., 11–10.

Home-style cooking is the draw at this popular family restaurant. Try their famous seafood stew or barbecued ribs, or one of the blackboard specials. The decor is casual but nice and the children's menu has an all-star lineup of chicken fingers, fish 'n' chips, hot dogs, and burgers.

● Four Seas Ice Cream

360 S. Main St., Centerville, (508) 775-1394. Late May–mid-Sept., daily, 9–10:30.

Still praline after all these years. When it comes to ice cream, Four Seas rules; they've won so many "Best of Cape" awards, they've lost count. A PBS special singled them out, among a scoopful of other ice cream shops elsewhere, as one of the best in the U.S., no less. No need to gussy it up with Reese's pieces. Try the penuche pecan or cantaloupe (all the fruit flavors are made with real fresh fruit).

■ Lower Cape
(Includes Harwich, Brewster, Chatham, Orleans)

● New England Fire and History Museum

Rte. 6A, Brewster, (508) 896-5711, www.nefiremuseum.org. Memorial Day– Labor Day, Mon.–Fri., 10–4; Sat. and Sun., 12–4; Labor Day–mid-Oct., Sat. and Sun., 12–4. Adults, $4; 5–12, $2.50; 4 and under, free. **All ages.**

This museum contains a fascinating assortment of antique fire engines, one of the largest collections in the country. "They put out fires with buckets of water?" "They had to pull this by hand?" "How fast could the horses get them to the fire?" Children are full of questions as they view this interesting exhibit of 18th- to 20th-century fire engines and related memorabilia. Kids can climb aboard a fire truck, a fire engine, and a fireboat, complete with hoses.

● Cape Cod Museum of Natural History

869 Main St., Rte. 6A, Brewster, (508) 896-3867, www.ccmnh.org. Year-round, Mon.–Sat., 9:30–4:30; Sun., 11–4:30. Adults, $5; 5–12, $2; 4 and under, free. **Ages 3 and up.**

Set on 300 acres of conservation land, this museum is a gem. Play nature detective and discover mysterious species of sea life; put your hand in a secret box and try to figure out what lurks within; test your knowledge of underwater creatures when you take the hands-on discovery quiz. Watch live marine animals scuttle around in their tanks, and see bees at work (can you spot the queen?) in an indoor, working beehive. Small fry adore creating impromptu puppet shows with the family of animal puppets. Outside, three nature trails invite rambling through woodlands, salt marsh, and coastal habitats. Ask about the archaeological dig, taking place on Wing Island in July and August. The museum runs several creative and fun kids' programs and special events, like Bubble-Blowing Day, Make Your Own Kite Day, field walks, and museum sleep-overs.

● Stony Brook Mill and Herring Run

Stony Brook Rd., Brewster. **All ages.**

If you're visiting in springtime (March through June), join local Cape Codders as they watch spawning herring run upstream. The herring swim against the current through a series of ladders that run from Cape Cod Bay to Upper Mill and Lower Mill Ponds. A restored 19th-century grist mill shares the property; it grinds corn every Thursday through Saturday from 2 to 5 P.M., May and June and (on Friday only) July through August.

● Nickerson State Park

Off Rte. 6A, Brewster, (508) 896-3867, www.state.ma.us/dem. Free for day use. **All ages.**

This lovely, 1,750-acre park is perfect for hiking and biking (part of the Cape Cod Rail Trail passes through it). Freshwater swimming (with life-guards on duty), camping, fishing, and paddling are available for sports-minded families. Insider tip: Your best bet for catching trout and landlocked salmon is at Cliff Pond. (Kids over 14 need a license.) Our favorite thing to do here: Rent a kayak from **Jack's** (508-896-8556) and enjoy a leisurely paddle on Flax Pond. It's also an awesome—if lively—place to camp.

● Chatham Fish Pier

Shore Rd. and Bar Cliff Ave., Chatham. Daily, after 12. **All ages.**

Bring your camera and watch salty New England fishermen unload their daily catch at this working fish pier. You'll stand atop a visitors balcony and see nets full of haddock, flounder, halibut, cod, and more being pulled in and readied for shipping to local markets and restaurants. Boats return shortly after noon, depending on the tide, and the action continues for hours.

● Kate Gould Park

Main St., Chatham Center. July and Aug., Fri. at dusk (around 8 P.M.). **All ages.**

If you're in Chatham and it's Friday night, catch the Chatham Band concert at Kate Gould Park. Bring a blanket and refreshments and join right in. It's a terrific, fun freebie. Hanging in Harwich? The Harwich Town Band performs at the Brooks Park Bandstand, Tuesday nights in July and August at 7:30 P.M.

● Beaches

Skaket Beach, on Skaket Beach Rd. (off Main St.) in Orleans is great for kids, thanks to long, shallow tidal flats. Another lovely option is **First**

Encounter Beach, off Rte. 6 in Eastham. This is the place where the Pilgrims first encountered the native Wampanoags (look for the plaque); plus it's a nice shallow stretch of sand with gentle surf.

● Boat Cruises

Chatham Water Tours offers some intriguing options for families. Their 90-minute lobster/nature cruises offer hands-on experience in hauling lobster pots, with narration that focuses on the coastline, wildlife, and ecology. They also take nature lovers out to watch seals frolic in the waters off the coast of Chatham near Monomoy Island. Call (508) 432-5895. Other companies offer seal-watching trips to Monomoy Island, including **Beachcomber Boat Tours** (508-945-5265) and **Monomoy Island Excursions** (508-430-7772). Monomoy Island is a wildlife refuge on the spit of land off Chatham. It is home to more than 400 gray seals, and many species of birds. The **Wellfleet Bay Wildlife Sanctuary** sponsors trips, too, even during winter months. Call (508) 349-2615.

■ Outer Cape
(Includes Eastham, Wellfleet, Truro, Provincetown)

● Salt Pond Visitor Center
Cape Cod National Seashore headquarters, Eastham, (508) 255-3421. Summer, open daily, 9–6; spring and fall, daily, 9–4:30; weekends only, Jan.–mid-Feb. Call to confirm tour schedule. Free. **All ages.**

Early birds: Take a guided, 8:30 A.M. Beach Walk and learn about the shoreline of Nauset Beach. Night owls: Plan to join an Evening Campfire Walk along the beach. Meet back at the campfire to tell stories and enjoy the aroma of wood smoke and salt air. More than 40 tours are offered in summer, including beach and inland walks and fishing and shellfishing demonstrations. Children's Hours, held two to three times weekly in summer, feature fun projects like scavenger hunts for kids up to age six. Most activities are free, and they offer a great way to get acquainted with the Cape Cod National Seashore. (Note: The Salt Pond Visitor Center recently received federal funding for major renovations and may be closed when you visit. The hiking trails will remain open, however. Please visit the National Seashore's Race Point Visitor Center, in Provincetown.)

● Clam Digging
This is the home of the world-famous Wellfleet oyster. For a true New England experience, roll up your pants cuffs, grab a bucket, and go clam digging. The shellfish beds here are abundant. Be sure to adhere to local laws regarding shellfish harvesting here and elsewhere on the Cape, especially if

there's a red-tide alert. This means it's unsafe to collect any shellfish. Check the local paper for times of low tide, when you can pick steamers, quahogs, mussels, oysters, cherrystones, and scallops from the shellfish beds along the shoreline. Shellfish licenses are available at the town shellfish offices near Mayo Beach and at Town Hall. You might ask local enthusiasts about recommendations for the best places to go, as these vary throughout the year.

● Wellfleet Bay Wildlife Sanctuary

West Rd., Rte. 6, S. Wellfleet, (508) 349-2615, www.wellfleetbay.org. Visitors Center open daily, May–Oct., 8:30–5; Nov.–Apr., Tues.–Sun., 8:30–5. Trails open year-round, dawn–dusk. Nonmember adults, $3; nonmember children, $2. Free to members of the Massachusetts Audubon Society. Tour costs vary. **All ages.**

This 1,000-acre sanctuary offers nature trails winding through moors, marshes, forests, beaches, tidal flats, ponds, and fields. Guided and self-guided walks are available. They also offer a host of nature programs, kids' classes, and marine cruises. Naturalist-led cruises on Cape Cod Bay are great for kids; dragnets and trawls bring aboard lots of interesting, touchable creatures, like crabs, sponges, snails, and plankton. The sanctuary also runs seal-watching cruises, coastal birding trips, and other terrific programs. Reserve in advance; these can fill up quickly.

● Wellfleet Drive-In

Rte. 6, north of Eastham-Wellfleet line, Wellfleet, (508) 349-2520, www.wellfleetdrivein. com. Late Apr.–early Oct., 7 P.M. Rain or shine. Ages 12–59, $6.50; 5–11 and 60–plus, $4; 4 and under, free. **All ages.**

Introduce your kids to the joy of watching a movie in the car, with one of those wonderfully scratchy speakers attached to the window. (Actually, they have an FM stereo sound system.) This Cape Cod classic has been entertaining families since 1957. As if the 700-car first-run, drive-in movie theater wasn't enough, there's a playground, a snack bar, and minigolf. By day, the place is transformed into a giant flea market.

● Highland Light and Highland House

Off Lighthouse Rd., N. Truro, (508) 487-3397. Early June–Sept., 10–5. **All ages.**

Sometimes called Cape Cod Light, this is one of the most powerful beacons on the Atlantic Ocean. The lighthouse dates back to 1795 and is the first one seen by seafaring visitors traveling from Europe to Boston. It's a pretty drive to the lighthouse, which sits atop a bluff in a quiet, country setting. Nearby, the Highland House museum houses a small collection of materials on shipwrecks and other local lore.

● Pilgrim Monument and Provincetown Museum

High-Pole Hill on Winslow St., off Bradford, Provincetown, (508) 487-1310, www.pilgrim-monument.org. Apr.–Nov., daily, 9–4:15; July and Aug., 9–6:15. Adults, $6; 4–12, $3. Admission includes monument and museum. **Ages 4 and up.**

This impressive monument—the tallest all-granite structure in the United States—was built to commemorate the landing of the Pilgrims here in 1620. Climb to the top of this 252-foot tower for a commanding view. (It's a stamina-testing 116 stairs and 60 ramps.) On a clear day, you'll see Boston skyscrapers as you look across the bay and, to the southeast, the Atlantic Ocean. Even if you choose not to climb the monument, you'll get a nice overview of Provincetown from this site.

Located at the base of the Pilgrim Monument, the Provincetown Museum houses some unique items of interest to adults and children. You'll see model ships (the *Mayflower* exhibit is especially good), marine and whaling artifacts, and a collection of toys and children's books from the 17th and 18th centuries. Another exhibit features the early days of modern American theater in Provincetown with Eugene O'Neill. One of the newest exhibits highlights the building of the Pilgrim Memorial Monument.

● Provincetown Shuttle

From MacMillan Wharf through town and to beaches, (508) 385-8311. Call for current fees and schedule.

Great news for visitors who arrive via ferry from Boston (or those who'd rather not navigate their car through P-Town's congested streets): A shuttle service makes it easy to get around town and to the beaches, without a car.

● Whale-Watching Cruises

Given that Stellwagen Bank, a major feeding ground for whales, is just six miles from Provincetown, you'd better believe there are plenty of whale watching tours available. Whale-watching boats from up the coast head to the same place; from P-Town, you spend less time getting to the cetaceans and more time watching them—yea! Cruise companies include **Portuguese Princess Whale Watch,** (800) 442-3188 or (508) 487-2651; **Boston Harbor Cruises,** (877) SEE-WHALE, www.bostonharborcruises.com., **Cape Cod Whale Watch,** (800) 448-6074, www.capecodwhalewatch.com.; and **Dolphin Fleet,** (800) 826-9300 or (508) 349-1900.

● MacMillan Wharf

Commercial St., Provincetown. **All ages.**

This busy wharf on Provincetown Harbor is the perfect spot to park your car and watch the fishing boats and yachts come and go. (Leave your car here and explore the rest of the town on foot.) If you'd rather nibble outdoors than eat in a restaurant, look no farther; there are lots of snack options on both sides of the wharf. This is also the place where you'll find charter fishing boats, harbor cruise excursion boats, and whale-watching tours. (See Whale-Watching Cruises.)

● Cape Cod National Seashore

The Cape Cod National Seashore is more than a beach; it's a unique national park (run by the National Park Service) that encompasses private residential and commercial land. Private businesses and residents are subject to strict building regulations and restrictions as part of an effort to protect the 400-mile coastline of the Cape's outer arm. The government owns about 27,000 of the 44,000 acres of land within the boundaries of the National Seashore. Six towns have boundaries within it: Chatham, Orleans, Eastham, Wellfleet, Truro, and Provincetown. Now for the fun part: The Seashore offers a wonderful variety of self-guided tours, bike trails, and ranger-guided activities, and they extend over six spectacular beaches.

● Province Lands and Salt Pond Visitors Centers

Salt Pond Road Visitors Center, off Rte. 6, Eastham, (508) 255-3421. Province Lands Visitors Center, Race Point Rd. off Rte. 6, Provincetown, (508) 487–1256. Summer, open daily, 9–6. Spring and fall, daily, 9– 4:30. Salt Pond Visitors Center only, open weekends, Jan.–mid-Feb. **All ages.**

Visit either of these two National Seashore Visitors Centers and pick up information, maps, and a schedule of activities and programs. The centers offer exhibits and introductory audiovisual programs on the area. Nature films are shown on summer evenings in the amphitheaters. (Note: Salt Pond Visitors Center will be closing for renovations. Call before you visit. Trails will be open, however.)

● Beaches

Of the six National Seashore beaches, **Race Point Beach,** off Rte. 6 in Provincetown, is tops for families. It's a protected beach and also a prime spot for watching the sun set. **Coast Guard Beach,** on Doane Rd. in Eastham, and nearby **Nauset Light Beach** (on Cable Rd., Eastham), are pretty, but the surf is rough. The former is good for boogie-boarding, the latter is known as the surfers beach, having the highest waves of the National Seashore beaches. **Herring Cove Beach,** on Province Lands Rd., in Provincetown, is another option; the left-hand side draws a gay and lesbian crowd, while the right attracts a mix of singles and families. Other National Seashore beaches are **Marconi Beach** in Wellfleet and **Head of the Meadow Beach** in Truro, which is not recommended because of seaweed. On Cape Cod Bay, in Truro, **Corn Hill Beach** is great for families, offering superb shelling. (Watch for off-road vehicles on Corn Hill Beach; they're allowed after 5 P.M.)

● Beachcombing

Even when Cape beaches are deserted, they're teeming with life. When the tide is out, see for yourself. Look for horseshoe crabs, starfish, sea urchins, sand dollars, periwinkles, and shellfish (wearing a pair of reef shoes isn't a bad idea, since it's fun to dig in the sand with your toes). The best beaches for beachcombing are the ocean beaches from Chatham to Provincetown, although there's plenty to see along the beaches of Cape Cod Bay, Nantucket Sound, and Vineyard Sound.

● Bicycling

The following bike trails are within the Cape Cod National Seashore. Trail maps are available at the Visitors Centers in Eastham and Provincetown. Bike rentals are available at several shops, including **Nelson's Bike Shop,** 43 Race Point Rd., Provincetown (508) 487-8849; and **Little Capistrano Bike Shop,** on Salt Pond Rd. in Eastham, (508) 255-6515.

● Nauset Trail

Salt Pond Road Visitors Center, off Rte. 6, Eastham.

This 1.6-mile paved bike trail offers views of the cedar banks, Nauset Marsh, old Nauset Coast Guard Station, and other points of interest. The trail ends at Coast Guard Beach.

● Head of the Meadow Trail

High Head Rd., Truro.

This two-mile marshland bike trail begins on High Head Road in Truro and heads toward Head of the Meadow Beach (you can also pick it up at the beach parking lot). Venture off the trail to the spring where the Pilgrims took their first drink of fresh water in America (follow signs to Pilgrim Lake and Pilgrim Spring Trail).

● Province Lands Trail

Herring Cove Beach, Provincetown.

This eight-mile paved bike trail crosses forests, ponds, bogs, and some of the most spectacular sand dunes along the Atlantic coast. Segments include a 5.25-mile loop trail; Herring Cove Beach spur (1 mile); Race Point Beach spur (.5 mile); Bennett Pond spur (.25 mile); and Race Point Road spur (.25 mile.)

● Hiking

Self-guided nature walks and ranger-guided tours and activities are offered throughout the year. You don't have to be an expert trail blazer— many are short but interesting nature walks suitable for beginners and children. Particularly enjoyable are some of the National Park Service hikes, such as the Seashore Surprise (parents and kids learn about the sea through scavenger hunts, stories, and games along the way); the Sunset Beach Walk, featuring stories around a campfire at sunset; and Cape Cod Whales and Historic Beach Apparatus Drill (divers demonstrate the methods once used to rescue shipwrecked mariners). Call the Province Lands Visitors Center for times and starting points, (508) 487-1256.

RESTAURANTS

● The Lobster Claw

Rte. 6A, Orleans, (508) 255-1800. Apr.–mid-Nov., daily, 11:30–9.

This sprawling, rustic eatery is a real visit to Crustacean Land; the gift shop has more than 250 lobster-themed knickknacks, the menu is shaped like a lobster claw . . . you get the idea. It's extremely popular. We recommend it for families with a caveat: Dine early, especially on weekend nights. You'll avoid long waits and get an incentive: free chowder, beverage, and ice cream with dinner between 4 and 5:30. That's a good deal, and the prices are pretty reasonable to begin with. Lobster, mussels, and steamers are good buys, as are fish dinners, and the food isn't bad at all. There's a kids' menu, too. This is a good option when you want a step up from an eat-in-the-rough place.

● The Mayflower Cafe

300 Commercial St., Provincetown, (508) 487-0121. First Sun. in Apr.– third Sun. in Oct., 11:30–9:30.

Need a break from seafood? This wonderful family-run place has served P-Town natives and tourists for almost 70 years. The Italian and Portuguese specialties are delicious, and the waitresses fuss over you (well, over your adorable children) like doting aunties. Kale soup and pork chops *vinho dahlos* are house specialties, and for the kids, you can't go wrong with spaghetti and meatballs or pizza. (Children's portions are available.) Prices are remarkably low. Decor is plain-Jane, but what the Mayflower lacks in looks it makes up for in friendliness.

● Bayside Lobster Hut

Commercial St., Wellfleet, (508) 349-6333. Memorial Day–Columbus Day, daily, 4:30–9.

Inside this old oyster shack you'll find some of the best seafood on the Cape. Eat in the rough and enjoy lobster, steamers, fried oysters, broiled flounder, or whatever else is fresh that day. Yes, there are cheeseburgers and hot dogs—sort of an unofficial kids' menu—but why not split up the generous Fisherman's Platter instead? Veggie lovers can opt for corn on the cob and a trip to the salad bar.

■ The Islands

Martha's Vineyard and Nantucket, accessible only by air or sea, are vacation playgrounds for thousands of travelers each year. Both islands offer miles of splendid beaches, sand dunes, nature trails, picturesque harbors, fishing villages, and bustling main streets lined with trendy boutiques and fine restaurants. And yet each island has a unique personality and charm of its own.

Martha's Vineyard, located just seven miles off Cape Cod, is the largest island in New England—20 miles long and 10 miles wide. The Vineyard, as it's commonly known, is full of surprises; its textures, rhythms, and amenities are as diverse as the people who visit it. Of course, one is never far from the sea, so the preferred pastimes are swimming, sunbathing, surfing, sailing, and exploring. Surrounding the sea are forests and salt marshes, meadows and cliffs, hills and plains. Much of the action—shopping, restaurants, attractions—centers in the towns of Edgartown and Vineyard Haven (also known as Tisbury). Oak Bluffs is famous for the Flying Horses antique carousel and charming gingerbread cottages in the center of town.

You'll find as much or as little to do as you want on this island, from bustling Edgartown to the rustic harbor village of Menemsha, where the current generation of fishermen still hauls in the daily catch.

Nantucket, meaning "faraway land," is 30 miles off the coast and offers a 100-year flashback in time. You'll step off the ferry to enter a perfectly preserved 19th-century village of cobblestone streets and red-brick mansions. Elegant sea captains' homes, reminiscent of a time when Nantucket was one of the great whaling centers of the world, now house fine restaurants, boutiques, and country inns. Pack up a picnic lunch and venture beyond the village to the shoreline, where cedar-shingled homes hug the coast. Swim in the surrounding island waters—the calm Nantucket Sound to the north, the mighty Atlantic to the south.

Travelers who plan ahead (book your accommodations as far in advance as possible) and avoid summer traffic congestion (consider leaving your car behind) can find the vacation they want in the islands. Most return revitalized, refreshed by the clear salt air that has the therapeutic power to wash away stress.

Hy-Line Cruises, (508) 778-2600 or (888) 778-1132 (www.hylinecruises .com), and the **Steamship Authority,** (508) 477-8600, provide regular ferry service to the islands from Hyannis and Woods Hole. Nantucket is 2 hours and 30 minutes from Hyannis and 3 hours from Woods Hole. If you're willing to pay a higher price to save time, a high-speed ferry, run by Hy-Line Cruises will whisk you and yours from Hyannis to Nantucket in just 1 hour. Martha's Vineyard is 45 minutes from Woods Hole and 1 hour and 45 minutes from Hyannis. Call for schedules. You can bring your car on the

Steamship Authority ferries, or rent a car on the islands, but you might want to consider bringing (or renting) bicycles, instead. Martha's Vineyard, in particular, is very bike-friendly, with paved bike paths covering much of the island (and more miles of pathway to come). (See Bicycling.)

For visitor information regarding Nantucket, contact the Nantucket Visitors Services and Information Bureau at (508) 228-0925, located at 25 Federal St. Also helpful is the Nantucket Island Chamber of Commerce at 48 Main St., (508) 228-1700, www.nantucketchamber.org. (They also have the only public rest rooms downtown.) For information on Martha's Vineyard, contact the Martha's Vineyard Chamber of Commerce at (508) 693-0085, www.mvy.com.

MARTHA'S VINEYARD

● Flying Horses Carousel
Circuit Ave., Oak Bluffs, (508) 693-9481. Easter Sun.–Columbus Day, daily, 10–10; weekends only before Memorial Day and after Labor Day. Per ride, $1. **All ages.**

Doing the island thing with little ones? This may be the highlight of their visit. Grab the rings as you whirl around this antique carousel—nab the brass one and you win a free ride. The challenge is as exciting as the ride for most children. Located a short walk from the ferry dock in Oak Bluffs, the Flying Horses carousel is said to be the oldest operating carousel in the country. It has been designated a national landmark.

● Felix Neck Wildlife Sanctuary
Edgartown–Vineyard Haven Rd., Edgartown, (508) 627-4850, www.massaudubon.org. Grounds open year-round, daily, dawn–7 P.M.; nature center, June to Sept., Mon.–Sun., 8–4; Oct.–May, Tues.–Sun., 8–4. Adults, $4; children 3–12, $3. Free to members of the Massachusetts Audubon Society. **All ages.**

A wonderful place to commune with island wildlife, this 197-acre property offers two miles of self-guided nature trails and a small exhibit center. Natural features include a pond (home to native waterfowl), salt marshes, barrier beach, woods, and wildflower-studded meadows. Look for nesting ospreys and a tree swallow colony.

● Cedar Tree Neck Wildlife Sanctuary
Off Indian Hill Rd., W. Tisbury, (508) 693-5207. **All ages.**

Walk off the effects of those ice cream cones from Mad Martha's with a day of hiking. This 300-acre preserve has 250 acres of North Shore headlands, with woods, ponds, brooks, dunes, and several scenic trails.

● State Lobster Hatchery and Research Station

Shirley Ave., Oak Bluffs, (508) 693-0060. June to Labor Day, Mon.–Fri., 9–12 and 1–3. Free. **All ages.**

A trip to New England wouldn't be complete without a real close look at one of these crustaceans. You'll see baby lobsters and large lobsters and learn all about the lobster life cycle. (Did you know it takes seven years for a lobster to grow to one-pound size in our waters?) And just wait til the next time you try to boil one. . . .

● Aquinnah Cliffs

State Rd., Aquinnah (aka Gay Head). **All ages.**

Formed by glaciers, this mile-long expanse of multicolored cliffs is a national landmark. They rise 150 feet above the shore, affording spectacular views. These russet-hued layers of clay, sand, and gravel tell the tale of the island's geologic past, as do the fossils revealed by the cliffs' erosion. Fossils of great sharks, ancient whales, camels, and wild horses have been found on the beach and in the cliffs. Many year-round residents are descendants of the Wampanoag Indians. The Wampanoag people have lived on the island for at least 600 years. The name Gay Head, referring to the vivid colors of the cliffs, was coined by British sailors who cruised past in the 17th century. There's a small parking lot at the top of the cliffs and a trail that leads to the beach.

● World of Reptiles

Bachelder Ave. off Edgartown–Vineyard Haven Rd., Edgartown, (508) 627-5634. Please call for current hours. Adults, $3; under 12, $2. **All ages.**

Get acquainted with snakes, including a 20-foot python, turtles, and an alligator.

● Polly Hill Arboretum

State Rd., W. Tisbury, (508) 693-9426. $5. **All ages.**

Once a local secret, now open to the public, this privately owned 60-acre property features lush meadows, stone walls, and flowering trees and shrubs. Take a nature walk amid blooming dogwoods and other dazzling flora, and bring some goodies; this is one of the island's prettiest places for a picnic.

● Nip 'N Tuck Farm

State Rd., W. Tisbury, (508) 693-1449. Open for pony rides on summer afternoons. $1.50. **All ages.**

Visit a working farm, where the featured attraction in summer is pony-cart rides for small fry.

● Mytoi Japanese Garden

Wasque Rd., Chappaquiddick, (508) 693-7662. Year-round; sunrise–sunset. Adults, $5; children, $2. Parking fee. **All ages.**

Little ones are fascinated by the fish in the koi pond, while grown-ups enjoy the riotous blooms of color at this 14-acre garden. Daffodils, Japanese maple, dogwood, azalea, and sweet gum make this a lovely nature escape.

● Beaches

In general, the beaches on the Vineyard's south shore offer rougher surf but better body surfing than those on the north shore. (**Katama Beach,** or **South Beach,** is one example.) Beaches to the east and north offer gentler stretches of sand and shallow water. Good family beaches include **Bend-in-the-Road Beach** on Nantucket Sound, Edgartown; **Joseph A. Sylvia State Beach,** off Beach Rd. between Oak Bluffs and Edgartown (accessible by bike path); narrow **Menemsha Public Beach,** at the mouth of the harbor on Vineyard Sound (try to forget that the movie *Jaws* was filmed in Menemsha); and **Owen Park Beach** in Vineyard Haven, a calm public beach that's right next to a park and great for kids. Other nice beaches, requiring a bit more effort to get to, are **East Beach** (Cape Pogue Wildlife Refuge and Wasque Reservation) on Chappaquiddick Island, a wilderness barrier beach on the southeast tip of Martha's Vineyard. Much of this area is accessible by four-wheel-drive vehicle. **Lambert's Cove Beach,** on the north shore, is one of the island's best, but it is reserved for West Tisbury residents and guests only. To use it, obtain a permit from the West Tisbury town hall.

● Story Hours

What's not to like about an island that boasts seven libraries? Some offer story hours for little people, an especially nice outing on a rainy day. These include **Edgartown Public Library,** at 58 N. Water St., offering story hour on Wed. at 10:30 A.M.; **Oak Bluffs Public Library,** on Circuit Ave. (call 508-693-9433 for current schedule); **Chilmark Public Library,** on South St., year-round on Saturday from 10:30 to 11:30 for kids ages three and older (they host professional storytellers in July and Aug.); and **Vineyard Haven Public Library,** on Main St., hosting a preschool story hour on Tues. at 10 A.M.

● Bicycling

Vineyard regulars agree: You haven't really *done* the Vineyard til you've biked it. Roads are mostly level, and paved bike paths run between Oak Bluffs and Edgartown, Vineyard Haven and Edgartown, and Edgartown to South Beach, with more on the way. Bikes can be rented in the three main towns: Edgartown, Oak Bluffs, and Vineyard Haven. (Check out **Anderson's** on the

Circuit Ave. extension in Oak Bluffs, [508] 693-9346; they've been in business for more than 30 years.) For a look at the unspoiled heart of the island, head to **Manuel F. Correllus State Forest.** The forest encompasses 5,000 acres of scrub oak barrens and pine forest at the center of Martha's Vineyard. A paved bike trail follows the perimeter of the forest. Access it from parking lots, located in Oak Bluffs (on Airport Rd.); W. Tisbury (Old County Rd.); and Edgartown (W. Tisbury Rd.) As always, obey traffic laws. Keep to the right, single file, obey one-way street signs, and wear a helmet (they're required by law for kids 12 and under).

● Hiking

For the loveliest nature walks on the island, head inland. **Manuel F. Correllus State Forest** (see Bicycling) offers great hiking. Another superb spot is **Menemsha Hills Reservation,** on North Rd. in Chilmark. Wild and beautiful, it offers a peek into the past, a view of what the vineyard looked like before development.

RESTAURANTS

● Among the Flowers Café

Mayhew Ln., Edgartown, (508) 627-3233. Open May–June and Sept.–Oct., daily, 8–4; July–Aug., daily, 8 A.M.–10 P.M.

Located near the dock, this outdoor café offers the best breakfast in town (kids love the waffles) and—good news—you can order those same items at lunchtime. Dinners are affordable compared to other Vineyard options and rely heavily on comfort food, like pasta dishes and baked haddock.

● Giordano's Restaurant

107 Circuit Ave., Oak Bluffs, (508) 693-0184. June–Sept., daily, 11:30–10:30.

Cheerful and unpretentious, this is a place to plop down and relax with the kids. No matter how many island restaurants come and go, this one's a perennial favorite, thanks to kid-pleasing pasta and pizza, and the island's best fried clams and onion rings.

● Vineyard Foodshop Bakery

State Rd., N. Tisbury, (508) 693-1079.

This tiny shop, called "Humphreys" by local folk, is *the* place to go for mammoth, overstuffed deli sandwiches.

● The Bite

Basin Rd., off North Rd., Menemsha, (508) 645-9239. July–Aug., daily, 11–9; call for off-season hours. No credit cards.

When dining with kids, we'll choose al fresco over indoors any day! This clam shack features awesome chowder, fried fish and shellfish, and salads.

● Mad Martha's

12 Circuit Ave., Oak Bluffs, (508) 693-9151; 8 Union St., Vineyard Haven, (508) 693–9674; and 7 N. Water St., Edgartown, (508) 627-8761. Hours vary.

It is probably illegal to visit the Vineyard without stopping at Mad Martha's. Everybody loves this place, with two dozen flavors and a Presidential Seal of Approval—President Clinton was a frequent guest when he vacationed here with the First Family. (Rumor has it, he rode in a Mad Martha's truck when his entourage drove around on the island.)

NANTUCKET

● Whaling Museum

Broad St., head of Steamboat Wharf, (508) 228-1894, www.nha.org. Memorial Day–mid-Oct., daily, 10–5; reduced schedule off-season. Adults, $10; 5–14, $8. **Ages 3 and up.**

Learn what it was like during Nantucket's great whaling era as you study the museum's collections of maritime artifacts. Learn all about whales, every kid's favorite giant marine mammal; see how they were caught and, well, processed. More fun are a whaleboat, scrimshaw, and the skeleton of a 43-foot finback whale. The collection includes rare artifacts from the *Essex,* a ship rammed by an enraged sperm whale. This event inspired Herman Melville's *Moby Dick.* A lecture on the history of whaling is offered three times a day (few kids make it through this, in our experience!).

● Gail's Tours

(508) 257-6557, www.nantucket.net/tours/gails. Van tours at 10, 1, and 3 daily, year-round. $13 per person in group tours, ages 5 and under, free; $130 for private tour. **All ages.**

If you really want to get to know the island, Gail Nickerson Johnson is the gal to see. She's been giving tours for ages, is a sixth-generation Nantucketer, and she'll give you a lively ride. Air-conditioned vans can accommodate 13 people; tours last about 1 hour and 30 minutes.

● Maria Mitchell Aquarium

28 Washington St., (508) 228-5387, www.mmo.org. Early June–Aug., Tues.–Sat., 10–4. Adults, $3, children, $1. **All ages.**

This teeny-tiny aquarium and the Hinchman House (see listing) honor Nantucket astronomer Maria Mitchell, America's first female astronomer. See marine life collected from around the island here; during a recent visit, we viewed 7 types of crabs, 15 kinds of fish, eels, and baby sharks. Some specimens can be taken out to touch; aquarium staffers will tell you all about them. You can even add to the collection here—join a marine life collecting trip (run twice a week), and you'll go out with nets and buckets to look for examples of local sea life. Your specimens may join the other inhabitants of the aquarium. Call for information and reservations. Nature walks are offered on Monday, Wednesday, and Friday at 9 A.M. Call (508) 228-9198 for details.

● Nantucket Lifesaving Museum

158 Polpis Rd., Nantucket Center, (508) 228-1885, www.nantucket.net/ museums/lifesaving. Mid-June–Columbus Day, 9:30–4. Adults, $4; 6–15, $2. **Ages 3 and up.**

Step into this authentic recreation of Nantucket's Surfside Station, built in 1874, and see lifesaving boats and displays of rescue equipment. Their motto: "You have to go out, but you don't have to come back." Chilling. Check out the exhibit of treasures from the sunken ship *Andrea Doria*, which sank more than 40 years ago off Nantucket's southeast coast.

● Old Mill/Living History for Children

At the intersection of Prospect, W. York, and S. Mill Sts., (508) 228-1894, www.nha.org. Mid-June–Labor Day, daily, 10–5; Labor Day–Columbus Day, daily, 11–3, weather permitting. Adults, $8; 14 and under, $5. (Pass good for all Nantucket Historical Association sites.) "Living History for Children" program: $25. **Ages 6 and up.**

Built in 1746, this is one of the last operating wind-powered mills in the country. It's preserved by the Nantucket Historical Association and is the sole survivor of four mills on the island. Watch the impressive-looking wooden gears turn the millstone, grinding the corn, and take home a freshly ground bag of cornmeal.

In summer, kids ages 6 to 10 can join the children's living-history program: Kids run the old windmill and help the miller make cornmeal. Then the group heads to the island's oldest house to bake cornbread, ending the session with some nautical knot-tying (and making sailors' valentines) at the Oldest House. The program runs on Wednesdays, July and August, twice daily, from 10 to 12, and again from 2 to 4 P.M. Reservations are required.

● Hinchman House

7 Milk St., (508) 228-0898, www.mmo.org. June–Aug., Tues.–Sat., 10– 4. Adults, $3; children, $1. **Ages 3 and up.**

This building houses a unique natural history museum, featuring a collection of living reptiles and mounted birds and fauna from the island.

There are also native wildflower and plant displays; exhibits focus on environmental issues of Nantucket. Tours are self-guided. Call for the schedule of bird and nature walks.

● Beaches

Children's Beach, on the North Shore (and an easy walk to town), is aptly named—it may well end up your family's favorite. On Nantucket Sound, the water is calm. Facilities include a playground, park, concessions, even tie-dying sessions, run Fridays at noon, from July 4th to Labor Day. (Bring your own T-shirt!) Other good choices include **Dionis Beach** (with sand dunes) and **Jetties Beach** (with sailboat rentals), both on the North Shore. Jetties Beach is an easy bike ride (or a long walk) from town and worth it—it's an inviting stretch of sand with a snack bar/ice cream take-out, sailboat and kayak rentals, and swimming lessons for kids ages six and up, 9:30 to noon, from July 4th to Labor Day. Looking for a beautiful beach for meandering? Take the shuttle bus from town to **Madaket Beach,** at the West End of Nantucket. The surf's heavy, but the views (and the sunsets) are splendid.

● Getting Around

Don't you dare bring a car to Nantucket! You haven't seen gridlock til you've seen Nantucket Town's narrow cobblestone streets in the height of tourist season. (They don't call it "Manhattan East" in August for nothing.) Who needs that on vacation? Better to stay someplace not far from the action, or near the beach, and vow to walk it, bike it, take taxis, or take advantage of the best, cheapest way to get around the island, the NRTA shuttle. These buses make regular runs all over—around town, out to Madaket and Siasconset—for a nominal fee. Little kids ride free.

● Bicycling

Nantucket has several paved bike paths, leading to Surfside, Siasconset, Madaket, and Polpis. Look for bike signs on sign posts, with destinations designated by color (e.g., Siasconset, red). Be sure to follow the rules of the road, stay off the soft sand and wildflowers along the path, and wear a helmet (required by law for kids 12 and under). For bike rentals, try **Young's Bicycle Shop** at Steamboat Wharf, (508) 228-1151. They'll also provide a dandy map of bike trails.

● Nobadeer Mini-Golf

12 Nobadeer Farm Rd., (508) 228-8977. Daily, in season, 9–11. **All ages.**

Even quaint Nantucket has a miniature golf course, nicely manicured, naturally. The 18-hole course features several lagoons; plus, there's an on-site Mexican restaurant, Patio J.

● Pirate Adventure/Friendship Sloop Adventure

Slip #1015, Straight Wharf, (508) 228-5585; www.endeavorsailing.com. July and Aug., $25. **Ages 3 to 7.**

Treat your little mates to a wild-and-woolly adventure at sea. They'll sail under the *Jolly Roger,* fire the ship's cannon, and follow a treasure map to pirate booty. Trips are 90 minutes long; call for details.

● Scenic Overlook

First Congregational Church and Old North Vestry, 62 Centre St., (508) 228-0950. Church and tower open to visitors, mid-June–mid-Oct., Mon.–Sat., 10–4. Adults, $2; children, $.50. **Ages 4 and up.**

Get a bird's-eye view of the island from the tower of the church. With sweeping views of the moors to Madaket, this is the loftiest view in town. It's 93 steps up, but you get a break halfway—there's an exhibit room at midpoint in the climb.

RESTAURANTS

First, a few words about Nantucket dining: To say that Nantucket has a bounty of wonderful dining establishments doesn't do it justice. Two of top-rated fine-dining restaurants in all of New England are on-island, The Chanticleer and Toppers at the Wauwinet. Of course, unless you brought the au pair along, you won't be setting foot in these bastions of gourmet-dom. No matter—you'll still eat well. Nantucket has more than 50 eateries, offering everything from bean burritos to classic clambakes. Prices are on the high side. In general, if your kids aren't always restaurant-civilized, stick with cafe-type places like the Fog Island Café, Brotherhood of Thieves, and Atlantic Café—these are fun, moderately priced, and casual.

● Fog Island Café

7 S. Water St., (508) 228-1818. July and Aug., Mon.–Sat., 7 A.M.–2 P.M., 5–10 P.M.; Sun., 7 A.M.–1 P.M., 5–10 P.M. Call for off–season hours.

Fresh, wholesome, and tasty—that describes the food at this local fave. The food is so good, they sell copies of their cookbook on-site. Homemade soups and salads are always good; for dinner, they offer creative takes on seafood, pasta, and veggie dishes.

● Brotherhood of Thieves

23 Broad St. (no phone). Mid-May–mid-Oct., Sun.–Thurs., 11:30 A.M.– midnight; Fri. and Sat., 11:30 A.M.–12:30 A.M.; mid-Oct.–mid-May, Sun.–Thurs., 11:30 A.M.–10:30 P.M.; Fri. and Sat., 11:30–11:30. No credit cards.

Our kids wanted to try this place because they liked the name; once inside the 19th-century brick tavern, they discovered the awesome burgers and great curly fries. What's not to like? This is, however, a pub, as well as a local institution, so it can be a lively scene as the evening progresses. With kids, go early. Warm up beside the brick hearth on nippy nights.

● Atlantic Café

15 S. Water St., (508) 228-0570; www.atlanticcafe.com. Year-round, lunch and dinner.

You know you won't feel out of place with small fry when you discover there's a children's menu; $5.95 for the usual suspects ($3.50 extra if you spring for a "kiddie colada"!) On the grown-up side, they offer a range of pasta and seafood options, plus some BBQ items. Try the tasty pulled-pork sandwich.

● Claudette's

Post Office Sq., Siasconset, (508) 257-6622. Open for breakfast and lunch, June–Oct.

Enjoy fresh baked goods on the outdoor terrace, or take 'em to go and head for the beach.

● Do-It-Yourself-Picnic

Local restaurateurs won't appreciate this insider's tip, but here goes: If you want to concoct your own fabulous picnic by-the-sea, stop by a local seafood market. Most will cook and crack lobster to go. Pick up some extras at the big A&P grocery store in Nantucket town (they even have ready-to-go items like chicken wings for kids who think lobster is yucky), then head to your favorite spot (say, Madaket Beach at sunset), relax, and enjoy.

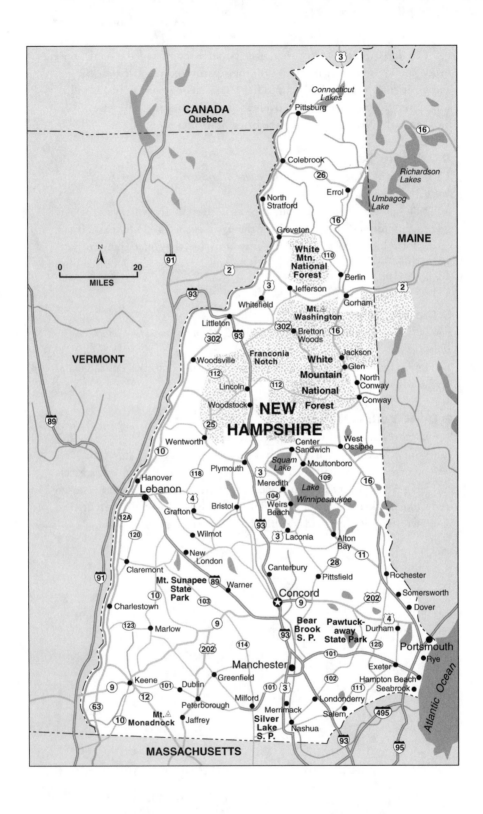

New Hampshire

■ Portsmouth

There aren't many better places for a family to spend a day or two than in Portsmouth, New Hampshire. This gem of a city, New Hampshire's only seaport, is tucked away between the Maine and Massachusetts borders and often gets bypassed by hurried tourists.

In Portsmouth, being a visitor is just plain easier than in most other popular New England towns. In this pretty, historic seaport, you'll find more than 70 restaurants (some are rated the best on the seacoast), boutiques, art galleries and shops, and a list of activities to keep even the busiest of families happy. It also manages to maintain an unpretentious, relaxed atmosphere.

Don't rush through this town. Plan to spend at least a day visiting its unique museums (including a quaint hands-on museum just for kids), strolling lovely Prescott Park, cruising to the Isles of Shoals, or zipping down the wild Geronimo! water slide at Water Country. Be sure to stop by the town pier, where you'll see the massive tugboats, and have fine views of the harbor.

● Strawbery Banke

Marcy St. (opposite Prescott Park and the Portsmouth waterfront), (603) 433-1100, www.strawberybanke.org. May–Oct., daily, 10–5; Nov.–Apr., Thurs.–Sun., 10–2. (Annual Christmas Stroll held in Dec.) Adults, $12; 6–17, $8; under 6, free. **Ages 6 and up.**

This unique living-history museum draws history buffs from around the country. When the first settlers landed in Portsmouth they found wild strawberries growing along the banks of the Piscataqua River and so named this seaport Strawbery Banke. During the next 150 years, the site became a thriving waterfront town and later an immigrant neighborhood known as Puddle Dock.

Today, you'll see 30 of the 35 original buildings, all salvaged from demolition and in various stages of restoration. A number of archaeological and restoration exhibits illustrate how historians are able to piece together facts about the past. Part of the fun is seeing restoration projects still going on, in various stages of completion.

Some of the houses are furnished to reflect time periods ranging from the 17th to the 20th centuries; others contain exhibits and craft shops. You're likely to see gardeners at work on the grounds, as well as boat builders, barrel makers, archaeologists, carpenters, quilt makers, weavers, and more. Older children (six and older) can get firsthand knowledge of what it might have been like to live in an earlier time by signing up for daily workshops. During these sessions, they might make a basket, spin yarn, or perform other 19th-century tasks.

● Port of Portsmouth Maritime Museum and Albacore Park

600 Market St., (603) 436-3680, www.asme.org. Columbus Day–Memorial Day, Thurs.–Mon., 9:30–4; late May–Columbus Day, daily, 9:30–5. Adults, $4; 7–17, $3; under 7, free. **Ages 5 and up.**

Climb aboard on the USS *Albacore,* dubbed the world's fastest submarine. You get to go below to its tiny engine room, captain's quarters, radio room, and dining area. A short film describes the history of the 1,200-ton submarine, and a tour guide explains things as you go along. Where else can you sit at the controls of a real submarine?

● Children's Museum of Portsmouth

280 Marcy St., (603) 436-3853, www.childrens-museum.org. Year-round; Tues.–Sat., 10–5; Sun., 1–5; mid-June–Aug., Mon.–Sat., 10–5; Sun., 1–5. Admission, $4; under 1, free. **Ages 10 and under.**

Watch as your children don rain slickers and fishing hats, jump aboard a lobster boat, and pull up a trap full of plastic flounders, lobsters, haddock, bass, and shrimp. Then, they can take their "catch" over to the fish market, where their playmates become make-believe customers. This cozy home-turned-museum is a child's paradise. When they're done fishing, children can head up to the rocket ship, taking turns at the controls, while a video screen helps them imagine their journey through space. A fun place for toddlers; older kids will enjoy the daily scheduled arts-and-crafts projects.

Many children never make it past the big yellow submarine—the first thing they see when they walk in the door. This three-story play structure contains tunnels, platforms, peek holes, slides, and poles. Relax in the adjacent sitting area—your children are bound to come out sooner or later.

● Water Country

Rte. 1 (3 mi. south of downtown Portsmouth), (603) 427-1111, www.watercountry.com. Memorial Day–mid-June, weekends, 10–6; mid-Jun–July 1, daily 10–6; July–mid-Aug., daily, 9:30–7; late Aug.–Labor Day, daily, 10–6. Over 4 ft. tall, $27.99; under 4 ft. tall, $18.99; 2 and under, free. Lower evening rates available. **Ages 7 and up.**

What's summer vacation without at least one trip to a water park? In the seacoast area, this is the place to go. Tube down a quarter-mile river through waterfalls and caves; speed down the dips on the double dive–boggin slide; bank around the curbs on the triple giant slides; or swallow your stomach down Double Geronimo, the fastest water slide in New England. There are 18 attractions in all, spread over 47 acres. Expect crowds and lines on the hottest summer days, especially for the popular high-rise Vortex slide and High Five, a group tubing exprience. If that sounds too active, there are simple pools to soak in and lots of lawn chairs. For kids under four feet tall, there are three large kiddie areas, including the Octopus Lagoon with mini water slides, wading pool, whirlpool, and playground equipment. But it's the older kids and daredevil parents who get the most for the money here.

● Prescott Park
Marcy St. on the Portsmouth waterfront, (603) 436-2848. **All ages.**

This lovely waterfront expanse is full of flower gardens and fountains and room to roam. Snack pushcarts are here if you need some quick replenishing, and often you'll see a variety of arts-and-crafts exhibits displayed throughout the park. Family art and music festivals are held during the summer; lots of folks turn out here on sultry summer nights to listen to concert music and watch the stars splash across the sky.

● Boat Cruises
There's no better place to view the coastline, harbors, and islands than from a boat. **The Isles of Shoals Steamboat Company** at 315 Market St., (800) 441-4620 or (603) 431-5500, offers a variety of cruises, including fall foliage and naturalist tours, whale-watching expeditions, and a special lighthouse cruise that takes you to five lighthouses in the area. The Steamboat Company also offers a special excursion to Star Island (part of the Isles of Shoals) on which you'll be able to explore the island and learn its interesting history.

Portsmouth Harbor Cruises, 64 Ceres St., (800) 776-0915 or (603) 436-8084, offers a 90-minute cruise aboard the small (40 passengers) wooden *M/V Heritage*. Because of its size, the *Heritage* is able to travel to areas not accessible to a larger boat. You'll get an intimate look at the seacoast area, including its picturesque inland rivers and the Great Bay.

● Isles of Shoals
Discovered in 1614 by Captain John Smith, the nine shoal islands are natural havens for birds, wildflowers, and animals. You'll see several species of gulls on the islands; the most common is the herring gull. The largest is the black-backed gull, with a wing span of five feet. Harbor seals raise their young on one of the islands, and whales have been observed a few hundred yards offshore. Four of the five islands are in New Hampshire and five belong to Maine. Sign up for one of the harbor boat cruises to reach them.

● Horse and Carriage Rides
Market Sq., (603) 427-0044. May–Oct., daily; Nov.–Apr., weekends. 20-minute ride, $20; 30-minute ride, $25; 40-minute ride, $30. Prices are per carriage ride; carriages fit up to 4 adults or 2 adults and 3 children. **All ages.**

What kid doesn't like a horse-and-buggy ride? Mom and dad will enjoy it, too, in these quaint, historic horse-drawn open carriages that tour Portsmouth in style. The ride is particularly special during the winter holidays when the downtown area is decked out in its old-fashioned finery, and the sleigh bells add the perfect touch.

● Bow Street Theater
125 Bow St. **Ages 5 and up.**

Both the Portsmouth Academy of Performing Arts, (603) 433-7272, and the Seacoast Repertory Company of PAPA, (603) 433-4472, perform at this intimate, comfortable theater. There's lots of quality, live theater going on here year-round, including a top-notch Saturday and Sunday children's series. Call for a schedule.

● Urban Forestry Center
45 Elwyn Rd., (603) 431-6774. Year-round, daily til dusk. Free. **All ages.**

This center is a peaceful nature escape just outside the city where you can walk Brook Trail alongside native wildflowers and herb and perennial gardens. Try your skill at identifying local trees—many are noted along the trail.

 RESTAURANTS

● The Stockpot
53 Bow St., (603) 431-1851. Daily, 11–11:30.

The Stockpot began in 1982 as a soup-and-stew hangout for local artists. Today it draws a more diverse crowd that comes for its good, relatively cheap food and waterfront location. Housed in a remodeled 19th-century brewery, it offers nice views of Portsmouth Harbor and freshly made, simply prepared food, including lots of great homemade soups, salads, and sandwiches.

● The Friendly Toast
121 Congress St., (603) 430-2154. Sun.–Thurs., 7 A.M.–11 P.M.; Fri.–Sat., open 24 hrs.

This funky, eclectic restaurant, filled with '50s memorabilia and retro decor (Elvis posters and Formica-topped tables), is a local favorite. The menu is creative, ingredients are fresh. Lots of kid favorites like the Almond Joy pancakes, stuffed with chocolate chips, coconut, and almonds. There are skads of breakfast items (breakfast is served all day), including a number of creative egg dishes and a variety of vegetarian choices; salads, burgers, and sandwiches grace the lunch menu.

■ New Hampshire Seacoast

This small, condensed region of New Hampshire encompasses only 18 miles of shoreline and centers on the busy resort area of Hampton Beach. Nearly 150,000 sunbathers crowd this long stretch of beach on sunny summer days. The hardy ones swim in the cold waters of the Atlantic (which average only 55 degrees in July); the rest soak up the sun's rays and the area's frolicking, carnival atmosphere. This is the Daytona Beach of the Northeast, full of noisy fun and enough activities to fill your days and nights.

If you're in need of a bit more solitude, don't despair. Visit the seaside town of Rye, where you can picnic at Odiorne Point State Park and take a quiet oceanside nature walk. Stroll the cobblestone streets of quaint downtown Exeter, or pick fruit at a nearby orchard. If you venture just a few miles from Hampton Beach in either direction, you're back in storybook New England.

● Hampton Beach

Ocean Blvd., (800)-GET-A-TAN or (603) 926-8717. Year-round. Free.
All ages.

Your kids will love this place. There are three miles of white, sandy beach surrounded by restaurants, games rooms, arcades, souvenir shops, water slides, and hot dog, pizza, candy, fried dough, and ice cream stands. Don't try to drive around town; you'll spend too much time stuck in traffic. Hop the town trolley car (on which you'll hear about the day's list of area activities), or walk the boardwalk on Ocean Boulevard. Each night stars something different—talents shows, fireworks, concerts, and sing-alongs.

● Hampton Beach Casino

169 Ocean Blvd., Hampton Beach, (603) 926-4100, www.casinoballroom.com.
All ages.

This is where just about everything cool happens at Hampton Beach—at least according to kids. This seven-acre playground includes shops, food (like cotton candy, hot dogs, slushes, fried dough, clams, and sausages), minigolf, kiddie rides, arcades, water slides, and a teen club. Always jam-packed and noisy. The 2,000-seat Casino Ballroom hosts top-rated bands and entertainers.

● Odiorne Point State Park

Rte. 1A, Rye, (603) 436-7406, www.nhparks.state.nh.us. Year-round.
All ages.

Located only a few minutes from Hampton Beach is this lovely, 230-acre oceanside park, the largest undeveloped stretch of shore on New Hampshire's coast. The area is expansive, offering great views and lots to do. Be sure to wear a pair of shoes that you don't mind getting wet. Odiorne is one of the best places around to go tide pooling. As you hop and peer into the pools, you'll likely find an abundant array of marine creatures, including sea urchins, snails, starfish, lobsters, shrimp, and more. (It's okay to pick them up, even to put them in a bucket for viewing—but everything needs to be put back before leaving.)

There are wading areas, picnic tables, grills, and a small playground. There are also a number of trails (lots of people bring their bikes) that take you along the rocky coastline or inland through salt marshes, ponds, and woodlands. The Science Center is a must-see, too.

● Seacoast Science Center

Odiorne Point State Park, Rte. 1A, Rye, (603) 436-8043, www.nhparks.state.nh.us. Year-round, daily, 10–5. Admission, $1; 5 and under, free. **Ages 3 and up.**

Get your hands on a starfish, snails, sea urchins, and more at this pretty marine center that sits atop a bluff overlooking the ocean. The best strategy is to stop at the Science Center first to see and learn all about the creatures that inhabit the nearby ocean waters. Then go exploring the hundreds of tide pools outside for a look at some of the same critters.

The center houses a number of aquariums and marine exhibits that interpret the seven habitats found at the park, including a tide pool touch tank, a 1,000-gallon Gulf of Maine tank, and a "Look Under" tank. Local schoolkids act as volunteer guides during the summer and are eager to answer any questions.

● Boat and Whale-Watching Cruises

New Hampshire Seacoast Cruises, Rye Harbor State Marina, Rte. 1A, Rye Harbor, (603) 964-5545, offers two-hour tours of the nine Isles of Shoals and six-hour whale-watch excursions, led by research biologists.

The **Atlantic Fishing Fleet and Whalewatching,** also at the Rye Harbor State Marina on Rte. 1A, (603) 964-5220, offers sunset cruises on its 80-foot M/V *Atlantic Queen II.* The evening whale watches offer a close-up view of these ocean giants. On the narrated trips, you're likely to spot dolphins, seals, and an array of seabirds. For deep-sea fishing adventures, check out **Al Gauron Deep Sea and Whale Watching** at (800) 905-7820 or (603) 926-2469.

● Wallis Sands

Rte. 1A, Rye, (603) 436-9404, www.wallissandsplace.com. Memorial Day– Labor Day. **All ages.**

This white, sandy beach is 800 feet long, 150 feet wide, and a popular summertime swimming spot. There are refreshments, rest rooms, and changing facilities. From the rocky bluff on the north end of Wallis Sands you can see Seal Rocks. During colder months, you might spot seals, who often sun themselves here. On the horizon, you'll be able to see the Isles of Shoals, nine tiny islands off the coast.

● Fort Stark and Fort Constitution

Fort Stark, Rte. 1B (take Wild Rose Ln. to the fort), Newcastle, (603) 436-6607, www.nhparks.state.nh.us.com. Memorial Day–Labor Day. Free. Fort Constitution, Rte. 1B (follow signs to Coast Guard Station), Newcastle. Memorial Day–Labor Day, weekends only. Free. **Ages 5 and up.**

These two sites in Newcastle provide a peek at early military installations and offer great views of the Atlantic coastline.

Fort Stark is a 10-acre former U.S. coastal harbor defense facility, where you'll get a historical look at the state's fortification system and a spectacular view of the Atlantic Ocean, Little Harbor, Odiorne Point State Park, and the Isles of Shoals. Be careful as you walk through the site: There are lots of rough ground and slippery rocks.

On December 13, 1744, Paul Revere rode from Boston with a message that the fort at Rhode Island had been dismantled and troops were coming to take over Fort Constitution (then named Fort William and Mary). The fort was damaged in the raid, which was an important link in the chain of events leading to the Revolution. Today, you can walk the site and enjoy the coastal views.

● Seacoast Science and Nature Center

Seabrook Station, just off Rte. 1, Seabrook, (800) 338-7482, www.seabrookstation.com. Year-round, Mon.–Sat., 10–4. Free. **Ages 5 and up.**

Okay, this is a nuclear plant. That said, let's go on. The science center set up here contains a number of informative, hands-on exhibits and sensitively presented educational programs about energy and the environment. There are more than 30 exhibits and displays, drawing some 30,000 visitors a year. You'll take an imaginary journey nearly 260 feet below the sea level to Seabrook's cooling tunnels. Kids can test their "Energy IQ" with computer quizzes, and their "Pedal Power" at the bicycle-powered generator. There are also aquariums and a touch pool for a look at regional marine life, and a short nature trail through surrounding salt marshes and woodlands. Note: Call ahead for hours and schedules; the center may be closed for security reasons.

● Sandy Point Discovery Center

Depot Road, off Rte. 33, Stratham, (603) 778-0015, www.greatbay.org. May–Sept., Wed.–Sun., 10–4; grounds open year-round during daylight hours. Free. **All ages.**

This beautiful natural area rests on the shores of Great Bay. Trails and boardwalks meander through forest, wetlands, salt marsh, and mudflats (look for herons, wintering bald eagles, and osprey along the way!) There are gardens to explore, a replica of 19th-century gundalow, and observation points. Inside the Discovery Center, you'll find interpretive exhibits and an estuarine touch tank full of lobsters, horseshoe crabs, mud snails, and other native creatures. Special programs and activities are held throughout the summer, including guided kayaking trips on the Great Bay.

● Little Bay Buffalo Company

Langley Rd., Durham, (603) 868-2632. Daily, 9–sunset. **All ages.**

Home, home on the range . . . can this be right? Yes, native New Englanders don't have to head west to catch a glimpse of the mighty American bison. Come see the unexpected at this farm. There are tours and a small shop (anyone care for a bison burger?), but just a stop for a close-up look at these hefty beasts is enough.

● Emery Farm

Rte. 4, Durham, (603) 742-8495. Mid-May–Dec.; daily, 9–6. **All ages.**

There are more than 12 acres of pick-your-own fruit on this family farm, established in 1655 in Durham. A small animal petting farm and an old-fashioned country store are also on the grounds. During the summer, there are scheduled children's reading hours and activities, too.

● Kingston State Park

Off Rte. 125, Kingston, (603) 452-9621, www.nhparks.state.nh.us.com. **All ages.**

Swim in the fresh waters of Great Pond and have a picnic in this 44-acre state park; it's just outside Exeter.

❡ RESTAURANTS

● Captain Newick's

431 Dover Point Rd., exit 6W off Spaulding Tpke., Dover, (603) 742-3205, www.newicks.com. Sun.–Thurs., 11–8:30; Fri.–Sat., 11–9.

A great family place, especially if you have a taste for fresh fried seafood or lobster in the rough. This always-crowded, quick-service place serves hefty portions at fair prices. You'll sit at long picnic tables, probably eat most of your food with your fingers, and take home a doggie bag of leftovers.

● Loaf & Ladle

9 Water St., Exeter, (603) 778-8955. Mon.–Wed., 8–8; Thurs.–Sat., 8–9; Sun., 11–9.

Help yourself, cafeteria style, to an assortment of homemade breads, soups, chilis, and salads. Grab your plate and head outdoors to the deck overlooking the tumbling river. This is hearty, healthy fare, with great breads, vegetables, soups, and salads. At dinner, the chef prepares a couple of special entrees to choose from (like fresh veggie pasta dishes or lemon-baked herb chicken).

● Ron's Landing

379 Ocean Blvd., Hampton Beach, (603) 929-2122. Daily, 11:30-11.

This family-friendly, beachfront restaurant offers a large menu of classic American fare: steaks, seafood, chicken, pasta. It's casual enough for families to be comfortable with enough meal choices to please everyone. Snag a table on the enclosed, second-floor deck where you'll have views of the ocean.

■ Merrimack Valley

More than half the population of New Hampshire lives in the Merrimack Valley region, and most visitors see it only in passing on their way north to the more popular tourist destinations. Nashua, Salem, Manchester, and Concord offer an abundance of fun-filled family activities. You'll find a host of interesting museums, from the Children's Metamorphosis Museum in Londonderry to the larger Christa McAuliffe Planetarium in Concord. And just outside the city centers, you'll find rolling, peaceful countryside, clear rivers and lakes, and some very scenic state parks.

Next time you're driving by get off the highway for more than a stop at a fast-food chain. Spend the afternoon at the Canobie Lake Amusement Park, take a refreshing swim at Silver Lake, a canoe trip down the Merrimack River, or go mountain biking at Pawtuckaway State Park. You'll return to the car refreshed, and the kids will be tuckered out for the rest of the journey. Or you might just decide to stick around the area awhile to discover more of its hidden gems.

● Canobie Lake Park

Exit 2 off I-93, Salem, (603) 893-3506, www.canobie.com. Late May–Labor Day, daily, noon–10; Labor Day–Sept., Sat.–Sun., 11–8; mid-Apr.–late May, Sat., noon–10; Sun., noon–6. Adults, $22 (includes all rides and shows), under 48 in. tall, $15. **All ages.**

A delight for kids: All their favorite amusement rides, boats, games, haunted house, live puppet shows, music revues, and more are here. In all, you'll find 25 rides, including 4 popular roller coasters. There's a large kiddie area with pint-size rides for young park visitors. Bring your bathing suit; there's a swimming pool and a wild log ride. You can also take a boat cruise around the lake or a train ride around the park. The park features a wide variety of entertainment, including fireworks, live shows, and specialty acts.

On your way home, head north a few miles for a look at America's Stonehenge.

● America's Stonehenge

Mystery Hill, off Rte. 111, North Salem, (603) 893-8300, www.stonehengeusa.com. Year-round, daily; Feb.–mid-June, 9–5; mid-June–Labor Day, 9–7; Labor Day–Oct., 9–5; Nov.–Jan., 9–4. Adults, $8; 13–15, $6; 6–12, $5; 5 and under, free. **Ages 5 and up.**

Some claim this series of unusual rock formations is the 4,000-year-old astronomical complex built by Celts who came here from the Iberian peninsula. It is most likely the oldest man-made construction in the United States. Formerly known as Mystery Hill, it has presented an intriguing puzzle to archaeologists and historians. It was, and still can be, used to determine specific lunar and solar events of the year. There are a few trails for the kids to run on while you ponder the site and take in the view.

● Massabesic Audubon Center

Audubon Way, Auburn, (603) 668-2045, www.nhaudubon.org. Daily, Mon.–Sat., 9–5; Sun., 1–5. Free. **All ages.**

Bring your binoculars and keep a lookout for flying and diving osprey! You'll find miles of scenic trails to roam at this Audubon Center. In warmer months, there's hiking and bird-watching. When the mercury drops, don snowshoes or skis and head to the woods in search of animal tracks. There's a large nature store, refreshments, live animals, and exhibits on-site. There are snowshoes and binoculars to rent at the center.

● Museum of New Hampshire History

Eagle Sq., Concord, (603) 226-3189, www.nhhistory.org. Year-round, Tues.–Sat., 9:30–5 (open Thurs. 9:30–8); Sun., noon–5; open Mon. in Dec. and from July–Oct. 15, 9:30–5. **Ages 7 and up.**

If you want to learn about New Hampshire's state history, this is the place to go. Interactive exhibits and programs teach about the Granite State's rich past and traditions. Kids and grown-ups alike will discover something new from the ongoing and traveling exhibits and collections. The museum store is a real treat, too, full of books, crafts, and New Hampshire–made products.

● Charmingfare Farm

774 High St., Candia, (603) 483-5623, www.visitthefarm.com. May–mid-Oct., Wed.–Sun., 10–4. Admission, $7.50 (includes hayride); under 1, free. **All ages.**

This popular 180-acre destination boasts the largest collection of farm animals and North American wildlife in the state. You'll roam among the animals—more than 200 in all, representing 30 different species. There are traditional barnyard animals, and wolves, fox, porcupines, black bears, mountain lions, and more . . . oh, my! A hayride completes the fun.

● Busch Clydesdale Hamlet

Anheuser-Busch Brewery, Rte. 3, Merrimack, (603) 595-1202. May–Nov., daily, 9:30–3:30; Dec.–Apr., closed Mon. and Tues. Free. **All ages.**

Get a close-up and personal look at the famous Clydesdale horses on this free tour through the stables. Also on display are wagons, harnesses, and other riding equipment.

● Children's Metamorphosis Museum

217 Rockingham Park, Londonderry, (603) 425-2560, www.discoverthemet.com. Tues.–Sat., 9:30–5; Fri., 9:30–8; Sun., 1–5. Admission, $5; under 1, free. **Ages 1–8.**

Curiosity the Caterpillar, the museum's mascot, is always waiting to show children around. Best for kids ages two to eight, the Metamorphosis features a variety of hands-on, fun-filled activity rooms.

In the World Cultures Room, you're surrounded by giant maps and will learn about people from around the world. You can try on regional clothing, play traditional games, and listen to music. In the Emergency Room, kids take pulses, listen to heartbeats, give shots, and use a wheelchair and crutches. At the Construction Site, future achitects, builders, and engineers work a bulldozer, design with blocks, and use tools at the workbench. Other exhibits include the Sticky Room (full of Velcro boards and Legos), Five Senses Room (touch it first and then see if you can guess what's hiding in the box), Grocery Room, Nature and Science Area, Puppet Theater, and an arts and crafts activity area. A great place for kids.

● Amoskeag Fishways

Amoskeag Dam, Fletcher St., exit 6 off I-293, Manchester, (603) 626-FISH. Year-round, Mon.–Sat., 9:30–5. Free. **All ages.**

Don't miss this site in the springtime when several species of ocean fish return to spawn in the Merrimack River. An underwater viewing window gives you a fish-eye's view of what's going on below. Dioramas and displays teach about fish migration.

● SEE Science Center

200 Bedford St., Manchester, (603) 669-0400, www.see-sciencecenter.org. Year-round, Mon.–Fri., 10–3; weekends, noon–5. Admission, $4; 1 and under, free. **Ages 4 and up.**

This popular science center has moved to its new location and tripled in size. It now encompasses more than 15,000 square feet of hands-on fun. Popular exhibits include the Chemistry Lab and The Fountain (expect to get wet!). Kids love to take a spin on the momentum chair or join a kid-friendly workshop or special activity where they might learn how to build their own rocket or make a bongo drum. (Call for a list of specific projects and the days they're offered.) The center also features a variety of special exhibits.

● Christa McAuliffe Planetarium

3 Institution Dr., off I-93, Concord, (603) 271-7831, www.starhop.com. Sat.–Tues., 10–5; Wed., 10–2; Thurs.–Fri., 10–7. No charge for exhibits. Show admission: adults, $8; 1–17, $5. **Ages 5 and up.**

Named after one of the *Challenger* teacher-astronauts who was a Concord native, the museum is a pleasing mix of small hands-on exhibits and razzle-dazzle video presentations. Call ahead to get reservations for the shows; these sell out quickly and you're likely to be disappointed if you go without reservations. Once you enter the theater, you'll sit back for a self-guided tour of the universe and an up-close look at the moon, planets, stars, comets, and more. You press buttons and answer questions as you plot your journey through space. Everyone is likely to learn lots and have fun doing it.

● State House Center

107 N. Main St., Concord, (603) 271-2154. Mon.–Fri., 8–4:30. Free. **Ages 5 and up.**

The hub of activities in downtown Concord is the State House Plaza; here, New Hampshire's most famous sons (Daniel Webster and Franklin Pierce) are immortalized in bronze. The gold-domed captial building can be seen from around town, and its picturesque grounds are inviting. Inside, visit the Hall of Flags and view a variety of displays and interesting dioramas that depict New Hampshire historical events. You'll be greeted by a friendly staff of guides; come with questions—they love to answer them. If the legislature is in session, you can catch a glimpse of state government in action.

● Audubon Society of New Hampshire Headquarters

3 Silk Rd., Concord, (603) 224-9909, www.nhaudubon.org. Mon.–Sat., 9–5; Sun., noon–5. Free. **Ages 5–15.**

What are those small black-and-white birds we see all the time? What kind of woodpeckers peck in New Hampshire? How far do shorebirds go? What birds will we see in the mountains? Stop by the Audubon Society headquarters to learn all about native feathered friends. You'll find a number of exhibits, a nature store, and trails to explore. The society also hosts a variety of programs throughout the year. Write or call for its brochure.

● Silver Lake State Park

Rte. 122, Hollis, (603) 465-2342, www.nhparks.state.nh.us.com. **All ages.**

This is a popular family picnic area and beach in the Merrimack Valley region. The sandy, 1,000-foot beach is great for toddlers. Older swimmers will enjoy racing to the raft. The park has a bathhouse, rest rooms, and concession stand. Picnic tables and grills are nestled in the pine groves surrounding the park.

● Bear Brook State Park

Rte. 28, Allentown, (603) 485-9874, www.nhparks.state.nh.us.com.
All ages.

This 9,000-acre park offers a playground, picnic area, swimming beach, and rental boats. You'll also find the Museum of Family Camping located at the park. The museum houses exhibits, memorabilia, and documents on family camping dating back to early days. But you won't spend much time in the museum; this is a great spot to play outdoors, and that's where you'll want to be.

● Pawtuckaway State Park

Off Rte. 156, Nottingham, (603) 895-3031, www.nhparks.state.nh.us.com.
All ages.

This is a favorite among locals—the park boasts lots of room to roam and lots of things to do. There's a swimming beach, picnic areas, boats, and a number of trails to explore. Mountain bikers will love it; a number of back-road and off-road places to pedal are ideal for all levels of bikers. Strap your bikes to the rack, pack your swimsuits and a picnic basket, and you have the makings for a great outdoor adventure.

 RESTAURANTS

● Shorty's Mexican Roadhouse

Rte. 3A, Litchfield, (603) 424-0010. Mon.–Thurs., 11:30–10; Fri.–Sat., 11:30–11; Sun., 1–9.

These Mexican restaurants have begun to pop up across New Hampshire; that doesn't make them any less appealing, however. Go easy on the basket of tortilla chips and salsa, because you'll want to save room for the chicken pendaja (marinated chicken breast in spicy tomato sauce, cilantro, and jalapeno peppers). The kids will like the typical taco, burrito, and nachos fare. Lots of great choices, reasonable prices, and a casual, lively atmosphere.

● Hermanos Cocina

11 Hills Ave., Concord, (603) 224-5669, www.hermanosmexican.com. Daily, 11:30–11.

If your family likes Mexican food, this is the place to go. Hermanos, located in downtown Concord, is considered the best Mexican restaurant in New Hampshire, serving up authentic south-of-the-border fare. Everyone can munch on cripsy nacho chips dipped in fresh salsa, while Mom and Dad sip a Hermanos margarita, made from just-squeezed lemons and limes. There's the standard Mexican fare: tacos, tortillas, and enchiladas. Or, try one of the chef's other specialties, like chicken in green chili cumin sauce, topped with fresh avocado.

■ Lakes Region

This region in central New Hampshire is dominated by Lake Winnipesaukee, the state's largest lake, encompassing 72 square miles and more than 280 miles of shoreline. The picturesque lake is surrounded by three mountain ranges and speckled with 274 islands. Claiming to be home to the country's oldest summer resort (Wolfeboro), it also lays claim to having New Hampshire's "most popular vacation spot" (Weirs Beach), although the tourist folk in Hampton Beach and the White Mountains region might have something to say about that. But a look at the level of activity and number of visitors on any summer weekend makes the claim hard to dispute.

On the western side of the lake is busy Weirs Beach, often crowded but full of amusements. For a slower pace, visit nearby Lakes Waukewan and Winnisquam, or Lake Squam, the setting for the movie *On Golden Pond.*

Especially popular in the summer, this area by no means closes down the rest of the year. With the crowds gone, this is a great spot to spend a warm autumn day admiring the fall foliage, and winter brings cross-country and downhill skiing enthusiasts to the Gunstock ski area.

● Winnipesaukee Boat Tours and Rentals

The best way to appreciate this area is to get out on Lake Winnipesaukee; merely driving around its borders is not enough. Several cruise ships operate from the Weirs Beach pier. The **M/S Mount Washington,** (800) 843-6686, offers daily summer cruises on the majestic 230-foot yacht, or aboard the classic **Sophie C.** Lake cruises are also offered on the **M/V Judge Sewall,** (603) 569-3016, and **Mille B's,** (603) 569-1080, classic boats, both departing from the Wolfeboro town docks.

If you prefer to go it alone, you can rent an 18-foot bowrider from **Thurston's Marina,** (603) 366-4811. It's located on Rte. 3 at the Bridge, Weirs Beach.

Ready to get away from it all? Load a day pack with some goodies and a can of bug repellent, and catch the Stoneham Island boat from Weirs Beach.

Now, relax. This is a 112-acre, unspoiled island in Lake Winnipesaukee, with 2.5 miles of nature trails.

● Squam Lake Tours

The serene, picturesque setting of Squam Lake was the site of the classic movie *On Golden Pond.* The best way to see the lake's pristine beauty is on a boat tour. In fact, the lake is not easily seen from the roadside—you need to get on the lake to appreciate it.

Cruise the lake with **Golden Pond Tours,** (603) 968-7194, www.nhnature/goldenpondtours.org, departing from the dock on Rte. 3 in downtown Holderness. Once on board, Captain Pierre Havre will take you to the movie's actual locations and entertain with his knowledgeable and friendly narration. **Squam Lake Tours,** located on Rte. 3 just south of the center of Holderness, (603) 968-7577, www.SquamLakeTours.com, also takes passengers out on a 28-foot pontoon boat.

● Fishing Charters

Lake Winnipesaukee is known for its great fishing waters. But you'll need to know how to get away from the crowds and find the hidden holes. Check out **Gadabout Golder Guide Service,** (603) 569-6426, at 79 Middleton Rd. in Wolfeboro, or **Landlocked Fishing Guide Service,** (603) 253-6119, at P.O. Box 1382, Centre Harbor.

● Kayaking

With 280 miles of shoreline and more than 250 islands, Lake Winnipesaukee is a kayaker's paradise. Never kayaked before? Not to worry; this sport is for everyone. A few short instructions and a couple of minutes on the water, and you'll get the knack. Even young children are able to conquer this sport. **The Lake Winnipesaukee Kayaking Company,** (603) 569-9926, www.winnikayak.com., offers half-day, full-day, and multiday guided tours. They also have plenty of kayak and canoes for rent.

● Beaches

Despite its size, Lake Winnipesaukee has few public access points; most of the lodging places have their own private beaches for guests' use. Here are your choices:

Endicott Rock Beach, Rte. 3, Weirs Beach, (603) 524-5046, is a small, sandy beach located next to the Weirs Beach Water Slide.

Ellacoya State Park, Rte. 11, Gilford, (603) 293-7821, is a small beach on the southwest shore of Lake Winnipesaukee. There are rewarding views of the Ossipee and Sandwich mountain ranges from the shoreline.

Wentworth State Beach, Rte. 109, Wolfeboro, (603) 569-3699, is a small park located on the shore of scenic Lake Wentworth.

● Molly the Trolley

P.O. Box 119, Wolfeboro, (603) 569-1080. July–Aug., daily, 10–5. Adults, $5; 4–12, $2; under 4, free. **All ages.**

Hop aboard a turn-of-the-century trolley car for a narrated tour of Wolfeboro. The all-day pass is also good for getting from one side of the town to the other and a quick history of the town.

● Weirs Beach Water Slide

Rte. 3, Weirs Beach, (603) 366-5161. Memorial Day–mid-June, weekends, 10–5; mid-June–Labor Day, daily, 10–5. 7-ride ticket, $8.99; 14-ride, $14.99; 2-hr. unlimited, $14.99; all-day, $19.99. **Ages 3 and up.**

There are water slides for every level of bravery, from the 70-foot-long Tunnel Twister to the high-acceleration Sling Shot ("reserved for the slider seeking the ultimate sliding experience"). Or try Super Slide, billed as the longest and highest water slide in New England. Daredevils will love the Pipeline Express; it drops you down into a black hole and around underground curves, then blasts you up into daylight and down the flume. Whew! Let's do it again.

● Surf Coaster

Rte. 11B, Weirs Beach, (603) 366-5600, www.surfcoasterusa.com. Mid-June–Labor Day, daily, 10–6. Over 4 ft. tall, $24.95; under 4 ft. tall, $17.95. **Ages 5 and up.**

If you're tired of sand in your shoes but still want to cool off in the surf, a visit to Surf Coaster is in order. This 11-acre attraction, overlooking Lake Winnipesaukee, boasts a giant wave pool (nearly a half acre in size), four water slides, lagoons, lazy rivers, a wave pool, and a Kiddie Play Park and minislides.

● Winnipesaukee Scenic Railroad

Trains depart from Weirs Beach or Meredith, (603) 279-5253, www.hoborr.com. Memorial Day–Aug., daily. Sept.–Columbus Day, Weds. and Sat.–Sun. Trains depart Meredith on the half hour, 10:30–6:30. Trains depart Weirs Beach on the hour, 11–6. Limited hours in the fall; special events held during the winter. Call for schedules. Adults, $8.50; 4–11, $6.50; under 3, free. HOBO picnic, $6.95. **Ages 5 and up.**

The railroad's specialty is the kid-pleasing HOBO picnic. Lunch is packed up in a bundle on a stick to be enjoyed along the way. The train travels along the shores of Lake Winnipesaukee. There are lots of special programs offered, including fall foliage tours and Santa Claus rides.

● Squam Lakes Natural Science Center

Rte. 113, Holderness, (603) 968-7194, www.nhnature.org. May–Oct., daily, 9:30–4:30. July–Aug., adults, $9; 5–15, $6; May–June and Sept.–Oct, adults, $7; 5–15, $4; 4 and under, free. **Ages 3 and up.**

Live native bear, deer, raccoons, owls, eagles, reptiles, bobcats, and other animals roam the 200-acre sanctuary, contained by natural enclosures. Don't miss the raptor exhibit display, the bird aviary, and an outside bird-feeding station. Discover the wonders of nature, learning about plant and animal life through a number of unique indoor and outdoor displays and interactive exhibits. Children can push buttons, solve puzzles, and skip along a nature trail lined with exhibits. In the summer, attend the "Up Close Animals" program, a live demonstration held twice a day. Special workshops and hands-on activities are held throughout the season.

● New Hampshire Farm Museum

Rte. 125, Milton, (603) 652-7840, www.farmmuseum.org. June–Oct., Wed.–Sun., 10–4. Adults, $5; 3–12, $1.50; 2 and under, free. **All ages.**

Ever wonder what it was like in the old days, growing crops for your food, weaving your clothes on a loom, churning butter, pumping water from a well? You'll find out here. Children get a chance to see and touch a large collection of old farm tools and equipment as they tour the museum. You'll see a blacksmith shop, cobbler shop, old house and tavern, herb garden, country store, and two large barns full of all sorts of harvesting, planting, and woodworking tools. Often children are invited to work the equipment— making butter in an old churn, working an antique loom, or cleaning clothes in the wash basin. Special family events are held each weekend throughout the summer.

● Castle Springs

Rte. 171, Moultonborough, (800) 729-2468 or (603) 476-2352, www.castlesprings.com. Mid-May–June 1, weekends; June–Labor Day, daily, 9–5; Labor Day–mid-Oct., daily, 9–4. Admission, grounds only, adults, $6; 10 and under, free. Admission and tour: adults, $10; 7–18, $8. Horseback riding, $35/hr. **All ages.**

Thomas Plant, an eccentric millionaire, wanted to own a piece of land "from the mountains to the water." This 5,000-acre site in the middle of the Ossipee Mountain range is testimonial to his desires. There are guided tours of Plant's spacious retirement home, but the real attraction is outside—this is a pretty spot. There are views everywhere you look, and lots of ways to enjoy them. Take the short path (off the driveway entrance road) to the Fall of Song or Bridal Veil waterfalls. Even if you opt to forgo the house tour, be sure to walk the grounds surrounding the castle. It sits on the highest point of the site, and you'll have fabulous views of mountains, woods, and lakes.

Guided trail rides on horseback are offered, covering some of the more than 80 miles of bridle paths on the property. The shorter half-hour or hour-long tours are best for younger children. If you have time, have a picnic at Shannon Pond. There are tables, grills, and paddleboats to rent. Castle Springs is especially beautiful in the fall, when the mountainside is ablaze with color.

● Polar Caves

Rte. 25, Plymouth, (603) 536-1888 or (800) 273-1886,
www.polarcaves.com. May–late Oct., daily, 9–5. Adults, $10; 6–12, $6;
under 6, free. **Ages 6–14.**

Get your first taste of spelunking as you sink through the narrow passageways and climb rocky inclines. You'll explore an area where giant boulders were deposited by glaciers many years ago, forming a maze of caves. Kids who love a challenging climb and don't mind getting their knees dirty will enjoy finding hidden Smuggler's Cave, squirming through Lemon Squeeze, and screaming in dark Fat Man's Misery. You can back out along the way; there are detours to get you around some of the more challenging spots. A picnic area, museum shop, cafeteria, and ice cream bar are also on the grounds.

● Funspot Amusement Center

Rte. 3, Weirs Beach, (603) 366-4377, www.funspotnh.com. Year-round,
10–10; mid-June–Labor Day, 9–midnight. Admission free. **Ages 3 and up.**

A rainy day is the perfect excuse to visit Funspot, although kids need no excuse at all. This 60,000-square-foot facility is said to be the second-largest arcade in the country, home to more than 500 electronic games—and more. You'll find all the latest machines, along with 20 lanes of bowling (10 pin and candlepin), and an indoor golf center with minigolf and a driving range. The preschoolers in your group will love the Aqua Blasta splash guns and kiddie bumper cars. You'll go through a lot of quarters.

● Mount Major

Rte. 11, Alton Bay. **Ages 5 and up.**

It's a steep climb to the summit but worth every grunt and groan along the way. The trail begins at a marked parking area on Rte. 11, about five miles north of Alton Bay, and climbs 1.5 miles to the summit. It takes about two hours to reach the top. From here, you'll see commanding views over the mountain ranges and across Lake Winnipesaukee. You're likely to see groups of people along the way, including many small children. There are many alternate paths—choose any way; they all lead to the top.

● Hyde-Williams Petting Farm

9 Federal Corner Rd., Center Tuftonboro, (603) 569-9991, www.thepettingfarm.com. June–Labor Day, Wed.–Sun., 10–6; Labor Day–Oct., Fri.–Sun., 10–6. Adults, $4; 12 and under, $2. **All ages.**

This delightful 200-year-old farm is a hit with small children and adults alike. You'll ooh and aah at the baby animals in the maternity ward and spend hours petting and feeding the menagerie of farm animals that roam the grounds. There are baby llamas and pygmy goats, cows, pigs, horses, donkeys, sheep, birds, and more. In all, more than 160 animals live here and the kids will want to take them all home.

● Loon Center

Lee's Mills Rd., Moultonborough, (603) 476-5666, www.loon.org. July–Columbus Day, daily, 9–5; Columbus Day–June, Mon.–Sat., 9–5. Trails open until dusk. Free. **All ages.**

Did you know that loons are among the oldest groups of birds still living today, dating back some 50 million years? Or, that loons' closest living relatives are penguins and albatrosses? These are just some of the things you'll learn at the Loon Center. You'll find a number of exhibits, videos, activities, and programs, and a network of nature trails to explore.

● Gunstock Ski Area

Rte. 11A, Gilford, (603) 293-4341, www.gunstock.com. Lift tickets: adults, $32, night skiing, $16; 6–12, $18, night skiing, $14; 5 and under, free with an adult purchase. SKIwee (5–12), $65/day; Buckaroo (3 yrs.), $55/day; child care (6 mos. and up), $40/day. Rates listed are for weekends and holidays; special packages available. **All ages.**

This area offers more skiing than you might think at first glance. Tucked away in the Lakes Region, the area has trails for all levels of expertise, with 39 trails and 7 lifts. It's a good, solid intermediate area, with a special user-friendly section for beginners, and a handful of black diamonds thrown in.

The staff shows a commitment to family and children's services. The Buckaroos Children's Center is located at the heart of Gunstock's base complex so parents can drop in frequently throughout the day, if they wish. The nursery and day-care programs include arts and crafts, outdoor play, and social activities. Children 3 to 12 years can join the SKIwee program.

RESTAURANTS

● Hart's Turkey Farm and Restaurant

Rtes. 3 and 104, Meredith, (603) 279-6212, www.hartsturkeyfarm.com. Daily, 11:15–8.

Every day is Thanksgiving at this turkey-farm-turned-restaurant. On a busy day, Hart's serves more than a ton of turkey. It has all the trimmings, too, like mashed potatoes, cranberries, and squash pie. The children's menu includes the "Tiny Tot Turkey Plate"—a real feast.

● Yankee Smokehouse

Rtes. 16 and 25, West Ossipee, (603) 539-RIBS. Late June–Labor Day, daily, 11:30–9; rest of the year, Thurs.–Sun., 11:30–9.

The Yankee Smokehouse proudly proclaims it will "serve no swine before its time," and it does not disappoint. This is real barbeque (not the kind you get out of a bottle). You eat at picnic-style tables among the Smokehouse's vast collection of pig paraphernalia. All the meat is smoked slowly over hardwood coals in an open pit out back. The top seller is the Smokehouse Sampler for two—chicken, ribs, beef, and pork, served with fries, beans, cole slaw, corn on the cob, and garlic toast.

● Weirs Beach Lobster Pound

Rte. 3, Weirs Beach (across from the water slide), (603) 366-4630. Mid-May–mid-June and Labor Day–Columbus Day, Thurs.–Fri., 4:30–8; Sat.–Sun., noon–8. Summers, daily, noon–9.

No need to dress up; just shake the beach sand out of your shoes and grab a table. This is a perennial favorite, serving up chicken, ribs, and lobster in the rough. Popular with families.

■ Sunapee Area

The Sunapee area has been called the best-kept secret in New England. No boardwalks, no T-shirt and tacky souvenir shops, no fast-food stands. It's a relaxing, beautiful place to vacation, void of the typical tourist trappings.

Nestled high in the mountains of western New Hampshire, the Lake Sunapee area extends a quiet, slow welcome to its visitors. You'll find nothing pretentious or fancy. Despite natural beauty and bountiful opportunities for sports and activities, the Lake Sunapee area is fairly noncommercial, retaining much of its rural charm. Aware of its increasing appeal, its citizens have adopted the motto Preserve the Best of the Past. They're doing a good job. That's not to say you have to spend your entire time sitting under a giant white pine tree, skipping stones on Lake Sunapee (unless, of course, you want to). There are plenty of things to do: aerial rides, band concerts, boat cruises, hikes, waterskiing and snow skiing, apple picking, horseback riding, science and art museums, forts, and playhouses.

● Mount Sunapee State Park

Rte. 103, Newbury, (603) 763-5561, www.nhparks.state.nh.us.com. Beach open Memorial Day–mid-June, weekends, 9:30–8; mid-June–Labor Day, daily, 9:30–8. **All ages.**

Start your vacation in Sunapee with a visit to the State Park. The entire family will enjoy the sandy park beach. Swimmers in the family will have fun racing to the raft; toddlers are safe along the calm, shallow banks. There are picnic areas in the park, a playground, and a small concession stand at the beach.

● Sunapee Harbor

Off Rte. 11. **All ages.**

Sit at the edge of the lake and watch the boats come and go, picnic on the lawn that stretches from the lake to the road. Nobody hurries here. During the day you can rent boats and waterskiing equipment from a nearby marina. (Sailboat, canoe, and motor boat rentals are also available a few miles north of the harbor.) Don't miss the free outdoor band concerts held every Wednesday evening during the summer. Bring a blanket—the kids can dance and play on the lawn while you listen to the music float across the lake.

● M/V Mount Sunapee

Sunapee Harbor, off Rte. 11, (603) 763-4030. Mid-May–mid-June, Sat.– Sun., 2:30; mid-June–Labor Day, daily, 10 and 2:30; Labor Day–mid-Oct., Sat.–Sun., 2:30. Adults, $12; 5–12, $7. **Ages 5 and up.**

"Who wants to take the wheel?" Captain Hargbol yells. By the end of the boat ride, nearly every child has taken the helm and played out the fantasy of "sea captain." This 1.5-hour cruise, departing from Sunapee Harbor, takes you around the lake, past beaches, lighthouses, and summer homes. Captain Hargbol gives a lively narration on history, points of interest, and lore. It's a relaxing way to see this crystal-clear mountain lake.

● Ruggles Mine

On Isingglass Mountain, off Rte.4, Grafton, (603) 523-4275, www.rugglesmine.com. Mid-May–mid-June, weekends, 9–5; mid-June–mid-Oct., daily 9–6; Labor Day–mid-Oct., weekends, 9–5. Adults, $15; 4–11, $7; under 4, free. **Ages 2–14.**

Hammer and pound and chisel away as you look for precious stones. Prospecting in Ruggles Mine is a real adventure, no matter what your age.

The more than 200-year-old mine pit is big, full of caves and tunnels, high ledges, and water pools. You're allowed to pick away at the walls and take whatever you extract. The kids are sure to leave with a heavy load of "precious" souvenirs. In fact, more than 150 types of minerals have been found in the cave. You can rent hammers, chisels, picks, flashlights, and carrying sacks, or bring your own. Consider packing a lunch; the scenic view of mountains and valleys makes this a nice setting.

● The Fort at No. 4

Rte. 11, Charlestown, (603) 826-5700, www.fortat4.com. Mid-May–Oct., 10–4:30. Adults, $8; 6–12, $4.50. **Ages 3–14.**

This living-history museum is a reproduction of the original fortified settlement at No. 4, Charlestown, New Hampshire, during the French and Indian Wars era. The 20-acre site on the Connecticut River includes a stockade surrounding 14 buildings: a watchtower you can climb into, plus a blacksmith shop, cabins, and barns. As you walk through the village, you'll meet costumed guides demonstrating a variety of early crafts, such as musketball molding and candle dipping.

● Shaker Village

288 Shaker Rd., Canterbury, (866) 783-9511 or (603) 783-9511, www.shakers.org. May–Oct., daily, 10–5. Adults, $10; 6–15, $5. **Ages 5–15.**

Walking through this historic communal village, you'll get a glimpse of what life was like for the Canterbury Shakers. Watch artisans make a broom, spin yarn, or weave a rug in the self-sufficient tradition of Shaker life. Skilled craftspeople use other traditional Shaker skills to make baskets, tinware, herbal sachets, and ladderback chairs. There are six buildings on the spacious grounds, and walking tours are given, interpreting 200 years of Shaker history.

● Mount Kearsage Indian Museum

Exit 8N off I-89, Warner, (603) 456-2600, www.indianmuseum.org. May–Oct., Mon.–Sat., 10–5; Sun., 12–5. Nov.–Dec., Sat., 10–5; Sun., 12–5. Free (nominal charge for guided tours and special activities). **Ages 3 and up.**

Indian lore comes alive at this interesting indoor/outdoor museum. Walk along the paths in Medicine Woods, where you'll learn about medicinal plants and how they were used by the Indians. Imagine yourself living the life of an Eastern Woodlands Indian as you sit in the teepees. Or put on one of the wolf robes, the kind the Indians used to wear on their buffalo hunts. There are 100 acres of forest, fields, and wetlands to explore, guided tours, and special activities. The museum displays artifacts and exhibits covering the lives and lore of the Eastern Woodlands, Southwest, and Plains Indians. A great place for kids and adults alike.

● Barn Playhouse
Main St., New London, (603) 526-4631. July–Aug. **Ages 5–12.**

The summer stock theater in New London is a great way to introduce your family to the stage. The theater extends a warm welcome to children. Catch the magical Monday series throughout July and August. All programs are held in a refurbished barn. Call ahead for program information and schedule.

● Gould Hill Orchards
Gould Hill Rd., off Rte. 103, Hopkinton Village, (603) 746-3811. Aug.– May, daily, 9–5. **All ages.**

If you're in the Sunapee area in the fall (and what a nice place to be), take a side trip to the Gould Hill Orchards for apple picking and fresh cider. The farm's scenic mountain setting is a good place to view fall foliage.

● Winslow State Park
Exit 10 off I-89, toward Wilmot, (603) 526-6168, www.nhparks.state.nh.us.com. **All ages.**

Take the auto road from the park entrance up to Mount Kearsage (2,937 feet), and you'll find a peaceful picnic area with a great mountain view. From here you can take a short hiking trail to the summit. This is an extra special spot at twilight, when the sunset is likely to be wonderful.

● Wadleigh State Park
Rte. 114, Sutton, (603) 927-4727, www.nhparks.state.nh.us.com. **All ages.**

The 52-acre beach and picnic area on the south shore of Kezar Lake makes this park a special spot for families. It's rarely crowded.

● Pillsbury State Park
Rte. 31, Washington, (603) 863-2860, www.nhparks.state.nh.us.com. **All ages.**

This 5,000-acre hideaway is a great place for fishing, hiking, and camping. There are nine picturesque woodland ponds and several hiking trails in the park. Walk to Balance Rock, a large glacial erratic in such a teetering position that it's said one can actually move it by hand.

● Cross-Country Skiing
Young and old, big or little, novice or expert, if you're thinking of cross-country skiing, you'll find what you're looking for in the Sunapee area. Head

for **Norsk Touring Center,** on Rte. 11 in New London, (603) 526-4685, www.skinorsk.com. Well known for its kid-friendly teaching staff, this facility has 34 trails on 72 kilometers in a pretty location with lots of amenities on site: lodging, restaurant, and ski shop. The **Eastman Cross-Country Center** in Grantham, (603) 863-6772, offers plenty of novice terrain on 40 kilometers of trails.

● Mount Sunapee Ski Area

Rte. 103, Mt. Sunapee, (603) 763-2353, www.mtsunapee.com. Lift tickets: adults, $49; 7–12, $33; 6 and under, free. Snowstars, 4–7, $79/day. Mountain Explorers, 8–12, $85/day. Day care, $50/day. Rates listed are for weekends and holidays; special rates and packages are available. **All ages.**

This small, friendly area has undergone lots of recent improvements making it bigger and better without losing its relaxed charm. You'll find 220 skiing acres with 60 trails. If you're looking for a place away from the crowds, consider Mount Sunapee Ski Area. This is a great place to learn—or to perfect your skills. The majority of the trails are for intermediate skiers, with a special area for beginners and handful of black-diamond runs. The pace is relaxed; the scenery inspiring.

● Pat's Peak

Rte. 114, Henniker, (603) 428-3245, www.patspeak.com. Lift tickets: adults, $40, night skiing, $20; 14 and under, $28, night skiing, $16; 5 and under, free. Learn to ski program, ages 3–5, $50/day; 4–14, $65/day. **All ages.**

For 30 years families have been going to southern New Hampshire's Pat's Peak ski area. The modest area has 19 trails and seven lifts and is a local favorite with families and school groups. On selected evenings, Pat's offers night skiing; be prepared to share the trails with lots of hot-dogging teens. This is a great place to get started. Most of the terrain is gentle and three isolated areas are just for beginners. It's also a great place to have fun and keep costs down. Look for specials offered throughout the season. Pat's Peak hosts a number of family events, including an early-season free learn-to-ski week, family day, and a number of other themed celebrations.

 RESTAURANTS

● Peter Christian's Tavern

186 Main St., New London, (603) 526-4042. Daily, 11–10.

This 19th-century tavern-style eatery serves up hearty soups and stews and hefty sandwiches. Its relaxed, casual atmosphere is a favorite with families. There are lots of menu options, from full dinners to lighter soup-and-sandwich fare.

● Four Corners' Grille & Flying Goose Brew Pub

Crockett's Corner, 155 Rte. 11, New London, (603) 526-6899, www.flyinggoose.com. Daily, 11:30–11.

We love the slow-cooked, pit-style barbecue they serve at this lively, lakeview restaurant. Try the Potter Place Park platter, all natural, locally raised pork, slow-cooked over apple wood and hickory, then pulled into melt-in-your-mouth bite-size pieces. There's beef and chicken barbecue dishes, too, plus an array of sandwiches and salads. The kids' menu includes the usual favorites: fun-shaped chicken nuggets, spaghetti and meatballs, burgers, dogs, and grilled cheese.

■ Lincoln and Franconia Area

This picturesque mountain area on the western flanks of the White Mountain National Forest is a pine-scented, four-season playground. Summer is the most popular season, when the valleys are full of flowers and the streams run with cool, clear mountain water. Each summer, thousands come to see the natural beauty of the White Mountains; to visit the Franconia Notch State Park gorges, flumes, and waterfalls; and to drive the scenic Kancamagus Highway, lined with mountain and valley vistas. Outdoor activities abound—take a hike to tumbling falls, swim in pristine mountain lakes and pools, canoe or kayak the Swift River, or take an aerial ride to the 4,200-foot summit of Cannon Mountain. The children can explore caves, zip down water slides and roller coasters, visit haunted houses and petting zoos, and learn about nature, music, and history at a variety of local museums. In the winter months, there are sleigh rides, ski runs, and rinks and ponds, perfect for skating.

● Lost River Reservation

Rte. 112, N. Woodstock, (603) 745-8031, www.findlostriver.com. Mid-May–mid-Oct., weather permitting; May, June, Sept., Oct., 9–5; July–Aug., 9–6. Adults, $8.50; 6–12, $5. **Ages 2–14.**

Your children will be dirty, tired, and happy when you leave this place. You'll become explorers and navigators as you climb your way up and down ladders, belly-slide under rock ledges, and slither through caves. You can also take the easy way around—on the boardwalk—and simply enjoy the scenery. (But really, what fun is that?) The .75-mile trip will take about an hour as you follow the river as it appears and disappears through giant glacier boulders. You'll learn about the geological and ecological history of the river along the way. Be sure to wear comfortable shoes and outdoor clothing. A cafeteria/snack bar, picnic area, garden, and nature trails are also on the grounds. Note: Strollers are not allowed.

● Clark's Trading Post

Rte. 3, Lincoln, (603) 745-8913, www.clarkstradingpost.com. Memorial Day weekend–mid-June and Labor Day–mid-Oct., weekends, 10–6; late June–Labor Day, daily, 10–6. Admission, $9; 3–5, $3. **All ages.**

From an adult's point of view, Clark's Trading Post is a hodgepodge of amusements, its best being the performance of a family of trained black bears. But the kids will skip along in amused bliss, laughing at the slanted floors in Tuttle's Haunted House and the flying pianos in Merlin's Mystical Mansion. They will enjoy the antics of Wolfman, who jeers at them as they ride aboard the White Mountain Central Railroad.

● The Whale's Tale Water Park

Rte. 3, Lincoln, (603) 745-8810, www.whalestalewaterpark.com. Early June, weekends only, 11–5; mid-June–Labor Day, daily, 10–6. Admission, $21; under 4, free. **Ages 5 and up.**

Brave souls can zip down the Blue Lightning Speed Slide or the Serpentine Flume Slide. Or try the 360-degree Beluga Boggin' Tube Ride. For a more relaxing pace, you can soak in the giant wave pool or unwind on the Lazy River. Young children have a special pool set aside for them. A fun place on a hot day.

● Hobo Railroad

Rte. 3, Lincoln, (603) 745-2135, www.hoborr.com. Memorial Day– Halloween. Trains leave at 11, 1, 3, 5, and 7 in summer; as needed in spring and fall. Adults, $8; 3–11, $6.50. **Ages 2 and up.**

For outstanding mountain views (and a fun way to have lunch), consider taking the 14-mile trip along the Pemigewasset River aboard the Hobo Picnic Train. Your picnic lunch comes packed hobo-style—wrapped in a bandana and tied to the end of a stick. (If you can't make lunch, there are other rides throughout the day and evening.) Your children will probably not let you get away without a ride on Diamond Eddie's Ferris Wheel. This giant wheel takes you for a gentle 10-minute ride as you sit on benches in enclosed compartments.

● Loon Mountain Park and Skyride

Rte. 112 (Kancamagus Hwy.), Lincoln, (603) 745-8111, www.loonmtn.com. Memorial Day–mid-June, weekends; mid-June–foliage season (early Nov.), daily. Adults, $9.50; 6–12, $5.50; 5 and under, free. **Ages 2 and up.**

The beauty of the New Hampshire mountain ranges, forests, and lakes is spectacular from the mountain summits. In the Lincoln area, ride the Loon Mountain Gondola to the top of Loon Mountain, where you get a panoramic view of White Mountain peaks. The enclosed gondola ride takes about 10 minutes. On top, there's a four-story observation tower, cafeteria, and lots to explore: glacial caves, trails, and ongoing nature programs. At the base area, you'll find mountain biking, an in-line skating park, pony and horseback riding, climbing walls, archery, and a lodging and dining area.

● Franconia Notch State Park

Franconia Notch Parkway, Lincoln/Franconia; (603) 823-8800, www.nhparks.state.nh.us.com. Free. **All ages.**

Travel for eight miles through a spectacular mountain pass—the Franconia Notch Parkway—and through the 6,440-acre state park. The Notch Parkway is located between the high peaks of the Kinsman and Franconia Mountain ranges. As you travel through the notch, from the Flume at the south end to Echo Lake at the north, you'll see wonderful vistas, waterfalls, mountain lakes, and natural attractions. Visit the Flume, then stop for a peek at the Basin. This beautiful waterfall has a granite pothole of 20 feet in diameter at its base. Below the Basin, look for the Old Man's foot rock formation. Show the kids Boise Rock, where Thomas Boise, a teamster from Woodstock, New Hampshire, sought shelter during a blizzard in the early 1800s. Boise killed his horse, skinned it, and wrapped himself in the hide. Searchers cut away the frozen hide and found him alive.

Just north of Boise Rock, you'll see Profile Lake, headquarters of the Old Man's Washbowl. Look up; hovering above Profile Lake is the Old Man in the Mountains. This natural rock formation was formed nearly 200 million years ago. The Old Man is made of five separate granite ledges arranged to form a man's profile. At the northern side of the Notch Parkway, you'll find beautiful Echo Lake, the perfect spot to stop for a swim or picnic.

● Flume Gorge

Rte. 3, Franconia Notch, (603) 745-8391, www.nhparks.state.nh.us.com. Mid-May–June. (weather permitting), daily, 9–5. July–Labor Day, daily, 9–5:30; Labor Day–mid-Oct., daily, 9–5. Adults, $8; 6–12, $5; under 6, free. **All ages.**

One of the most popular attractions in the area, this natural 800-foot chasm is a must-stop along the way. The rushing waters of the Pemigewasset River carved the wonder thousands of years ago, leaving walls that rise as high as 70 feet. If you don't mind sharing space with the inevitable summer crowds, you'll enjoy the cool, misty mountain air and marvel at the surrounding natural beauty. Walk boardwalks and hiking trails across covered bridges to waterfalls, cascades, river basins, and pools.

● Cannon Aerial Tramway

Rte. 3, Franconia Notch, (603) 823-5563, www.cannonmt.com. Mid-May– mid-Oct., daily, 9–5. Adults, $10; 6–12, $6; under 6, free. **All ages.**

In Franconia Notch, the Cannon Aerial Tramway whisks you to the summit of 4,200-foot Cannon Mountain; on a clear day, you'll be able to see into Maine, Vermont, and Canada. The ride takes 6 minutes, but plan to spend some time at the top. Consider packing snacks or lunch (or buy something at the summit cafeteria) to enjoy along one of the summit trails. The Rim Trail is perfect for families. You'll be treated to some great mountain views, and you'll find plenty of picnic spots along the way. At the end of the trail is an observation deck for more viewing. It'll take about 20 minutes to walk, not counting time out for picnics and viewing. Summit cookouts are held July through Labor Day, Thursday through Sunday.

● New England Ski Museum

Base of Cannon Mtn., Franconia Notch, (603) 823-7177, www.skimuseum.org. Memorial Day–Columbus Day and Dec.–Mar., daily, noon–5. Free. **Ages 5 and up.**

Older children who have been bitten by the ski bug might enjoy a visit here. The exhibit that traces the evolution of ski equipment is particularly interesting. The museum also features changing ski-related exhibits and displays and archival film footage on video that outlines the history of New England skiing.

● Robert Frost Place

Ridge Rd., Franconia, (603) 823-5510, www.frostplace.com. Memorial Day–June, Sat.–Sun., 1–5; July–Columbus Day, daily, 1–5 (closed Tues.). Adults, $3; 6–12, $1.25. **Ages 8 and up.**

The Frost farm homestead is an unpretentious, quiet tribute to the renowned poet. You'll find a small museum and an interpretive nature trail highlighting some of Frost's poems.

● Swimming

On hot days, head for **Echo Lake** (Rte. 3, Franconia Notch), a pristine, spring-fed lake at the base of Cannon Mountain. The white, sandy beach, cool mountain waters, and picturesque background make a hard-to-beat combination. There are changing and bathhouse facilities.

Travel the **Pemigewasset River** along Rte. 112 and you'll find a number of great swimming holes.

Other cooling-off spots include **Russell Pond,** in Woodstock, and **Franconia Notch State Park.**

● Horseback Riding

Horseback rides through meadows and forests, offering beautiful views of Mount Lafayette, Mount Moosilauke, and the Franconia Range, are available at the **Franconia Inn,** Rte. 116, Franconia, (800) 473-5299 or

(603) 823-5542, www.franconiainn.com. You'll ride with a guide on trails through the 117-acre estate in the Easton Valley. Children must be at least 54 inches tall to reach the stirrups properly.

Trail riding is also available at **Loon Mountain Park,** Rte. 112, Lincoln, (800) 229-5666 or (603) 745-8111, www.loonmtn.com; and at **Waterville Valley Resort,** Rte. 49, Waterville, (800) GO-VALLEY or (603) 236-4666, www.waterville.com.

● Cross-Country Skiing

If you like to be on your own, skinny skiing through the countryside, check out the Echo Lake area. Cross-country skiing along Echo Lake is a visual treat. You'll see Cannon Mountain in the background and a glimpse of the Old Man in the Mountains. Or there are lots of cross-country opportunities in Franconia Notch State Park, where you can follow the bike paths.

The Loon Mountain Cross Country Center, on Kancamagus Highway in Lincoln, (800) 229-5666 or (603) 745-8111, www.loonmtn.com, maintains more than 30 kilometers of groomed trails that run along the Pemigewasset River and traverse the mountains. There are lots of gentle trails for beginners and children. Information on trails, lessons, and rentals is available at the headquarters in the base lodge at Loon. There's also a skating rink and skate rentals available.

Waterville Valley, on Rte. 49, (800) GO-VALLEY, www.waterville .com, selected as one of the top cross-country ski resorts in North America, offers a vast trail network laid out over 7,000 scenic acres. There's a variety of terrain; 70 kilometers of trails are groomed, 35 kilometers provide wilderness ski access. At the Cross Country Ski Center, in Town Square, you'll find services and amenities, including refreshments, ski rentals, lessons, and special programs and activities.

Other cross-country ski opportunities can be found at the **Franconia Inn Ski Touring Center,** (603) 823-5542, www.franconiainn.com, which offers 50 kilometers of groomed trails.

● Waterville Valley Ski Area

Rte. 49 (Waterville Valley Access Rd.); (800) GO-VALLEY, wwwwaterville.com. Lift tickets: adults, $39; 13–18, $29; 6–12, $19; 5 and under, free. Learn to ski, ages 3–6, $65/day; child care, 6 mos.–4, $51/day. Rates listed are for weekends; holidays are more; discounts and special packages are available. **All ages..**

Waterville knows how to treat families. Come for the day and ski the 53 trails serviced by 13 lifts. But it won't be enough—to get the best out of Waterville you'll have to stay overnight to browse the Town Square, ice skate in the indoor arena, soak in a hot tub, or enjoy the twilight sleigh ride. Despite its amenities, this resort manages to retain a cozy, New England village atmosphere.

Waterville Valley offers a professionally run nursery for infants six months and up, located at the ski area. If your children are old enough, however—that's three years and up at Waterville—enroll them in one of the children's learn-to-ski programs. Kids have their own small ski area and kinderlift.

In recent years, Waterville has gained a well-earned reputation as one of the best places for snowboarders in the East. On Mount Tecumseh, the Boneyard Snowboard Park is for experienced riders featuring gaps, tabletops, kickers, and railsides. (If you have to ask, don't go there.) Across the street is Snow's Mountain, a 2,050-foot peak for snowboarders only. Features include steep pitches and a half pipe. Riders have their own base lodge at Snow's Mountain. If you have riders in your family, they're going to love it here.

Remember, this resort gets crowded on the weekends. Your best bet? Play hookey and head up midweek.

● Loon Mountain Ski Area

Kancamagus Hwy., Lincoln, (800) 229-5666 or (603) 745-8111, www.loonmtn.com. Lift tickets: adults, $51; 13–17, $45; 6–12, $33. P.K. Boo Bear (3–4), $79/day; Kinderbear (5–6), $79/day. Adventure Camp (7–12), $89/day; child care (6 wks.–8 yrs.), $59/day. Rates listed are for weekends and holidays; discounts and special packages are available. **All ages.**

Loon Mountain is a popular Northeast ski resort, offering 41 trails for skiers of every level. Loon's trails ski long. Even a beginner can ride to the top of the mountain and take a gradual easy run down to the base. That's what makes it so appealing to intermediate and beginner skiers.

Don't plan on having the place to yourself—it gets crowded. Some tips to get more skiing for your dollars include getting your lift ticket the night before, getting to the mountain early, avoiding the gondola during peak usage (10:30–11:30 and 1–2:30), and heading to the less-crowded West Basin double chairs.

● Cannon

Franconia Notch State Park, Franconia, (603) 823-8800, wwwcannonmt.com. Lift tickets: adults, $44; 12 and under, $27; Learn to ski, ages 3–12, $65/day; day care, $45/day. Rates listed are for weekends and holidays; discounts and special packages are available. **All ages.**

Cannon has thousands of ardent followers and loyal return skiers. It's earned a reputation as a "skier's mountain," and you won't find a lot of frills and developments. Predominately known for its challenging ski runs, and its ungroomed, off-trail skiing in heavy snow seasons, Cannon also offers some of the best views in the East.

Cannon has made several changes in recent years to lure families. The small, manageable area now has Peabody Slopes, offering a variety of intermediate and beginner trails. You'll find 31 trails in all, serviced by six lifts. If it's a windy, cold day, best to stay away. But if the sun is shining in the White Mountains, head straight for Cannon, hop the chair to the 4,200-foot summit, and enjoy the view of surrounding mountains and forests and the glistening Echo Lake below. Then, cruise down.

 RESTAURANTS

● Jigger Johnson's
On the Green, Plymouth, (603) 536-2992. Mon.–Sat., 11–10; Sun., 4–10.

Named after the New Hampshire folk hero and logger Jigger Johnson, this place works hard at not taking itself too seriously. Full of memorabilia and bad jokes, posters and souvenirs, it's casual, fun, and the food suprisingly good. There's a big menu—pizza, burgers, nachos, sandwiches, salads, and a full selection of dinner entrees. Kids have their own menu, and the chocolate milk comes with cherries.

● The Common Man
Main St., Ashland, (603) 968-7030. Lunch, Tues.–Sat., 11:30–2; dinner, daily, 5:30–9.

Rustic charm abounds in this restaurant. The old mixes with the new, and you'll get a feast for your eyes as well as your palate. Neon clocks mix with lobster traps, Shaker baskets, and white tablecloths. Upstairs, you'll find a relaxing lounge with comfy chairs, books, board games, and puzzles. The place to go if there's a wait for a table. Or elect to eat in the lounge, where young toddlers may feel more comfortable. The food is good old American fare—steaks, baked potatoes, salad. There's a handful of nicely prepared fish and poultry dishes, too.

■ Conway and Jackson Area

If your family has a love of the great outdoors, you'll revel in the natural beauty and abundance of activities at the pretty village of Jackson. This is the home of the Appalachian Mountain Club and center for hiking, mountain climbing, and cross-country skiing. The beauty of the area is best seen on a hike into the White Mountain National Forest, a picnic on the shores of a mountain lake, or a horse-drawn sleigh ride through a covered bridge and past a white-steeple church in the village center. There's fishing, swimming, hiking, canoeing, rafting, kayaking, golf, tennis . . . and more, more, more. Come winter, there's some of the best cross-country and downhill skiing in New England.

Drive a few miles south to North Conway, however, and you're in a different world of factory outlets, discount shopping, outdoor gear shops, and boutiques . . . and restaurants, minigolf, inns, hotels . . . and traffic. The end-of-day and Sunday afternoon bottlenecks are legendary.

Amid the surrounding natural beauty of the area, you'll find an abundance of commercial attractions to delight children. Your family can visit Cinderella at her castle, ride a gondola to the top of a mountain, and zip down it on a water slide. It's a wonderfully diverse and popular area for family vacationing.

● Heritage New Hampshire

Rte. 16, Glen, (603) 383-9776, www.heritagenh.com. Memorial Day weekend–mid-June, weekends, 9–5; mid-June–Columbus Day, daily 9–5. Adults, $10; 4–12, $4.50; under 4, free. **Ages 6–14.**

This museum puts you in the middle of history-in-the-making as you journey through time, from 1634 to the 20th century. You'll be carried across the ocean aboard the ship *Reliance.* From there you'll walk through history, as special effects and audiovisual techniques do a good job of putting you right in the middle of the action. Not quite Disney World, but you'll learn about early American history.

● Story Land

Rte. 16, Glen, (603) 383-4293, www.storylandnh.com. Memorial Day weekend–mid-June and Labor Day–Columbus Day, weekends only, 9–6; mid-June–Labor Day, daily, 9–6. Admission, $19; 3 and under, free. **Ages 1–10.**

Look, it's Cinderella and Little Bo Peep with her sheep. Youngsters will squeal with delight as they meet their favorite storybook characters. Take a ride on a pirate's ship, set sail on a swan boat, or travel around the track in a miniature Model T. You can also take a voyage to the moon or a rolling journey on the Polar Coaster. Cool off on Bamboo Chutes, a water flume ride. There are other amusement rides, a castle, live animals, and daily shows. A mixed bag of amusements, ultrafriendly staff, and well-done attractions make this destination one of the top in New Hampshire for families with young ones.

● Attitash Bear Peak and Fields of Attitash

Rte. 302, Bartlett, (603) 374-2368, www.attitash.com. Late May–early June, weekends, 10–5; mid-June–Aug., daily, 10–6; Sept.–Columbus Day, weekends, 10–5. Rates and packages vary. **All ages.**

You can't beat this place for easy summer fun on the mountain; it has something for everyone. Take a scenic chairlift ride to the White Mountain Observation Tower for a spectacular panoramic view of surrounding mountains and valleys. Too slow a pace for your family? No problem—zip down on a water slide. Or rent mountain bikes and follow the network of trails. At the Fields of Attitash, guided horseback rides along the scenic Saco River are offered. Special events are held throughout the summer.

● Conway Scenic Railroad

Rte. 16, North Conway, (800) 232-5251 or (603) 356-5251, www.conwayscenic.com. Valley train: mid-Apr.–mid-May and Nov.–mid-Dec., weekends; mid-May–late Oct., daily. Notch train: late June–early Sept., Tues.–Sat.; mid-Sept.–mid-Oct., daily. Adults, from $9.50; 4–12, from $7; under 4, free. **Ages 5 and up.**

Hop aboard for a relaxing, nostalgic ride through the New Hampshire countryside. A variety of trips are offered. The Valley Train offers round-trip rides to Conway and Bartlett, and the Notch Train travels through pretty Crawford Notch. On both, you'll see wonderful mountainside scenery. For a special treat, book the Pullman Parlor Car or a seat in the dining car "Chocorua" on the Valley Train. The Notch Train offers coach and first-class seating.

● Community Center Playground

Main St., North Conway. **Ages 1–10.**

This is where all the kids hang out. The outdoor playground is full of monkey bars, tunnels, slides, swings, and jungle gyms, and it's right next to the Conway Railroad Station in the center of North Conway Village. You can't miss it; just follow the sounds of children at play.

● Eastern Slope Playhouse

Main St., North Conway, (603) 356-5776. Tues.–Sat., 8. **Ages 10 and up.**

For a special evening, consider attending a performance of the Mount Washington Valley Theater Company, held throughout the summer at the Eastern Slope Playhouse. The renowned summer theater performs first-rate productions of Broadway musicals. A nice, upbeat, toe-tapping night out with older children. Call starting mid-June for schedule, reservations, and ticket prices.

● Arts Jubilee

Box 647, North Conway, (603) 356-9393. Performances held at Schouler Park in North Conway. **All ages.**

You're likely to see anything under the Arts Jubilee tent in North Conway: magicians, dragons, and acrobats; folk dancing and ballet; barbershop quartets, jazz reviews, classical orchestras, knee-slapping country music, and bagpipes. This ongoing arts festival is well known for its weekly summer family entertainment series (monthly events are held the rest of the year) and free evening concerts. Call for a schedule of events.

● Wildcat Mountain Gondola

Rte. 16, Jackson, (800) 255-6439 or (603) 466-3326, www.skiwildcat.com. Mid-May–July 4, weekends, 10–5; July 4th–Columbus Day, daily, 10–5. Adults, $9; 6–12, $4.50. **All ages.**

Enjoy the views atop the 4,062-foot summit at Wildcat Mountain without having to walk up or ski down it. Take a 15-minute sky ride to enjoy fabulous views of the White Mountain National Forest and beyond. Observation deck, picnic areas, snacks, and nature trails are at the summit.

● Echo Lake State Park

Rte. 302, just off Rte. 16, North Conway, (603) 356-2672. June–Labor Day. **All ages.**

This small park is the perfect spot to stop for a refreshing swim or a relaxing day outing. The clear, spring-fed lake has a good swimming area for children. There are trails to take you around the lake and to ledges above, depending on your time and inclination. There are picnic tables, grills, and boats for rent. This is a very popular summer spot.

● Swimming

There are plenty of places to pull off the road for a refreshing dip in the pristine mountain rivers and falls. On hot summer days, you'll see lots of people sunning on the rocks and swimming in the clear waters of the **Saco** and **Swift Rivers,** accessed from the Kancamagus Highway and Rte. 302. If you want to avoid the crowds, prowl around a bit. You'll find many good swimming holes a bit off the highway that are easily accessible. Tip: Ask a friendly local about his or her favorite spot.

● Canoeing

Saco Bound, Rte. 302, Center Conway, (603) 447-2177, www.sacobound.com. **Ages 5 and up.**

The Saco River is well known for its excellent canoeing. You don't need experience. Stop by the Saco Bound offices in North Conway, where you'll get all the equipment and instruction you need to go for a few hours or a day (or more) of it. The scenery is wonderful, the waters are calm (in spots) and shallow, and you'll find lots of great places along the way to stop for a picnic and swim. In the spring, when the waters are swifter, you might consider an exhilarating kayaking or white-water trip (for more experienced paddlers and older children).

Be sure to plan several weeks ahead for weekend rentals; the river gets crowded and rentals can be scarce.

● Gold Panning

The locals swear there's gold in them thar rivers—the Saco and the Swift, that is. But the rangers are quick to add that while many have found gold, no one's struck it rich yet. Pack a couple of shallow pans and try your luck. It's a fun way to spend a few hours on the river. And who knows?

● Hiking

Many who come to this area find they want to go farther into the woods and mountains. To really appreciate this part of New England, you have to get off the roads. Your first stop should be a visit to the Pinkham Notch Camp at the base of Mount Washington. This is the hub of White Mountains hiking activity, and it serves as the northern New England headquarters for the Appalachian Mountain Club. Everyone is welcome to use its facilities and services. The AMC is a nonprofit organization offering a variety of recreation and conservation activities, including guided expeditions, research, backcountry management, trail and shelter construction and maintenance, mountain search and rescue, book publishing, and outdoor recreation.

At Pinkham Notch you'll see mountain climbers and backpackers, downhill and cross-country skiers—novices and experts—all gathering about, planning the day's activities. You'll want to talk to the people on staff for updated information on trail conditions and recommendations for families, and to pick up trail maps.

There are literally hundreds of hiking trails in the White Mountains area, and many are appropriate for the inexperienced hiking family. (Most, however, do not accommodate wheelchairs or strollers; put baby in a backpack.) Here's a selection of family-friendly hikes in the area:

Glen Ellis Falls. Off Rte. 16 (.8 mile south of the Pinkham Notch Camp), this trail is an easy walk to Glen Ellis Falls. The trail passes under the highway through a tunnel and reaches the falls in .3 miles. The main fall is 70 feet high, with many pools and smaller falls below.

Winneweta Falls. This trail leaves Rte. 16 three miles north of Jackson. You'll cross the Ellis River (watch out in the spring when the water is high) and follow the Miles Brook until you get to Winneweta Falls. A refreshingly wet, hot-day hike, this is about one mile long and takes about 40 minutes.

Mountain Pond Trail. This trail begins .6 mile up the road that leaves Maine Highway 113 at a spot .2 mile north of the Congregational Church in Chatham. You'll walk through a birch and fir forest to the pristine Mountain Pond. From here, take the northerly route around the pond and head back (stop first for a dip in the pond or a picnic along its shores). If you continue south past the AMC cabin, you'll be in for a much longer hike, about three hours. Otherwise, it's a short, easy hike to the pond and back.

Sawyer Pond Trail. This trail leaves the Kancamagus Highway two miles east of the Sabbaday Falls Picnic Area. You'll head north and cross the Swift River, pass between Coreens Cliff and Owls Cliff, and cross Sawyer Brook. The walk takes you through the woods (bring bug repellent!). Just about the time you've had enough of walking, Sawyer Pond will come into view. The pond is clear and inviting—a great place for a swim after your hike. You can continue on the trail and end up on Sawyer Pond Road (AMC runs a shuttle service; arrange for it before you start out). A less complicated option is just to head back the way you came. This will take about 2.5 hours on an easy four- to five-mile trail.

Sabbaday Falls Trail. This is a pleasant, easy walk to a picturesque series of cascades. The trail begins off the Kancamagus Highway (about 15 miles west of Rte. 16) and has a number of descriptive signs along the way pointing out wildlife and rock formations. It'll take about a half hour to go the .4 mile.

Black Cap Mountain. Drive to the top of Hurricane Mountain Rd. There's an easy hike from here to Black Cap Mountain, where you'll be rewarded with great views of the national forest, mountain peaks, and Maine to your east. Watch for migrating hawks often spotted here. The 1.2-mile trail will take about an hour.

● Cross-Country Skiing

The Jackson, New Hampshire, area has been rated as one of the four best places in the world for cross-country skiing. **The Jackson Ski Touring Center,** (603) 383-9355, www.jacksonxc.org, boasts a 154-kilometer trail system in the North Conway area. The trails are well maintained and marked for all abilities. There are a number of beginner and kid-friendly trails and a warming cabin along the way.

Many of the trails of the **Appalachian Mountain Club,** Pinkham Notch, (603) 466-2727, are open to cross-country skiers who love natural snow. Ask for trail descriptions and recommendations at the center.

You'll also notice a number of cross-country skiers and snowshoers right in the middle of Jackson as they traverse the town golf course.

● Mount Cranmore Ski Resort

Off Rte. 16, North Conway, (800) SUN-N-SKI or (603) 356-5544, www.cranmore.com. Lift tickets: adults, $32; 6–12, $18; 5 and under, free. Learn to ski, ages 4–12, $78/day; child care, $50/day. **All ages.**

Conveniently located in North Conway, Mount Cranmore has old-time appeal, nothing too flashy or fancy. In fact, this is where skiing began nearly 60 years ago. Today, Cranmore is a big hit with families, where they enjoy easygoing and gentle skiing on 36 trails, serviced by six lifts. Snowboarders like Bad Dog Snowpark, and everyone seems to love the night skiing.

● Attitash Bear Peak Ski Resort

Rte. 302, Bartlett, (603) 374-2368, www.attitash.com. Lift tickets: adults, $49; 13–18, $44; 6–12, $32. Learn to ski, ages 4–12, $75/day; child care (6 mos.–6 yrs.), $45/day. Prices listed are for weekends; special packages and rates available. **All ages.**

This is a nice intermediate area offering 45 trails, serviced by 10 lifts. Recent improvements have expanded snowmaking on the mountain and added the more challenging Bear Peak area. It can get crowded on the weekends, but the area tries to avoid congestion by limiting lift ticket sales. Skiers and riders have more than 200 acres to explore, most of them on intermediate runs.

● Wildcat Mountain

Rte. 16, Jackson, (800) 255-6439 or (603) 466-3326, www.skiwildcat.com. Lift tickets: adults, $52/day; 13–17, $42; 6–12, $25; Learn to ski, ages 3–5, $70/day; 5–12, $79/day; child care (2 mos.–5 yrs.), $44/day. **All ages.**

Wildcat's 2,100-foot drop and its 4,100-foot elevation make it an exciting ski area for the more experienced skier. The trails here run steep and narrow. There are concessions to beginners: a handful of easier trails, lessons, and nursery and learn-to-ski programs. And intermediate skiers will have a blast. You'll find all the amenities of a top-notch ski resort—base lodges, child care, services, and a number of special programs and events.

● Black Mountain

Rte. 16B, Jackson, (800) 698-4490 or (603) 383-4490, www.blackmt.com. Lift tickets: adults, $32; 18 and under, $20; 5 and under, free. Kids ski school (3–5), $50/day; 6–12, $70/day; child care (6 mos.–5 yrs.), $40/day. **All ages.**

Billed as the "Great American Family Ski Place," Black Mountain offers gentle, sheltered slopes and a slow, relaxed atmosphere that are welcoming for family skiers. There are 30 trails, serviced by four lifts, and a snowboard park to entice riders. This is a great place to learn.

Tired of skiing? Black Mountain also has a lift-serviced snow-tubing park offering day and night tubing during the weekends and holiday periods. Sleigh rides and dogsled rides are also offered. Great fun.

RESTAURANTS

● Elvio's
Main St., North Conway Village, (603) 356-3307. Sun.–Thurs., 11–9;
Fri.–Sat., 11–11.

If you're in the mood for pizza (and when is your child not in the mood for pizza?), head to Elvio's. Locals argue that it's the best pizza in the world. You decide. Three different types are offered: the regular, round, thin-crust pizza baked in a stone deck oven; the rectangular, thick-crust, Sicilian pan-cooked pizza; and white pizza, a round-pie made with white cheeses, olive oil, garlic, and spices. Dine in or take out.

● Merlino's Steakhouse
Rte. 16, North Conway, (603) 356-6006. Daily, 11–9:30.

You can't miss the giant cow grazing atop the Merlino's Steakhouse sign on busy Route 16. This restaurant has been a mainstay on the North Conway dining scene for years. Pleasant atmosphere, serving the standard fare of steak, salad, and potatoes. Prime rib is their specialty. Children's portions are available.

■ Mount Washington Area

Majestic Mount Washington, the highest peak in the Northeast, looks down upon an area rich in natural beauty and abundant with family-friendly activities. The Presidential Range, a string of mountain peaks named after U.S. presidents, and the surrounding national forest offer miles of fine hiking trails, cascades, waterfalls, and mountain lakes. Chug along in a steam-powered railroad car, or take the slow, climbing auto road to the top of Mount Washington. The view, of mountain peaks and valleys below, is breathtaking.

Families who ski will enjoy the relaxing Bretton Woods ski area for cross-country and downhill skiing. Young children will enjoy a visit with Santa, and the entire family can get a taste of the Old West at Six Gun City in nearby Jefferson. Always, no matter what your day's agenda may be, you'll be surrounded by beautiful mountain scenery.

● Santa's Village
Rte. 2, Jefferson, (603) 586-4445, www.santasvillage.com. Memorial Day
weekend–mid-June, weekends, 9:30–5; mid-June–Labor Day, daily, 9:30–6;
Labor Day–Columbus Day, weekends, 9:30–5. Thanksgiving–mid-Dec.,
Sat., noon–8. Admission, $17; 3 and under, free. **Ages 1–8.**

Santa is never out of season with young children. If you can tolerate the "When is Christmas coming?" questions that will inevitably follow, stop in to see Santa and his elves. Besides a visit with the host of honor, children will enjoy splashing down the log flume, riding on the enchanted train, and circling on the old-fashioned carousel. There are music and bird shows, and Santa's Skyway Sleigh, a monorail ride that encompasses part of the park. The attraction sounds a bit hokey, but it's actually nicely done.

● Six Gun City

Rte. 2, Jefferson, (603) 586-4592, www.sixguncity.com. Late May–mid-June, weekends, 10–5; mid-June–Labor Day, daily, 9–6. Admission, $15.45; 3 and under, free. **Ages 1–10.**

This is a kid's fantasy come true—a visit to the Old West when cowboys ruled the land, sheriffs caught the bad guys, and horses were the mode of transportation. Children will love becoming deputies, helping the sheriff go after law-breaking outlaws, or taking a ride on a pony or burro. The live cowboy skits and Frontier Show are fun family-style entertainment. Throughout Six Gun City, you'll see more than 100 horse-drawn vehicles and many Old West antiques. And there are plenty of rides, bumper boats, and a miniature golf course. Be sure to bring your bathing suit for a trip down the Tomahawk Run Waterslide.

● Mount Washington Auto Road

Rte. 16, Gorham, (603) 466-3988, www.mt-washington.com/autoroad. Mid-May–late Oct. (weather permitting), daily, 8:30–5. Car and driver, $16; each additional adult, $6; 5–12, $4. Guided tours, adults, $22; 5–12, $10. **All ages.**

This winding, steep, eight-mile toll road offers some of the most scenic views in the Northeast. The 45-minute trip to the summit—at 6,288 feet it's the highest in the Northeast—takes you through mountain forests til you reach the top, where on clear days views stretch across six states. Don't count on it being clear, though. It's usually not, and it's almost always windy and chilly. There's a weather station and observatory at the top, plus a cafeteria and small museum. If you prefer not to drive yourself, there are guided tour vans that will take you up, or you can catch a ride on the Cog Railway.

● Mount Washington Cog Railway

Rte. 302, Bartlett, (800) 922-8825 or (603) 278-5404, www.thecog.com. May–Oct. Adults, $44; 6-12, $30; 5 and under (on an adult's lap), free. **All ages.**

The mountain railway to the summit of Mount Washington is a lot like an old-fashioned wooden roller coaster ride. The steam-powered train, dating back to 1869, hits inclines that reach a 37 percent grade, making it the steepest railway in the world. It will chug, spit, and spew black smoke up the side of the mountain, threatening to give up each inch of the way. Get a window seat and enjoy the mountain scenery. Be sure to dress warmly; the summit (where you'll find an observatory, cafeteria, displays, and small museum—and spectacular views!) is nearly always windy and cold. It takes about three hours to make the round-trip.

● Great Glen Trails Outdoor Center

Rte. 16, Pinkham Notch, Gorham, (603) 466-2333, www.mt-washington.com. Year-round, daily, 8:30-4:30. Rates vary. **Ages 5 and up.**

This year-round activities center, at the base of mighty Mount Washington in northern New Hamsphire, is a great place for families who love the outdoors. In summer, there's mountain biking on hard-packed gravel trails or single track paths through scenic backcountry mountains and forest. Guided kayaking and canoeing excursions are also offered. In winter, there's cross-country skiing, snowshoeing, and snow tubing. Or catch a ride on the SnowCoach, an eight-passenger van with snow claws for tires. The SnowCoach travels the legendary Mount Washington Auto Road to above treeline for spectacular views of the Great Gulf Wilderness and snow-covered Presidential Range. From here, you can ski or snowshoe down, or ride the SnowCoach back.

● Hiking

Don't miss the chance to hike one of the many trails in the Mount Washington area; it's the best way to enjoy its natural beauty. Stop by one of the Appalachian Mountain Club camps or U.S. Ranger Stations for trail maps, recommendations, and up-to-date trail conditions. The following trails are short, easy hikes appropriate for families:

Jackson-Webster Trail. There are a few steep spots along the way, which make this trail best for families with older children. The trail, marked in blue, leaves the east side of Route 302 just south of the Crawford Depot. (You'll see a side trail, Elephant's Head, veering to the right. Take this short side trip to the top of the ledge overlooking Crawford Notch for some fine views.) The main trail runs above Elephant Head Brook, crosses Little Mossy Brook, and rises, rather steeply, to Flume Cascade Brook. It's about 45 minutes and .9 mile to this point. Head back now, or continue on the Webster branch (to the right) to a beautiful cascade and pool. That'll be enough for most families.

Sylvan Way. This is a great trail for families, particularly in the fall when foliage is spectacular. Pick it up at the Link at Memorial Bridge on Rte. 2, .7 mile from the Appalachian parking area in Randolph. You'll pass falls and brooks on this easy 2.5-mile trip. It should take about an hour and a half.

● Jefferson Notch

A drive through Jefferson Notch is not recommended for the faint-hearted, but it's worth the effort. The narrow, steep road is one of the highest in New Hampshire, reaching almost 3,000 feet. From U.S. 2, three miles east of Jefferson Highlands, you'll turn south on the road heading from Labyan to the Mount Washington Cog Railway Station. You'll be rewarded with great mountain and valley panoramas, and a fine view of Jefferson Notch.

● Cross-Country Skiing

There are many natural, ungroomed trails in the **Appalachian Mountain Club** network open to cross-country skiers. Stop by the AMC headquarters in Pinkham Notch, (603) 356-5541, for information on conditions and for detailed trail maps.

Nordic skiers will also enjoy the well-maintained course at **Bretton Woods Ski Area,** Rte. 302, Bretton Woods, (603) 278-3320, www.brettonwoods.com, ranked as one of the top cross-country centers in the state. The trails, including 100 kilometers of groomed paths, are generally old logging roads or rail beds that head through forests, over bridges, and down picturesque lanes. There are lots of nice views of Mount Washington, Crawford Notch, and the Ammonoosuc River along the way. There are also a handful of lift-serviced trails, a yurt warming hut, and a backcountry cabin on Mount Stickney.

● Bretton Woods

Rte. 302, Bretton Woods, (603) 278-3320, www.brettonwoods.com. Lift tickets: adults, $53; 13–18, $43; 6–12, $33; 5 and under, free. Learn to ski, $79/day; child care (2 mos.–5 yrs.), $55/day. Rates listed are for weekends and holidays; special packages are available. **All ages.**

The slow and easy atmosphere and the wide-open beginner and interme-diate terrain make Bretton Woods a favorite with families—or with anyone looking for a relaxing ski getaway. You'll be skiing Mount Rosebrook, which has a 1,500-foot vertical drop mostly felt in long, cruising runs. There's not much of a challenge at this area for experienced skiers, but everyone will enjoy its views and happy-go-lucky ease. In recent years, Bretton has expanded its expert terrain (you'll find a couple of mogul-strewn, ungroomed trails) and added 25 wonderful acres of glade skiing.

The resort boasts lots of amenities: lessons, restaurants, nursery, special events, and programs. Locals tell us the area gets twice as much snow as do other resorts, a phenomenon they call the "Bretton Woods flurries."

RESTAURANTS

● Fabyans Station
Rte. 302 (next to the Cog Railway Rd.), Bretton Woods, (603) 846-2222. Daily, 11–9:30.

Housed in a restored railroad depot, this restaurant offers a selection of appetizers, salads, burgers, and sandwiches. Dinner entrees feature chicken, ribs, steak, pasta, and fish dishes. Ask for half portions for children. Pleasant decor, reasonably priced, and tasty food.

● Darby's Restaurant
Rte. 302, Lodge at Bretton Woods, (603) 278-1500. Late May–Columbus Day, daily, 7:30 A.M.–9 A.M. and 5:30 P.M.–9 P.M. Rest of the year, daily, 5–7 P.M.

This casual restaurant in the lodge at the Bretton Woods Resort offers great views of the Presidential Range. In winter, you'll be warmed by two fireplaces. The menu offers veal, chicken, steaks, and seafood. Make reservations for weekend dinners; it can get crowded.

■ Monadnock Region

White-steepled churches set in village centers, old-fashioned country stores, covered bridges, and rolling hills all set in quiet meandering valleys and farmlands welcome you to rural New Hampshire. You'll want to stroll the Main Street in the town of Peterborough, the model for Thornton Wilder's *Our Town,* or Main Street in Keene, the widest paved Main Street in the world. And if you like a parade, this is the place—the Monadnock region may well hold the most parades per capita in the country. Stay more than a day or two in the summer, and you'll likely see one. This is small-town USA.

The area surrounding Keene is classic New England countryside. You won't find neon lights, flashy hotels, or amusement parks. This is the place to come for lazy summer drives (be sure to drive Rte. 10 from Keene to West Swanzey, where you'll see six covered bridges along the way), hikes in the woods, swimming in the rivers, casting in lakes, and sleigh rides in the snow.

● Friendly Farm
Rte. 101, Dublin (a half-mile west of Dublin Lake), (603) 563-8444, www.friendlyfarm.com. May–Labor Day, daily, 10–5 (weather permitting); Labor Day–mid-Oct., weekends, 10–5. Adults, $5; 1–12, $4.25. **Ages 1–10.**

Young children will enjoy a visit to this five-acre farm where they can pet and feed their favorite animals. At the hen house, you may see eggs hatching, and you can hold and cuddle baby chicks. Brilliantly plumed peacocks strut their stuff alongside a pen housing baby bunnies. Take a look at the observation beehive, too. You can bring a packed lunch to enjoy in the picnic area.

● Greenville Wildlife Park

18 Blanch Rd., Greenville, (603) 878-2255, www.greenvillewildlifepark.com. Apr.–July 4th, Wed.–Sun., 10–5; July 4th–Labor Day, daily, 10–5; Labor Day–Oct., Wed.–Sun., 10–5. 7 yrs. and older, $5; 3–6, $4; 2 and under, free. **All ages.**

Dubbed New Hampshire's only wildlife park, this natural habitat zoo is full of wild beasts your children will love, including bears, tigers, leopards, lions, wolves, hyenas, wild boars, prairie dogs, and more. Kids can feed and pet sheep and goats and visit baby animals in the maternity ward. There are lots of exhibits on wildlife and endangered species, live demonstrations, and special activities and programs throughout the summer season.

● Mount Monadnock State Park

Rte. 124, Jaffrey, (603) 532-8623. **Ages 5 and up.**

Getting to the top of Mount Monadnock is a popular pursuit. First scaled by settlers in 1725, Grand Monadnock is the single most climbed mountain in North America! If you have the energy (sure you have!) for the two-mile trek up to the 3,165-foot summit, you'll be rewarded with lovely views of Boston to the east and Mount Washington to the north. It will take about three hours to complete the round-trip hike (plus time for viewing and picnicking). If that sounds too ambitious for your group, there are more than 30 miles of other trails to choose from in the park. You'll also want to stop in the Ecocenter, where you'll find exhibits and programs on nature and ecology, as well as information on the various hikes.

● Ashuelot River Park

West St., Keene. **All ages.**

For a nice stroll along the river, you can't beat this pleasant town park. You can meander the trails, get in a good workout (look for the fitness markers along the way), sit in the gazebo, have a picnic, or simply admire the pretty plantings maintained by the Keene Garden Club.

● Sleigh Rides

Take a winter sleigh ride through snow-covered country lanes, rolling fields, and pine-scented forests. At **Silver Ranch,** Rte. 124E in Jaffrey, (603) 532-8870, you can ride in a covered carriage, take a sleigh ride, or hop aboard a wagon for a fun-filled hayride. At **Stonewall Farm,** 243 Chesterfield Rd., in Keene, (603) 357-7278, you'll be pulled by Belgian draft horses through the 124-acre working farm.

● Greenfield State Park

Rte. 136, Greenfield, (603) 547-3497, www.nhparks.state.nh.us.com.
All ages.

This is a nice family park of more than 350 acres along Otter Lake. The sandy beach is great for swimming, and children enjoy the small playground. If you'd like to do some rowing or fishing, you can rent small boats. The picnic area includes tables, grills, and a refreshment stand. There are also hiking trails in the park. Pack your trout-fishing gear and head for Hogback or Mud Ponds; locals say the fishing is good.

● Cross-Country Skiing

Many of the trails in the **Greenfield State Park** (see entry above) and at **Pisgah State Park** (off Rte. 63 in Chesterfield or Rte. 119 in Hinsdale) are good for cross-country skiing. There are also a number of ski touring areas, including **Temple Mountain** ski area in Peterborough, (603) 924-6949; **Tory Pines Resort** in Francestown, (603) 588-2000; **Inn at East Hill Farm** in Troy, (603) 242-6495; **Windblown Ski Touring** in New Ipswich, (800) 262-6660 or (603) 878-2869; and **Woodbound Inn** in Jaffrey, (603) 532-8341.

 RESTAURANTS

● Peterborough Diner

10 Depot St., Peterborough, (603) 924-6202.

This favorite diner, always ranked as one of the top diners in New England, has been feeding locals and visitors for more than five decades. If you like comfort food and classic diner digs, you'll enjoy your meal here. Expect friendly, fast service and typical diner fare, like club sandwiches, hot turkey platters, spaghetti and meatballs, macaroni and cheese, meat loaf, and more. Breakfast is served all day.

● Nonie's Food Shop

28 Grove St., Peterborough, (603) 924-3451. Mon.–Sat., 4 A.M.–2 P.M.

This is where the townies gather for a hearty breakfast or lunch, and all the local gossip. No one needs a menu—it's bacon and eggs, pancakes, and french toast; sandwiches and burgers for lunch. The blackboard announces daily specials, food like macaroni and cheese, or a long dog and slaw. Good prices, casual setting.

● Acqua Bistro

9 School St., Peterborough, (603) 924-9905. Wed.–Sun., 5 P.M.–11 P.M.

There's no need to give up fine food just because you're traveling en famille. Head to this trendy bistro-style restaurant that is fast becoming the most popular place to dine in Peterborough. The kitchen serves up simply prepared Mediterranean cuisine and an array of creative, wood-fired pizzas. Casual, affordable, and tasty.

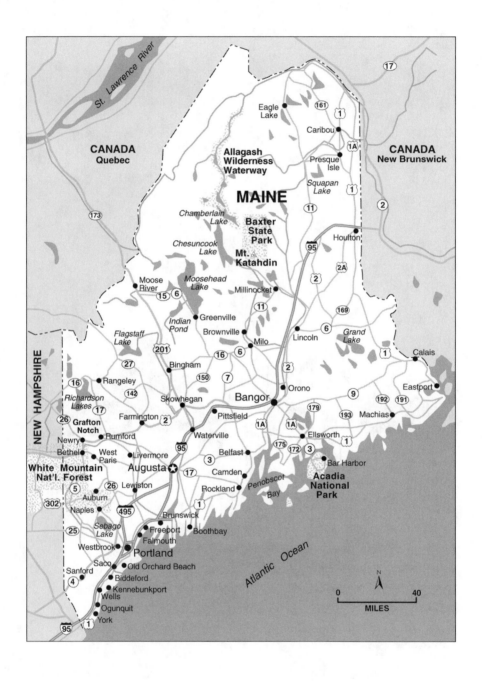

Maine

◼ Southern Coast

If the word Maine conjures up visions of rocky shores, picturesque villages, and freshly caught lobsters, you won't be disappointed when you visit. Maine's southern coast is a favorite with vacationing families for those reasons and more. First, it's not difficult to get here. Many visitors to Boston are surprised to learn that Maine is only 55 miles away. Then there are the sandy beaches. That's right—sandy. Although there are 3,500 miles of shoreline in Maine, fewer than 100 miles are sandy beach. Southern Maine has a lot of them—long, silvery strands that stretch for miles. When it comes to swimming, some adults find the ice-cold North Atlantic waters a tad too brisk to be pleasurable. If you prefer being on the water to being in it, you'll find plenty of options, including a quintessentially Maine lobstering cruise on which you'll help pull up the traps.

Most families try to visit a museum or two while they're here, and rainy weather usually means a pilgrimage to family amusement centers and arcades along Route 1. A better remedy for less-than-sunny weather? Dress for it, then head outdoors so you won't miss the dramatic, foggy beauty that is Maine at its best.

● York's Wild Kingdom

Rte. 1, York Beach, (207) 363-4911, www.yorkzoo.com. Zoo: Memorial Day–Labor Day, daily, 10–5; adults, $12.50; 4–10, $8.25; 3 and under, $1. Amusement park: Memorial Day–late June, weekends only, noon–6; late June–Labor Day, daily, noon–6. Combination tickets (zoo and amusement park): adults, $15.25; 4–10, $11.75; 3 and under, $3.50. **All ages.**

This zoo/amusement park combination is a bit bedraggled, but your children will hardly notice. Kids have a terrific time gazing at the lions, tigers, monkeys, llamas, the zebra, elephant, and more. Children can feed goats and deer in the petting area. On the amusement side, there are 25 rides, including a Ferris wheel, a merry-go-round, bumper cars, the Octopus, and the Jaguar—the park's most popular ride.

● Old York Historical Tour

Lindsey Rd., off Rte. 1A, York, (207) 363-4974, www.oldyork.org. Early June–mid-Oct., Mon.–Sat., 10–5. Admission for all buildings: adults, $7; 6–16, $3. **Ages 5 and up.**

The Old York Historical Society offers guided tours of seven historic buildings, dating back to the days when York was a colonial village and seaport. You'll start at Jefferd's Tavern (1750), where you'll find period furnishings and a tap room. You're likely to see a demonstration of hearth cooking, basket weaving, or candle making during your visit.

Children enjoy touring the Old Gaol Museum, built in 1719 as the King's Prison for the Province of Maine and used as a prison until 1860. You can wander through the dungeons and cells that once housed criminals and debtors, and see the "gaoler's" living quarters. An exhibit room features the Museum of Colonial Relics, a turn-of-the-century display with old dolls, toys, and unusual objects. Other sites on the tour include the Elizabeth Perkins House; the Emerson-Wilcox House; the George A. Marshall Store, a 19th-century general store; the John Hancock Warehouse; and the Old Schoolhouse, a one-room school built in 1745.

● Wiggly Bridge Footpath
Rte. 103, York Harbor. **All ages.**

For a lovely view of the York River that few tourists see, stroll the footpath that starts at Wiggly Bridge. Walk over the bridge, passing over an inlet to the York River, and follow the path along the river to Stedman Wood.

● Lobstering Cruise
Barnacle Bill's Dock, Perkins Cove, Ogunquit, (207) 646-5227. July–Labor Day, daily except Sun., 9–3. Call ahead for limited schedules in May–June and Sept.–Oct. Adults, $9; 4–11, $7. **All ages.**

If you've ever wondered what it's like to trap lobsters for a living, this is your chance to find out. Take a 50-minute trip with Finestkind Cruises and learn how to bait lobster traps, read the markings on lobster buoys, and determine whether a lobster is a "chicken." Children are warmly welcomed. **Second Chance** in Kennebunk, (800) 767-2628, also offers lobstering cruises.

● Sailing and Whale-Watching Cruises

The best way to see the Maine coastline is to get out on the water. There are a number of cruises offered from southern coastal towns and ports. You're likely to spy humpback and finback whales, dolphins, seals, and porpoises on the half-day whale-watching cruises aboard **First Chance** cruises in Kennebunk, (800) 767-2628. Or check into the scenic and wildlife-watching cruises offered by **Cape Arundel Cruises,** Kennebunkport, (877) 933-0707 or (207) 967-5595, and **Saco Bay Sailing,** in Saco, (207) 283-1624.

● Marginal Way
Shore Rd., Ogunquit. **All ages.**

This 1.25-mile-long shoreline footpath is not to be missed. You'll see spectacular ocean views, tidal pools, wildflowers, rock formations, and, at high tide, waves crashing against the rocky shore. The benches that have been placed along the way are perfect when little feet need a rest. The footpath begins on Shore Road, near the center of Ogunquit, and continues to Perkins Cove.

● Bald Head Cliff

Shore Rd., Ogunquit. **All ages.**

Be sure to stop and take a look at this fascinating rock formation. Just south of Ogunquit, on Shore Road, you'll see the signs pointing out Bald Head Cliff. The cliff rises more than 100 feet from the edge of the Atlantic. Surrounded by stretches of sandy beach and rocky outcrops, the cliff is a striking spectacle.

● Sightseeing Tours

Lighthouses, ghost stories, shipwrecks . . . you'll hear lots of ghastly and goodly tales of land and sea on a number of special tours. Candlelit walking tours through historic York Village are given by a hooded tour guide, where you'll hear the folklore of the 18th and 19th centuries as you stroll the historic streets. Call **Ghostly Tours,** Rte. 1A, York, (207) 363-0000. Take the **Tour of the Old Gaol,** (207) 363-4974, and hear fun-filled tales of prisoners, escapes, and legends. The tour is offered by the York Historical Society on Friday evenings throughout the summer.

● Wells Auto Museum

Rte. 1, Wells, (207) 646-9064. Mid-June–Sept., daily, 10–5; open weekends only in May–mid-June and Labor Day–mid-Oct., 10–5. Adults, $3.50; 6–12, $2. **All ages.**

More than 70 antique cars are on display here, some dating from the turn of the century, including gas, steam, and electric models. (Look for the 1963 Studebaker and the 1907 Stanley Steamer.) Kids will love taking a ride in a Model-T Ford. Arcade games and nickelodeons add to the fun.

● Wells Reserve at Laudholm Farm

342 Laudholm Farm Rd., off Rte. 1, 1.5 miles north of Wells Corner, Wells, (207) 646-1555, www.wellsreserve.org. Trail hours: May 15–Sept. 15, daily, 8–8; Sept. 16–May 14, daily, 8–5. Visitors Center hours: Jan. 16–Apr. 30, Mon.–Fri., 10–4; May 1–Oct. 31, Mon.–Sat., 10–4; Sun., noon–4; Nov. 1–Dec. 15, Mon.–Fri., 10–4; Dec. 16–Jan.-15, closed. **All ages.**

Budding bird-watchers can get their life list started. The sanctuary is also a good place to commune with nature while enjoying a picnic. This 1,600-acre site—mostly marshland—includes the Rachel Carson Wildlife Refuge and Laudholm Farm. The sanctuary includes fields, woodlands, tidal rivers, salt marshes, dunes, and beaches, and offers a protected environment for wildlife. Seven miles of marked nature trails lead through the woods and along the marsh. There are exhibits, video, and a gift shop in the farmhouse. Planned activities and programs are scheduled throughout the year.

● Cape Neddick Light

Off Rte. 1A. **All ages.**

Perhaps one of the most photographed lighthouses on the East Coast, the Nubble Light (as the locals call it) personifies the style of lighthouse for which Maine has become famous. Its white cast-iron tower, built in 1879, stands "atop the nubble," just off the shore, striking a beautiful pose against the rocky shoreline and blue waters of the Atlantic. Take Rte. 1A to Long Sands Beach; from the north end of the beach, a local road leads east to the tip of Cape Neddick and the lighthouse. The annual holiday lighting of Cape Neddick in December is a popular event, drawing more than a thousand onlookers.

● Old Orchard Beach

Rte. 1, Old Orchard Beach, www.oldorchardbeachmaine.com. **All ages.**

Kids love the lively, carnival-like atmosphere of this seaside resort. At more than seven miles long, it's one of the longest stretches of beach on the Atlantic Ocean, lined with boardwalks full of fast food and fun. In fact, it's been called the Coney Island of Maine. The Atlantic waters here are shallow and warm, and the surrounding amusements are a hit with youngsters.

● Palace Playland

1 Old Orchard St., Old Orchard Beach, (207) 934-2001, www.palaceplayland.com. Late June–Labor Day, Mon.–Fri., noon–10; Sat.–Sun., 11–10. Memorial Day–late June, weekends. Admission to the park is free; charge for rides. Unlimited ride pass, $16.50; kiddie ride pass, $11. **All ages.**

All a little heart desires for thrills are here at this beachfront amusement park: 26 rides—14 major ones and 12 for the kiddies—and arcade games aplenty, an antique carousel, a water slide, junk food, and more. Bet you can't pass by without going in. Look for fireworks on Thursday nights beginning in late June.

● Seashore Trolley Museum

Log Cabin Rd., off Rte. 1, Kennebunkport, (207) 967-2800, www.trolleymuseum.org. Memorial Day–mid-Oct., daily, 10–5; May 1–Memorial Day and mid-Oct.–late Oct., weekends, 10–5. Adults, $7.50; 6–16, $5; 5 and under, free. **Ages 3 and up.**

More than 200 antique trolley cars are housed here—the world's largest collection. You'll see a slide show and tour the cars on exhibit, but the real fun here is an old-fashioned trolley ride. You can hop aboard the authentically restored trolley cars from all over the world. All aboard!

● Ocean Drive

A ride along Ocean Drive to Cape Porpoise and Goose Rocks Beach is a pleasant way to view Kennebunkport's coastline. Along the way, you'll see two unmarred natural wonders, too—Spouting Rock, a spectacular ocean fountain, and Blowing Cave, a rock formation where the waves roar in dramatically. Look closely so you don't miss them. When you reach Cape Porpoise, park the car and stroll around this quaint fishing village.

● Scarborough Marsh Nature Center

Rte. 9, Scarborough, (207) 883-5100 from June–Sept. or (207) 781-2330, Oct.–May, www.maineaudubon.org. Trails open year-round, dawn–dusk. Nature Center: May–June, Sat., 9:30–5:30; June–Labor Day, daily, 9:30–5:30. **All ages.**

Bring your bug spray and old sneakers—and a pair of binoculars. This 3,100-acre natural area, the largest salt marsh in the state, contains a number of salt-marsh nature trails perfect for bird-watching and canoe routes through the inlets. The center offers guided nature walks, hands-on exhibits, and canoe tours. Canoe rental is available at the park. The park puts on lots of special naturalist programs for children throughout the summer.

● Rachel Carson Wildlife Refuge

321 Port Rd., Wells, (207) 646-9226. Open year-round; trails, daily, dawn–dusk; headquarters, Mon.–Fri., 8–4:30; limited weekend hours in the summer. **All ages.**

This 77,000-acre refuge is dedicated to Rachel Carson, renowned marine biologist and environmentalist. You'll find a delightful one-mile trail meandering through pine forest, with fabulous views of sweeping salt marshes, mudflats, and open ocean. Dusk and dawn are the best times for wildlife watching; look for herons in the marshes and osprey in the open waters.

● Mount Agamenticus

Mountain Rd., York, (207) 361-2840. Open year-round, dawn–dusk. Free. **All ages.**

This wildlands jewel in southern Maine is a great place to spend the day. There are a variety of trails to roam, through hardwood forest, wetlands, and fields, and longer, more challenging treks up the foothills. The undeveloped area is home to deer, turtles, snowshoe hare, fisher, black bear, wild turkey, and the great horned owl. The trails are open for horseback riding (there's a stable at the park), mountain biking, skiing and snowshoeing, and hiking. Our favorite time to visit is in the fall to watch for migrating hawks, peregrine falcons, osprey, and bald eagles.

● Smiling Hill Farm

Rte. 22, Westbrook, (207) 775-4818 or (800) 743-7463,
www.smilinghill.com. Farm open May–late Sept., daily, 10–5. Winter trails
open for skiing throughout winter, weather permitting. Adults, $6; 1–15,
$4.50. **Ages 1–14.**

You might as well head directly to the ice cream barn upon arrival and grab yourself a fresh, farm-made cup of ice cream. Now, everyone can relax and visit the rest of this 500-acre working dairy farm. Meet the friendly barn animals in the petting area. More than 200 animals can be seen and touched at the farm, including some exotic farm animals from around the world. Plan to participate in a number of ongoing activities, like pony rides, horse-drawn hayrides, milk-a-cow, "Llead a Llama," or "Llunch with a Llama." During the winter, there's cross-country skiing and sleigh rides.

● Aquaboggin Water Park

Rte. 1, Saco, (207) 282-3112, www.funtownsplashtownusa.com. Late June–
Labor Day, daily, 10–6. Over 4 ft. tall, $16; under 4 ft. tall, $13. **Ages 5**
and up.

This water park is part of the Funtown/Splashtown complex and combination tickets to both amusements are available. But if it's a hot summer day and you're only looking for cool water fun, check this place out. If your children love water slides (and what kid doesn't?), this place is sure to please. Attractions include a wave pool, bumper boats, a swimming pool, and a go-cart race track. Gentler souls can tool around the pond on paddleboats.

● Funtown/Splashtown U.S.A.

Rte. 1, Saco, (207) 284-5139 or (800) 878-2900,
www.funtownsplashtownusa.com. May–mid-Sept., daily, 10–10 (Funtown)
and 10–6 (Splashtown). Call for limited hours in May and June. Funtown:
over 4 ft. tall, $23; under 4 ft. tall, $15.50. **Ages 3 and up.**

Family fun is the name of the game here at Maine's largest theme amusement park. The Thunderfalls Log Flume is most popular and is very tall and very wet. There's also a high-speed roller coaster, tilt-a-whirl, bumper cars, and kiddie rides galore. And what better to go with those tummy-twisting roller coasters than Mexican food, taffy, and cotton candy? Mellower folk will enjoy antique car rides and minigolf.

● Beaches

Maine's southern coast is dotted with several public beaches. Most are well marked; look for signs leading to beaches on the side roads off Route 1. Arrive early to snare a parking space. The best beaches for families with small children—offering gentler surf—are **Ferry State Park Beach** in Saco,

(207) 781-2330; **Crescent State Park Beach** in Cape Elizabeth, (207) 767-3625; and **Long Sands Beach** in York Harbor. The surf can be lively at **Ogunquit** beaches, but toddlers can wade safely at a protected area near the mouth of the Ogunquit River.

● Harris Farm Cross Country Ski Center

280 Buzzell Rd., Dayton, (207) 499-2678, www.harrisfarm.com. Winters, weather permitting. Trail fees: adults, $12/weekends, $8/midweek; 7–18, $10/weekends, $7/midweek. **All ages.**

You'll find more than 40 kilometers of trails at this delightful farm, from groomed cruisers to more challenging rolling terrain. You'll cross open fields and sheltered forests, as you explore this 500-acre working dairy and tree farm. If you have young ones in tow, consider renting a sled. There's also snowshoeing, sledding, and ice skating on the property. A nice way to spend a winter's day.

 RESTAURANTS

● Mabel's Lobster Claw

Ocean Ave., Kennebunkport, (207) 967-2562. Daily, 11:30–9:30.

Known locally as Mabel's, this restaurant was featured in *Time* magazine for serving the best lobster rolls in the country. Adults can enjoy a glass of wine with their fresh seafood dinner, which might be the stuffed sole (a house specialty) or lobster prepared in one of several ways. Children can choose from the many sandwiches and fish items on the menu. Be sure to try the onion rings: "Fresh, not frozen." After dinner, the family can stroll next door to Mabel's ice cream shop for dessert.

● Foster's Downeast Clambake

Rte. 1A, York Harbor, (207) 363-2213. Memorial Day–Labor Day, daily, noon–8. Reservations required.

This is the place in southern Maine to enjoy an old-fashioned clambake. It's just what you'd expect: lobster, steamed clams, corn on the cob, slaw, and melted butter. Steak and chicken are offered if you're not a crustacean fan. Eat in the rough, then join in the old-fashioned sing-along. Little kids will love this; older children will, of course, be mortified, especially if you sing along.

● Barnacle Billy's

Perkins Cove, Ogunquit, (207) 646-5575, www.barnbilly.com. Memorial Day–mid-October, daily, 11:30–11.

Even former president George Bush has dined here, but that doesn't mean this place is too fancy for the commoners. The specialty at this casual, harborside restaurant is what you'd expect: fresh seafood. Steamed clams and lobsters are popular items, and so are the lobster rolls and stews and the creamy clam chowder. There's a children's menu, too. On warm summer nights, grab a table on the outdoor deck for pretty views of the harbor. Anytime, expect to wait in line for a table.

■ Portland

Maine's largest city is an intriguing blend of old and new. Wander around the waterfront and you'll see fish-processing plants and warehouses just around the corner from specialty shops and fancy restaurants. Many stores and eateries are housed in renovated old warehouses, giving a quaint appeal to even the newest. This booming little city is rapidly becoming a cultural presence in New England, with museums, concerts, and festivals aplenty. After visiting Portland, you'll see why it keeps cropping up on those lists of "most livable" cities. The same factors make it a great place to visit.

● Children's Museum of Maine

142 Free St., (207) 828-1234, www.childrensmuseumofme.org. Memorial Day–Labor Day, Mon.–Sat., 10–5; Sun., noon–5; Labor Day–Memorial Day, Tues.–Sat., 10–5; Sun., noon–5. Admission, $5; under 1, free.
Ages 1–10.

"Please touch" is the operative slogan here. This terrific museum has so many things to do that your children will have the happy dilemma of deciding where to head first. Young ones will want to head to the Our Town exhibit where they can work an ATM machine, hop on a fire truck, shop in the grocery store, and visit an animal farm. Older children will like the Star Lab and Space Shuttle, TV studio, and hands-on art and science projects. There's the perennial favorite "Bubbles" exhibit and the human skeleton, where kids can learn how "dem bones" really work. Don't miss the Camera Obscura, one of three of its kind in the United States.

● Southworth Planetarium

96 Falmouth St., Science Bldg., University of Southern Maine, (207) 780-4249, www.usm.maine.edu/~planet.com. Astronomy shows: Fri. and Sat., 7 P.M.; adults, $4.50; 12 and under, $3.50. Laser light concerts: Fri. and Sat., 8:30; adults, $5; 12 and under, $4. Matinees are sometimes held on Sat. and Sun. at 3 P.M. **Ages 3 and up.**

Astronomy goes 20th-century tech at this planetarium. The sky dome theater is the perfect setting for high-tech light shows with full-color motion and sound effects. Constellations and other objects currently visible in the sky are shown at the end of each show. There are also general astronomy shows— a good introduction to this dazzling science—and a special program for young children on Saturday (and sometimes Sunday) afternoons. Call ahead for information and reservations.

● Children's Theater of Maine

25A Forest Ave., Portland, (207) 874-0371. Rates and schedule vary.
Ages 3 and up.

This is the oldest children's theater in the country and count on it to present top-notch performances and thought-provoking presentations. Classic and child-pleasing shows are the mainstay, including longtime favorites like *The Velveteen Rabbit* and *The Secret Garden*. Older children and teens will appreciate the more updated—and often controversial subjects—tackled throughout the year.

● Peak's Island

Don't miss the popular day excursion to this small island off the coast from Portland. A 15-minute ferryboat ride will take you to the 720-acre island. When you hop off the ferry, head to the rental shops for bikes—this is the best way to get around the island. The small community boasts only three restaurants, a gift shop, a market, and a library. But you'll find a nice sandy beach near the ferry landing and lots of scenic vistas and fresh salt air. Take a quick look in the Civil War Museum. It's also possible to see where Longfellow's "Wreck of the Hesperus" was inspired by the 1869 wreck of the *Helen Eliza* on the rocks off the island's south shore. Peak's is the closest major island to Portland, and it can get crowded in the summer.

● Two Lights State Park

Off Rte. 77, Cape Elizabeth, (207) 799-5871. May–Oct., dawn–dusk. 12 and older, $2. **All ages.**

It's too cool for swimming, but you want to stay outdoors? Head to this state park to stroll the walkway, which offers great ocean views and picnic sites along the way. It's located south of the city on the Cape Elizabeth shore.

● Crescent Beach State Park

Rte. 77, (207) 767-3625. May–Oct., dawn–dusk. 12 and older, $2.50.
All ages.

A popular beach with Portland locals, Crescent has a 4,000-foot sandy area. You'll find it south of Portland on the Cape Elizabeth shore.

● Portland Head Light and Museum

1000 Shore Rd., off Rte. 77, Cape Elizabeth, (207) 799-2661. **All ages.**

Just off Cape Elizabeth's Shore Road you'll find the Portland Head Light, Maine's oldest lighthouse (built in 1791) and one of the most frequently photographed. You'll enjoy the scenic coastal setting. There's a small maritime museum here, also.

● Boat Cruises

The Atlantic Ocean beckons. Why not take a harbor tour, or cruise to an island for a clambake? Or if you want a real getaway, take the ferry to Nova Scotia. A number of cruise companies offer a variety of options; you'll find many along Commercial Street in the Old Port section of Portland. Some possibilities: **Casco Bay Lines,** (207) 774-7871, www.cascobaylines.com; **Bay View Cruises,** (207) 761-0496, www.bayviewcruiseme.com; **Atlantic Yacht Charters,** (207) 775-5082, www.atlanticyachtcharters.com; and **Prince of Fundy Cruises, Ltd.,** (207) 775-5616, www.princeoffundy.com.

● Portland Sports

Major-league sports tickets are high-price items, often out of reach for the average family of four. That doesn't mean you have to give up the action. In Portland, families can catch a **Sea Dog** game at Hadlock Field for about $6, (207) 874-9300. The **Sea Dogs** are the AA Farm team for the **Florida Marlins.** Hockey fans can watch the **Portland Pirates,** (207) 838-4665, an AHL affiliate of the NHL **Washington Capitals,** at the Cumberland County Civic Center.

RESTAURANTS

● The Great Lost Bear

540 Forest Ave., (207) 772-0300. Mon.–Sat., 11:30–11:30; Sun., noon–11:30.

The toughest part about dining at TGLB is selecting a choice off the extensive menu. The offerings are seemingly endless: more than 25 appetizers, chili, soups, salads, and four pages of entrees, sandwiches, and more. There's something here to please even the picky eaters in your brood. Relaxed, casual atmosphere and hearty meals make this a favorite among locals and visitors.

● Cap'n Newick's Lobster House

740 Broadway, (207) 799-3090. Tues.–Thurs., 11:30–8; Fri.–Sun., 11:30–9.

This popular family restaurant offers delicious seafood at reasonable prices. The atmosphere is casual, so you don't have to worry if baby uses the drawn butter as a finger bowl or if junior discovers several unusual things to do with a used lobster leg.

● Ricetta's Pizzeria

29 Western Ave., South Portland, (207) 775-7400. Sun.–Thurs., 11:30–10; Fri.–Sat., 11:30–11.

Locals love the brick oven specialty pizzas served up here, voting it Maine's best in local magazines and surveys. Deciding what kind of pizza to order will be your biggest problem; there are lots of creative, delicious combinations, like "Melanzano Diavolo—the devil's eggplant, hot cherry peppers, pepperoni, and cheeses." Or the "Scampi Pie" with shrimp, butter, scallions, basil, and cheeses. Or create your own. There are also antipasti platters, salads, calzones, and a full menu of pasta entrees.

● Gilbert's Chowder House

92 Commercial St., (207) 871-5636. Sun.–Thurs., 11–8; Fri.–Sat., 11–9.

If you're hankering for fresh seafood in casual digs, head to this longtime favorite in the Old Port district. Locals love this place for its fast service and simple food. Award-winning chowders and just-caught seafood are its claim to fame.

■ Midcoast

You could spend a lifetime exploring the midcoastal region of Maine and still you'd leave some hidden gem undiscovered. This area, running from Portland to Belfast, covers some of the prettiest spots in the country, characterized by quaint New England seaside villages, rocky coastlines juxtaposed against sandy beaches, idyllic peninsulas jutting out into the Atlantic, tidal rivers, classic Maine lighthouses, and more. And in each village you'll visit along the way, recreation and adventure abound.

You'll find outlet shopping in busy Freeport, home to the famous outdoor-goods company, L.L. Bean, and also island hopping. Busy harbors have lots of choices for families who wish to try out their sea legs; just walk to any harbor and check out the offerings. You'll find charming, popular harbor villages, like Camden, Boothbay, and Rockport, with galleries, boutiques, and exquisite seaside dining, and others like Brunswick and Bath that are steeped in nautical history. There are numerous museums to explore, trails to hike, and trains to board, and lots of places to learn about the sea. There's even a scorching hot desert.

The downside of all this is the crowds. On a summer weekend, you'd better have a reservation for a bed and a meal waiting when you roll into town.

● **Gilsland Farm Environmental Center and Sanctuary**

20 Gilsland Farm Rd., (off Rte. 1, Falmouth, (207) 781-2330, www.maineaudubon.org. Trails: year-round, daily, dawn–dusk. Environmental Center: Mon.–Sat., 9–5; Sat., 9–5; Sun., 1–5. Admission, $1. **All ages.**

This is the home of the Maine Audubon Society and a great place to visit if you're in the area. You'll learn about solar energy through a variety of displays and, of course, about native birds. Pack a picnic; there are lots of nature trails and places to stop along the way. The Environmental Center offers guided walks and programs year-round.

● **Desert of Maine**

95 Desert Rd., off Rte. 1 and I-95, Freeport, (207) 865-6962, www.desertofmaine.com. Early May–mid-Oct., daily, 9–dusk. Adults, $7; 13–16, $5; 6–12, $4. **All ages.**

The desert of Maine? Yep. Give your kids a real lesson in what happens when you don't respect Mother Earth. This spot was once the Tuttle Farm, located on a glacial sand deposit. After years of tree cutting and planting, the topsoil eroded, exposing the sand beneath. Today this sand, covering more than 50 acres, forms dunes that tower over the trees and buildings. But at Desert of Maine you'll also see rebirth. Surrounding the desert are lush forests. After a hot walk through the desert (this area sees temperatures that exceed 100 degrees), cool off with a walk on the forest trails, which are abundant with wildflowers. In fall, visitors can see 30 to 50 different kinds of mushrooms along the nature trail. Narrated tram tours give a good overview of the area. There's also a farm and sand museum, and a variety of sand design artists are at work.

● **Maine Bear Factory**

294 Rte. 1, Freeport, (207) 865-0600, www.mainebear.com. Mon.–Sat., 10–5:30; Sun., noon–5. Free factory tours; bears extra. **Ages 1–12.**

The Maine Bear Factory is one of the last makers of stuffed animals in the United States. The kids will love a peek at how these cuddly, furry friends are "born." In the factory, you can pick your own unstuffed bear. The staff will then help you stuff him or her. Next comes sewing and grooming, and your new friend is ready to go home with you. At the store, you can pick out a special outfit from a large selection of clothes and accessories.

● **Kayaking**

There is no better way to explore the coast of Maine than by sea kayak. Never done it? No problem. The folks at **Maine Sport Outdoor School** in Rockport, (800) 722-0826, will show you how. Sign up for a four-hour, full-day, or multiday kayak tour that will take you on Muscongus Bay, paddling the coves and coastline. You're likely to see lots of shorebirds, marine animals, and great scenery. There are a number of special family tours offered, too. Other companies to check out include **Riverdance Outfitters,** (207) 763-3139, www.riverdanceoutfitters.com, and **Seaspray Kayaking,** (888) 349-7772, www.seapraykayaking.com, or visit www.maineguides.com for a complete listing of registered Maine guide services in the state.

● Day Sails and Windjammer Cruises

Penobscot Bay is famous for its stunning coastline and sailing waters. Short cruises out of most towns and harbors along the coast, on motor vessels and traditional sailboats, are offered. Or hop aboard a working lobster boat. Local ferries also run daily in the summer to many of the islands in the bay. Day sails are offered by **Freeport Sailing Adventures,** (207) 865-6399; **Captain Hays Coastal Boat Co.** from Orrs and Bailey Islands, (207) 833-7825; **Captain's Watch Sail Charters** in Harpswell, (207) 725-0979; and **Sea Escape Charters** in Harpswell, (207) 833-5531.

● Winslow Park

Staples Point Rd., South Freeport (207) 865-4198. Memorial Day–Sept., 8–9. Free. **All ages.**

When you're tired of outlet shopping in Freeport, head to this park for some cheap outdoor fun. Romp in the sand on the beach, rest at the picnic area overlooking the bay, or take a short walk on the nature trail that runs along the park perimeter.

● Reid State Park

Rte. 127, Georgetown, (207) 371-2303. Year-round, dawn–dusk. **All ages.**

This 770-acre park is a favorite with families. You'll find a 1.5-mile-long sandy beach on the Atlantic Ocean. Midcoast Maine waters are always chilly, even in the dog days of summer, but this park boasts a lovely, warm saltwater pond that's perfect for swimming. There's also changing rooms, snack bar, and picnic area with grills.

● Boothbay Railway Village

Rte. 27, Boothbay, (207) 633-4727, www.railwayvillage.org. Memorial Day–early June, weekends only; early June–Columbus Day, daily, 9:30–5. Adults, $7; 3–12, $3. **Ages 3 and up.**

This 10-acre turn-of-the-century village is sure to delight young visitors. The main attraction is a two-gauge railway with a working 1911 steam train that kids can ride. After purchasing a ticket at the railroad Station (relocated from Freeport), you'll board the Boothbay Central and chug your way on a 1.5-mile, 15-minute ride. At the other end, there are old train cars, antique autos, and trucks to explore. Eat in the diner, or bring your own food and eat at the village's picnic area.

● Marine Resources Aquarium

McKown Point, W. Boothbay Harbor, (207) 633-9559. Memorial Day–Sept., daily, 10–5. Adults, $3; 5–18, $2.50. **All ages.**

Your child's first encounter with a lobster will probably be rather unpleasant for both parties, the lobster having been trapped and boiled, and the child thinking, "I'm supposed to eat this thing?" A visit to this small but interesting aquarium will provide a more complete picture of native sea life. A wonderful 20-foot touch tank is filled with sea urchins, starfish, periwinkles, and other inhabitants of the Gulf of Maine. Even more thrilling is a large, live shark tank with dogfish—some as long as two feet—and unusual lobsters that brave children can reach in and pat. Toddlers will love pressing their noses against the "baby tank" filled with tiny, squirmy sea creatures. Be sure to pack a picnic; the Seaquarium has a pretty picnic area right on the water.

● Brunswick Fishway Viewing Area

CMD Dam, Maine St., off Rte. 201, Brunswick, (207) 725-6631. May and June, Sat. and Sun., 10–2; Wed., 7–9 P.M. Free. **All ages.**

This is a fun place to visit when the fish runs are in progress, usually in early spring. There's a fish ladder, a counting room, and a viewing area. You'll see salmon, alewives, and shad as they migrate up the Androscoggin River.

● Peary-MacMillan Arctic Museum

Hubbard Hall, Bowdoin College Campus, Brunswick, (207) 725-3416, www.bowdoin.edu/dept/arctic. Year-round, Tues.–Sat., 10–5; Sun., 2–5. Donations accepted. **Ages 5 and up.**

When the snow falls some things just come naturally to kids: snowball fights, snowman making, and building their own version of an igloo. Kids are naturally interested in igloos and Eskimos, and at this museum they can feed that curiosity and learn more about the Eskimo culture. Actually, the museum is a tribute to two Bowdoin College alumni, Admiral Robert E. Peary and Admiral Donald B. MacMillan, and also contains equipment from and information about their arctic explorations.

● Maine Maritime Museum

243 Washington St., Bath, (207) 443-1316, www.bathmaine.com. Year-round, daily, 9:30–5. Adults, $9; 6–16, $6; under 6, free. **All ages.**

Here the imagination and fascination of Maine's maritime past are captured in a very child-friendly manner. Kids can get their hands on the capstan and into Morse Code and the World Trade Game, all equipment meant to be touched and played with. The museum hosts a number of changing exhibits celebrating the seafaring past, with lots of hands-on components for children. There are boat models and paintings on display as well. Be sure to stop by and talk to the apprentices in the boat-building school. During the summer there are also tours of the historic shipyard, visits to vessels, demonstrations of seafaring techniques, and a lobstering exhibit. Visitors to the area are invited along with locals to enjoy the weekly lobster bakes and special waterfront activities such as concerts, fairs, and parades.

● Thomas Point Beach

Cooks Corner, off Rte. 24, Brunswick, (207) 725-6009, www.thomaspointbeach.com. Mid-May–Sept., daily, 9–sunset. Adults, $3.50; under 12, $2. **All ages.**

Ready to kick back and relax? Enough sightseeing for the day? Spend the afternoon at pretty 80-acre Thomas Point Beach (it's also a campground) on a sandy ocean inlet. There are picnic spots, a calm beach area, playground, and lots of room to stretch out. Take in a deep breath of that fresh, salty ocean air while the kids run, play, and splash in the surf.

● Popham Beach State Park

Rte. 209, Phippsburg, (207) 389-1335. May–Oct., daily, dawn–dusk. 12 and older, $2. **All ages.**

A favorite of visitors and locals alike, this pretty beach on the Phippsburg peninsula is the perfect spot for a sunny picnic and a refreshing dip in the ocean. The rocky coastline combines with a sandy beach area to make this a perfect place to spend a hot summer Maine day. Visit the granite fort that guarded the Kennebec River during the Civil War and World War II.

● Camden Hills State Park

Rte. 1, Camden, (207) 236-3109. May–Oct., daily, dawn–dusk. 12 and older, $2. **All ages.**

This park spreads across 5,000 acres at the foot of Mount Battie. Be sure to drive the road to Mount Battie's 900-foot summit. While not the tallest mountain in New England, from its summit you'll still get wonderful panoramic views of Penobscot Bay and the surrounding countryside. There are more than 30 miles of hiking trails to explore, too.

● Owl's Head Transportation Museum

Rte. 73, Owl's Head, (207) 594-4418, www.ohtm.org. Apr.–Oct., daily, 10–5; Nov.–Mar., daily, 10–4. Adults, $6; 5–12, $4; under 5, free. **All ages.**

Cars, trains, planes, boats . . . transportation vehicles make every kid's list of favorite things. Adults, too, will enjoy this collection of historic aircraft, automobiles, and engines—one of the world's top displays. Stop by the restoration workshop, where work on pre-1940s vehicles is in progress. Often you'll be able to hop aboard one of the antique autos for a ride. There are also energy exhibits, a small gallery, picnic areas, and nature trails.

● Fort Knox State Historical Site

Rte. 174, off Rte. 1, Hancock, (207) 469-7719. Nov.–Apr., 9–5; May–Oct., 9–sunset. 12 and older, $2. **All ages.**

Your kids can hide in the secret passageways, climb the underground stairways, shoot the giant cannons, and, along the way, learn about 19th-century armies, battles, and life. Fort Knox is a massive granite and brick fortification dating from 1844 (Maine's largest historic fort); it's now a state park. There's a guided tour each day at 1 P.M. Bring a picnic; there are tables and charcoal stoves. And bring a flashlight for exploring the underground passageways.

● Steve Powell Wildlife Management Area

Swan Island, (207) 547-5322 (reservations) or (207) 287-8000 (informa-tion), www.state.me.us.com. May–Labor Day, daily, 9–sunset by reservation only. **All ages.**

For a day in the wilderness and some exceptional animal watching, take the ferry from Richmond to Swan Island. This 1,755-acre area, run by the Maine Department of Inland Fisheries and Wildlife, offers an opportunity for successful wildlife viewing. Quiet, observant walkers are likely to see deer, eagles, and several types of native waterfowl. Bring binoculars and bug spray. There's camping on the island, too. Be sure to call ahead for reservations and ferry arrangements.

● Belfast Moosehead Lake Railroad

11 Water St., Belfast, (800) 392-5500, www.belfastrailroad.com. May–Oct. Call for up-to-date departure listings and rates. **Ages 5 and up.**

What a fun way to see the Maine countryside—chug-chugging along in a vintage 1924 Pullman Day Coach. You'll start at the water's edge and travel up the banks of the Passagassawakeag River. Pulling away from the river, you'll go farther inland, into the forests, across hills and fields. You'll be in the countryside once populated by Native American tribes and later farmed by the earliest settlers. Bring along some hands-on materials for young tots who may become antsy after the novelty of the train ride wears off and the thrill of scenic vistas wanes. The railroad features two excursions: one departing from Belfast, Maine, another from Unity, Maine. Or try their unique Rail and Sail excursion: a train ride through the countryside and a sail in beautiful Penobscot Bay.

 RESTAURANTS

● The Brown Bag
606 Main St., Rockland, (207) 596-6372. Mon.–Sat., 6:30–4; Sun., 7–2.

This is a bright, cheery little eatery with great tasting food. If you're around the area for breakfast, don't bother to go anywhere else. The small street facade belies the open, airy inside dining space with exposed brick, pine flooring, and country decor. You can feast on fresh Maine blueberry muffins, cinnamon swirl french toast, homemade sausages, three-cheese omelets, and smoked salmon, capers, and cream cheese bagels. The Brown Bag also serves great soups, salads, and sandwiches.

● Mama & Leenie's Cafe and Bakery
27 Elm St., Camden, (207) 236-6300. Summer, Mon.–Sat., 7 A.M.–8 P.M.; Sun., 8–4. Winter, Wed.–Mon., 7–2.

Bet you can't pass this place up. You'll smell the home-baked cooking— fresh breads, simmering soups, and pastries. How about fresh blintzes filled with cheese, fruit, and sour cream or a slice of spinach and bacon quiche? Lunch brings a list of daily blackboard specials that include hearty soups and chowders, salads, and sandwiches. During evening hours, the blackboard announces the nightly specials, like fresh seafood and cheese pasta, marinated chicken breast with veggies, chili, or an assortment of pizzas.

● Moody's Diner
Rte. 1, Waldoboro, (207) 832-7785. Daily, 24 hrs.

This landmark restaurant has been feeding locals and visitors alike since it opened its doors in 1927. You can't miss the flashing neon sign above the diner: Eat . . . Eat . . . Eat. And eat you will, on classic diner food (hot turkey sandwiches, meat loaf, honey-dipped chicken), followed by homemade pies, Jell-O, or pudding.

■ Downeast, including Acadia National Park

The Downeast region of Maine includes beautiful Acadia National Park and the prestigious resort community of Bar Harbor. Here you'll see striking stretches of coastline where ragged cliffs meet pounding surf. The combination of fresh salt air, fragrant pines, towering cliffs, and sparkling ocean is a sensory feast you're not likely to forget.

There's more to this area than spectacular scenery. Think of it as the ultimate place to play outside: You can hike, bike, camp, swim, paddle, cruise, or ski. Even the museums are of the hands-on variety. At the Natural History Museum, for example, you can help assemble a 20-foot whale skeleton. And the local zoo has the largest petting area in the state of Maine.

The village of Bar Harbor, formerly a vacation mecca for wealthy East Coast families, is full of shops, restaurants, and galleries. While many of its mansions were destroyed in the Great Fire of 1947, some still exist and are now in use as inns. It's a fun place to stroll, with its streets at their liveliest during the Art Show and Musical Festival in late June and the Seafood Festival in early July. Enjoy.

● Acadia National Park

Park headquarters located on Rte. 233, near Eagle Lake, (207) 288-5262, www.acadia.national-park.com.

It's 22 square miles of wildlife, woodland, mountains, lakes, and valleys surrounded by the Atlantic Ocean. You'll call it paradise. The park is part of Mount Desert Island, a chunk of primitive beauty that owes its unique contours to the action of Ice Age glaciers. In 1919, President Woodrow Wilson set aside much of this lovely island as a national park. Acadia is eminently seeable, with more than 57 miles of car-free paths for hiking, bicycling, horseback riding, and, in winter, cross-country skiing. By car, a trip along scenic Ocean Drive follows the island's entire eastern perimeter.

Begin your visit at the Visitors Center, Rte. 3, Hull's Cove. Open from May through October (although the park is open year-round), the Visitor's Center offers a free 15-minute film to introduce you to Acadia. Here you'll find information about Acadia's Naturalist Program, which has activities especially for children. The program offers several guided walks, ranging from easy to strenuous. You might want to join a "Night Prowl," for a glimpse of the nocturnal animals who share the park. Others might include guided nature walks and photography workshops, all free of charge. Or sign up for "Nature's Way for Children," a program offered two to three times weekly.

Riding a bike is a wonderful way to see the park, which has more than 50 miles of car-free paths to traverse. Bicycle rental shops are located in Bar Harbor.

While the ocean surrounds and beckons (especially on a hot summer's day), even the kids might find the waters here a bit too frigid for fun. Better to swim and play in Echo Lake, which has a nice sandy beach and warmer freshwater. Lifeguards are posted, too. Open mid-June through Labor Day, the lake is located along Rte. 102, Southwest Harbor.

There are lots of places to get on the water as well, from a variety of ocean-bound boat cruises to a pleasant paddle in a canoe. (Canoe rentals are available at the northern end of Long Pond, located within the park.)

● Park Loop Road

Consider starting your Acadia National Park visit with this scenic 27-mile drive through the park. The road begins at the Hull's Cove Visitors Center and will take at least three hours or more, allowing for stops along the way. There's plenty of spectacular scenery of the rocky and dramatic Maine coastline and island mountains. But kids won't have time to complain about the car ride; there are a number of places you'll want to visit along the route. The road allows access to pretty Sand Beach, a great place for toe dunking, though the waters may be too frigid for full-body swimming. Stop to see Thunder Hole, where the rising tide and rough seas send out thunderous sounds. The road also passes Otter Cliffs, Jordan Pond, and Cadillac Mountain.

● Boat Cruises

Park naturalists conduct hourly or half-day cruises aboard privately owned boats out of Bass Harbor, Northeast Harbor, and Bar Harbor. Naturalists will describe geological history and area wildlife. (Bring binoculars so you won't miss anything.) You'll see seabirds and—to the delight of children—you may spot seals and porpoises. A variety of other sightseeing cruises are also available, including seal watching, whale watching, and lobstering trips. Try **Downeast Windjammer Cruises,** (207) 288-4585; **Atlantis,** (800) WHALES-4; **Island Cruises,** (207) 244-5785; **Acadian Whale Watch Co.,** (800) 421-3307.

For a more active excursion, consider a coastal kayak or canoe tour. **Acadia Bike and Canoe Company,** (207) 288-9605; **Coastal Kayaking Tours,** (207) 288-9605; and **Acadia Kayak,** (800) 347-0940, offer guided tours, rentals, and island camping trips of varying lengths.

● Abbe Museum

Sieur de Monts Spring, (207) 288-3519. Mid-May–mid-Oct., daily. Spring and fall, 10–4; July and Aug., 9–5. Adults, $2; 6–15, $1. **All ages.**

This tiny museum, located within Acadia National Park at Sieur de Monts Spring, contains more than 50,000 decorative and practical items representing more than 10,000 years of Native American life in Maine. Artifacts include unusual jewelry (fashioned from animal bones), pottery, baskets, and tools made of stone and bone. A museum shop offers Maine Indian crafts, books, and tapes.

● Cadillac Mountain

Ocean Drive follows the eastern perimeter of Mount Desert Island. Follow it from Sieur de Monts Spring, stopping along the way at scenic lookouts including Thunder Hole, until you reach Seal Harbor. There, a park road will take you north to the summit of Cadillac Mountain (1,530 feet), the highest point on the eastern seaboard. From this 360-degree vantage point, you'll see the surrounding ocean, distant mountains, and offshore islands. It's breathtaking. For a special treat, set the alarm clock for predawn, pack a breakfast in a bag, and arrive at the top for sunrise. You may be the first in America to see the sun come up that day.

● Somes Sound

From Northeast Harbor, take Sargent Drive to the fjord at Somes Sound. The fjord was formed when Ice Age glaciers cut through existing mountains. Stunningly beautiful, Somes Sound is the only natural fjord on the East Coast.

● Mount Desert Oceanarium/Southwest Harbor

Clark Point Rd., off Rte. 102, Southwest Harbor, (207) 244-7330. May–Oct., Mon.–Sat., 9–5. Adults, $6; 4–12, $4.50. Combination tickets for the two Oceanariums and Lobster Hatchery (see below): adults, $11.95; 4–12, $8.75. **All ages.**

Why does the tide go out? Why is the sea salty? What do lobsters eat? If questions like these have come up during your trip to Maine, help is at hand. The Oceanarium's interactive displays offer a lively look at sea life, answering the questions kids might ask. And there's more. In the lobster room, a lobsterer explains how a lobster eats, reproduces, and gets caught. The See and Touch room has sea urchins, starfish, and sea cucumbers that children can handle. In the Living Room, live specimens of local marine life are displayed in tanks.

● Mount Desert Oceanarium, Lobster Hatchery/Bar Harbor

Rte. 3, Thomas Point, Bar Harbor, (207) 288-5005. Oceanarium: May–mid-Oct., Mon.–Sat., 9–5. Adults, $6; 4–12, $4.50. Lobster Hatchery: early June–mid-Oct., Mon.–Sat., 9–5. Adults, $3.95; 4–12, $2.75. Combination tickets for two Oceanariums and Lobster Hatchery: adults, $11.95; 4–12, $8.75. **All ages.**

There's no better place than this Downeast waterfront location to learn about lobsters. The Lobster Hatchery was opened in 1990 to enhance Maine's lobster landing. At this facility, lobsters are hatched from eggs and raised for their first few tender weeks, then released in the local waters. You'll see thousands of tiny crustaceans in all stages of growth. You'll even get a microscopic view of very tiny lobsters. Friendly staff people are on hand to explain the whole process.

The Oceanarium, located on pretty Thomas Bay, is an expansion of the Southwest Harbor Oceanarium. You can visit both—this facility offers exhibits not available in the Southwest Harbor Oceanarium. The kids will enjoy the harbor seal program, where they get a chance to see the seals during feeding times, and the Maine Lobster Museum, where you'll learn everything there is to know about lobsters and lobster fishing.

● George B. Dorr Museum of Natural History

College of the Atlantic, Rte. 3, Bar Harbor, (207) 288-5395, wwwcoamuseum.org. Mid-June–Labor Day, Mon.–Sat., 10–5; Labor Day–mid-June, Thurs.–Sat., 1–4; Sun., 10–4. Adults, $3.50; teens, $1.50; children, $1; under 3, free. **All ages.**

This small college museum is housed in the original headquarters of Acadia National Park. Exhibits are designed and produced by college students and portray native animals in natural environments. There's an indoor tide pool for a close view of tidal creatures and a small gift store on the premises.

● Acadia Zoological Park

Rte. 3, Trenton, (207) 667-3244. May–Christmas Eve (or until the first large snowfall), daily, 9:30–sunset. Adults, $6.50; 3–12, $5.50. **Ages 1–14.**

Heading north on Route 3, over the causeway from Mount Desert Island to the town of Trenton, you'll find this 100-acre nature preserve and petting farm. More than 150 native and exotic animals make their homes here, amid the woodlands, streams, and pastures. Children will delight in the petting area—the largest in Maine.

● Island Soaring Glider Rides

Hancock County–Bar Harbor Airport, Rte. 3, (207) 667-SOAR, www.airnav/airport/bhb/island_soaring.com. May–Oct., daily til sunset. Rates vary. **Ages 5 and up.**

You can't miss this place on busy Route 3 heading into Acadia National Park. You'll see the glider planes, you'll be tempted . . . go ahead, stop in. What a thrill to soar in these one- to two-passenger aircraft! Great for kids and adults alike.

● Craig Brook National Fish Hatchery

Hatchery Road, off Rte. 1, East Orland, (207) 469-2803. May–Sept., daily, 8–8. Free. **All ages.**

This is the oldest salmon hatchery in the country. You'll find exhibits at the Visitors Center, display pools, and an aquarium. It's also a nice little park, with a beach area, boat launching facilities, and nature trails. Stop by.

⑪ RESTAURANTS

● Jordan Pond House

Park Loop Rd., Acadia National Park, (207) 276-3316. Late May–Oct.,
11:30–8; July–Aug., until 9.

A trip to Acadia wouldn't be complete without a visit here. Enjoy huge
popovers and homemade ice cream on the lawn, with magnificent views all
around. Elegant dinners are served in the evenings with classical music
accompaniment.

● Beal's Lobster Pier

Clark Point Rd., Southwest Harbor, (207) 244-3202 or (800) 245-7178.
Year-round, daily, 9–sunset.

For more than 50 years, families have enjoyed seafood "in the rough"
here, on picnic tables along the pier. Fresh fish, lobsters, shrimp, clams, and
crab meat are available at reasonable prices. You'll soak up the atmosphere of
a busy fish pier, while feasting on the freshest fish around.

■ Bangor and Augusta

Just off the major interstate (I-95) in Maine, you'll find the two bustling cities
Augusta and Bangor, the state's commercial and cultural hubs. While most
vacationers closely hug the jagged coastline of Maine, much of the state's
business is done inland.

The mighty Kennebec River cuts through the center of capital city
Augusta. Here, you can get a close look at Maine's government in action. The
state capitol building dominates this lively city; its towering gold dome can
be seen from afar.

Traveling north, you'll discover Bangor, with its big-city-style shopping, restaurants, and lodging, and also Orono, where the University of
Maine makes its home. Visitors are welcome to tour the pretty 1,200-acre
campus and take advantage of its cultural and sports offerings.

Despite their modern-day conveniences, both cities retain historic
architecture and respect for their rural pasts. Venture just a short distance
from these hubs and you'll find forests, lakes, and streams abundant with
outdoor recreational opportunities.

● Maine Discovery Museum

74 Main St., Bangor, (207) 262-7200, www.mainediscoverymuseum.org.
Tues.–Sat., 9:30–5; Sun., 11–5. Admission, $5.50. **All ages.**

This recently opened museum, the largest children's museum north of
Boston, is getting raves from local families and visiting vacationers. Located

in downtown Bangor, the museum offers hands-on fun for little ones; it's a great place to romp, roam, and learn. You'll find three floors, chock-full of interactive exhibits, covering nature, geography, literature, music, science, anatomy, and more. Don't miss it, if you're in the area.

● Maine State Museum

Capitol Complex, Rte. 201, Augusta, (207) 287-2301. Year-round, Mon.– Fri., 9–5; Sat., 10–4; Sun., 1–4. Free. **Ages 5 and up.**

Located in the impressive Capitol Complex, this museum offers a thorough look at Maine, past and present. "Made in Maine," the museum's central exhibit, includes a water-powered woodworking mill, a textile factory, and more than 1,000 Maine-made products. The "12,000 Years in Maine" exhibit features more than 2,000 artifacts and specimens dating from the last Ice Age to the 19th century. Kids will enjoy peeking at "This Land Called Maine," including five nature scenes that show many of the plants and animals found in the state. Other exhibits reveal Maine's agriculture, fishing, granite quarrying, lumbering, and shipbuilding activities.

● State Capitol Tours

Capitol Complex, Rte. 201, Augusta, (207) 287-2301. Year-round, Mon.– Fri., 8–5. Free. **Ages 5 and up.**

The impressive Maine State Capitol Building can be seen rising above the mighty oak and elm trees that surround it from just about any point in Augusta. Constructed of native granite in 1829, the building's front facade, with its towering arcade, is a fine example of the work of noted American architect Charles Bulfinch. You'll enjoy a walk through the rotunda, where you'll see a large display of Maine battle flags. Also, for a firsthand look at government in action, visit the Legislative Chambers and the Office of the Governor.

● Fort Western Museum

City Center Plaza, Augusta, (207) 626-2385, www.oldfortwestern.org. First weekend in May–July 4th, daily 1–4; July 4th–Labor Day, Mon.– Fri., 10–4; Sat.–Sun., 1–4; Labor Day–Columbus Day, weekends, 1–4; Nov.–Apr., open first Sun. of every month, 1–3. Adults, $4.75; 6–16, $2.75. **All ages.**

What child doesn't like a fort? And there's no better way to learn about early American fortification and history than with a close-up look at the real thing. Fort Western, on the eastern bank of the Kennebunk River, was built in 1754 for protection from the Indians. The fort's original main house, once the barracks and the store, is still standing. You'll also see reproduction blockhouses and watchboxes. In the adjacent City Hall, visit the Museum

Services building with exhibits depicting military, settlement, trade, and family themes.

● Maynard Planetarium and Observatory

Wingate Hall, University of Maine Campus, off Rte. 2, Orono, (207) 581-1341, www.ume.maine.edu/~lookup.com. Public showings throughout the school year. Call for current shows and prices. **Ages 5 and up.**

The moon, the planets, the Milky Way, flashing comets, and falling stars . . . the nighttime sky has always held mystery and fascination for people of all ages. You can learn more about starry nights and space exploration at this small university planetarium. Shows on varied topics in astronomy, space exploration, and other sciences are offered year-round, but you'll need to call ahead for information on programs, schedule, and prices.

● Waterville-Winslow Two Cent Bridge

Front St., Waterville. Year-round. Free. **All ages.**

What will you give me to pass? This is one of the few remaining original toll footbridges in the United States. The toll taker's house is on the Waterville side, but you'll be able to walk across free.

 RESTAURANTS

● Miller's Restaurant

427 Main St., Bangor, (207) 942-6361. Daily, 11–10.

Families love Miller's famous buffet. This inexpensive all-you-can-eat feast includes more than 200 hot and cold items. Soups, salads, sandwiches, seafood . . . plus, you'll find an Italian section with spaghetti, lasagna, chicken, pizzas; a Mexican section with tacos, enchiladas, nachos; and classic American cuisine. Save room for the dessert table; you can make your own sundae, strawberry shortcake, cakes, pies, and more. Come hungry.

● The Greenhouse Restaurant

193 Broad St., Bangor, (207) 945-4040. Tues.–Fri., 11:30–9; Sat., 4–9.

This popular restaurant is on Bangor's waterfront, overlooking the Penobscot River. The kids will enjoy the jungle-like feel to it; there are floor-to-ceiling plants—more than 300 in all. The kids' menu features familiar favorites like chicken fingers, sandwiches, burgers, and small orders of fried fish. Entrees run the gamut from seafood, chicken, lamb, and beef. Top sellers include the baked Riverside Chicken, a moist, cheesy, melt-in-your mouth chicken breast and the charbroiled prime rib with horseradish dipping sauce.

■ Western Lakes and Mountains

As spectacular as Maine's rugged coastline is, there's more to the state than this, as those who've traveled its western lakes and mountain region can attest. This inland area encompasses the Sebago and Long Lakes area, the beautiful Grafton and Evans notch regions of the White Mountain National Forest, and, farther north, the outdoor-recreation-rich Rangeley Lake and Carrabassett River Valley.

Sebago Lake, the second largest in Maine, covers 46 square miles and offers plenty of vacation facilities and recreational opportunities, including swimming, boating, fishing, floatplane rides, and more.

Traveling north, you'll find the classic New England town of Bethel (Hallmark once used the town for a Christmas card commercial). The town boasts a host of fine restaurants and country inns and also Sunday River, one of Maine's top ski resorts. Surrounded by the Mahoosuc Mountain Range and Grafton State Park, the region has also grown very popular with hikers and outdoor enthusiasts.

The Rangeley Lakes area has long been a mecca for vacationers, with a wide range of hotels, lodges, restaurants, and shops. Swim and picnic at lovely Rangeley State Park, attend the town cookouts in the square, play golf, or hike the numerous trails.

If you're a skiing family, no doubt you've heard of downhill giant Sugarloaf USA, near the Carrabassett River Valley. When your legs need a break from skiing, take an adventurous ride on a dogsled. Or come here in the summer for golf, tennis, mountain biking, horseback riding, canoeing, hiking, and more.

● Grafton Notch State Park

Rte. 16, north of Newry, (207) 824-2912, www.state.me.us/doc/prklnds/ grafton.com. May 15–Oct. 15, daily, dawn–dusk. 12 and older, $1. **All ages.**

Located 14 miles north of Bethel, Grafton Notch is a great place to commune with nature and is one of Maine's best spots for picnicking, hiking, and swimming. Be sure to visit Screw Anger Falls; its rocky ledges are fun to climb, and the falls make a perfect backdrop for a picnic. Other points of interest: the Moose Cave nature walk and Mother Walker Falls.

● White Mountain National Forest

Rte. 2, Bethel, (207) 824-2134. **All ages.**

The Evans Notch Ranger District of the White Mountain National Forest is located here. Evans Notch is one of the five districts in the forest, which has lands in both Maine and New Hampshire. The U.S. Forest Service maintains a number of hiking trails that connect with the Appalachian Trail.

Pick up trail maps at the Visitors Center. Take a short loop hike or make a day of it, enjoying magnificent mountain scenery.

● Artist's Covered Bridge

Rte. 5, 2 mi. beyond Sunday River Ski Resort Access Road, Newry. **All ages.**

This frequently photographed 1872 bridge marks a great family swimming hole. Have a picnic on the rocky ledges beneath the bridge, downstream.

Special Note: This is private property, so please use discretion.

● Washburn-Norlands Living History Center

Norlands Rd., off Rte. 4, Livermore, (207) 897-2236. Year-round for overnight learning vacations. General tours: July–Labor Day and on Columbus Day, daily, 10–4. 14 and older, $6; under 14, $3. **Ages 5 and up.**

When you check into this living-history center, you are assigned an identity—and from then on you live it. You'll remain in costume. You'll probably be sleeping on cornhusk mattresses. No showers, no bathrooms (that's how it was in the old days!). In fact, this living-history museum allows visitors only two concessions to modern-day conveniences: window screens in the summer and toilet paper all year. Norlands is continually lauded as the best of the best in family learning vacations.

Of course, the ideal way to experience Norlands is to sign up for one of its multiday learning vacations. But throughout the summer, the center also conducts 1.5 to 2-hour tours. You'll find an 1853 one-room schoolhouse and Maine's only living-history farm. On 445 acres and complete with barns, horses, oxen, cows, sheep, pigs, and poultry, the farm operates year-round. The kids can lend a hand with outdoor farm chores and later visit the library and Victorian home of the Washburn family, one of the country's greatest political dynasties. Bet you'll want to return for one of the vacation programs.

● Mountain Biking

If you want to skip the thigh-burning, uphill climbs and go directly to the cruise down, check out the two area ski resorts. Come summer, **Sugarloaf/USA,** RR 1, Box 5000, Carrabassett, (800) THE-LOAF, and **Sunday River,** P.O. Box 450, Bethel, (800) 543-2SKI, turn into fat-tire paradises.

At Sugarloaf/USA, the 53-mile mountain bike park includes its Nordic ski network and some of its alpine trails. Maps, tours, rentals, and shuttle drop-off and pick-up service are available from the Sugarloaf Bike Shop.

The Sunday River Mountain Bike Park has 35 miles of single track and wide-open dirt roads to cruise. With or without a guide, riders have access to a variety of terrain, with the western mountains of Maine as a backdrop.

● *Songo River Queen II*

Rte. 302, Naples, (207) 693-6861. July–Labor Day, daily; June and Sept., weekends. Songo River tour: adults, $10; 4–12, $6. Long Lake tour: adults, $7; 4–12, $4. **Ages 5 and up.**

Take a lazy one-hour riverboat ride on Long Lake or a 2.5-hour cruise across Brandy Pond and through the hand-operated Songo Locks before reaching Sebago Lake. Both are on a lovely 92-foot sternwheel riverboat. It's very relaxing and scenic. In the summer, several trips are made each day. There are sunset cruises, too. In June and September, one trip is offered each weekend day at 9:45 A.M.

● Willowbrook at Newfield

Off Rte. 11, Newfield, (207) 793-2784. May 15–Sept., daily, 10–5. Adults, $8; 6–18, $4. **All ages.**

History comes alive here, and the kids will enjoy looking at the toys, nurseries, schoolhouse, carriages, bicycles, and other artifacts of days gone by. The beautiful 1894 Armitage-Herschell Carousel is eye-catching for all—24 horses and 4 chariots fully restored and animated. You'll also see an early stagecoach, old-fashioned country store, and, in a nod to the present, restaurant, gift store, and ice cream parlor.

● Fish and Wildlife Visitors Center

Rte. 26., Gray, (207) 657-4977, www.state.me.us.ifw/education/ wildlifepark.com. Mid-Apr.–Nov.11, daily, 9:30–4:30. Adults, $4.50; 5–12, $3; 4 and under, free. **All ages.**

Don't miss this charming and educational facility, operated by the Maine Department of Inland Fisheries and Wildlife. You'll see an array of native wildlife, including bald eagles, moose, black bear, lynx, mountain lions, and more. The animals have been injured or orphaned and are unable to return to the wild. You are free to roam the farm and to look at the displays of native animals, birds, and wildlife educational exhibits. There also are trout pools and picnic areas. Guided tours are offered, too.

● Perham's

Rtes. 26 and 219, West Paris, (207) 674-2341. Year-round, daily, 9–5. **Ages 3 and up.**

This area of Maine is noted for its wide variety of mineral and gem deposits, including tourmaline, mica, feldspar, and various types of quartz. At Perham's, you'll find out all about gem hunting and at its Mineral Museum alone have plenty of things to touch. Bring a bag and a shovel and pick—Perham's quarry is open to the public and you're free to take home what you find. Kids love this treasure hunt.

● Mount Blue State Park

From Wilton or Dixfield, 15 mi. off Rte. 2, in Weld, (207) 585-2261.
Mid-May–mid-Oct. 12 and older, $2. **All ages.**

This large scenic park nestled in the mountains of western Maine is popular with mountain climbers, hikers, and families looking for outdoor fun. Swim at Webb Lake and join in ranger-led activities that include gold panning, nature walks, canoe trips, and mountain hikes. There's also a boat launch, and canoe rentals are available.

● Rangeley Lake State Park

Rumford, (207) 864-3858. Year-round, daily, dawn–dusk. 12 and older,
$2. **All ages.**

Located on the south shore of Rangeley Lake, this 691-acre recreation area offers picnicking, swimming, fishing, camping, and boat launching facilities.

● Sunday River Ski Resort

Rte. 2, north of Bethel, (207) 824-3000, www.sundayriver.com. Lift tickets:
adults, $52; 13–17, $47; 6–12, $34; under 6, free. Tiny Turns, 3 yrs.,
$30 for 1.5 hrs.; Learn to Ski, 4–12, $89/day; young adult, 13–17,
snowboard clinics, $61/day; child care, $45/day. Ticket prices listed are for
weekends; special packages and discount rates are available. **All ages.**

Sunday River is one of the premier ski resorts in the East, if not in the country. Continually upgrading and improving, the resort now encompasses eight interconnected mountains, 660 skiable acres, with 127 trails. While skiing at Sunday River is geared toward the intermediate skier, it continues to expand its expert terrain with mogul runs, ungroomed steeps, and glade skiing. Beginners' action is centered in the South Ridge Slope area, but novices can also ski from the top of the mountain and back to the South Ridge Base via Three Mile Trail. There are eight snow parks and playgrounds for riders.

Sunday River does a great job of welcoming families, offering a variety of programs for kids of all ages and abilities. A Children's Ski Center adjacent to the South Ridge Center serves as the base for children's programs. A special off-mountain fun area, with tubing, ice skating and arcade games, is popular with the young set. You won't find too many families who don't like skiing at Sunday River. It's one of the best.

● Sugarloaf USA

Rte. 27, Kingfield, (207) 237-2000, www.sugarloaf.com. Lift tickets:
adults, $52; 13–18, $47; 6–12, $35. Mountain Magic (3–6), $62/day;
Mountain Adventure (7–12), $48/day; child care (10 wks.–5 yrs.), $46/
day. **All ages.**

Skiing families who are tired of long waits in lift lines, crowded ski trails, and jammed parking lots should give serious thought to Sugarloaf. It's a bit off the beaten path, and that's why it's so relaxed. The closest major cities are Portland, two and a half hours away, and Montreal, four hours away, so you miss the big crowds that head to more southerly ski mountains. Located in Kingfield in the Carrabassett Valley, Sugarloaf is a destination resort. Drive up, park your car, and spend the rest of your time on skis, on foot, or riding the Sugarloaf Shuttle to the resort's shops and restaurants.

You'll find plenty to do. The resort has a well-equipped health club (including six indoor and outdoor hot tubs), an Olympic-size ice skating arena, and a host of eateries and shops.

Now, about that mountain: It's big, challenging, and rough and tumble if you want it, slow, easy, and relaxed if you prefer. The vertical drop is 2,820 feet for above treeline skiing, with 129 trails, 14 glades, and lots of varied terrain. Black-diamond skiers love it at Sugarloaf, where they find lots of big bumps, steeps, glades, chutes, and off-trail, out-of-bounds skiing.

Sugarloaf also works hard at pleasing families, and succeeds. Friendly staff, a top-ranked kids' program, an outdoor center with tubing, skating, sleigh rides, and more, and plenty of beginner terrain are hits with vacationing families.

 RESTAURANTS

● Cole Farms Restaurant

Rte. 100, Gray, (207) 657-4714, www.colefarms.com. Daily, 5 A.M.–10:30 P.M.

This restaurant has been pleasing diners for more than 45 years with old-fashioned, home-style cooking at very reasonable prices. They take pride in preparing most dishes on the premises, including salad dressings, sauces, soups, chowders, pies, and more. This is the stuff your Momma used to cook for you (if she was good at it!). You'll find a large selection of choices on the menu, including hot roast beef sandwiches, American chop suey, meat loaf, fried fish platters, grilled dogs and burgers, cold sandwiches, salads, soups, and more. Stop here on your way to and from the Bethel/Sunday River resort area. And bring your appetites.

● Hugs

Rte. 27, Carrabassett Valley, (207) 237-2392. Summer, Thurs.–Sat., 5–10; winter, Tues.–Sat., 5–10. Closed mid-Oct.–Nov.

This is a great place to come with friends and family. The food is nothing less than fabulous, and the staff makes you feel right at home. This friendly place dishes up big baskets of just-baked pesto bread, bowls of fresh salad, and platters full of fine northern Italian cuisine. Select different entrees to pass at the table, mixing and matching to fit tastes and budgets. Dinners are served family style, and you can get all you want to eat. Save room for dessert.

● Matterhorn Wood-fired Pizza and Pasta

Sunday River Rd., Bethel, (207) 824-OVEN. Open Nov.–Apr., 11:30–10.

Ultrafresh ingredients piled high on a wood-fired, smoky thin crust is what makes skiers and winter vacationers crowd the doors of this casual restaurant. Specialty pizzas are offered in a variety of creative combinations, but you'll find traditional combos to please the finicky eaters in your group. There's pasta dishes, too; how to go wrong with a plate of spaghetti and meatballs? If you're looking for something a little more hearty, try the **Great Grizzly American Steakhouse,** in the same building, where you'll have choices of hefty platters of beef, ribs, chicken, and more. It's a popular place to dine after a day on the slopes.

■ Moosehead and Katahdin Region

If you have a love for the great outdoors and an appreciation for the beauty of unspoiled wilderness, this northern lakes region of Maine is for you.

This is considered one of the greatest hunting, fishing, and canoeing regions in the country. You'll see few commercial tourist attractions or concessions to modern-day extravagances. Rather, it's the wealth of natural resources that draws people to the shores of mighty Moosehead Lake or into the wilderness of Baxter State Park.

You'll stand in the shadows of Mount Katahdin, one of the highest peaks in the Northeast and the legendary home of the sacred spirits of the Abenaki Indians. Mount Katahdin, meaning "greatest mountain," rises nearly one mile above Baxter State Park. You'll get a good taste of northern Maine wilderness in this 201,018-acre park, where you can swim in secluded mountain ponds, hike through forests, and picnic along babbling brooks.

You'll get your thrills not from a water slide or a roller coaster, but from a white-water raft trip down the West Branch of the Penobscot River, or on a floatplane ride over the undeveloped shores of Moosehead Lake. It's easy here—and relatively inexpensive—to hire a seaplane for island exploring or to rent a canoe to get around the lakes and rivers. In the winter, you'll join snowmobilers, snowshoers, and ski tourers who traverse the surrounding forests on a network of trails and old logging roads. But whenever you come, be prepared to spend the time outdoors.

● Moosehead Lake

Moosehead Lake is Maine's largest lake, more than 40 miles long and up to 20 miles wide. There are several large islands, bays, and inlets in the lake, surrounded by rugged mountains and miles of dense forests. Much of the 420-mile shoreline remains undeveloped and accessible only by floatplanes, boats, or canoes. But don't despair; all these are easy to rent or hire. Stop in Greenville, on the southern tip of the lake, where you'll find lots of local seaplanes for sightseeing tours. There's nothing formal here; just walk up to the plane of your choice and talk to the owner. In Greenville you'll also find a number of places to rent canoes and rowboats. This is a great way to see the lake and explore its many islands.

Be sure to bring a pair of binoculars for moose watching. More than 10,000 moose reportedly live in the Moosehead Lake region. The best time to see them is early morning or twilight, when they come out to feed in the lake's swampy areas. If you feel adventurous, explore some of the old logging roads around the lake; they will take you to secluded bogs.

Special Note: Though moose will seldom approach people, it's a good policy to watch from a distance.

● Mount Kineo

While you're exploring the lake, you'll notice Mount Kineo rising dramatically out of it for more than 700 feet. Located about a mile from the lakefront town of Rockwood, Mount Kineo is made entirely of green flint. Many years ago, the Abenaki Indians sought its flint to make arrowheads and tools. From here, you'll also get great views of the lake and surrounding mountains and forests.

● Lily Bay State Park

East side of Moosehead Lake, 8 miles north of Greenville, (207) 695-2700. Early May–mid-Oct. 12 and older, $2.50. **All ages.**

This park, located on the shores of Moosehead Lake just north of Greenville, is a fine recreation center. Its 942 acres include a small beach for swimming, canoe rentals, and boat-launching facilities. The kids will enjoy taking the short path to the playground or picnicking in the pines.

● SS Katahdin *and Moosehead Marine Museum*

Main St., Greenville, (207) 695-3390, www.katahdincruises.com. Memorial Day–June, weekends only; July–mid-Sept., Tues., Thurs., Sat. and Sun.; mid-Sept.–Sept. 30, weekends only. 3-hr. cruise departs at 12:30: adults, $20; 6–15, $12; under 6, free. 5-hr. cruise: adults, $26; 6–15, $15; under 6, free. **All ages.**

Known locally as Kate, this restored 1914 steam vessel has been converted into the floating Moosehead Marine Museum. There are exhibits, displays, and photographs to see, but the highlight is taking a cruise around Moosehead Lake. You'll have a choice of a five-hour tour of the lake (best for older children) or the shorter three-hour cruise. Both feature great views and a look at the logging industry in the area, past and present.

● Baxter State Park

North of Millinocket, (207) 723-5140, www.baxterstateparkauthority.com. Year-round. **All ages.**

This premier 202,064-acre park was given to the state by Maine governor Percival Baxter in 1941, with one condition: "That it forever shall be held in its natural, wild state." The park is an unspoiled wilderness area dominated by Mount Katahdin, the highest mountain in the state. It includes 46 mountain peaks and ridges (18 exceed an elevation of 3,000 feet) and a network of about 150 miles of trails, all surrounded by natural wildlife, mountain streams, ponds, lakes, and dense forests. Visitors can wind their way through the park on a narrow road. The auto trip through the park takes about two and a half to three hours, but this doesn't include the stops you'll want to make for picnics, swimming, and hiking along the way.

There are trails for everyone in the park, and even families with small children can enjoy a number of hikes. Daicey Pond Nature Trail is perfect for small children. The trail is level and an easy trip around Daicey Pond. Be sure to pick up the free pamphlet on the trail that points out wildlife as you go. It's available from the ranger station at Daicey Pond Campground. Little Niagara and Big Niagara Falls Trail is part of the Appalachian Trail, and it's a great one to walk on a hot summer's day. (The Appalachian Trail, the only trail in Baxter blazed in white, terminates in the park at Mount Katahdin.) You'll pick up the trail at the Daicey Pond Campground and hike along the Nesowadnehunk Stream. There are lots of places to take a refreshing dip along the way. You'll pass a logger's dam before reaching Little Niagara Falls. Go a little farther down the side trail to Big Niagara Falls, a picturesque spot for a picnic. From the campground to Big Niagara Falls is 1.2 miles. Families with older children will enjoy a 3.2-mile hike up Sentinel Mountain on the Kidney Pond Sentinel Mountain Trail. It's not too steep, and the summit view, overlooking a range of mountains, is beautiful. The trail leaves from the southwest corner of Kidney Pond.

There are lots of mountain pools and streams to swim in throughout the park. Families will also enjoy South Branch Pond; this is a busy camping and picnic area also open for day use. You'll find a nice swimming area and canoes for rent. Abol Pond is a popular spot for swimming and picnicking at the southern end of the park. Take Abol Pond Road three miles in from the park's southern gatehouse entrance. Togue Pond is open for general use. It's located just outside the entrance of the park.

Baxter State Park is a great place for animal watching. There are more than 170 bird species, and you're likely to see deer and moose in the ponds feeding on aquatic vegetation. (Look for them at Daicey and Elbow Ponds.) There's also a large bear population in the park. People are warned not to feed the bears or leave waste around.

Parents should be warned that there is a serious bug population from May into August, and everyone will need the protection of insect repellent, nets, or both. Finally, there are no running water, electricity, lights, food, or supplies in the park.

● Patten Lumberman's Museum
Shin Pond Rd., Patten, at the northern entrance to Baxter State Park, (207) 528-2650, www.lumbermansmuseum.org. Memorial Day–June, Tues.–Sun.; July–Aug., Fri.–Sun.; Sept.–Columbus Day, Tues.–Sun.; 10–4. 12 and older, $5; 6–11, $1. **Ages 5 and up.**

You'll learn about the active lumbering industry at this museum. The complex of nine buildings contains a working model of a sawmill, a blacksmith shop, old tractors, and 3,000 artifacts of the lumbering industry.

● Canoeing and White-Water Rafting
This area boasts some of the most spectacular white-water rivers in the East, including the West Branch of the Penobscot River, the Kennebec, and the Allagash Wilderness Waterway. Canoe trips can last for a day, a few days, a week, or longer and are designed for beginners as well as experts. A number of licensed outfitters can arrange canoe trips. The adventurous can try a thrilling ride down rushing waters in a rubber raft. Licensed outfitters arrange and guide the trips. Many outfitters offer family trips, suitable for children, on the lower Kennebec River. Minimum age on other white-water rivers is usually 12 years. For a list of canoe trips, white-water raft expeditions, and licensed outfitters, write to the Maine Department of Inland Fisheries and Wildlife, 284 State St., Augusta, ME 04333, (207) 289-2043.

● Blacksmith Shop Museum
Park St., off Rte. 153, Dover-Foxcroft, (207) 564-8618. Memorial Day– Oct., daily, sunrise–sunset. Free. **Ages 5 and up.**

Do your children know what a blacksmith's shop is? Here's a good place to find out. This 1863 restored Civil War period blacksmith shop retains much of the original equipment, and kids will get a quick look into the past, when four-legged animals—not engines—were the mode of transportation.

● Gulf Hagas
Millinocket Rd., just north of Milo and Brownville. **Ages 10 and up.**

Gulf Hagas, accessible only by a four- to five-mile hike down a trail, has been called the "Grand Canyon of the East." This is where the west branch of the Pleasant River is deeply entrenched in a slate canyon, and waterfalls, sheer walls, and unusual rock formations form a spectacular site. Don't attempt this with young tots. But if you have older children and you've got the time, don't miss it.

 RESTAURANTS

● Lost Lobster Seafood Café

422 N. Main St., Greenville Junction, (207) 695-3900. Late May–Columbus Day; 11:30–10.

So what if you're miles from the ocean, you are in Maine and seafood reigns—especially at this casual, family-friendly restaurant in the Moosehead Lake region. Try the lobster stew with cornbread or thick clam chowder. You can get lobster a half-dozen different ways, plus other seafood, ribs, and chicken. For lunch, there are sandwiches, salads, and wraps, and kids have their own menu of standard kid fare (chicken bites, hot dogs, and shrimp boats) served with fries and flavored applesauce. There's indoor and outdoor seating. Want your meal delivered? Check into the restaurant's clambakes, prepared at your cabin or other site.

● Auntie M's

Main St., Greenville, (207) 695-2238. Summers, daily, 5 A.M.–8 P.M.; winters, daily, 5 A.M.–6:30 P.M.

Yes, you read that right . . . this place opens at five all year round. Auntie M's wants to be sure all those day hikers, hunters, snowmobilers, skiers, and fishing enthusiasts get a good, strong start on the day. Everyone knows Auntie M's, where you'll get homemade doughnuts and muffins, large-size breakfast specials, and hearty lunches and dinners. You'll find unfussy, home-style meals offering all the basics, like fried seafood platters, steaks, chicken, sandwiches, and burgers. Breakfast anytime.

● The Birches Resort and Restaurant

Birches Rd., Rockwood, (207) 534-7305. Daily, summers, 7 A.M.–10 A.M. and 6 P.M.–9 P.M.; winters, 7 A.M.–10 A.M. and 5 P.M.–8 P.M.

You'll first look at this room, a turn-of-the-century log building with giant stone fireplaces, and then, look at the view, a panorama of Moosehead Lake and surrounding mountain ranges. This is a great setting for a meal, and you'll likely share the dining room with fellow outdoor enthusiasts and vacationers. Actually, the food isn't bad, either. Dinners include appetizer, dessert, salad, vegetables, and potatoes. Standard menu items (steak, fish, chicken, and pasta) are offered, plus three or four daily specials.

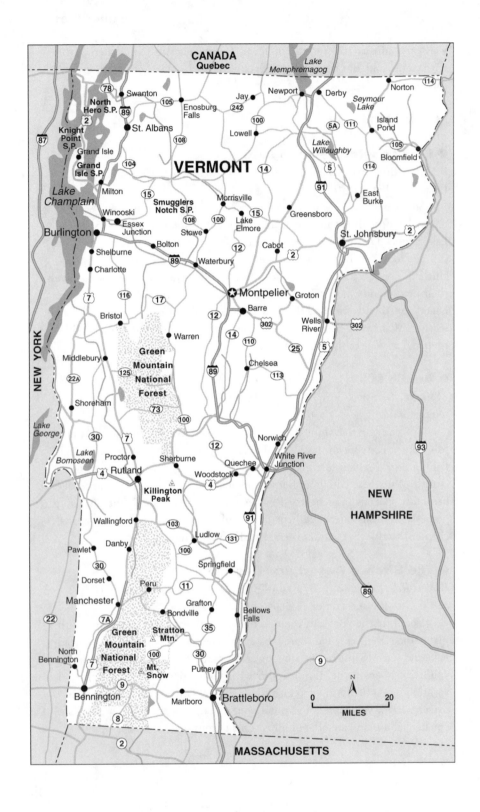

Vermont

■ Manchester and the Mountains

Long before there were ski lifts and condominiums, Manchester was an elegant summer resort—Vermont's answer to Newport, Rhode Island, and Saratoga, New York. Instead of waiting in lift lines, guests queued up for a game of croquet. Then, as now, the combination of fresh mountain air and charming countryside proved too enticing to resist.

Happily some of that gentility remains today. Visiting families can tour Manchester Village in a horse-drawn carriage complete with a top-hatted driver. Guests can picnic on the manicured lawns of Hildene, the Robert Todd Lincoln estate, as past presidents once did. Or you can bundle up for a sleigh ride, stopping back at the mansion for hot mulled cider.

In Manchester Center, a more modern pastime predominates—shopping. You'll find a plethora of specialty stores, antique shops, craft studios, and designer outlets. In recent years, outlet shopping has also reared its (we won't say it) head.

But if you spend too much time poking around in the shops, you'll miss what this area has best to offer—ample opportunity to play outside. Southern Vermont is a great place for trout fishing, canoeing, camping, swimming, hiking, skiing, horseback riding—you name it.

There's also a prominent resident your children will want to meet: Santa. Where else would the Claus family choose for a summer home?

● Santa's Land

Rte. 5, between exits 4 and 5 off I-91, Putney, (802) 387-5550 or (800) 726-8299. Memorial Day–Christmas, daily, 10–5; Labor Day–Christmas, weekends only, 10–5. Adults, $8; 3–15, $6. **Ages 1–8.**

This very merry park has lots of child-pleasing features, including a petting zoo, a train ride, a carousel, and a playground. The highlight of your child's visit will likely be a chat with the Jolly Old Elf himself, who'll ask, "Do you take care of your toys?" not, "What do you want for Christmas?" And there's a close-up look at Rudolph and his animal friends. Marionette and puppet shows are featured on the weekends.

● Southern Vermont Natural History Museum

Rte. 9, Marlboro, (802) 464-0048, www.vermontmuseum.org. Memorial Day–late Oct., daily, 10–5; late Oct.–Memorial Day, weekends only. Adults, $3; 5–18, $1. **All ages.**

Don't miss this hidden gem tucked in behind the Vermont Country Market. This top-notch natural history museum has recently expanded and now includes nearly 600 different animals. Critters roam the forest, and birds fly the skies of New England in a collection of more than 80 dioramas. The native bird collection is astounding, featuring a very complete example of birds native to New England, including three extinct birds. Kids will love the big cases—one with four bald eagles, and another with at least 10 owls.

● Green Mountain Flyer

8 Depot St., Bellows Falls, (802) 463-3069, www.rails-vt.com. Late June–Aug., Tues.–Sun; Sept.–Oct., daily. Trains depart 11 and 2. Call about special winter and spring trips. Adults, $2; 3–12, $8. **Ages 3 and up.**

Climb aboard and journey through central Vermont's scenic countryside. The restored coaches, pulled by vintage diesels, travel 26 miles, from Bellows Falls to Chester. You'll view Brockways Mill Gorge, two covered bridges, and lots of rolling hills and valleys and pretty tumbling waterfalls.

● Hildene

Rte. 7A, Manchester, (802) 362-1788, www.hildene.org. Mid-May–Oct., daily, 9:30–4. Grounds only: adults, $5; 6–14, $2; 5 and under, free. Tours: adults, $10; 6–14, $4; 5 and under, free. **Ages 5 and up.**

This place is probably not number one on your children's "top fun things to do" list, but promise them an ice cream cone on the way home and they might go along. And you'll get to see this gracious Georgian Revival mansion, built by Robert Todd Lincoln, the only one of Abraham Lincoln's four sons to live to maturity. Lincoln's descendants lived at Hildene until 1975. The kids will find the toy room, decorated with fairy-tale scenes, and the 1908 player pipe organ the most interesting. When they begin to get antsy, you can take them for a walk on one of the nature trails. There are also picnic areas on the grounds, and open air concerts, performed by the Vermont Symphony Orchestra, are often scheduled in the summer.

● Bennington Museum and Grandma Moses Gallery

Rte. 9, Old Bennington, (802) 447-1571, www.benningtonmuseum.com. Nov.–May, daily, 9–5; June–Oct., daily, 9–6. Adults, $6; under 12, free. **Ages 5 and up.**

You'll take a trip back to the 19th century when you view this collection of paintings, furniture, military artifacts, and toys. But most come for a look at the gallery devoted to Anna Mary Robertson, better known as Grandma Moses. This legendary woman began painting seriously at age 78 and continued to do so until her death at age 101.

● Bromley Mountain Thrill Zone!

Rte. 11, Manchester, (802) 824-5522, www.bromley.com. Memorial Day–Columbus Day, weekends, 10–5; mid-June–Labor Day, daily, 10–5. Rates vary depending on activities. **Ages 2 and up.**

It's been dubbed the largest fun park in Vermont, an all-in-one mountain center that's jam-packed with kid-pleasing activities. Older kids will love the Adrenaline Zip Line and Volcano Peak. There are three alpine slides, including the longest in North America, two trampolines, an 18-hole minigolf course, climbing wall, water rides, kiddie bumper boats, play areas, and more.

● Southern Vermont Arts Center

West Rd., Manchester, (802) 362-1405, www.svac.org. Mid-May–Oct., Tues.–Sat., 10–5; Sun., 12–5; Nov.–mid-May, Mon.–Sat., 10–5. Adults, $6; children under 13, free. **Ages 5 and up.**

This lovely arts center sits on 407 acres on the slope of Mount Equinox. There are ten galleries of exhibits with a collection of more than 700 paintings. Kids will especially enjoy the outdoor sculpture gardens in the lower meadow of rolling lawn and the Boswell Botany Trail. Along this half-hour woodsy walk, you'll discover a variety of wildflowers, ferns, and trees (all identified), including a 285-year-old sugar maple.

● Adams Family Farm

15 Higley Hill, Wilmington, (802) 464-3762, www.adamsfamilyfarm.com. Tues.-Sun., 10-5. Adults, $6.50; 3-12, $5.50. **All ages.**

A day at Adams Farm is one of Vermont's favorite family excursions. There are more than 150 animals at this sixth-generation family farm and plenty of hands-on activities. Goat milking and bottle feeding the calves are among the favorites. There are hayrides, pony rides, and tractor pulls and a number of special workshops, demonstrations, and programs held through-out the summer. In winter, there are sleigh rides, too. Biggest thrill: a high-flying jump into a giant hay pile!

● Swimming Holes and Picnic Spots

When it comes time to cool off and stretch out, you'll have plenty of choices:

Hapgood Pond Recreation Area, Rte. 11, Weston (2 mi. north of Peru), is part of the Green Mountain National Forest, and a popular spot for swimming, hiking, fishing, and picnicking.

Emerald Lake State Park, Rte. 7, North Dorset, is a 430-acre play-ground offering swimming, boating, and fishing. Picnic tables, snack bar, and boat rentals are available.

Stoughton Pond in Weathersfield is great for a quick dip. You'll find changing rooms here.

Jamaica State Park, Rte. 30, Jamaica, is on the banks of the West

River, where you can fish, hike, canoe, kayak, or swim. A nice nature trail leads to pretty Hamilton Falls. Boat rentals are available.

Lake Saint Catherine State Park, Rte. 30, Poultney, has swimming, fishing, and boating. A marina on the west shore of the lake rents canoes and motorboats. You'll also find a nature trail, nature museum, playground, and picnic tables. Bring barbecue fixings; there are fireplaces, grills, and wood available.

Townscend Lake Recreation Area, Rte. 30, Townsend, has swimming, boating, picnicking, and hiking trails. There are boat rentals available.

● Hiking

Check in with the Manchester Ranger District, U.S. Forest Service, Rte. 11, Manchester, (802) 362-2307, for trailhead directions and information on local hiking opportunities. **All ages.**

You're likely to see a number of backpackers and hikers in this area. Two legendary trails merge here: the Appalachian Trail and the Long Trail. But you don't have to be an avid mountain climber to enjoy the trails.

There are plenty of opportunities for day hikes. Here are some easy treks in the area for families:

Grout Pond Trails is a series of easy loop trails that pass Grout Pond and provide access to the north end of Somerset Reservoir. You'll find camping, picnicking, and swimming at Grout Pond. Catch the trailhead off Kelley Stand Rd., just east of Rte. 71.

Hapgood Pond Trail begins at the Hapgood Pond Recreation Area, Forest Highway 3. The trail loops around the north edge of the pond to a dam. (Summer admission is charged at Hapgood.)

Griffith Lake Trail begins at the end of Forest Road 58 and heads north on an old road to Griffith Lake. It's just over two miles and well marked.

● Connecticut River Safari Canoe Touring Center

451 Putney Rd., Rte. 5, Brattleboro, (802) 257-5008. May–mid-Sept., daily, 8–6; mid-Sept.–mid-Oct., weekends by appointment. **Ages 2 and up.**

Even small children will enjoy a paddle on the beautiful Connecticut River. This long, 412-mile stretch of water, flowing from the Canadian border to Long Island Sound, is wide and meandering. You'll paddle peaceful waters, sometimes around islands and under bridges. The overnight downriver trip from Bellows Falls to Brattleboro is the most popular water adventure. You'll camp on the river shores, or, if you prefer, stay overnight at the Putney Inn, a short walk from Putney Landing. The company also offers rentals and shuttle service.

● Batten Kill River

The infamous Batten Kill, known for its great trout fishing, weaves through this southern Vermont region, inviting passersby to dip their toes or drop a line. Originating in Dorset and East Dorset, the Batten Kill flows into New York State and the Hudson River. Its waters are lively, clear, and perfect for canoeing and fishing. Your best bet is to stop in at the **Orvis Company** in town (Rte. 7A, Manchester) and pick up a detailed map of the river. Or just chat with the sales folk here. They'll tell you the best place to access the water, whether you want to sit on a rock and get your legs wet, or get serious about fishing. The store is a great place to browse, too, full of fishing gear and gadgets. You're likely to see a class outside by the Orvis Pond learning the finer points of fly casting.

Canoe rentals are available at the **Battenkill Canoe Company,** Rte. 7A, Arlington (800) 421-5268 or (802) 362-2800, www.battenkill.com. Shop staff will provide you with a map, go over your route, and point out interesting spots to watch for along the way. At the end of your trip, one of the shuttle vans will meet you and bring you back to your car. Guided excursions and inn-to-inn trips are also offered.

● Mount Snow Mountain Biking

Rte. 100, Mount Snow, (800) 245-SNOW, www.mountsnow.com. June–Oct. Rates vary. **Ages 5 and up.**

Whether you're a beginner or a fat-tire maniac, you're going to love Mount Snow. And if you haven't tried this fast-growing sport, this is the place to do it. Mount Snow is famous for its world-class biking trails. The Bike Center offers more than 140 miles of terrain on single-track, old town roads, and ski trails. You'll find lots of variety, from meandering, scenic back roads to rugged and steep up-and-down runs. The staff is always available to help you choose which way to go, providing maps and advice. Private and group instructional tours are also available.

If you'd rather peddle downhill than uphill, buy a chairlift pass and ride it to Mount Snow's 3,600-foot summit. After a great four-state view, point those fat tires down one of the many trails.

● Sun Bowl Ranch Horseback Riding

Stratton Mountain, off Rte. 30, (802) 297-9210, www.sunbowlranch.com. Mid-June–Columbus Day, daily, 8–6. One- or 2-hour rides, $27–$50. **Ages 8 and up.**

Take a guided horseback ride through the rolling Vermont countryside, past rippling streams, through forests, and to secluded spots. Parents ride on gentle horses; children eight years and older hop on a donkey.

● Cross-Country Skiing

Southern Vermont is a Nordic skier's paradise. There are numerous ski-touring centers nearby; these are great for families because you get detailed maps, advice, rental equipment, groomed trails, and lessons. Here are some possibilities:

Hildene, Rte. 7A, Manchester Village, (802) 362-1788, www.hildene.org, offering 15 kilometers of trails through the hardwoods on the historic Robert Todd Lincoln estate; **Stratton Nordic Centers** at Stratton Mountain, Rte. 30, Bondville, (802) 297-4114 or 800-STRATTON, www.stratton.com, with more than 30 kilometers of terrain at two centers—the Sun Bowl for secluded forest trails and the Country Club for more gentle rolling terrain; **Viking Nordic Center,** Little Pond Rd., Londonderry, (802) 824-3933, www.vikingnordic.com, with 35 kilometers of groomed trails through woods and open fields; **Wild Wings Ski Touring Center,** North Rd., Peru, (802) 824-6793, a family-friendly center with 25 kilometers of beginner through expert trails in wooded terrain; and **Grafton Ponds Nordic Center,** 802-843-2400, with 60 kilometers of trails, ice skating, tubing, kids' park, and more.

For those who want more natural terrain, head to **Merck Forest,** Rte. 315, Rupert Mountain, (802) 394-7836, for some fine backcountry skiing. Merck has 2,820 acres with 27 miles of ungroomed trails.

● Mount Snow/Haystack Ski Resort

Rte. 100, Mount Snow, (802) 464-3333, or (800) 245-SNOW, www.mountsnow.com. Lift tickets: adults (13 and up), $56; young adults (13–18), $50; junior (6–12), $38. Mountain Camp and Mountain Riders (7–12), $69/day (rentals extra); Snow Camp (4–6), $81/day (rentals extra); child care (6 wks.–6 yrs.) $64/day. Rates are for weekends and holidays; discounted midweek rates and special packages are offered. **All ages.**

Recent expansions and improvements have put a fresh face on this southern Vermont favorite. Families with beginner skiers and riders will find an expanded learning area and lots of beginner terrain. For those looking for a challenge, Mount Snow added 16 acres of tree skiing for a total of 137 acres and 12 specific acres devoted to expert skiers. In all, you'll find 132 trails and about 50 miles of slopes spread across five separate mountain faces, including Haystack, located two and a half miles from the main area (open weekends and holidays only).

The resort is doing its best to welcome vacationing families. Special ski and stay packages and annual Teddy Bear Weeks are offered, and a host of kids' programs are available. Families will find lots of off-slope activities, including the Teen Extreme Program (coaching during the day for skiers and riders and social activities in the evening); the Planet 9 After Dark (a teen club for ages 15-20); and the Cave Club (ages 10-14). Both clubs feature DJ entertainment, adult supervision, and refreshments.

Riders will find a mix of beginner and expert trails. Un Blanco Gulch, one of the first snowboard parks in the East, runs about 2,700 feet long, with an average trail width of about 80 feet, and features more than 25 freestyle elements. The Gut is a 400-foot competition-size half pipe, featuring lights for night riding.

The resort can be a hoppin' place; very popular with the New York and Connecticut crowds.

● Bromley Mountain

Rte. 11, Peru, 6 miles east of Manchester, (802) 824-5522, www.bromley.com. Lift tickets: adults, $35; 13–17, $44; 7–12, $34; under 6, free. Mighty Moose (ages 3–5) and Mountain Club (6–12), $91/day. Kids Center (day care for 6 wks.–3 yrs.), $49/day. Rates are for weekends and holidays; discounted midweek rates and special packages are offered. **All ages.**

Tired of the crowds, the hassle, and the hustle-and-bustle of the big resorts? Then you're going to love this place. Bromley is low-key, friendly, and the perfect spot for beginners, or for those looking for a relaxing getaway. There's another great thing about Bromley: its southern exposure, which makes the alpine experience a tad warmer than at other New England ski resorts. It's also a bit kinder on the family budget; lift prices are about $8-$10 less a day than those at other, larger resorts.

There are 43 trails, mostly beginner and intermediate terrain, with a handful of expert runs. Riders will find two parks with lots of man-made obstacles, whales, and snow beasts.

On-mountain lodging is available, for ski-in, ski-out ease, and Manchester Center is just a few miles away if you're hankering for fine cuisine and apres-ski fun.

● Stratton Mountain

Stratton Mountain Rd., Bondville, (800) 843-6867, www.stratton.com. Lift tickets: adults, $62; 13–17, $50; 7–14, $42; 6 and under, $5. Snowkids (3 yrs.), $57/day; Little Cub (4–6), $89/day; Big Cub (7–12), $109/day; child care (6 wks.–5 yrs.), $89/day. Rates are for weekends; discounted midweek rates and packages are available. **All ages.**

Stratton believes in comfort—on and off the slopes. The mountain: the highest peak in southern Vermont, with a summit elevation of 3,875 feet, 92 trails, and 14 lifts including four 12-person gondolas and a 6-person, high-speed lift. The resort: a slopeside alpine village with dining and shopping options; and a mega sports center with swimming, racquetball, tennis, and more. Stratton draws crowds from the Big Apple.

● Ascutney Mountain Resort

Rte. 44, Brownsville, (800) 243-0011, www.ascutney.com. Lift tickets: adults, $49; 7–16, $26; 6 and under, free. Ski programs for children ages 3–12, $75/day; child care (6 wks.–6 yrs.), $55/day. Rates are for weekends and holidays; discounted midweek rates and packages are available. **All ages.**

This small, family-oriented resort is a hit with vacationers looking for a relaxed, friendly, and less expensive mountain getaway. Recent expansions on the mountain have improved the conditions and variety of skiing; you'll find 56 trails, six lifts, including the mile-long North Peak Express Quad, and a pleasant self-contained village at the base. Most of the trails are easy or intermediate level, all dropping down to the same base area (so it's easy to keep track of the children!). On-mountain lodging adds to the convenience and ease.

Come summer, the resort turns to warm-weather fun like biking, hiking, tennis, swimming, and a host of outdoor children's programs.

RESTAURANTS

You won't go hungry in this region; there are plenty of dining options from fast-food chains, delis, and family restaurants to upscale dining establishments. Head to Manchester Center or Brattleboro and take your pick. Here are a few notables:

● Laney's

Rtes. 11 and 30, Manchester, (802) 362-4465. Daily, 5–10.

This lively, popular restaurant features an open kitchen with a wood-fired brick oven. You'll be surrounded by lots of show-biz, sports-biz memorabilia, including signed movie posters and sports equipment. You can't go wrong with the barbecued ribs or chicken dishes, or one of their specialty pizzas. Noisy and fun.

● Mother Myrick's

Rte. 7A, Manchester Center, (802) 362-1560. Fri.–Sat., 10–10; Sun.–Thurs., 10–6.

This is goody heaven: an ice cream parlor, bakery, and chocolate shop all in one. Children will enjoy watching the candy makers prepare fudge and dip chocolates in the candy room. (Tell yourself this is an educational trip.) Can't decide what you want? Indulge in a scrumptious ice cream sundae now, and take some fudge home for later.

● Blue Benn

*Rte. 7, North Bennington, (802) 442-5140. Mon.–Tues., 6 A.M.–5 P.M.;
Wed.,–Fri., 6 A.M.–8 P.M.; Sat., 6 A.M.–4 P.M.; Sun., 7 A.M.–4 P.M.*

This is a classic diner complete with barreled ceiling, Formica countertops, and lots of stainless steel and chrome. But this is not your typical greasy spoon. Blackboard specials might include cheddar cheese and asparagus or watercress and cream cheese omelets, whole wheat pancakes, veggie enchiladas, falafel, and nut burgers. There's lots of traditional diner fare, too, like hot dogs, meat loaf and mashed potatoes, and Jell-O. Often crowded, but worth the wait.

■ Woodstock Area

If your family loves the outdoors, start packing. This gorgeous slice of Vermont mountains and valleys is a treasure trove of recreation.

Many visitors are attracted to this region for downhill skiing; most come to mammoth Killington with its six mountains and the nearby rollicking nightlife. Certainly, you could spend days on skis, while your kids are merrily making snowmen or perfecting their wedge turns. (Or more often than not, waiting for you at the bottom of the hill.) Not a bad way to beat the winter doldrums.

Come summer, ski trails and the maze of old logging and carriage roads open to hikers, bikers, and strollers. And summer visitors meander the quaint towns that existed before the ski resorts arrived, especially picturesque Woodstock; visit a world-class museum; or gaze down Quechee Gorge, a natural wonder that dates back to the Ice Age.

● Billings Farm and Museum

Rte. 12, Woodstock, (802) 457-2355, www.billingsfarm.org. May–Oct., daily, 10–5; selected weekends throughout the winter. Adults, $9; 13–17, $7; 5–12, $4; 3–4, $2; under 3, free. **All ages.**

Watch cows being milked, churn cream into butter, nuzzle a sheep, pet newborn calves—these are some of the pleasures awaiting your family at Billings Farm. This working dairy farm has prize Jersey cattle, sheep, draft horses, oxen, and a petting nursery. You'll explore the busy life on this real working Vermont dairy farm, getting a good look at the rigors and traditions of farm life in the 1890s. Be sure to visit the 1890 farmhouse, featuring an old-fashioned creamery. It's also the home of a farm museum, complete with an authentically restored farm home, workshop, and general store. There are demonstrations of how to hook a rug, spin wool, and do other country chores. Special events are scheduled each month, including an annual Children's Day.

● Vermont Institute of Natural Science

27023 Church Hill Rd., Woodstock, (802) 457-2779, www.vinsweb.org.
Mon.–Sat., 10–4; closed Sun. Adults, $7; 12–18, $4; 5–11, $3; 3–4, $1.
All ages.

This unique living museum, a favorite among adults and children alike, houses 26 species of birds of prey native to northern New England. This is your chance to get up close and personal with an owl, hawk, or eagle. All the raptors at the center are permanently injured and unable to survive in the wild. You'll also see injured birds in the infirmary. The institute treats hundreds of injured birds of prey each year; most are released back to the wild.

Leave time for a walk on one of the many self-guided nature trails (there are 77 acres of nature preserve), and for a look at the Visitors Center. Housed in a remodeled dairy barn, it usually has a small display of nature exhibits.

● Montshire Museum of Science

Rte. 10A, Norwich, (802) 649-2200, www.montshire.net. Daily, 10–5.
Adults, $6.50; 3–17, $5.50; under 3, free. **All ages.**

This peaceful setting has been called "one of the finest museum sites in New England" by the American Association of Museums. The natural world is the focus at Montshire, featuring a wide range of hands-on exhibits and programs, and outside exhibits on the museum's 100-plus acres of forest along the Connecticut River.

Inside, the two-story museum offers dozens of exhibits on astronomy, natural history, and general science. One exhibit is a self-contained colony of more than 250,000 leaf-cutter ants. Other live animals include boa constrictors, a see-through beehive, and an aquarium with freshwater fish found in northern New England.

The museum continues outside. A footbridge connects the building with the trail system, which has exhibits on cloud formations, ultraviolet light, and other weather-related phenomena. Other trails offer opportunity to see native wildlife, or to learn about geology, trees, insect life, and more. The short walks are perfect for families with even young children and offer lots of scenic overlooks of the Connecticut River.

● Wilson Castle

W. Proctor Rd., near Rutland, off Rte. 4, Proctor, (802) 773-3284.
Mid-May–late Oct., daily, 9–6 (last tour, 5:30). Adults, $7.50; 6–12, $3.
Ages 5 and up.

If you've ever imagined living in a fairy-tale castle, you might have envisioned a place like this. Built by a local physician and his monied British wife, Wilson Castle boasts turrets, arches, parapets, and balconies, the whole thing made of imported materials, including the bricks. On the grounds are cattle barns, stables, and, to the delight of children, an aviary with Indian peacocks. The Wilson Castle fairy tale, alas, has an unhappy ending. Soon after the castle was built, the lady of the house fled, taking all her money with her.

● The New England Maple Museum

Rte. 7, Pittsfield, (802) 483-9414, www.maplemuseum.com. Late May–Oct., daily, 8:30–5:30; Nov.–Dec. 23 and mid-Mar.–late May, daily, 10–4. Closed Jan.–Feb. Adults, $2.50; 6–12, $.75; under 6, free. **Ages 2 and up.**

Vermonter's call it "nature's gold." And you won't want to miss a sample of the state's sweetest product. Visitors learn how the Native Americans first taught Vermonters to tap the trees and turn sap into syrup. Go during maple sugaring time, from about the end of February until early April, when you'll get a hands-on lesson.

● Sugarbush Farm

591 Sugarbush Farm Rd., Woodstock, (802) 457-1757 or (800) 281-1757, www.sugarbushfarm.com. Year-round, daily, 9–5. Free. **All ages.**

This working farm is a great place to learn about cheese making and the maple sugaring process. You'll get to sample a variety of cheeses, pet the farm animals, and take home your favorite products. There's a pleasant nature trail, too.

● Killington Adventure Center

Rte. 4, Killington Ski Resort, Sherburne, (802) 422-3333, www.killington.com. Rates vary for activities. **Ages 2 and up.**

Families love this all-in-one activity center, nestled at the foot of Killington's mountain peaks. You'll find skateboard and in-line parks, an alpine slide, climbing wall, 18-hole golf course, and 45 miles of hiking and biking trails (bike rentals available, too). Summer, winter, or fall, you can ride to the summit of Killington Mountain without ever putting on a pair of skis. During the foliage season, the enclosed gondola, or, in the summer, the chairlift will take you three and a half miles up. At the peak you'll find a lounge, cafeteria, and an observation deck. From the deck, you'll see the Green Mountains, the White Mountains (see if you can spot majestic Mount Washington in the distance), the Berkshires, and the Adirondacks. The views, especially during foliage season, are spectacular.

● Vermont Marble Exhibit

52 Main St., Proctor, (802) 459-2300 or (800) 427-1396, www.vermont-marble.com. Mid-May–late Oct., daily, 9–5:30. Adults, $6; 15–18, $2.50; 15 and under, free. **Ages 5 and up.**

You'll learn about marble formation, quarrying, and finishing at the world's largest marble museum. An informative film, exhibits, and interpretive displays show the history of the marble industry inVermont. The kids will enjoy seeing the sculptor at work. There's also an interesting outdoor display and gallery, including carved marble busts of several U.S. presidents.

● Quechee Gorge

Rte. 4, Quechee, (802) 295-7600. **All ages.**

One of Vermont's most intriguing natural wonders, Quechee Gorge is a mile-long, 162-foot-deep channel that dates back to the last Ice Age. From the bridge spanning the gorge on Route 4, you can stare down into the seemingly bottomless chasm. If your group includes older children, try the shaded mile-long trail to the bottom. It's a fairly easy hike along the fenced-in edge of the precipice. Or take the short stroll to the falls at the top of the gorge and indulge in a picnic.

● Horseback Riding

From horse-drawn wagon rides to pony rides and trail riding, there's something for all ages and experience levels. You can ride for hours through pastoral valleys, pine-scented forests, and along lakes and streams. At **Kedron Valley Inn & Stables,** Rte. 106, Woodstock, (802) 457-1473, guided trail rides and hourly and daily rentals are offered. Other places to check out if you're hankering to get in the saddle include: **Pond Hill Ranch,** Rte. 4A, Castleton, (802) 468-2449; **Riverside Farm** in Pittsfield, (802) 746-8544; and **Mountain Top Stables,** Mountain Top Inn, Mountain Top Rd., Chittenden, (802) 483-6089.

● White River

Be sure to throw your bathing suit or an extra change of clothes in the trunk when you're traveling this area. The beautiful White River snakes its way through central Vermont, around bends and over rocks. There are lots of places along its banks to stop for a dip, to jump across its width on rocks and fallen logs, or to picnic next to a picturesque waterfall. A favorite summer-time sport among locals and visitors alike is tubing down the river on a hot summer's day. Runs can last two to four hours, covering between 2 and 10 miles. There are several places in the area to rent tubes (watch for the hand-scrawled signs and piles of rubber) or check out **White River Tubing Adventures,** (802) 234-6361, www.tubevermont.com. The company provides transportation and tube rentals.

● Hiking

Hiking opportunities abound, from easy strolls to rigorous mountain climbs. The trail around **Quechee Gorge,** for example, offers easy hiking with great views into the gorge.

At **Mount Tom** in Woodstock, there's a graded footpath with benches along the way. Start at Faulkner Park and follow the switchback trail to the top of Mount Tom. Or for an easier way up, start at the Woodstock Inn on the Green. The walk follows paved paths, leading gently to the summit with a rewarding 360-degree view. For more hiking and walking trails, contact the local chamber of commerce. Several old carriage roads, constructed by the Rockefeller family, crisscross the Woodstock area and make beautiful backcountry strolls.

● Cross-Country Skiing

Nordic skiers will find abundant trails, varied terrain, and plenty of extras at the **Woodstock Ski-Touring Center,** Rte. 106, Woodstock, (802) 457-6674, www.woodstockinn.com; **Mountain Meadows,** Thundering Brook Rd. (off Rte. 4), Sherburne, (802) 775-7077 or (800) 221-0598; **Fox Run,** Ludlow, (802) 228-8871; **Trail Head,** Stockbridge, (802) 746-8038; and **Wilderness Trails,** Quechee, (802) 295-7620, www.quecheeinn.com. **Killington and Okemo ski resorts** resorts also have cross-country ski centers.

● Killington Ski Resort

Killington Rd., off Rte. 4, Sherburne, (800) 621-MTNS, www.killington.com. Lift tickets: adults, $62/day; young adult, 13–18, $57/day; junior, 6–12, $39/day. SnowZone, ages 13 and up, $154/day, including ski or snowboard instruction, rentals, and lunch; Superstars (7–12), $121/day, including ski or snowboard instruction, rentals, and lunch; Ministars (4–6), $110/day, including ski or snowboard instruction, rentals, and lunch; First Tracks (2–3), $97/day, including on-snow instruction and indoor games. Child care (6 wks.–6 yrs.), $67/day. Rates listed are weekend and holiday rates; midweek discounts and special packages are available. **All ages.**

Killington is undeniably a popular place with skiers, and for good reason: It's huge. With seven mountain peaks and 200 trails, it's the largest resort in the East. Even those who are new to the sport will find plenty of territory to cover from top to bottom. Killington Peak, the highest mountain of the six, has a vertical rise of 3,000 feet. Since it gets crowded here, plan to hit the slopes early. Also, you may want to head over to the less populous Sunrise Mountain or Bear Mountain areas, where you'll get more runs in. Some complain that you spend too much time just trying to get from one trail to another. Killington has made it easier for families with the addition of its new Rams Head Family Mountain. The self-contained area has a family center, child care, food emporium, and other services, and the Snow Play Park has beginner and intermediate terrains. An underpass from Rams Head to Snowshed makes it easy for families to access the rest of the mountains.

Beginner riders will like the eight-foot minipipe, offering an easy, less intimidating route to drop in and learn the sport. More advanced riders can twirl, flip, and soar in the 12-foot half pipe on Snowdon Mountain. Freestylers will also like the 1,300-foot snowboard park at Bear Mountain (for riders only). Jimburritos, a food and music hut, is located at the base of the half pipe. Lots of rock 'n' rollin'.

● Okemo Mountain Resort

Mountain Rd., Ludlow, (802) 228-4041 or (800) 78-OKEMO, www.okemo.com. Lift tickets: adults, $59/day; 13–18, $50/day; 7–12, $38/day. Ministars (3–4), $80/day, lift tickets extra; Snowstars (4–7), $78/day, lift tickets extra; Mountain Explorers and Young Riders (8–12), $70/day, lift tickets extra. Child care (6 wks.–8 yrs.), $60/day. Rates listed are weekend and holiday rates; midweek discounts and special packages are available. **All ages.**

If you're thinking of a family ski vacation at Okemo, you better book early. This popular ski resort draws crowds from New York, New Jersey, and southern New England. It's the biggest area in southern Vermont—88 trails and 13 lifts. It's a wonderful place for families, offering a variety of terrain. Beginners will find lots to ski, including a 4.5-mile trail from the summit and one of the longest and widest novice slopes in the country. The upper mountain glades are challenging (and the views are great), and more experienced skiers will be challenged on the mogul-strewn black-diamond runs like Sel's Choice, Punch Line, and The Plunge.

Okemo is becoming a hot spot for snowboarding, too. Boarders can catch the waves on The Pipe, a 420-foot half pipe; The Park, a giant snowboard park; and The Pull, a new riders-only surface lift.

 RESTAURANTS

● The Grist Mill

Summit Pond on Killington Road, Killington, (802) 422-3970, www.gristmillkillington.com. Open lunch and dinner, year-round; breakfast, lunch, and dinner, during winter.

The food is classic New England—hearty steaks, seafood, and chicken dishes. But the view is wonderful. The dining room is surrounded by windows on three sides overlooking Summit Pond, with Killington Peak in the distance. If it's a nice day, grab a chair on the deck, and order from the lounge menu.

● Mother Shapiro's

RFD 1, Box 3175, Killington, (802) 422-9933, www.mothershapiros.com. Daily, 7 A.M.–10 P.M.

It's been called one of the best family-style eateries in the East. Both early risers and serious night owls haunt this place. This is the spot to go for breakfast, especially if you're a hash lover. Shapiro's made-from-scratch hash is its best-selling item. Other traditional breakfast items are also available. Sandwiches, soups, and burgers sell at lunch, and dinner entrees include the popular prime rib plate and chicken and seafood dishes. There's also an extensive kosher menu offered. Children's portions are available.

● Ludlow Cooking Company
29 Main St., Ludlow, (802) 228-3080. Daily, 11:30–9.

Homemade soups, sandwiches, stews, salads, and more are the specialties at this deluxe deli. You can order in or have them pack it to go for your own classic New England roadside picnic. Don't forget dessert—lots of scrumptious baked goods.

■ Lake Champlain Valley

Burlington, the largest city in Vermont, reigns over the Lake Champlain Valley region, blessed with spectacular views of mountain peaks on both sides and a large, glistening lake in the middle. The most urban of Vermont's cities sits on the eastern slope of Lake Champlain and is home to nearly a quarter of the state's population. But "urban" to most of us does not mean what it does to Vermonters. You'll find a thriving, vibrant city but one that has not lost its small-town charm and rural influences.

The rejuvenated waterfront area, once one of the country's busiest ports, is a nice place to stroll; at dusk you'll be rewarded with breathtaking sunsets across the lake. Nineteenth-century buildings have been restored and now house cafes, specialty shops, and pedestrian marketplaces. There are five public parks from which to enjoy water views and lake activities.

If you have time, be sure to visit Champlain's Grand Islands, only a short half-hour drive from downtown Burlington. You'll discover the rural town of South Hero, the countryside of Grand Isle, the tiny village of North Hero, and the beautiful seashore of Isle La Motte. The islands are connected by bridges, surrounded by mountains, and laced with lovely state parks and lakeside beaches.

Everywhere there are opportunities to enjoy the sparkling, 110-mile-long Lake Champlain. Beaches are plentiful; there are powerboats, sailboats, kayaks, and windsurfing equipment to rent; ferries and schooners to carry you across; and scenic vistas everywhere you look. Be on the lookout for Lake Champlain's legendary sea monster—Champ. In 1609, Samuel de Champlain noted in his diary the sighting of a strange creature in the lake. Since then, other sightings have been made, prompting the Vermont House of Representatives to pass a resolution in 1982 protecting Champ from "injury or harrassment." The Lake Champlain Chamber of Commerce annually hopes for a banner year of sightings.

Waterlogged and happy, you can travel inland to visit horse and dairy farms, a 1783 log cabin, and the popular Shelburne Museum and Farm.

● Champlain Ferries

Lake Champlain Transportation Co., King St. Dock, Burlington, (802) 864-9804, www.ferries.com. **All ages.**

An easy way for the family to see Lake Champlain is to hop on one of the ferries that cross the lake to New York. Along the way you'll be treated to beautiful vistas of the New York Adirondacks on one side and the Green Mountains of Vermont on the other.

There are three crossings on Lake Champlain. Catch the ferry in Charlotte just south of Burlington for the 20-minute ride to Essex, New York. You'll enjoy the stopover in Essex; it's a charming lakeside village. The drive from Burlington to Charlotte is worthwhile, too, and you might want to visit a few sites (Wildflower Farm, Mount Philo State Park) in Charlotte, before or after the ferry ride. The ferry leaving Charlotte is open year-round.

A 12-minute ferry between Grand Isle and Plattsburgh, New York, is open all year, 24 hours a day. This is a good side trek to remember on your visit to Grand Isle.

A longer, one-hour ferry between Burlington and Port Kent operates mid-May through October and provides great views of Lake Champlain.

The boat charter company also offers daily, historic cruises in the summer. You'll trace the path of Samuel de Champlain and hear tales of battles, shipwrecks, and heroes. Several cruises depart daily throughout the summer from the King Street Dock.

● *Spirit of Ethan Allen*

Departs from the Burlington Boathouse, Burlington, (802) 862-8300, www.soea.com. Late May–mid-Oct. Adults, $7.95; 3–11, $3.95; under 3, free. **Ages 3 and up.**

This is a lively, 1.5-hour narrated lake excursion aboard a replica of a vintage sternwheeler. With small children, you might want to opt for the shorter day cruise or, perhaps, a sunset ride. On either one, you'll see fine scenery. Keep your eyes and ears open for the elusive Lake Champlain sea monster, Champ, whom only a few have seen. The sea serpent is said to be about 20 feet long with a horselike head.

● *M/V Carillon*

Departs from Whitehall, New York, or Shoreham, Vermont, (802) 897-5331, www.paxp.com/carillon.com. Mid-May–Oct., daily. Adults, $8.50; 3–12, $4.50. **Ages 3 and up.**

While other Champlain boat charters opt for the wide-open waters and expansive lake views, this special excursion boat takes a different route. The

Carrillon, a 1920s lakeboat, moves up and down the narrowest stretch of Lake Champlain. In a vivid history lesson along the way, the boat makes stops at Fort Ticonderoga on the New York side and at several Revolutionary War battlefields in Vermont.

● Shelburne Museum and Heritage Park

Rte. 7, Shelburne, (802) 985-3344, www.shelburnemuseum.com.
Mid-April–mid-May, daily, 1–4. Adults, $10; 6–18, $5. Mid-May–Oct.,
daily, 10–5. Adults, $18.75; 6–18, $7. **All ages.**

The Shelburne, one of the world's great museums of American folk art, artifacts, and architecture, is often referred to as New England's Smithsonian. This is a museum for people of all ages. The children will enjoy its parklike setting, covering 45 acres and filled with an interesting collection of buildings and memorabilia. You'll be able to board the 220-foot steamboat *Ticonderoga,* cross a covered bridge, peek in a typical New England one-room schoolhouse, shop in an 1840s general store, circle the round barn, and climb the lighthouse.

There are 37 exhibit buildings, seven furnished historic houses, more than 200 horse-drawn vehicles, and 80,000 pieces of Americana in all. The museum grounds leave lots of room to roam and are perfect for strolling. Lilac gardens, some of the finest in New England, and perennial and herb gardens grace the grounds. A fun peek at the past, and a great family outing.

● Shelburne Farms

Bay and Harbor Rds., off Rte. 7, Shelburne, (802) 985-8442,
www.shelburnefarms.org. Visitors Center and Farm Store open year-round,
daily, 10–5. Children's Farmyard and tours: mid-May–mid-Oct., daily,
10–4. General admission: adults, $6; 3–14, $4. Tours (includes general
admission): adults, $10; 3–14, $9. **All ages.**

This is a true gentleman's farm, with 1,000 acres of rolling hills, gracious gardens, and lake views. Always on the kids-favorite list, the open-air wagon tour stops at the dairy barns where you can try your hand at milking at the Coach Barn Education Center and at the beautiful Shelburne House gardens. You'll see cheese-making and dairy operations and majestic 19th-century buildings and landscapes along the way. Save time for the walking tour; it begins at the Visitors Center and winds through fields and woodlands about a mile, past the Farm Barn to the top of Lone Tree Hill for a magnificent view of Lake Champlain and the Adirondacks. Small children will like the up-close and personal look at the farm animals in the Farm Barn.

Stop by the gatekeeper's cottage on your way out to pick up some cheese courtesy of the herd of Brown Swiss on the farm.

● Birds of Vermont Museum

900 Sherman Hollow Rd., Huntington, (802) 434-2167,
www.birdsofvermont.org. May–Oct., daily, 10–4. Adults, $4; under 12, $2.
Ages 5 and up.

Bring your binoculars and hiking boots and try your luck at spotting some of Vermont's most common birds on the museum trails. Inside you'll find a lovely display of wood-carved Vermont birds—more than 170—and lots of information on these native friends.

● The Vermont Teddy Bear Company

Rte. 7, Shelburne, (802) 985-3001 or (800) 829-BEAR.,
www.vermontteddybear.com. Year-round, daily, 10–4. Adults, $2; 12 and
under, free. **All ages.**

The factory that makes the popular handcrafted Vermont teddy bears has opened its doors, allowing a look inside the magical business of teddy bear making. The colorful complex had its inspiration from the movie *Willie Wonka and the Chocolate Factory,* and kids of all ages enjoy the entertaining factory tour. The tour guides, or Bear Ambassadors as they are called, throw in lots of teddy bear history and lore, as you watch the Toymakers cut, sew, and stuff the bears. You'll wave as the bears "head off to their new home" inside a pretty box, complete with air hole. Kids can create their own bear in the Make a Friend for Life section of the factory (for $24.95). First, they'll select a "hungry" bear (unstuffed) and then fill him or her with love, dreams, wishes, and giggles on the stuffing machine. The bear, carrying case, and birth certificate is theirs to take home. After the tour, you'll have a chance to browse the Bear Shop, with more than 100 teddy bears for sale.

● UVM Morgan Horse Farm

Rte. 23, Middlebury, (802) 388-2011, www.ctr.uvm.edu/cals/farms/
mnfarm. May–Oct., daily, 9–4. Adults, $3.50; 13–18, $2; 12 and under,
free. **All ages.**

This farm, once owned by Joseph Battell, an eccentric landowner, was one of the first centers for the development of the purebred Morgan horse. Now operated by the University of Vermont, the stables are open for guided tours to see the Morgan descendants. From the short audiovisual presentation shown on the tour you'll learn that the Morgan was the first breed of horse developed in America.

● Lake Champlain Chocolates

750 Pine St., Burlington, (802) 864-1808 or (800) 465-5909,
www.lakechamplainchocolates.com. Mon.–Sat., 9–6; Sun., 12–5; tours:
Mon.–Fri., 9–2. Free. **All ages.**

This factory tour couldn't be sweeter . . . watch as a variety of mouth-watering morsels are being made and packaged. Of course, the best part of the visit is the sampling at the end. The tour is free, but few leave the store without a box of chocolate to bring home.

● Robert Frost Trail

Rte. 25, west of Middlebury Gap. **All ages.**

"[A]nd I—I took the one less traveled by . . . " Whatever road you travel, don't miss the short (three-quarters of the mile) walk on this commemorative trail. You'll wind through woods and across a beaver pond, coming upon seven mounted Robert Frost poems along the way. Why here? Poet Frost spent 39 summers in a log cabin just down the road and surely must have walked the same path years ago. While you're here, visit nearby Texas Falls.

● Texas Falls

Rte. 125, east of Middlebury Gap. **All ages.**

These falls must have been an inspiration to long-ago resident poet Robert Frost. You'll see a sign marking the falls on Route 125 and a designated parking area; walk across the bridges to view the series of falls. There are picnic tables along the way.

● Dakin Farm

Rte. 7, Ferrisburg, and 100 Dorset St., South Burlington, (802) 425-3971 or (800) 993-2546, www.dakinfarm.com. Year-round, daily, 9–5:30. Free. **All ages.**

Vermont is known worldwide for its farm products. At this family-owned farm, you'll gain a greater understanding of the processing of food between the farm field and the grocery store shelves. Farm products include corncob-smoked ham, bacon, poultry, syrup, and cheeses. Kids can watch the production of food products and taste free samples.

● Lake Champlain Maritime Museum

Basin Harbor, (802) 475-2022, www.lcmm.org. May–mid-Oct., daily, 10–5. Adults, $10; 5–17, $5. **Ages 2 and up.**

Lake Champlain's colorful nautical past comes to life at this museum dedicated to preserving the lake's heritage. Top on kids' lists are the working shops, where they can watch craftspeople carry on the traditional skills of boatbuilding and blacksmithing. You can view a large collection of original small watercraft, built over the past 150 years; learn about shipwrecks in the Nautical Archaeology Center; talk to conservators and archaeologists on current research being conducted in the lake; climb aboard a replica of Benedict Arnold's Revolutionary War gunboat, the *Philadelphia; and* take a look at marine technology. The museum has a pretty lakeside location, too.

● Ethan Allen Homestead

Off Rte. 127, Burlington, (802) 865-4556, www.ethanallen.together.com. Mid-May–mid-Oct., Mon.–Sat., 10–5; Sun., 1–5. Adults, $4; 5–17, $2; under 5, free. **Ages 5 and up.**

You'll learn all about Ethan Allen, Vermont's founder and hero of the American Revolution, as you tour his restored 1787 farmhouse. The struggles of 18th-century Vermont farm families come alive as you reconstruct their daily lives. (Maybe the kids will stop complaining about picking up their toys and making their beds after a visit here. . . . Sure.) Through exhibits and shows, visitors also learn about the Indians, French colonists, and English settlers in the Champlain region. There are authentic working gardens on the property, and in-progress archaeology projects. Bring a picnic basket of goodies to complete the outing; besides plenty of walking trails with river access, there's a picnic area.

● Swimming and Picnicking

There are a handful of public beaches in Burlington where you can enjoy the clear, cool waters of Lake Champlain. **North Beach** is the largest and most popular of the town's beaches. It has a sandy area for sunbathers and swimmers. You'll also get a view of the Adirondacks in the distance. **Oakledge Park** is a more rugged, scenic beach. It has a picnic area and rocky ledges to toss your towel on. **Red Rocks,** a small, sandy beach in South Burlington, is good for kids. Lifeguards are always on duty. **Leddy Park** has a playground and a small beach area. Our favorite is at **Alburg Dunes State Park.** The south-facing sandy beach is one of the longest on Lake Champlain, accessible by a short pedestrian and bike path.

Kingsland Bay State Park in Ferrisburg, (802) 241-3655, www.vt.stateparks.com, is a favorite summertime hangout for families visiting the Lake Champlain area. There's swimming, boating, fishing, and nice trails along the shoreline. **Mount Philo State Park,** off Rte. 7 in Charlotte, (802) 425-2390, is a great place for a picnic. Be sure to take a drive to Mount Philo's 980-foot summit. Sure, it's small, but you'll have some of the best views in the area. An access road in the park (there's a nominal fee) leads you to the summit.

Burton Island State Park is perfect for those who like a bit more solitude. There are no cars on the island; you reach it by boat or a launch service from **Kill Kare State Park,** off Rte. 36 in Saint Albans. There are hiking trails and a small nature center on the island.

● Catamount Family Center

592 Governor Caittenden Rd. Williston, (802) 879-6001 or (888) 680-1011, www.catamountoutdoor.com. Dec.–mid-Oct., daily, 9–5. Rates vary for activities and rentals. **All ages.**

At this 500-acre recreation center, you can run, mountain bike, hike, cross-country ski, ice skate, golf, and more. There is an extensive network of trails for all levels of experience. Ambience is friendly and casual, with a very helpful staff. Cross-country ski and mountain bike rentals are available. Also check out the wide array of sports programs offered. Refreshments and services are offered in the summer kitchen of the Catamount family's 1796 historic farmhouse.

● Ed Weed Fish Culture Station

14 Bell Hill Rd., Grand Isle, (802) 372-3171. Daily, 9-5. Free. **All ages.**

Take a self-guided tour of this state-of-the-art facility to learn about the amazing science of fish culturing. There's a small aquarium and exhibits, too. Added bonus: The station's picturesque setting on Grand Isle is a nice place to be.

● Burlington Bike Path

This 10-mile recreation path follows the lake from the mouth of the Winooski River. You'll share the route with strollers, joggers, and bikers. Pick up the path at Perkins Pier, Leddy Park, Oakledge Park, or North Beach.

● Champlain's Grand Islands

If you have time, take a drive through these peaceful lakeside gems. Traveling north from Burlington, you'll cross the lake to the islands of South Hero, Grand Isle, North Hero, and Isle La Motte. The island villages, connected by bridges, are 30 miles long and 8 miles wide. Surrounded by water, with views of the Adirondacks to the east and Mount Mansfield to the east, they offer some of the best in solitude and scenery. Parks and beaches on the islands include:

Grand Isle State Park, with great views, a small beach cove, and rowboats to rent, U.S. 2, Grand Isle, (802) 372-4300; **Knight Point State Park,** a good family beach with a large, sandy swimming cove, picnic area, nature trails, concession stand, and boat rentals, U.S. 2, North Hero, (802) 372-8389; and **North Hero State Park,** where the beach is only open to campers, but noncampers can fish, bike, hike, and rent boats, U.S. 2, North Hero, (802) 372-8380.

● Ice Skating

There are lots of places to ice skate along the shores and inlets of Lake Champlain. Also, you'll find skating at **Leddy Arena** in Leddy Park, Burlington, (802) 864-0123; **Essex Junction Education Center,** Essex Junction, (802) 878-1394; **Fenton Chester Ice Arena,** Lyndon, (802) 626-9361; and at the **Collins-Perley Sports Center,** Saint Albans, (802) 527-1202.

RESTAURANTS

Stroll through Burlington's downtown Church Street Marketplace and you'll find all kinds of things to eat at lots of delis, takeout stalls, candy shops, sidewalk cafes, and indoor and outdoor restaurants. Two family favorites are featured below.

● Carbur's

115 Saint Paul St., Burlington, (802) 862-4106. Sun.–Thurs., 11:30–10:30; Fri.–Sat., 11:30–11:30.

Like no other, this zany restaurant is perfect for families. From the moment you glance at the menu (a 16-page newspaper with more than 100 "granwich" combinations) til the moment you wipe your face with the fluffy hand towels, you'll enjoy your meal here. There are close to 200 items on the menu. (The staff recommends you glance at the table of contents, decide what you're in the mood for, and turn to the pages for descriptions.) The favorite items on the kids' menu are the peanut butter, jelly, honey, and sliced banana sandwich or the peanut butter and fluff sandwich (fluff of marshmallow). If these offend your good taste, there's the kids' bowl of tricolored pasta and sauce, minipizza, fish-and-chips, and more.

● Five Spice Café

175 Church St., Burlington, (802) 864-4045. Mon.–Thurs., 11:30–10; Fri.–Sat., 11:30–10:30; Sun., 11–10.

Looking for something more than burgers, fingers, and fries? Treat yourself—and expose the kids—to something a little more exotic. This relaxed and informal restaurant in downtown Burlington is a local favorite, serving a wide variety of Asian cuisine, from Myanmar to Korea, China to Thailand, and more. There are lots of vegetarian dishes on the menu, and plenty of spicy and not-so-spicy offerings, all made to order.

● Henry's Diner

Bank St., Burlington, (802) 862-9010. Daily, 11–10.

A real diner, with real diner food and pocket-pleasing prices. Try the pig-in-a-poke—a hot dog wrapped in bacon and cheese on a grilled roll. The kids will love swinging around on the stools at the counter.

■ Montpelier Area

As you gaze up at Montpelier's elegant, gold-domed capitol building, you'll get a sense that time has passed you by. The nation's smallest state capital is nestled in the valley of the Winooski River and surrounded by rolling green hills. There's a simple elegance and beauty about Montpelier. But it's not at all pretentious; it's a friendly place to be. Your family will feel comfortable running about the town streets or tumbling on the front lawn of the capitol. Best of all, from here you have all of Vermont to explore. You won't need to go far for recreation. The area mountains, forests, lakes, and streams offer great skiing, hiking, biking, swimming, fishing, and sightseeing.

Meander the back roads for a view of rural Vermont's rolling farmlands and tiny villages. Follow the winding mountain road through dramatic Smuggler's Notch or the twisting side road that follows the Lamoille River through scenic covered bridges. If you're looking for something more lively, visit the cosmopolitan, four-season resort town of Stowe.

This is also a great place to learn about how things are made. Visit the Cabot's Visitors Center to see cheese being made. At the Maple Grove Museum, you'll see a maple-sugaring operation. In nearby Barre, you can visit the world's largest granite quarries. Take the tour of the capitol and learn how laws are enacted. And everyone's favorite is a tour of Ben & Jerry's Ice Cream Factory.

● Vermont State House Tour

State St., Montpelier, (802) 828-2228, www.leg.state.vt.us/sthouse.com. July–mid-Oct., Mon.–Fri., 10–3:30; Sat., 11–2:30. Free. **Ages 5 and up.**

On this friendly, 20-minute tour of the State Capitol, visitors get an introduction to how state government works. You'll see old Civil War flags in the governor's ceremonial office and take a look at Representatives' Hall. If you are here when the Legislature is in session (January through April), you can watch the proceedings, although tours are not given at this time. Directly behind the capitol, there's pretty Hubbard Park. This 121-acre network of trails is a favorite place to go for short hikes. Pack a picnic to enjoy en route; there are scenic places along the way to stop.

● Morse Farm Sugar Shack and Woodshed Theater

County Rd. (3 miles from the state capitol), Montpelier, (802) 223-2740 or (800) 242-2740. Year-round, daily, 9–5; summers, 8–8. Free. **All ages.**

The Morse family members have been maple sugar makers for eight generations and they love to tell the story of maple sugar. The best time to visit this rustic sugarhouse is in March or April, when the sap is gathered and transformed into syrup. But you can tour the farm and learn about the process of maple sugaring at all times. You'll watch a short slide show in the unique Woodshed Theater, and get a chance to taste samples of the syrup. Few visitors leave without purchasing the traditional Vermont treat, Sugar on Ice ($2).

● Rock of Ages

Exit 6 off I-89, Barre, (802) 476-3121, www.rockofages.com. May–Oct. (closed July 4th), Mon.–Sat., 8:30–5; Sun., noon–5; mid-Sept.–mid-Oct., Mon.–Sun., 8:30–5. Adults, $4; 6–12, $1.50. **Ages 3 and up.**

You can stand atop an observation platform and look over the world's largest granite quarry. From a 350-foot pinnacle at the 20-acre quarry, you'll watch skilled granite miners carve out huge blocks with machines, then lift up to 150 tons with giant granite derricks towering 150 feet above the quarry's edge. Kids will enjoy the tour to the giant ice wall, created for the lair of Dr. Freeze, one of Batman's rivals. Warner Bros. shot one of its Batman movies at the quarry.

Rock of Ages has been operating since the Civil War, producing granite for buildings and monuments around the world. On the guided walking tour, you'll see and hear (this is a noisy place!) the work being done. You can also take an open-air rail car to the work areas farther uphill. Visit the Craftsman Center on your way out to see how granite is used in final products. Just the sheer size of things here will amaze you.

● Stowe Gondola and Alpine Slide

Mountain Rd., Stowe, (802) 253-7311 or (800) 253-4754, www.stowe.com. Gondola: late June–mid-Oct., daily, 10–5. Adults, $11; 6–12, $7. Slide: late June–Aug., daily, 10–5, weekends only Sept.–Oct. Adults, $9 (1 ride), $29 (5 rides); 6–12, $7 (1 ride), $24 (5 rides). **Ages 2 and up.**

Take a scenic ride to the summit of 4,393-foot Mount Mansfield aboard the enclosed, four-person gondola. Too tame? Hop a ride down on the alpine slide that zips down the face of Spruce Peak. You control your own speed through woods and fields and around the curves.

● Mount Mansfield Auto Road

This 4.5-mile gravel road twists and turns its way to the top of Mount Mansfield. At the top—put on your coats, it's likely to be cold—the 33,881-acre Mount Mansfield State Forest stretches before you. Because of the cold climate, you'll see alpine plants found only in arctic temperatures. (Stay on the marked trails to avoid damaging these fragile plants.)

● Stowe Aviation

RR 2, Morrisville, (802) 888-7845. May–mid-Nov., daily, 8–sunset. Rates vary. **Ages 3 and up.**

For a bird's-eye view of Mount Mansfield, and an experience you won't soon forget, stop by Stowe Aviation and inquire about its airplane, sailplane, and hot-air balloon rides. If you've always wanted to soar above the mountaintops or float sliently across the treetops, this is your chance. Even small children are welcome.

● Stowe Recreation Path

Hiking or biking the Stowe Recreation Path is, perhaps, the best way to get a look at this mountain city. The 5.3-mile, handicapped-accessible path meanders back and forth across the West Branch River and over 11 gracefully arched bridges. It connects and links a number of attractions in Stowe. In winter, it's a popular cross-country tour. The path begins behind the white-steepled Community Church on Main St.

● Ben & Jerry's Ice Cream Factory

Rte. 100 (exit 10 off I-89), Waterbury, (802) 244-5641, www.benjerry.com. Daily, Sept.–Oct., 9–6; Nov.–May, 10–5; June, 9–5; July–Aug., 9–8. Adults, $2; 12 and under, free. Note: There is no ice cream production on Sun. **All ages.**

It's not quite Willy Wonka's Chocolate Factory—but close enough. For ice cream lovers, it's next to heaven. The fun-filled tour takes you through the factory where all that famous Ben & Jerry's ice cream is made. You'll learn the steps it takes to produce the ice cream, and just when you think you can wait no longer, you'll reach the Scoop Shop. (The tour does include free samples of ice cream, but just enough to make you want more.) Enjoy your Chunky Monkey cone (or any of your other favorite flavors) at a picnic table overlooking a pasture of cows with a backdrop of Vermont's rolling Green Mountains. In the summer, Ben & Jerry's offers free outdoor family movies once a week at dusk. Call ahead for a schedule. If you're here in June, inquire about the timing of the Ben & Jerry's annual ice cream festival—lots of fun. In the winter, there are snowshoe tours.

● Cold Hollow Cider Mill

Rte. 100, Waterbury, (802) 244-877, www.coldhollow.com. Daily, 8–6; June–Oct., 8–7. Free. **All ages.**

Cold Hollow is Vermont's largest producer of fresh apple cider. Come to watch the cider being made and to partake of a barnful of homemade Vermont goodies, including fresh pies, doughnuts, jams and jellies, cheeses, hams, syrup, and more.

● Lamoille Valley Railroad

Rte. 100, Railroad Depot, Morrisville, (802) 888-4255, www.silveron.com/ lvrr.com. Mid-July–mid-Oct., daily, 10–1. Rates vary. **Ages 5 and up.**

Take a scenic mountain trip aboard 1920 rail cars. The 60-mile excursion takes about two hours and is very popular during foliage season. Call ahead for reservations.

● Cabot Creamery and Visitors Center

Main St., Cabot, (802) 563-2231 or (800) 837-4261, www.cabotcheese.com. June–Oct., daily, 9–5; winter, Mon.–Sat., 9–4; closed Jan. Adults, $1; under 12, free. **All ages.**

If your family has not yet tired of factory visits, go to the Cabot Creamery, where you'll see all kinds of dairy products being made. The cooperative is the largest in the region, owned by 1,800 farm families. From this small, quiet Vermont village comes award-winning, world-renowned cheddar cheeses. The countryside setting is pleasant, the staff always friendly, and the video presentation interesting. Of course, you won't want to leave without sampling the creamery's excellent products. An annex store is also located in Waterbury, between Ben & Jerry's Ice Cream Factory and Cold Hollow Cider Mill.

● Groton State Forest

Rte. 232, Groton, (802) 584-3822, www.state.vt.us/anr/for/parks. **All ages.**

This is one of the best places in the area for outdoor family recreation. The 25,000-acre area is the state's largest recreational center, covering six towns and including six state parks. There are several lakes in the forest for swimming and boating (you can rent boats and canoes in the park), and more than 40 miles of hiking trails. The summer nature programs are fun for the entire family.

● Elmore State Park

Rte. 12, Lake Elmore, (802) 888-2982, summer; (802) 479-4280, winter; www.vermontstateparks.com. Late May–Columbus Day. **All ages.**

A pleasant park about 25 miles from Stowe, you can swim, rent boats, hike, and walk up a lookout tower for a view of the Green Mountains here.

● Smuggler's Notch

If you can endure the hairpin turns and narrow curves on this steep, winding scenic drive, you'll be rewarded with a dramatic view of Smuggler's Notch. Travel Route 108 just beyond Spruce Peak, where you'll begin your climb to the top of the notch. It is said to have been used as a hideout and, during the War of 1812, as a passageway between Canada and the United States. At the top, there's a small rest area from which to view the gnarled chasm created by glacial waters. You'll be at an elevation of 2,162 feet, where the air begins to cool. On the way down the back side, you'll pass a waterfall before reaching the Smuggler's Notch Resort. The road is closed from late fall until May.

● Smuggler's Notch Resort

Rte. 108, Smuggler's Notch, (802) 644-8851 or (800) 451-8752, www.smuggs.com. The resort specializes in multiday family packages, offering a variety of options. Write or call for free brochures, listing packages and rates.
All ages.

Smuggler's has accumulated just about every "best family resort" award given out. It's always rated at the top of the list for quality and fun. It has everything children want—lots of activities, lots of freedom, and lots of other kids. Drive your car to the resort (the drive itself is beautiful) and park. You'll need to go no farther to find dining, swimming pools, games, sledding, ice skating, movies, arcades, saunas, hot tubs, tennis, parties, bonfires, parades, and top-notch resort lodging. The really nice part? While the kids are off having fun (everything is within walking distance), the parents are free to do the same. Smuggler's takes care of your kids, and all the details, so you can relax and have fun, too.

In the winter, there's plenty of skiing on 60 trails across three intercon-nected mountains. Most of the terrain is beginner to intermediate, but black-diamond skiers will find a handful of runs to get the adrenaline going, including the first triple black-diamond run in the East. In a good snow season, Snuffy's Trail opens, connecting Smuggler's with the Stowe ski area. (Interchangeable tickets are available.) Kids have their own Learning and Fun Park. Kids are Smuggler's specialty. The smallest children do their first skiing indoors on the carpeted ski ramp. They get the feel of sliding on skis before they head outdoors for their first 20- to 30-minute lesson. Children, ages 3 to 5, learn to ski in Discovery Dynamos; 6- to 12-year-olds ski or snowboard in Adventure Rangers; and teens, 13-17, have their own program, Mountain Explorers. Everyone graduates with the appropriate degree—bachelor of skiing or snowboarding for novices; master's for intermediates; and a Ph.D. for those who've conquered the black diamonds.

In summer, a variety of nature, hiking, and exploration programs and activities are offered.

● Sugarbush Resort

RR 1, Warren, (802) 583-2381 or (800) 53SUGAR, www.sugarbush.com. Lift tickets: adults, $57; 13–18, $55; 6–12, $37; 6 and under, free. Microbears (3), $70/day; Minibears (4–6), $70/day; Sugarbears (7–12), $80/day. Child care (6 wks.–6 yrs.), $52/day. Programs include instruction, *lift tickets, lunch, and rental equipment. Rates are for weekend and holidays; special discount packages are available.* **All ages.**

With the recent infusion of improvements, Sugarbush has become one of the premier ski resorts in the East. The world's longest, fastest quad chair now travels from the Mount Ellen area in the north to Lincoln Peak area in the south. Skiers and riders have more than 4,000 acres to explore, including 115 trails. Experts will find some of the best runs in the region, including the legendary Castlerock runs—bumpy, gnarly, steep, narrow, unpredictable. But there's plenty for intermediate and beginner skiers, too: lots of blue-square cruisers, plenty of pretty glades, and a separate learning area for beginners. Small children will enjoy the Sugarbush Forest, a special kids' area with a covered bridge, obstacles, and artificial bumps and rolls. (Adults must be accompanied by a child to enter.) Riders encounter rolls, waves, hits, and pipes on several trails. At the Mount Ellen area, the Wizard Bus blasts out tunes all day on Sid. At Lincoln Peak, riders can get their thrills on Nancy, a half-mile pipe.

The best part about the Sugarbush expansion is that it managed to maintain most of its character. Off the slope, vacationing families will find the quintessential Vermont countryside and quaint villages. Lots of pretty country inns, rustic taverns, and traditional charm surround the resort.

● Stowe Mountain Resort

Mountain Rd., Stowe, (802) 253-3000 or (800) 253-4SKI, www.stowe.com. Lift tickets: adults, $58; 6–12, $38; 5 and under, free. Children's ski programs (3–14), $85/day; child care, $68/day. Rates are for weekend and holidays; special discount packages are available. **All ages.**

You'll get real spoiled skiing at Stowe. It makes skiing as easy, convenient, and comfortable as possible. You'll find some of the finest on-mountain services. And you'll find some great skiing—big-time skiing. Experts can tackle a 2,360-foot vertical drop, offered in a variety of terrain. The intermediate runs at Stowe ski long and hard all the way down, and beginners have an entire mountain area to explore. Stowe has often been cited as one of the best vacation ski areas in the country, and its reputation draws plenty of trendy, lively crowds. In recent years, Stowe has actively targeted the family business, offering special family packages and top-notch day care and children's ski programs.

● Bolton Valley Ski Area

Bolton Valley Access Rd., off Rte. 2, Bolton, (802) 434-3444, www.boltonvalleyvt.com. Lift tickets: adults, $44/day; 7–17, $30/day. Mountain Explorer (4–6), $70/day; child care (6 wks.–6 yrs.), $45/day. **All ages.**

The friendly atmosphere of Bolton Valley is especially appealing to families. Tucked away high in the mountains of northern Vermont, Bolton offers two mountains to ski with 46 trails. This is a relaxing, effortless skiing experience, with gentle cruising runs and an emphasis on the slow and easy. Bolton loves families and goes that extra mile to welcome them. It was one of the first ski resorts in America to offer a full-service day care and instruction program for kids. Bolton is an all-inclusive, self-contained resort, offering dining, recreational facilities, and nightlife (making it even more pleasant for vacationing families). An added plus: night skiing.

¶ RESTAURANTS

Stowe, Mad River Valley, and Montpelier are all well known for a variety of eateries, from elegant to casual. In addition, the major ski resorts offer a wide selection of family-friendly restaurants. Here are a few of the most popular:

● The Shed

1859 Mountain Access Rd., Stowe, (802) 253-4364. Daily, 11:30–10.

This brew pub/restaurant is a perennial favorite; more families probably eat here than at any other restaurant in Stowe. It serves breakfast, lunch, and dinner—fast, friendly, and predictable. This place goes through a lot of barbequed baby back ribs and mighty Shed burgers (the best in town).

● J. Morgan's

100 State St., Montpelier, (802) 223-5252. Daily, 7 A.M.–10 P.M.

This classic 1990s-style steak house is casual and friendly serving up hefty portions at reasonable prices. Steaks are its specialty, but there's plenty of pasta, poultry, and seafood dishes, too. Model trains circle the dining room and keep young ones amused while you're waiting for your meal. Check out the special night buffets, like Fajita Thursdays.

● Hunger Mountain Café

Stone Cutters Way, Montpelier, (802) 223-8000, www.hungermtncoop.com. Daily, 8-8.

If you're looking for something healthy and quick, stop in at this small café overlooking the Winooski River. There are plenty of vegetarian dishes and a great salad and deli bar (with nonvegetarian choices, too). Everything's ultrafresh and prepared on-site.

● About Thyme Cafe

40 State St., Montpelier, (802) 223-0427. Mon.–Fri., 7–7:30; Sat., 9–3. Closed Sun.

This gourmet takeout/deli is the perfect antidote for a hungry crew. The sandwiches come on thick-sliced home-baked breads; the salads—an impressive array is always offered—are fresh, creative, and great tasting. Breakfast is homemade muffins, waffles, fresh fruit, and more. At dinner, there's a selection of daily entrees, reflecting the cafe's international flavor.

■ Northern Vermont

Some call it the Northeast Kingdom. Some call it the quiet corner. Some call it the last vestige left of "real" Vermont. Whatever you call it, you won't argue about its scenic, unspoiled beauty. The Vermont territory closest to the Canadian frontier offers the most variety of terrain and range of topography, from rolling hills to high mountaintops to wide, flat rural regions. There are places where you'll be able to see for miles, unbroken by the marks of civilization, and others where you'll find surprising pockets of lively culture, interesting museums, and frolicking activity. Your options for travel are just as diverse, from a hot-air balloon or gondola, a car, train, or mountain bike, to canoe or afoot. Poking about the vast rural lands, you'll discover some unexpected pleasures, such as an extraordinary natural history museum, a challenging ski resort, and a hidden mountain lake to enjoy.

● Fairbanks Museum and Planetarium
*1302 Main St., St. Johnsbury, (802) 748-2372,
www.fairbanksmuseum.org. Museum: year-round, daily, Mon.–Sat., 9–5;
Sun., 1–5. Adults, $5; 5–17, $3. Planetarium shows: Sat.–Sun, 1:30 show.
Admission, $3.* **All ages.**

This must-see museum was founded in 1891 by Colonel Franklin Fairbanks, a naturalist and born collector of wildlife. The building itself, a red sandstone Victorian with a 30-foot barrel-vaulted oak ceiling, is something to see. But you'll be more dazzled by the exhibits inside.

You'll be nose to nose with stuffed polar bears, wild boars, alligators, penguins, bison, foxes, moose, opossums, an armadillo, and more. You'll be surrounded by an unbelievable collection of mounted birds and mammals peeking out through holes, from under limbs, and from behind glass in environmental displays. The eclectic collection also includes Indian artifacts, dolls, photomicrographs of tiny snowflakes, dinosaur bones, Fairbanks scales, and lots of folklore . . . from doll furniture made by Mark Twain to colorful mosaic tapestries depicting the Revolutionary War— made out of bugs!

Be sure to visit the lower level, where you'll see one of the country's oldest continuously operated weather stations and get a glimpse of regional weather broadcasts being prepared. If you have time, travel to the stars at one of the ongoing planetarium shows, offered daily in July and August and on weekends the rest of the year.

● Maple Grove Maple Factory

1052 Portland St., St. Johnsbury, (802) 748-5141, www.maplegrove.com.
Museum: May–Oct., daily 9–5. Factory tours: year-round, Mon.–Fri., 8–4.
Adults, $1; under 12, free. **All ages.**

Vermont is maple syrup country, and you can't leave the area without at least one visit to where it is being made. Maple Grove is one of the world's largest. You'll learn how the sap is gathered—a tap is driven into the tree and a tin bucket hung from it. When the bucket is full, it's emptied into a vat, transported to a shack, and boiled down. The Maple Grove Museum re-creates this process. Housed in an original sugar shack, the museum includes the displays of both antique and modern sugar-making equipment. You'll also see how maple syrup is converted into candy (and get a free sample) on the tour.

● Bread & Puppet Museum

Rte. 22, off Rte. 16, Glover, (802) 525-3031. June–Oct., daily, 10–5.
Free. **All ages.**

Show us a kid who doesn't like a puppet or can resist the lure of full-size masks, and we'll show you a kid who hasn't seen them. As you travel the Northeast Kingdom and find yourself near the tiny town of Glover (just off I-91), stop by this enthralling museum. Housed in a 130-year-old barn, the museum shows off hundreds of puppets that have been used in past performances. On Sunday afternoons during the summer, there are special activities and workshops (like papier mache or bread making) offered.

● Lake Willoughby

Near Westmore. **All ages.**

Okay, you've been traveling through the northern region of Vermont, gazing at the gorgeous scenery, rolling hills, and rural pastures. Nice, but now it's time to get out of the car for fresh air, a little exercise, maybe even a swim. This is the place. Although a bit off the major highways, Lake Willoughby is worth the extra time it takes to get there. This is a 600-foot deep lake carved by ancient glaciers, tucked between two mountain ranges. Secluded and relatively undiscovered, it has great views and hiking trails, too.

● Jay Peak Ski Resort

Rte. 242, Jay, (802) 988-2611 or (800) 451-4449, www.jaypeakresort.com.
Adults, $52/day; juniors, $38/day. KinderSki (3–5), $30/half day sessions,
rentals extra; Jay Explorers (5–10), MiniRiders (7–10), Mountain Adventures
(10–15), and Mountain Expeditions (16–19), $47/day, rentals extra; child
care (2–7), $40; under 2, $8/hour. **All ages.**

Ready to get away from it all? Want to escape the southern crowds? Longing for some skiing on real, natural snow? Consider a trip up to Jay Peak.

This area is famous for receiving the greatest natural snowfall of any eastern resort. This is a relatively small resort, unpretentious and relaxed. You'll find 2,153 vertical feet of skiing, 40 diverse trails and glades, and numerous slopeside accommodations and amenities. Jay Peak welcomes families and offers unique programs for all ages and abilities. Family specials are offered, including "children stay free" programs and complimentary day and evening child care.

¶¶ RESTAURANTS

● Miss Newport Diner

E. Main St., Newport, (802) 334-7742. Mon.–Fri., 5:30 A.M.–1 P.M.; Sat., 6–noon; Sun., 7–noon.

This authentic 1947 dining car has been a favorite watering hole for many a year offering homemade, old-fashioned food at yesteryear prices. It's a great place for families. Hot turkey sandwiches, real mashed potatoes and gravy, fresh-baked breads, burgers and fries—even Jell-O.

● Miss Vermont Diner

Memorial Dr., Saint Johnsbury, (802) 748-9751. Mon.–Thurs., 6 A.M.– 8 P.M.; Fri.–Sat., 6 A.M.–9 P.M.; Sun., 7 A.M.–8 P.M.

This is the quintessential cheap-eats restaurant—and the kids will love the swivel seats. Clean, bright, and cheery, Miss Vermont serves up huge portions of homemade food at old-fashioned prices. You'll get jumbo eggs, thick slices of toast, and chunks of ham, or for lunch, a fresh, flaky haddock sandwich or thick, marinated chicken breast with roasted potatoes and cole slaw. At dinner, you're likely to find roast turkey, homemade soups and chowders, and fresh pies for dessert.

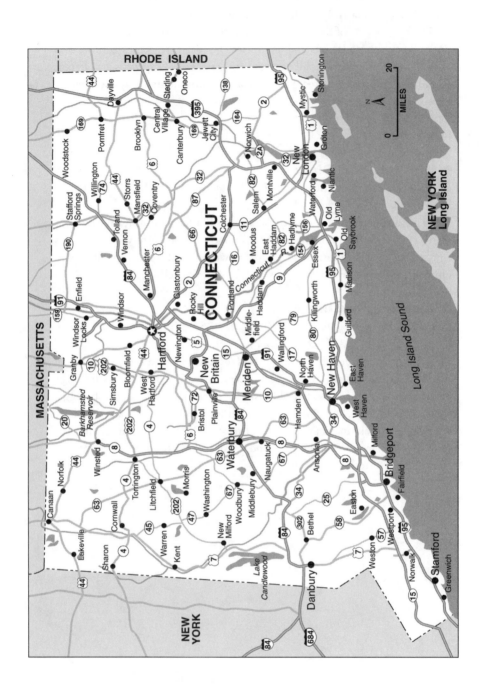

Connecticut

■ Mystic and the Shoreline

The Mystic area is tremendously popular with families, and for good reason: It boasts two awesome attractions, Mystic Seaport and Mystic Aquarium. Downtown Mystic—sliced down the middle by the Mystic River—has a seafaring charm all its own. Here you can participate in the town's most popular spectator sport, watching boats go by. You may not have a choice regarding this activity: The bridge goes up in the middle of downtown each hour from 7:15 A.M. to 7:15 P.M. (at a quarter past the hour) in summer.

Neighboring towns, including Stonington, Norwich, Groton, and New London, offer appealing attractions, too, such as the Science Center of Eastern Connecticut, the Nautilus Submarine Museum, and Ocean Beach Park.

Where there's lots of fun and activity, you can bet there'll be crowds. This is especially true of Mystic Seaport. So arrive early, and be prepared to spend some time waiting in lines if you visit in summertime. Or plan your trip to Mystic in the less-hectic spring or fall. Another possibility: Consider Christmastime. Mystic makes the most of it. Mystic Seaport holds Children's Victorian Christmas Tours, and downtown Mystic re-creates the spirit of a 19th-century Christmas, complete with carolers and yuletide refreshments.

For more information, contact Mystic & More at (860) 444-2206 or (800) TO ENJOY, or visit their website at www.mysticmore.com. For a Connecticut vacation guide and a statewide calendar of events, call (800) CT BOUND or visit www.ctbound.org.

● Mystic Seaport
75 Greenmanville Rd., exit 90 off I-95, Mystic, (860) 572-0711 or (888) 9 SEAPORT, www.mysticseaport.org. Year-round, daily, except Christmas Day. Open daily, 9–5; winter hours, 9–4. Adults, $16; 6–12, $8; age 5 and under, free. **All ages.**

This is the attraction that put Mystic on the map. Mystic Seaport is America's largest maritime museum, a 17-acre site boasting tall ships and a re-created 19th-century seaport village. If you're visiting Mystic Seaport in summer, stop at the gate for your copy of *Kids Today,* a chronological guide to all the fun stuff scheduled for kids. This might include a session on tying sailor's knots or helping set sails, and special planetarium shows. Small fry will adore the quaint Children's Museum (despite the long wait to enter it in high season). A treasure trove of 19th-century toys and games awaits inside; outside, on the green, children can try rolling a hoop or walking on stilts.

Your family could spend a whole day at Mystic Seaport and not be bored. For starters, you'll want to explore the seaport's historic homes and village, where role-players demonstrate such 19th-century skills as boatbuilding and wood carving. Climb aboard the 1841 whaleship, *Charles W. Morgan,* and you'll see the magnificent result of one of the lenghthiest resoration projects in the seaport's history. The *Morgan* is the last of the wooden whaleships. You won't want to miss a river cruise on the *Sabino,* the last coal-fired steamboat in America. The *Sabino* departs hourly for 30-minute cruises, from mid-May to mid-October.

A great way to end your day at Mystic Seaport: Give your legs a rest and take a ride on a horse-drawn carriage at Chubb's Wharf. Children will enjoy clip-clopping around the seaport village, and you'll get one last look at this special place before heading back to the present.

● Mystic Aquarium

55 Coogan Blvd., exit 90 off I-95, Mystic, (860) 572-5955, www.mysticaquarium.org. July 1–Labor Day, 9–6; rest of year, daily, 9–5. Closed Thanksgiving, Christmas, and New Year's Day. Adults, $15; 3–12, $10; ages 2 and under, free. **All ages.**

More than 3,500 marine animals live here, and the best part about this aquarium is that you can get really close to most of them. The aquarium houses 34 exhibits, with every kind of fish and sea creature you can imagine, including a blue lobster and a giant Pacific octopus. Plus, this is the only place in New England to see beluga whales.

Most kids are fascinated by sharks, and they'll love exchanging menacing stares with them, and Darth Vader-ish sting rays, in the Coral Reef exhibit, the aquarium's centerpiece. There's even a special step up, alongside the tanks, so that toddlers won't miss anything. Don't miss the antics of Coco, Tabor, and Surfer, three California sea lions who star in the show at the aquarium's Marine Theater. You can even take a virtual journey to the bottom of the sea. Plan to spend a couple of hours here to see it all.

● Denison Pequotsepos Nature Center

109 Pequotsepos Rd., Mystic, (860) 536-1216, www.dpnc.org. Open Mon.– Sat., 9–5; Sun., 10–4. Adults, $6; children under 12, $4. **Ages 3 and up.**

If you're worn out from fighting the crowds at Mystic Seaport and Mystic Aquarium, this peaceful nature center could provide the perfect respite. You'll find more than 200 acres of wildlife sanctuary and seven miles of hiking trails, with ponds, fields, and lowland and upland woods to explore. The Nature Center maintains a year-round trailside museum, where you'll learn about birds, insects, reptiles, and pond and marine life. The nonprofit center is dedicated to environmental awareness. Special programs are offered on weekends throughout the year; call ahead. Nearby, the Denison Homestead (1717) showcases heirlooms from several generations of the Denisons, one of Connecticut's first families.

● Mystic Carousel & Fun Center

Route 27, Mystic, (860) 572-9949. Open daily, 10–10. Free. Fee charged for activities. **All ages.**

For rainy-day fun, you can't beat it—this is one of the largest indoor fun spots in the state. Attractions include a working carousel, a ball pit, rides (check out the cute piggie ride), and games for little ones. An indoor/outdoor flea market operates here on Sundays.

● Scenic Stroll: Downtown Mystic's Bascule Bridge

You really can't miss this famous bridge; it runs right through the center of town, rising so that sailboats can navigate the Mystic River without snapping their masts off. Watch the boat traffic, wander into a shop or two, perhaps stopping for a meal at a riverfront eatery. One choice: Mystic Pizza, the setting for the movie of the same name, featuring an unknown actress named Julia Roberts.

● Old Lighthouse Museum

7 Water St., Stonington Village, (860) 535-1440. May and June, Sept. and Oct., Tues.–Sun., 10–5; July and Aug., daily, 10–5. Adults, $4; 6–12, $2. **Ages 3 and up.**

Drive out to the Lighthouse Museum on Stonington Point (a short trip from downtown Mystic on Rte. 1) and you can see three states at the same time: Fisher's Island, New York, to the south; Watch Hill, Rhode Island, to the east; and Connecticut, under your feet. Stonington Lighthouse was operated as a lighthouse until 1889; now it's a museum, housing a collection of whaling and fishing gear, swords, and firearms and, in the children's room, toys and a dollhouse. To most kids, the best part is just being inside a lighthouse.

● Rocky Neck State Park

Rte. 156, exit 72 off I-95, Niantic, (860) 739-5471. Daily, 8 A.M.– sunset. Parking fee. **All ages.**

The best feature of this park is a half-mile-long crescent beach. Enjoy hiking, fishing, picnicking, a boardwalk, and concessions.

● Children's Museum of Southeastern Connecticut

409 Main St. (Rte. 156), Niantic, (860) 691-1111, www.childmuseumsect.org. Tues.–Sat., 9:30–4:30; Sun., 12–5. Open Mon. in summer and on Connecticut school holidays. $4 per person; under 2, free. **Ages 1–12.**

"We all vis-it a yellow submarine." Kids from 1 to 12 will find plenty to engage, delight, and challenge them here, including a pipe organ to play;

an Amtrak train exhibit, "Kidsville," a kid-size town; and a real, 21-foot yellow submarine. Themed areas focus on science, the arts, safety and health, and culture and history. Play stations feature computers, Brio trains, Legos, and more. Live performances are often featured, including folksingers, storytellers, jugglers, magicians, and dancers.

● Millstone Discovery Center
278 Main St., exit 74 off I-95, Niantic, (860) 691-4670, (800) 428-4234. Year-round, Mon.–Fri., 10–4. Free. **Ages 3 and up.**

The Millstone Nuclear Power Station offers exhibits on nuclear energy and other energy sources, computer games, multimedia shows, bicycle generators, an aquarium, and marine touch tanks. Outside, stroll the Millstone Nature Trail, a one-mile walking path through woodlands and lagoons with views of native wildlife.

● Putts Up Dock Mini Golf
One Chelsea Harbor Dr., Norwich, (860) 886-PUTT. June–Sept., daily, 10–10; weekends only, spring and fall. Open weather permitting. **Ages 3 and up.**

While there are several miniature golf courses in southeastern Connecticut, this one claims to be New England's most challenging course. Features include an actual spouting volcano, a misty cave under a waterfall, and a play-through boathouse. Bumper boats, too.

● Norwich Navigators Minor League Baseball
Sen. Thomas W. Dodd Memorial Stadium, 14 Stott Ave., Norwich; (860) 887-7962 or 800-64-GATOR. Apr.–Sept. Tickets, $3.50–$9. **All ages.**

Catch all the action (and a fly ball, if you're lucky) of the New York Yankee's AA minor league affiliate team.

● Maple Breeze Park
Rte. 2, exit 92 off I-95, Pawacatuck (near Stonington), (860) 599-1232. May and June, weekends, 10–10; July–Labor Day, daily, 10–10. **Ages 3 and up.**

Here's just the place for the kids to expend some pent-up energy after a too-long road trip or museum session. This amusement park offers a water slide, bumper boats, and minigolf.

● Seal Watching and Eagle Watching
Wildlife watchers will want to check out these intriguing adventures, offered by the Sunbeam Fleet at Captain John's Dock in Waterford. From mid-March to mid-May, take a three-hour cruise aboard the *Sunbeam Express*

to visit harbor seals, departing from Waterford. In February and March, bald eagles are plentiful, and the boat captain knows the best places to go to see them. Trips depart from The Dock restaurant in Old Saybrook. For information, call (860) 443-7259 or visit www.sunbeamfleet.com.

● Historic Ship *Nautilus* and Submarine Force Museum

1 Crystal Lake Rd., exit 86 off I-95, Groton, (800) 343-0079 (recorded information), (860) 694-3174. Open mid-May–Oct., Wed.–Mon., 9–5; Tues., 1–5; Nov.–mid-May, Wed.–Mon., 9–4. Free. **Ages 3 and up.**

Many a child has fashioned a periscope out of a cardboard tube and played submarine. At the Nautilus Museum—part of the U.S. Naval Submarine Base—kids can peer through real periscopes and tour a real submarine, the USS *Nautilus.* The world's first nuclear-powered vessel, the *Nautilus* was commissioned into the U.S. Navy in 1954. Once on board (you might have to wait in line, as only 60 people are allowed aboard at one time), you'll carry an electronic wand that activates narration about each area of the submarine. You'll see the navigation center, the radar room, the attack center, and watch films about submarines past and present. Elsewhere in the museum, there are working periscopes, an authentic submarine control room, and several midget submarines.

● Project Oceanology Marine Studies Cruise

UConn/Avery Point, 1084 Shennecossett Rd., Groton, (860) 445-9007 or (800) 364-8472 (outside Connecticut). Mid-June–Labor Day, daily, 10 and 1. Seal watch cruise, Feb.–Mar., weekends. Please call for current rates. Reservations recommended. **Ages 5 and up.**

Climb aboard a 55-foot Enviro-Lab research vessel for a cruise you won't forget. Marine scientists and instructors will teach you how to use oceanographic instruments, help pull a trawl net, test seawater, identify lobsters, crabs, and fish, and measure lobsters. You'll also help take core samples of mud and sand (wonderfully messy work) from the bottom of the ocean and examine them. Best for kids ages 5 and up, the trips last two and a half hours. Project Oceanology is operated by a nonprofit association of public and private schools and colleges in Connecticut, Massachusetts, Rhode Island, and New York.

● Fort Griswold Battlefield State Park

Monument St., exit 85 off I-95, Groton, (860) 445-1729. Park open year-round. Museum and monument: Memorial Day–Labor Day, daily, 10–5; Labor Day–Columbus Day, weekends only, 10–5. Free. **All ages.**

This 17-acre park was the scene of a massacre in 1781. Benedict Arnold led an attack by the British forces, taking the fort and burning Groton and

New London. On the hilltop near Fort Griswold, a 135-foot monument dedicated to the victims of the massacre bears their names. Today you'll find the spot a considerably more pleasant place, with beautiful views of the Thames River and Fisher's Island from the memorial tower. Bring a picnic.

● Bluff Point Coastal Reserve

Depot Rd., off Rte. 1, Groton, (860) 424-3200. Open daily, 8 A.M. to sunset. **All ages.**

Located between Mystic and Groton on Long Island Sound, this unspoiled stretch of shoreline is a great place to take a hike or nature walk, have a picnic, or fish from the shore. Take to the trails on cross-country skis in winter.

● Lyman Allyn Dolls & Toys

165 State St., New London, (860) 437-1947. Open Tues.–Sat., 1–5. Adults, $4; 6–16, $3; 2–5, $2; under 2, free. Family fee, $10. **Ages 5 and up.**

This oversize dollhouse offers themed sections that tie into the history of southeastern Connecticut, and lots of touchable dolls and toys.

● Science Center of Eastern Connecticut

33 Gallows Lane off Williams St., exit 83 off I-95, New London, (860) 442-0391. Open Tues.–Sat., 10–6; Sun., 1–5. Adults, $6; under 12, $4. **Ages 3 and up.**

Discover scientific principles through play. Explore a jungle of microbes as a "microscope master," play with sound and light equipment, high-tech puzzles, touchable marine life, and more.

● Connecticut College Arboretum

270 Mohegan Ave. (Rte. 32), New London, (860) 439-5020. Open daily, dawn–dusk. Tours offered Sun., May–Oct., 2 P.M. Free. **All ages.**

Cool, fragrant, and beautiful, this 750-acre property features hiking trails through a variety of natural ecosystems, and landscape plants from around the world.

● U.S. Coast Guard Academy

15 Mohegan Ave. and Rte. 32, exit 83 off I-95, New London, (860) 444-8270. Visitors Pavilion: May–Oct., daily, 10–5. Tall ship Eagle open Fri.–Sun. when in port. Free. **Ages 3 and up.**

There are two advantages to visiting the academy in spring and fall: You might see the cadet corps on dress parade (usually on Friday afternoons), and you can board the 295-foot training barque, *Eagle,* Fridays through Sundays from 1 to 4 P.M. when it's in port. (Call first to avoid disappointment.) The Visitors Pavilion features a multimedia show depicting cadet life, while the museum at Waersbe Hall displays historical nautical items.

● Ocean Beach Park

1225 Ocean Ave., exits 75N and 83S off I-95, New London, (860) 447-3031, (800) 510-SAND. Memorial Day–Labor Day, 9 A.M.–11 P.M. Parking, $8. Fee for activities. **All ages.**

You'll have a rollicking good time at Ocean Beach Park, one of the most popular recreation areas on Long Island Sound. In addition to a wide sandy beach, you'll find a boardwalk, a café, a pool, a triple water slide, minigolf, a playground, and an arcade. The adorable 1979 carousel features 30 horses, and elephant, donkeys, and reindeer. The kids won't leave willingly.

● Harkness Memorial State Park

275 Great Neck Rd., Waterford, (860) 443-5725. Year-round, 8 A.M.– sunset. Mansion open Tues.–Sun., 10–3, for free guided tours. Parking fee in season. **All ages.**

Once a private summer estate, this grand Italian-style villa is set on 116 acres on Long Island Sound. Grown-ups will enjoy poking around the 42-room mansion and formal gardens; kids will like beachcombing, picnicking, and fishing.

● Garde Arts Center

325 State St., New London, box office (860) 444-7373, (888) ON-GARDE. **Ages 5 and up.**

The historic Garde Theatre, the region's last remaining vaudeville/ cinema house, offers a family theater series among its program of performances. Call for a schedule and showtimes.

● Mohegan Park

Judd Rd., Rtes. 2 and 32, Norwich, (860) 823-3759. Year-round, daily, 9 A.M.–sunset. Swimming, June 1–Labor Day. Free. **All ages.**

In season, don your suits for swimming in Mohegan Park Lake. A beautiful rose garden, honoring World War II dead, is in full bloom from late June to early July. Other features include hiking trails, fishing, picnic areas, and a playground.

● Slater Memorial Museum

108 Crescent St., Norwich, (860) 887-2505. Sept.–June, Tues.–Fri., 9–4; Sat. and Sun., 1–4. July and Aug., Tues.–Sun., 1–4. Closed holidays. Adults, $3; under 12, free. **Ages 5 and up.**

Visit the Norwich Free Academy with your kids for a look at the Slater Museum complex's Joseph P. Gualtieri Children's Gallery. Appointed with work that appeals to children, the gallery features authentic African masks, a parade of circus figures carved in wood, sculpture and painting, and porcelain dolls. The Romanesque Slater Memorial Museum houses sculpture; Egyptian, Greek, Roman, and Native American artifacts; American primitives; and African and Oriental art. Kids will be inspired to get out the Play-doh and modeling clay once they get home.

● Mashantucket Pequot Museum & Research Center

110 Pequot Trail (Rte. 2), Mashantucket, (800) 411-9671. Open daily, Memorial Day–Labor Day, 10–7 (last admission at 6 P.M.). Winter hours: Wed.–Mon. (closed Tues.), 10–6 (last admission at 5 P.M.). Adults, $12; 6–15, $8; under 6, free. **Ages 3 and up.**

In the shadows of the mammoth Foxwoods Resort Casino, this museum features permanent exhibits highlighting the native people and natural history of southern New England. Descend into a glacial crevasse from 18,000 years ago; walk through a 1550 Pequot village peopled by 51 lifelike figures. Interpretive films and interactive exhibits add to the experience.

● Boat Cruises

Windjammer cruises and sightseeing ferry trips are popular ways to explore the Connecticut coastline and Long Island Sound. Several companies offer trips; here's a sampling. **Mystic Whaler Cruises** offers one-, two-, three-, and five-day cruises (including a three-day pirate cruise) on a re-created 110-foot New England schooner. Kids ages 10 and up are welcome on the longer cruises, while kids 5 to 10 are appropriate on day sails and evening cruises. Trips are offered from Memorial Day through October. Call (800) 697-8420 or visit www.mysticwhaler.com for details. The *Mystic Whaler* departs from Whaler's Wharf in Mystic. The **Sea Pony,** a 36-foot lobster boat, cruises New London harbor, Fisher's Island Sound, and other ports, out of New London. Trips run daily from mid-May through October, and November to mid-May on a limited schedule. Call (860) 443-0795. **Mystic Seaport** offers a half-hour sail aboard the *Breck Marshall,* a 24-foot gaff-rigged vessel. And don't forget the steamboat *Sabino,* also at Mystic Seaport. Both trips are offered from mid-May to mid-October. Call (860) 572-5315 or (888) 9-SEAPORT.

● B. F. Clyde's Cider Mill

129 N. Stonington Rd., Mystic, (860) 536-3354. June–Dec., daily, 9–6. Free. **All ages.**

Looking for a way to mark the arrival of autumn? Visit the last steam-powered cider mill in New England and see the cider pressing operation in action. Of course, you'll want to take home a jug of cider and a fresh apple pie.

● Sugarhouses

Show your kids that some things are still done the old-fashioned way; maple sugaring, for instance. There are several places in southeastern Connecticut where you can watch sap being collected and boiled to make maple syrup and candy. The season typically runs from early February to late March. Call ahead for a boiling schedule. Places to visit include: **Bureau's Sugarhouse,** 60 Rowland Rd., Old Lyme, (860) 434-5787; and **Hannon's Sugarhouse,** 707 Exeter Rd., Lebanon, (860) 642-4566. For a complete list of Connecticut's Maple Sugar Houses, send a self-addressed stamped envelope to the Connecticut Department of Agriculture, Marketing Division, 765 Asylum Ave., Hartford, CT 06105, (860) 713-2503.

 RESTAURANTS

● Abbott's Lobster in the Rough

117 Pearl St., (2.5 miles south of Mystic off Rte. 215), Noank, (860) 536-7719, www.abbotts-lobster.com. Memorial Day–Labor Day, daily, 12–9; Labor Day–Columbus Day and first Fri. in May to Memorial Day, Fri.–Sun. only, 12–7.

This waterfront, eat-in-the-rough restaurant has won fans far and wide, including the folks at *Gourmet* magazine. Eat at a picnic table outdoors, where you might see lobster boats bringing in their catch, or grab a table indoors if the weather is foul. The bill of fare includes boiled lobster, hot lobster rolls (excellent), shrimp, clams, mussels—and hot dogs. Ice cream, too.

● Kitchen Little

135 Greenmanville Ave., Mystic, (860) 536-2122. Open for breakfast and lunch daily, 6 A.M.–2 P.M.

Don't blink or you'll miss this tiny little place, locally famous for great breakfasts. The regulars get their own personalized coffee mugs.

● Steak Loft

27 Coogan Blvd., Olde Mystick Village, Mystic; (860) 536-2661, www.steakloftmystic.com. for lunch and dinner, daily 11:30–9:30; Fri. and Sat., 11:30–10:30.

Shamelessly touristy, but big and noisy (perfect for rambunctious small fry), this steak place features a varied menu, fun drink concoctions, and a kids' menu featuring the usual suspects.

■ Hartford and Central Connecticut

Hartford calls itself "The Insurance Capital of the World," not "vacation wonderland." However, the city of Hartford—Connecticut's second largest—offers several attractions that will delight visiting families. Museums are the main event, with a wonderful hands-on science museum, the Mark Twain house, a fire museum, and an art museum with a super program for kids. Hartford also serves as a good base for exploring other sites in central Connecticut. They're varied and loaded with kid appeal, ranging from a state park with real dinosaur tracks to an aviation museum.

Looking for a cheap, easy way to get around Hartford? Here's a tip. Try a Scooter. Brightly painted Scooter buses zip around downtown Hartford to East Hartford from early morning to early evening, Monday through Friday. Call (860) 247-5329 for more information.

For visitor information, contact Greater Hartford Tourism at (800) 793-4480 or visit www.enjoyhartford.com.

● State Capitol and Legislative Office Building

210 Capitol Ave., exit 48 off I-84 or exit 29A off I-91, Hartford, (860) 240-0222. Free 1-hour tours Mon.–Fri., (except holidays), 9:15–1:15; July and Aug., Mon.–Fri., 9:15–2:15. Open Sat., Apr.–Oct., 10:15–2:15. Free. **Ages 5 and up.**

Visiting a state capitol building makes history lessons come alive. Connecticut's state executive offices and legislative chambers are housed in an impressive gold-domed structure built in 1897. See bullet-riddled battle flags and more on a guided hour-long tour.

● Mark Twain House

351 Farmington Ave., exit 46 off I-84, Hartford, (860) 493-6411. Year-round. Hour-long guided tours Mon. and Wed.–Sat., 9:30–4; and Sun., 12–4. Daily, Memorial Day–Columbus Day and month of Dec., Mon.–Sat., 9:30–4; Sun., 12–4. Closed Tues., rest of year. Open Monday holidays. Adults, $9.50; 6–12, $5. **Ages 6 and up.**

Twain's bright red Victorian Gothic house reflects the eccentricity of its owner. For example, Twain slept with his head at the foot of his bed so he could admire the ornate Venetian headboard, and he kept his telephone in the closet because it drove him crazy. You'll see the study where Twain wrote about Tom Sawyer and Huckleberry Finn—and took billiards breaks at the full-size pool table. Visitors soon realize that the author enjoyed drinking, smoking, and billiards at least as much as he liked writing. The Twain House is part of Nook Farm, an intellectual community formed in the mid-19th century by Twain and cultural luminaries Isabella Beecher Hooker, who was a women's rights activist; William Gillette, a playwright; author Harriet Beecher Stowe; and others.

● Harriet Beecher Stowe House

Nook Farm, 77 Forest St., Hartford, (860) 525-9258, www.hartnet.org/ Stowe. Year-round. Open Tues.–Sat., 9:30–4:30; Sun, 12–4:30. Open Mon., Memorial Day–Columbus Day and month of Dec. Adults, $6.50; 6– 16, $2.75. (Includes Katherine S. Day House.) **Ages 6 and up.**

Adjacent to the Mark Twain House is the restored Victorian cottage of *Uncle Tom's Cabin* author Harriet Beecher Stowe. Most of Stowe's original furniture is here, including the small desk where she wrote 33 books.

● Science Center of Connecticut

950 Trout Brook Dr., exit 43 off I-84, W. Hartford, (860) 231-2824. Tues. and Wed., Fri. and Sat., 10–5; Thurs., 10–8; Sun., 12–5. Open Mon., 10–4, in July and Aug. and school vacations. Adults, $6; 3–15, $5; under 3, free. Additional fee for planetarium and laser shows. **All ages.**

From kinkajoos to computers, this science center offers lots to see and do. Explore the mysteries of the solar system and the planetarium, shake hands with a starfish in the touch tank (part of a 25-tank aquarium), and learn by doing in the Discovery Room, where there's an echo tunnel and a giant 30-foot walk-in kaleidoscope. The center also has a computer laboratory, and a small indoor/outdoor zoo with 50 species of animals. Zoo inhabitants include a kinkajoo, a mountain lion, a raccoon, an eagle, ferrets, owls, and snakes.

● Hartford Whalers Hockey

Hartford Civic Center, 242 Trumbull St., Hartford, (860) 728-6637 or (800) WHALERS. Season: Oct.–May; games start at 7 P.M. Ticket prices range from $19–$42. **All ages.**

We New Englanders do love our hockey. Watch Connecticut's home team face off against NHL opponents at the Hartford Civic Center, downtown. Call for a schedule of home games.

● Travelers Tower

700 Main St., 1 Tower Sq., Hartford, (860) 277-4208. Tours: mid-May– late Oct., Mon.–Fri., 10–3. Free. **Ages 3 and up.**

At 527 feet, this building—home of Travelers Insurance Company—is one of the tallest in New England. Climb up 72 steps to the observation deck for a panoramic view of the city.

● Bushnell Park Carousel

Jewel St., Capitol Area exit off I-84, Hartford. Park, (860) 585-5411. May–mid-Oct., Tues.–Sun., 11–5. Carousel rides, $.50. **All ages.**

What child doesn't adore a carousel? And the one at Bushnell Park, built in 1914, is something special, with 48 hand-carved horses and ornate lovers' chariots. Also on the grounds are two Farragut cannons. Located in the center of the city, within steps of the capitol, this 37-acre municipal park is a great place to people-watch or just relax under a tree. Grab a hot dog and a juice from a pushcart vendor.

● Elizabeth Park

915 Prospect Ave. at Asylum Ave., exit 44 off I-84, Hartford, (860) 722-6514. Open daily, dawn–dusk. Greenhouse open weekdays, 10–4. Free. **All ages.**

An urban oasis, this park features gorgeous rose gardens (more than 14,000 plants of 90 varieties), in full bloom late June through early July. Lots of space to play; lawn bowling, perhaps? You can go ice skating in winter.

● Wadsworth Atheneum

600 Main St., Hartford, (860) 278-2670, www.wadsworthanteneum.org. Tues.–Sun., 11–5. Open first Thurs. of each month until 8 P.M. Adults, $7; children, $3; under 6, free. Free to individuals all day Thurs. and before noon on Sat. Tours on Thurs., 1 P.M., and Sat. and Sun., 2 P.M. **Ages 3 and up.**

America's first public art museum (more than 150 years old), the Atheneum features paintings, sculpture, furniture, costumes, bronzes, firearms, and—yikes!—mummies. Items date from prehistory to the present. For kids, the staff has prepared specials tours on cassette tapes, designed to make art more accessible. The tapes combine fun (treasure-hunt-type questions and clues about the works) and facts (design concepts, how art is made). Wearing the headphones makes kids feel involved, not merely dragged along. Adults can plug in, too. On your way out, don't miss Alexander Calder's huge stegosaurus exhibit.

● New England Air Museum

Bradley International Airport, 10 mi. north of Hartford on Rte. 75, off I-91, Windsor Locks, (860) 623-3305, www.neam.org. Year-round, daily, 10–5. Adults, $7; 6–11, $3.50. **Ages 3 and up.**

Older kids who think airplanes are neat will enjoy taking a look at the aircraft exhibited here. More than 80 examples are on display, including bombers, fighters, helicopters, and a modern commercial jet. All have been meticulously restored. Children (and adults) will get a kick out of playing with the flight simulator; a museum staffer will supervise you. Aviation-related films are shown several times a day.

● Connecticut Trolley Museum

58 North Rd., Rte. 140, exit 45 off I-91, E. Windsor, (860) 627-6540. Daily, Memorial Day–Labor Day, Wed.–Sat., 11–5; Sun., 12–5. Labor Day–late Nov., Sat., 10-5; Sun., 12–5. Late Nov.–Dec., Sat., 10–4; Sun., 12–4; Jan.–Mar., closed. Apr.–Memorial Day, Sat., 10–5; Sun., 12–5. Special events for Halloween and Christmas season. Adults, $6; 6–18, $3; under 5, free. Includes admission to Connecticut Fire Museum. **All ages.**

Take a 3.5-mile ride through scenic New England countryside on an antique trolley car. Cars date from 1894 to 1949. The Halloween special, "Rails to the Dark Side," is a howlin' hoot, but too scary for small fry.

● Connecticut Fire Museum

58 North Rd., Rte. 140, exit 45 off I-91, E. Windsor, (860) 623-4732. July and Aug., Wed.–Sat., 10–4; Sun., 12–5. May–June, Sat., 10–5; Sun., 12–5. Sept. and Oct., Sat.–Sun., 12–5. Adults, $6; 6–12, $3. Includes admission to Connecticut Trolley Museum. **Ages 3 and up.**

It's 100 years of choo-choo history, with old-time fire trucks and models dating from 1850 to 1950.

● Phelps Homestead

800 Hopmeadow St., Rte. 10, Simsbury, (860) 658-2500. May–Oct., Tues.–Sat., 10–4 P.M.; Nov.–Apr.: call for schedule. Adults, $6; 2–17, $3.50. **Ages 5 and up.**

This complex represents three centuries of local history. Older children will enjoy the Phelps House (1771, formerly a hotel and tavern), the one-room schoolhouse (1741), and the stocks and pillory. Also on the grounds is an herb garden, a 1683 meetinghouse, and a Victorian carriage house. Guided tours, from 1 to 3 P.M., are lively enough for most kids to tolerate.

● Talcott Mountain State Park and Heublein Tower

Rte. 185 at Bloomfield-Simsbury town line, (860) 242-1158. Grounds open year-round; tower open May–Aug., Thurs.–Sun, 10–5; Sept.–Oct., daily, 10–5. **Ages 3 and up.**

For the best view in the state, take a 1.5-mile hike to 165-foot Heublein Tower in Talcott Mountain State Park. Once the summer home of the Heublein family, the tower offers panoramic views of four states and the Farmington River.

● Stratton Brook State Park

Rte. 305, Simsbury. 8–sunset. **All ages.**

Have bikes, will travel? This small park is best known for its extensive bike trail, winding through white pines and over brooks. Hiking, swimming, fishing, and, come winter, cross-country skiing and ice skating are other possibilities here. There are boathouses and a concession stand, too.

● Flamig Farm

7 Shingle Mill Rd., W. Simsbury, (860) 658-5070. Open daily, 9–5. Admission $2. **All ages.**

From April through November, meet the barnyard creatures at this family-owned petting farm. They also offer horse-drawn hayrides, sleigh rides, and carriage rides, and pony rides for the kids, weather permitting.

● Northwest Park and Nature Center

145 Lang Rd., exit 38 off I-91, Windsor, (860) 285-1886. Year-round. Park: open dawn–dusk; nature center: Mon.–Sat., 9–5. Free. **All ages.**

A Native American teepee, a weather station, and an animal barn are the highlights here.

● Wethersfield Nature Center

30 Greenfield St., Wethersfield, (860) 529-7421. Call for current schedule. Free. **All ages.**

This 120-acre nature park is home to mammals, reptiles, and birds; plus, there's a log cabin and several hands-on science displays.

● Old Newgate Prison and Copper Mine

115 Newgate Rd., exit 40 off I-91, E. Granby, (860) 566-3005 or (860) 653-3563. Mid-May–Oct., Wed.–Sun., 10–4:30. Adults, $4; 6–17, $2. **Ages 6 and up.**

This colonial copper mine served as a Revolutionary War prison—the nation's first state prison—housing British sympathizers. This site served as Connecticut's state prison until 1827. Prowl the dungeonlike chambers to see where the prisoners ate and slept, and hear of their attempted escapes. You can take a tunnel stairway down to the celebrated Simsbury copper mine and walk the narrow mine paths. The mine was worked from 1707 to 1773. Later the Newgate prisoners were kept in the mine at night. It's an unusual glimpse of American history. Today the crumbling jail walls set against a backdrop of foothills and valley forests appear picturesque. The picnic area on the grounds is a pleasant setting. If you have time, take the Newgate Wildlife Trail from the parking lot. The six-mile self-guided nature trail winds around Newgate Pond.

● Lutz Children's Museum

247 S. Main St., Manchester, (860) 643-0949. Tues. and Wed., 12–5; Thurs. and Fri., 9:30–5; Sat. and Sun., 12–5. Admission $3. **Ages 1–12.**

Don't look, just touch . . . what is it? Yes, deer antlers. The "feel boxes" are just one of many exhibits children can get their hands on here. This little charmer is chock-full of fun possibilities: Children can put on life jackets and steer a boat through a storm, climb aboard the Alphabet Express, or put on their own puppet show. The museum also has a live animal exhibit. Many of the animals are part of a rehabilitation and release program, making this an ever-changing exhibit. Nearby, the museum's Oak Grove Nature Center offers self-guided trails through woods, swamps, a hemlock grove, and over a covered bridge. Little ones will want to run—not walk—to the outdoor playscape.

● Wickham Park

1329 W. Middle Tpke., exit 60 off I-84, Manchester, (860) 528-0856. Apr.–Oct., daily, 9:30–dusk. Parking fee. **All ages.**

An aviary, a small zoo, and a 1927 log cabin are the featured attractions at this unusual park, formerly a private estate. The 250-acre site has beautifully manicured grounds with ornamental gardens, toddler play areas, and picnicking facilities. Cross-country skiing in winter.

● Old Tolland Jail Museum & Warden's Home

Town Green, exit 68 off I-84, Tolland, (860) 875-3544. Hours limited; phone ahead. Donation suggested. **Ages 3 and up.**

This site on Tolland Green housed prisoners until 1968; now visitors can go into the jail's stone and iron cells (built in 1856) and tour the country house connected to it where the warden and his family lived. Refurbished in 1990, the warden's home contains farm tools and home furnishings. Across the street, the Hicks-Stearns Museum is worth a visit. This colonial-tavern-turned-Victorian-summer-cottage houses family heirlooms (including toys) and souvenirs of European travel. A Victorian Christmas open house and a summer lawn concert series are local traditions.

● Daniel Benton Homestead

Metcalf Rd., exit 68 off I-84, Tolland, (860) 872-8673. Hours limited; phone ahead. Donations accepted. **Ages 5 and up.**

This center-chimney colonial house, the oldest house in Tolland (constructed in 1720) housed Hessian prisoners during the Revolutionary War. Perhaps the best feature of this historic house is its romantic-yet-spooky ghost story. The guide tells it well, and locals swear it's true. Visit and decide for yourself whether or not the Benton house is haunted.

● Dinosaur State Park

400 West St., exit 23 off I-91, Rocky Hill, (860) 529-8423, www.dinosaurstatepark.org. Park: year-round, daily, 9–4:30. Free. Exhibit Center: year-round, Tues.–Sun., 9–4:30. Adults, $3; 6–17, $1. Track casting permitted May–Oct., daily, 9–3:30. Please call for instructions. **All ages.**

Imagine finding real, 185-million-year-old (Jurassic Period) dinosaur tracks! That's what happened here in 1966 during excavation for a new state building. The fossil tracks, three-toed impressions ranging from 10 to 16 inches in length, are now protected in a large geodesic dome. What type of dinosaur made these tracks? Nobody knows for sure, but you'll see a full-size replica of the scientists' best guess, a dilophosaurus, on display here. Bring 10 pounds of plaster of paris and one-quarter cup of vegetable oil, and make your own cast of a dinosaur footprint. The park also has two miles of nature trails (pick up a trail map at the office—no pets or bikes, please), an arboretum, and a gift shop.

● Connecticut Audubon Center at Glastonbury

1361 Main St., exit 7 off Rte. 2, Glastonbury, (860) 633-8402. Tues.– Fri., 1–5; Sat., 10–5; Sun., 1–4. Free. Discovery Room: $1 per person for nonmembers. **Ages 3 and up.**

"Green" tots (and aren't they all, these days?) will love connecting with nature here. The center has a small exhibit area and walking trails through a wooded park, adjacent to the Connecticut River. Best for kids up to the third grade or so, the hands-on Discovery Room offers do-it-yourself craft projects (make footprints with ink pads, for example), a skull collection, a puppet theater, and live animals. Other exhibits feature native flora and fauna and the Connecticut River ecosystem. Wear walking shoes and plan to hike the nature trails in 48-acre Earle Park; maps are available at the center.

● Mill Pond Falls

Garfield St., Newington, (860) 666-4661. Year-round. **All ages.**

Once surrounded by Indian wigwams, this area is now a lovely town park with its own natural waterfall. Enjoy a picnic here, as ducks paddle across the pond.

● New Britain Youth Museum

30 High St., New Britain, (860) 225-3020. July–Aug., Mon.–Fri., 1–5. Sept.–June, Tues.–Fri., 1–5; Sat., 10–4. Donations requested. **Ages 2–10.**

A doll collection, a miniature circus display, multicultural exhibits, and Americana are featured here, along with changing displays and hands-on activities.

● New Britain Youth Museum at Hungerford Park

*191 Farmington Ave., exit 35 off I-84, Berlin, (860) 827-9064. Tues.–
Fri., 1–5: Sat., 10–5. Summer hours: Tues.–Fri., 11–5, Sat., 10–5. Closed
holidays. Animal demonstrations in summer: weekdays, 2 P.M., and Sat., 11,
1, and 3. Adults, $2; 2–17, $1.* **All ages.**

Take a walk on Connecticut's wild side here, where there's plenty to see
and do at a family-friendly price. Meet the hedgehogs, ferrets, reptiles, and
other curious creatures at the indoor exhibits, then head outdoors to wander
the nature trails and view a pond from an observation station. Exhibits explore
Connecticut's geology and natural history, science, and agriculture. Live
animal demonstrations add to the fun.

● New Britain Museum of American Art

*56 Lexington St., New Britain, (860) 229-0257. Tues., Thurs., and Fri.,
1–5; Sat., 10–5; Sun., 12–5, Wed., 12–7. Adults, $4; students, $2; under
12, free.* **Ages 5 and up.**

American art from 1740 to the present is the focus here, with artists such
as Sargent, Benton, Whistler, and Wyeth represented among the 5,000
works. They've discovered a cool way to get small fry to look at the "big
picture"—a dress-up corner, featuring costumes copied from those worn in
famous portraits. Props include a bird cage and a baby doll. Then, kids look
for their "twin" in upstairs galleries.

● New Britain Rock Cats Minor League Baseball

*Willow Brook Park Complex, S. Main St., New Britain, (860) 224-8383.
Season runs Apr.–Sept. Tickets, $2–$10.* **All ages.**

With a name like the Rock Cats, how could they not be totally cool? Da
Cats are the AA Eastern affiliate of the Minnesota Twins. About 71 home
games are scheduled in the team's nifty $9.25 million stadium.

● Connecticut Wolves Soccer

*Willow Brook Park Complex, S. Main St., New Britain, (860) 223-0710.
Season runs Apr.–Sept. Tickets $8.* **All ages.**

Soccer is so hot these days, it's a thrill to watch the pros do it. Here's a
chance to watch a Division II men's pro soccer team in action.

● Stanley Quarter Park

*Stanley St., New Britain, (860) 826-3360. Park: open year-round. Rides:
mid-June–mid-Aug. Free admittance; fee for activities.* **All ages.**

Paddleboats, "funyaks" (sit-upon kayaks), a fishing pond, playground,
and skateboard park make this a lively scene. The pond is transformed into
an ice rink in winter.

● Tomasso Nature Park

Granger Ln., Rte. 72, Plainville, (860) 747-6022. Mid-Mar.–mid-Nov., daily, dawn–dusk. Free. **All ages.**

This 11-acre wetland area is home to a bounty of plant and animal life, including nearly 600 painted turtles. Nature trails, bridges, grassy knolls, and observation areas offer opportunities to view them.

● Barker Character, Comic & Cartoon Museum

1188 Highland Ave. (Rte. 10), Cheshire, (203) 699-3822. Tues.–Sat., 11–5. Free. **Ages 3 and up.**

Take a trip down Memory Lane when you visit Herb and Gloria Barker's 40,000-piece collection, including 350 lunch boxes! Popeye, Olive Oyl, and other cartoon and comic strip faves are featured among displays of memorabilia here, plus a slew of advertising characters you thought you'd forgotten. Besides the "don't touch" displays, there are child-friendly elements like a kiddie playhouse, storybook stage, Western corral, and Snow White's wishing well.

● Hot-Air Ballooning

Ever wonder what it would be like to hover over rivers and valleys in a hot-air balloon? Central Connecticut is home to several balloon companies, which specialize in sunrise or sunset flights (always followed by a champagne toast). This is a truly unbeatable way to view fall foliage. Most companies are happy to bring along children, even infants, with adult passengers, but it is quite a splurge—typically, $125 or more per person. Talk with your balloon pilot about group discounts. Some companies to try: **Emerald City Balloon Co.,** Manchester, (860) 647-8581; **Kat Balloons,** Farmington, (860) 678-7921; and **Berkshire Balloons,** Southington, (203) 250-8441.

● Fruit Picking

The pickings are far from slim in central Connecticut. Here are some possibilities: **Pickin' Patch,** Nod Rd., Avon, (860) 677-9552 (fruits and veggies in season; hayrides to pumpkin patch in Oct.); **Rose's Berry Farm,** 295 Matson Hill Rd., S. Glastonbury, (860) 633-7467 (strawberries, blueberries, pumpkins, and raspberries); and **Hickory Hill Orchards,** 3515 S. Meridan Rd., Cheshire, (203) 272-3824 (free hayrides to pick apples, peaches, pears, and pumpkins). For a complete directory, contact the Connecticut Department of Agriculture, Marketing Division, at (860) 713-2503.

RESTAURANTS

● City Steam Brewery Cafe
942 Main St., Hartford, (860) 525-1600. Mon.–Thurs. 11:30–10:30; Fri. and Sat. 12–12; Sun., 12–9:30.

Located in a historic building, this seven-level restaurant features innovative, upscale pub food at great prices; kids' menu, too.

● Shady Glen Dairy
840 East Middle Tpke., Manchester, (860) 649-4245. Mon–Thurs. 7 A.M.– 10 P.M.; Fri. and Sat., 7 A.M.–11 P.M.; Sun. 10:30–10.

This dairy bar is locally famous for great cheeseburgers and ice cream (made on the premises). Unless you're a cardiologist, what's not to like?

● Rein's N.Y. Style Deli Restaurant
435 Hartford Tpke., Vernon, (860) 875-1344. Open every day, 7 A.M.– midnight.

You've seen the bumper stickers for Rein's "famous" deli; one visit and you'll know why folks travel from miles away to nosh on Rein's traditional deli fare. Think huge, crisp garlic pickles, mounds of hot pastrami, and delectable New York-style cheesecake. There are about a million different deli sandwich combos, and bagels with cream cheese, so kids will always find something that pleases.

■ Essex and the Connecticut River Valley

A visit to charming, postcard-pretty Essex is like a trip to the past. Stroll down tree-lined Main Street, and you'll see gracious old colonial homes where sea captains and shipbuilders lived with their families, centuries ago. Once an important shipbuilding town, Essex is where America's first warship, the *Oliver Cromwell,* was built. Residents are happy to tell visitors that their little town crops up frequently on lists of "best small towns." It's easy to see why.

Stand at the lower reaches of the Connecticut River and you can almost picture an old side-wheeler riverboat churning up the river on its voyage from New York to Hartford. Although schooners have been replaced by pleasure craft and riverboats have given way to automobiles, it's possible for visitors to get a taste of the river's glory days. You can even take a ride on an authentic riverboat. Combine your cruise with a steam-train ride, and you'll get a delightful tour of the Connecticut River Valley. For more river lore, visit the River Museum. Or for something completely different, tour the fantasy castle-turned-state-park or bob along the Farmington River in a giant rubber doughnut.

For visitor information, contact the Connecticut River Valley & Shoreline Visitors Council at (860) 347-0028 or (800) 486-3346 or visit www.cttourism.org.

● Essex Steam Train and Riverboat Ride

Valley Railroad Co., exit 3 off Rte. 9, Essex, (860) 767-0103, (800) ESSEX-TRAIN, www.essexsteamtrain.com. May–Dec. Schedules change depending on season; check locally for exact departure times. Every train connects with the riverboat except the last train of the day. No boat service with Christmas train rides. Adults, $18.50 (train only, $10.50); 3–11, $9.50 (train only, $5.50). **Ages 3 and up.**

There's an old-fashioned magic about a steam train ride. Kids find it exciting—the smoke billowing and whistles blasting—while adults find it relaxing. This attraction combines a Valley Railroad steam-train ride from Essex to Chester with an hour-long riverboat cruise; the whole trip lasts about two and a half hours. The scenery is beautiful and includes rolling hills, flowering meadows, the Connecticut River shoreline, and local attractions such as Gillette Castle and the Goodspeed Opera House. Passengers transfer from steam train to riverboat at Deep River Landing, boarding the *Becky Thatcher* or *Silver Star* vessels. Bring a picnic to enjoy on the riverboat, if you wish. Off-season, visit in fall for an unforgettable view of autumn foliage. Or come at Christmastime, when you'll share the train with Santa, Mrs. Claus, and their elves.

● Connecticut River Museum

67 Main St., Essex, (860) 767-8269. Year-round, Tues.–Sun., 10–5. Adults, $4; 6–12, $2. **Ages 3 and up.**

At the foot of Main Street in Essex, where the old steamboat dock has been restored, you'll find a full-size replica of America's first submarine. Constructed in 1775, *American Turtle* was clumsy and ineffective against the British; still, it's interesting to look at. The River Museum also houses ship models, navigational instruments, shipbuilding displays, and special exhibits.

● Amy's Udder Joy Exotic Animal Farm

27 North Rd., exit 27 off I-91, Cromwell, (860) 635-3924. Open Apr.– Labor Day, Tues.–Fri., 11–5; Sat. and Sun., 11–5; Labor Day–Oct., Sat. and Sun., 11–4. Open weather permitting. Admission $3; under 1, free. **All ages.**

More than 50 species of exotic, rare, native, and endangered animals are on display at this recreational and educational facility. Take a self-guided tour; watch animals at feeding time.

● Kidcity Children's Museum

119 Washington St., Middletown, (860) 347-0495. Sun.–Tues., 11–5; Wed.–Sat., 9–5. Adults, $2; children, $5; under 1, free. **Ages 6 mos.–10.**

Climb to the top of a clipper ship, be the mayor of Main Street, and star in your own movie at this engaging children's museum.

● Gillette Castle State Park

River Rd., off Rte. 82, Hadlyme, (860) 526-2336. Castle: Memorial Day– Columbus Day, daily, 10–5. Columbus Day–Sun. before Christmas, week- ends, 10–4. Park: year-round, 8–7. Castle: admission fee charged. Park only: free. Note: Property is currently undergoing renovation; call before you visit for updated information. **All ages.**

Your kids may not know who actor William Gillette is—for that matter, you might not remember him, either. But visiting his 24-room fantasy castle is a fun way to get acquainted. Best known for his role as Sherlock Holmes, Gillette was a rather eccentric character himself, and the house is full of creative mechanical touches. It's also full of feline-themed artifacts; Gillette shared the castle with 15 cats during his residence from 1919 to 1937. After his death, the estate was designated a state park. Now, you can picnic here, take a hike, go fishing, or, for a real adventure, rent a canoe here and camp at Selden State Park, a 528-acre island near Gillette Castle that's accessible only by water.

● Goodspeed Opera House

Rte. 82, East Haddam, (860) 873-8668, www.goodspeed.org. Tours offered on Mon., 1–3 P.M., and Sat., 11–1:30, June–Oct. (with some exceptions; call to verify). Performances: Wed.–Fri., 8 P.M., Sat. at 4 and 9 P.M.; Sun. at 2 and 6:30 P.M.; Wed. matinee at 2:30. Season: Apr.–Dec. Tour only: Adults, $3; under 12, $2. **Ages 6 and up.**

This wonderful Victorian gingerbread structure was a popular riverside theater from the late 1800s to the 1920s. Nearly demolished in the 1950s, this unique landmark was rescued, restored, and now features musical theater productions. Take a behind-the-scenes tour of the opera house or take in a show. Older children who enjoy the performing arts will find a visit to the Goodspeed a real treat. Three musicals are performed here each season.

● Devil's Hopyard State Park

Three mi. north of junction of Rtes. 82 and 156, E. Haddam, (860) 873- 8566. Open mid-Apr.–Sept. **All ages.**

This scenic area offers 15 miles of hiking trails—one steep side, one gentler side. Hike along the stream to Chapman Falls, a 60-foot cascade. Fish in the trout-stocked stream, enjoy a picnic, or bring camping gear and spend the night. Beware: Legend has it that the devil lived here. That should inspire some interesting ghost stories around the campfire. . . .

● Haddam Meadows State Park
Rte. 154, Haddam, (860) 566-2304. Daily, 8–sunset. **All ages.**

Fly a kite, toss a Frisbee, or just stretch your legs; this 175-acre meadowland (the river floodplain) offers lots of room to roam from sunup to sundown, along with fishing, picnicking, boating, and, in winter, cross-country skiing.

Special note: While traveling through Moodus, Connecticut, listen for the Moodus Noises. These strange, subterranean rumblings have been variously explained as the threats of evil spirits (according to Indian legend), witches in the mountain (according to early white settlers), and emanations from pearls (according to a British scientist, who disappeared while researching the subject). Modern scientists believe the sounds are caused by movement along intersecting fractures in the earth's crust.

● Canoeing/Tubing

Exploring the serpentine Farmington River is a splendid way to spend a day. Canoeing and tubing are great ways to go with kids. **Farmington River Tubing,** (860) 693-6465 or (860) 739-0791, offers tube rentals, PFDs (personal flotation devices), and a ride back to your starting point. Season runs from Memorial Day to Labor Day. Kids must be ages 10 and over, 4 feet 5 inches tall or more, and weigh at least 50 pounds. Excursion starts at Satan's Kingdom State Recreation Area, Rte. 44, New Hartford. **Huck Finn Adventures** offers rental canoes (with extra seats for families) for paddling down a tranquil, wooded stretch of the Farmington. Some kids like to bring fishing gear to troll along while they ride. Shuttle service is available, too. Offered spring through fall. Call (860) 693-0385 for information.

● Fruit Picking

One of the busiest spots in the area is **Lyman Orchards,** Rtes. 147 and 157 in Middlefield, (860) 349-1566; they offer pick-your-own produce in more than 100 varieties, from June through October, including sweet corn, raspberries, pears, squash, pumpkins, apples, peaches, and strawberries in season. The farm store sells produce and baked goods and hosts special events in summer and fall. Check out the corn maze, open in September and October. For a complete directory of pick-your-own farms, roadside stands, and cider mills, call the Connecticut Department of Agriculture, Marketing Division, at (860) 713-2503.

● Chatfield Hollow State Park

Exit 63 off I-95, .5 mi. west of Killingworth Center on Rte. 80,
Killingworth, (860) 566-2304. Daily, 8–sunset. **All ages.**

An old waterwheel, a covered bridge, a pond, a brook, and red pine groves make this a truly exceptional park. Swim in Schreeder Pond, walk the nature trail along the brook, or hike the well-marked trails (a 4.5-mile loop passes points of interest). The pond is stocked with trout. There's ice skating in winter, weather permitting. The park is part of Cockaponset State Forest, where you'll find additional hiking trails, cross-country skiing, and snowmobiling in winter.

● Wadsworth Falls State Park

Rte. 157, Middlefield, (860) 566-2304. Daily, 8–sunset. **All ages.**

A beautiful waterfall with a scenic overlook is the most outstanding feature here. Also enjoy fishing, hiking, swimming, picnicking, and, in springtime, colorful laurel. Go iceskating and cross-country skiing here in winter.

● Hurd State Park

Rte. 151, E. Hampton, (860) 566-2304. Daily, 8–sunset. **All ages.**

Located on the east bank of the Connecticut River, this park features several hiking trails—some through the woods, some along the river, and some to high points with scenic views. Pack your gear and fish in the Connecticut River. Go cross-country skiing here in winter.

● Hammonasset Beach State Park

Exit 62 South off I-95, Madison, (203) 245-2785. Year-round, 8–sunset.
Parking fees daily, Memorial Day–Labor Day; fee weekends only, mid-Apr.–
Memorial Day and Labor Day–Oct.; off-season, free. **All ages.**

A two-mile stretch of sandy beach is the main attraction at this popular recreation area, Connecticut's largest (900 acres!) shoreline park. Swim in Long Island Sound, fish, or hike along marked trails through a salt marsh. This is a great spot for birding; more than 220 species fly through. There's also a nature center with interpretive programs, camping and boating, picnic areas, a boardwalk, and concessions.

● Boat Cruises

In addition to the riverboat ride previously described, several other cruise options are available. A pleasant day trip, if your kids can handle a leisurely boat ride: Cruise from Haddam to the ports of Sag Harbor and Greenport, New York, along the Connecticut River and across Long Island Sound aboard the *Camelot*. Explore for three hours, then return to Haddam. The trip lasts all day and is offered from June through Labor Day. Contact **Camelot Cruises** in Haddam; (860) 345-8591. Or take a narrated cruise along Connecticut's beaches and shoreline to Duck Island aboard the **Aunt Polly.** Departing out of Old Saybrook, the cruises run from June through Labor Day. Call (860) 526-4954 for details. Several cruise companies operate out of Branford, a coastal town on the western edge of this region. The **Volsunga IV** makes 45-minute tours of the Thimble Islands daily, with lively narration featuring pirate legends (kids love this, of course). Trips run from May to October; call (203) 481-3345. Also based in Branford, the **Sea Mist** offers daily, 45-minute sightseeing cruises of the Thimble Islands, including foliage cruises, and seal- and bird-watching cruises. Trips run from April through October; call (203) 488-8905. For an expanded list of tour boat operators, call (800) CT BOUND and ask for the *Connecticut Vacation Guide.*

 RESTAURANTS

Many of the restaurants in this area of Connecticut are found in fine country inns—lovely, but not the best of choices if you're dining with small fry. Your best bet is to head to Old Saybrook, where you'll find fast-food franchises and some casual family restaurants. Here are some restaurants—low-key and not touristy—favored by local parents.

● Pat's Kountry Kitchen

70 E. Mill Rock Rd., Old Saybrook, (860) 388-4784. Summer hours: daily, 7 A.M.–9 P.M. Winter hours: Thurs.–Tues., 7 A.M.–9 P.M.

There's a little bit of everything on the menu here: steaks, Italian specialties, seafood, soups, sandwiches. It's a quick breakfast stop, and great for early birds since it opens at seven. Children's lunch and dinner menus offer the usual burgers, dogs, and grilled cheese. The setting is casual; the daily specials are good and cheap. "Nothing changes much here," one of the waitpeople told us, and that's just the way the regulars like it.

● Hale-n-Hearty

38 Town St., East Haddam, (860) 873-2640. Open Mon.–Fri., 11:30 A.M.– midnight.

This old-fashioned, country-style restaurant offers steak, seafood, and pasta dishes, but what comes flying out of the kitchen most frequently? Retro classics like pot pies and meat loaf dinners, and, from the kiddie side of the menu, boomlet faves like chicken tenders and pasta.

● Oliver's Taverne

124 Westbrook Rd., Essex, (860) 767-2633, www.oliverstavern.com. Mon.– Thurs., 11:30–10:30; Fri. and Sat., 11:30–11; Sun. brunch, 11:30–4.

A bit fancier than the other two recommendations, this "eating and drinking emporium" (the tavern's words) is a big, multilevel barn-wood affair with lots of wood, brass, and cozy fireplaces. Blackboard specials include everything from fried clams to pot roast to baked stuffed lobster; prices are moderate.

■ Greater New Haven

The next time you lick a lollipop, munch on a burger, fish with a steel fishhook, or pop open a bottle with a corkscrew, thank the folks of New Haven. Those items were invented here, along with the first steamboat and rubber footwear. As if that's not enough "firsts," rumor has it that the first American pizza pie was tossed here, at Frank Pepe Pizzeria Napoletana. They still make a great pizza. The city also takes credit for creating the sports of football (dreamed up by a Yale rugby coach) and Frisbee throwing (inspired by Yalies tossing Mrs. Frisbee's pie plates into the air). Of course, New Haven residents have a couple of other reasons to boast. The most obvious is Yale University, one of the country's oldest and most respected colleges. Yale's outstanding museums are not to be missed, especially the Peabody Museum of Natural History.

New Haven is also a center for regional theater; the most famous is the Yale Repertory Theater, where many top-flight actors have honed their skills, and the Long Wharf Theater, birthplace of several Broadway plays over the years. Whether you're in town for museum hopping, theatergoing, or attending the Harvard-Yale game, you'll realize that New Haven is a college town—and more.

Don't forget your lollipop.

For information, contact Greater New Haven Convention & Visitors Bureau at (203) 777-8550 or (800) 332-STAY or visit www.newhavencvb.org.

● Peabody Museum of Natural History

Yale University, 170 Whitney Ave., exit 3 off I-91, New Haven, (203) 432-5050; www.peabody.yale.edu. Mon.–Sat., 10–5; Sun. and holidays, 12–5. Adults, $5; 3–15, $3. Free hours Mon.–Fri., 3–5 P.M. **Ages 3 and up.**

You don't have to know a pterodactyl from a triceratops to be impressed by this museum, one of the largest and oldest natural history museums in the United States. A massive mural provides a dramatic backdrop for life-size prehistoric creatures in the Hall of Dinosaurs. Youngsters will be amazed, and delighted, by the sight of the 67-foot brontosaurus skeleton, the first brontosaurus skeleton found in North America. Another amazing specimen here is a 75-million-year-old turtle. Elsewhere the natural history of our planet is traced through mineralogy, meteorites, and zoology. The Peabody is one of the best museums of its kind in the country. Don't miss it.

● The Only Game in Town

275 Valley Service Rd., exit 11N/12S off I-91, North Haven, (203) 239-GOLF. Apr.–mid-Oct., daily, weather permitting. Please call for current hours. Free admission; activities charges. **Ages 5 and up.**

Need to get physical after being on your best behavior in New Haven's museums and theaters? This is the place—it's one of those mega (20 acres!) sports complexes that attract older kids and sports-happy moms and dads. Miniature golf, a driving range, indoor batting cages—it's all here, waiting for you to test your prowess.

● New Haven Colony Historical Society

114 Whitney Ave., New Haven, (203) 562-4183. Tues.–Fri., 10–5; Sat. and Sun., 2–5. Closed Sun. in July and Aug. and on major holidays. Adults, $2; 6–16, $1. **Ages 6 and up.**

Local antiques are the focus here, including beloved playthings of New Haven children who lived 300 years ago. In addition to the antique dolls and toys, older children may enjoy seeing the photographs of old New Haven and comparing them to the city of today. Other noteworthy items are Eli Whitney's cotton gin and the sign from Benedict Arnold's drugstore on Chapel Street.

● Shore Line Trolley Museum

17 River Rd., exit 51E off I-91, East Haven, (203) 467-6927, ww.bera.org. Memorial Day–Labor Day, daily, 10:30–4:30. May, Sept., Oct. and late Nov.–late Dec., Sat. and Sun., 10–4:30. Rest of Nov. and Apr., Sun. only, 10:30–4:30. Adults, $6; 2–15, $3. **All ages.**

Kid-appeal is guaranteed here, where the highlight is a three-mile ride on a vintage 1911 trolley car. Adults will get a chuckle out of the old advertising slicks posted in the cars. Nearly 100 classic trolley cars are on view, many antique, from the United States and Canada. If you dare, sign up for a special Terrifying Trolley Trip at Halloween. Wear a suitably bewitching costume. Santa rides the trolley during the holiday season.

● Shubert Performing Arts Center

247 College St., New Haven, (203) 562-5666 or (800) 228-6622, www.shubert.com. Season: Sept.–June. Ticket prices vary. **Ages 5 and up.**

They call this 1914-era theater "the birthplace of the nation's greatest hits," since *Oklahoma!*, *South Pacific*, and *The Sound of Music*, all premiered here. Current productions include Broadway favorites, dance, music, and family entertainment. Take a backstage tour and see the famous graffiti wall, covered with autographs of the stars. Free tours are offered from September to June; reservations are required. Call (203) 624-1825 during business hours, Monday through Friday, to book a tour.

● New Haven Ravens Minor League Baseball

Yale Field, 252 Derby Ave. (Rte. 34), West Haven, (800) RAVENS-1, www.ravens.com. Season: Apr.–Sept. Tickets, $2–$15. **All ages.**

Come to the "Ravens Nest" at beautifully refurbished Yale Field (built in 1927) to see New Haven's boys of summer pick apart their opponents. The Ravens, an AA affiliate of the St. Louis Cardinals, play 70 or so home games a season.

● Yale University Student Guided Tours

149 Elm St., New Haven, (203) 432-2300. Guided tours daily, Mon.–Fri. at 10:30 and 2; Sat. and Sun. at 1:30. Free. **Ages 3 and up.**

Start at the Yale Visitors Information Center (the oldest surviving residence in New Haven, they tell us) and begin your hour-long guided tour of campus. See where former Yalies Eli Whitney, Nathan Hale, Noah Webster, and President George W. Bush—not to mention President Clinton and Hillary Rodham Clinton—studied, hung out, and brown-nosed their professors.

● Connecticut Audubon Coastal Center

1 Milford Pt. Rd., Milford, (203) 878-7440, www.ctaudubon.org. Tues.– Sat., 10–4; Sun., 12–4; gate closes at dusk. Adults, $2; 2–12, $1. **All ages.**

From this dazzling locale, add new species to your lifetime list of birds— this 8.4-acre bird sanctuary/wildlife refuge is one of the best birding sites in the state and a mecca for nature lovers in general. Located at the mouth of the Housatonic River, the property includes an indoor nature center with touch tanks, displays, and hands-on exhibits. Programs (usually free) include bird walks, storytelling, and sea creature demonstrations. Outdoors, a 70-foot observation tower offers panoramic views of Long Island Sound, the Housatonic River, and an 840-acre salt marsh.

● New Haven Crypt

250 Temple St., New Haven, (203) 787-0121. Open for tours Apr.–Oct., Thurs. and Sat., 11–1. **Ages 3 and up.**

We don't suppose you're dying to get in here . . . the good news is, you don't have to. This unique, historic crypt is located under the First Church of Christ on the New Haven Green, and bears tombstones that date back to 1687.

● Grove Street Cemetery

227 Grove St., between Prospect and Ashmun Sts., New Haven. Gates close at 4.
Ages 3 and up.

Visit the gravesites of Eli Whitney, Charles Goodyear, Noah Webster, and other famous figures here. Established in 1796, this cemetery is a good place to try your hand at grave rubbing.

● East Rock Park

At Orange and Cold Spring Sts., New Haven, (203) 946-6086,
www.newhavenparks.org. Park: daily, sunrise–sunset. Summit: daily, Apr.–
Nov., sunrise–sunset; closed to vehicles Nov. 1–Apr. 1, weekdays; open weekends,
weather permitting. Dec.–Mar., open weekends and holidays, sunrise–sunset.
All ages.

The best feature of this 420-acre city park is its summit. Drive up to the top of the Rock and you'll get an aerial view of the city, the harbor, and Long Island Sound. Also on the grounds are a bird sanctuary, playgrounds, nature trails (more than 10 miles of hiking paths!), and picnic facilities. Ranger-led programs include early-morning warbler walks and a kids' fishing derby.

● West Rock Ridge State Park and West Rock Nature Center

Wintergreen Ave., New Haven, (203) 946-8016, www.cityofnewhaven.com.
West Rock Park: daily, 9–sunset. Free. Nature Center: Mon.–Fri., 10–4.
Free. **All ages.**

Rock on, New Haven. West Rock Park surrounds West Rock, which is 428 feet high. Near the summit is Judges' Cave, a historic landmark. Reach the summit by hiking, biking, or by car. Along the ridge you'll enjoy excellent views of New Haven harbor and Long Island Sound. West Rock Nature Center has displays of native birds, insects, butterflies, reptiles, and mammals. The center is surrounded by 40 acres of woodland with nature trails, ponds, and meadows.

● Lighthouse Point Park and Carousel

2 Lighthouse Rd., exit 50 off I-95, New Haven, (203) 946-8005,
www.newhavenparks.org. Memorial Day–Labor Day, sunrise–sunset.
Carousel: daily, 10–6. Parking fee. Carousel rides, $.50. **All ages.**

This 82-acre waterfront park and beach, set on Long Island Sound, has several delightful features, including an antique carousel set in a turn-of-the-century beach pavilion. There's also a marine touch tank and bird sanctuary, with bird-watching programs in March and April, and hawk watching in September. You'll also find nature trails, playgrounds, picnic groves, and, when it's steamy outside, lots of happy kids playing on the beach and splashing in the ocean.

● Fort Nathan Hale and Black Rock Fort

Woodward Ave., exit 50 off I-95, New Haven, (203) 946-8790,
www.fortnathanhale.org. Daily, Memorial Day–Labor Day. Free. **All ages.**

These reconstructed Revolutionary War and Civil War forts give kids a
chance to play soldier with reasonable authenticity. Located on the eastern
shore of New Haven harbor, the forts have bunkers, gun emplacements, and
breastworks, and there's even a Civil War-era drawbridge that really works.
Another plus: awesome views of New Haven harbor.

● Edgewood Park

Edgewood Ave., exit 45 off I-95, New Haven, (203) 946-8028. Daily,
sunrise–sunset. **All ages.**

This 123-acre park is a popular place for local families to get out and play,
thanks to the in-line-skating rink, playground, nature trail, tennis courts,
and duck pond.

● Sleeping Giant State Park

200 Mt. Carmel Ave., Hamden, (203) 789-7489 or (203) 272-2841
(hiking information), www.sgpa.org. Daily, 8–sunset. Parking fee, Apr.–
Nov., weekends and holidays. **All ages.**

Two miles of mountaintop form the outline of a "sleeping giant" along
the skyline. This 1,500-acre park is a popular hiking area, with a 33-mile
network of nature trails, and ranger-led hikes throughout the season. Call
first; some hikes are designated for experienced hikers only, covering rough
terrain. Hikes depart from the bulletin board at the park entrance. A 1.5-mile
trail leads to a stone lookout tower on the peak of Mount Carmel, offering
great views of Long Island Sound.

● Eli Whitney Museum

915 Whitney Ave., Hamden, (203) 777-1833, www.eliwhitney.org. Open
Memorial Day–Labor Day, daily, 11–4. Rest of year, Wed.–Fri. and Sun.,
12–5; Sat., 10–3. Adults, $3; children, $2. **Ages 3 and up.**

"Exploring the passion for making things" is the theme here, where
features include a water learning lab and a covered bridge. After a visit here,
kids will tackle those Lego creations with renewed vigor. The 1816-era barn
is a venue for country dances, folk music, and summer theater; call for a
schedule.

● General David Humphreys House

37 Elm St., Ansonia, (203) 735-1908, www.electronicvalley.org/derby/
history/humphrey.htm. Year-round, Mon.–Fri., 1–4:30. $2 donation per
person suggested. **Ages 3 and up.**

Humphreys, a Revolutionary War hero and aide to General Washington, was born in this house, which was built in 1698. Now, it's a living-history museum, re-creating daily life in 1762 with demonstrations of open-hearth cooking and wool spinning. Worth a pass-through if you're in the area.

● Wharton Brook State Park

Rte. 5, North Haven–Wallingford line, (203) 269-5308. Open 8 A.M.– sunset. **All ages.**

Quiet and peaceful, this park is a pleasant out-of-the-city escape. Fish for trout (stocked), swim, or enjoy a picnic here in relative solitude. Ice skating in winter.

● Ansonia Nature & Recreation Center

10 Deerfield Rd., Rte. 243 or Rte. 115, Ansonia; (203) 736-9360, www.electronicvalley.org/ansonia/nature.htm. Park: daily, dawn–dusk. Center: daily, 9–5; closed major holidays. Free. **All ages.**

This lovely, 104-acre park boasts an interpretive center, two miles of nature trails, a fishing pond, picnic pavilions, and beautiful fern and wildflower gardens, even a butterfly/hummingbird garden. (Fun for kids to see hummingbirds in action!) Cross-country skiing in winter.

● Smiles Entertainment Center

1607 Boston Post Rd., exit 39B off I-95, Milford, (203) 877-3229; www.milfordamusementcenter.com. Open Sun.–Thurs., 10 a.m.–midnight; Fri. and Sat., 10 a.m.–2 a.m. Kiddie Land open Sun.–Thurs., 10–9 or 10; Fri. and Sat., 10 a.m.–midnight. **Ages 3 and up.**

When they've had enough wholesome outdoor activity and need a little high-tech fun, this is the place. You'll find amusements ranging from video and pinball games (300 or so) to a giant laser-tag arena. Kiddie Land has coin-operated games and rides; other options include miniature golf, bumper boats, and batting cages. (Some of these are outdoors, so kids will get a little fresh air in spite of themselves.)

● Boat Cruises

If you want to see the area by sea, you have a couple of interesting options. Great for kids: **Schooner, Inc.,** offers narrated tours on the colorful history of New Haven and its harbor, aboard the *Quinnipack,* a 91-foot, gaff-rigged wooden schooner. The boat sails from May through mid-October from Long Wharf Pier; call (203) 865-1737 for information and reservations. The Freedom schooner **Amistad,** a replica of the Spanish ship *La Amistad,* is a traveling museum that chronicles the story of the Amistad Revolt that began off the coast of Cuba and landed in New Haven, where the fight for freedom began. When in port, the ship serves as a floating classroom, offering lessons in leadership and racial harmony. The ship is also open to the public for evening sails on Monday through Friday from 5 to 8 P.M. Evening sails cost $25 for adults and $15 for kids ages 12 and under. For a schedule, visit their website at www.amistadamerica.org.or call (203) 495-1555.

● Hayrides and Family Farms

Who can resist the lure of a bumpity hayride in autumn? Here are some options: Operating for 10 generations, **Rose Orchard,** 33 Branford Rd. (Rte. 139), North Branford, has farm animals, a picnic area, pick-your-own pumpkins and other produce in season, and hayrides. Call (203) 488-7996. **Jones Family Farm,** Rte.110 and Israel Hill Rd., Shelton, has it all: pick-your-own produce in summer, pick-a-pumpkin (and hayrides) in October, and Christmas trees and Santa in December. Call (203) 929-8425.

Maple View Farm, 603 Orange Center Rd., Orange, offers hayrides and pony rides by appointment. Call (203) 799-6495. **Windy Hill Farm,** at 393 Amity Rd., Bethany, offers horse-drawn hayrides; call (203) 393-3179 for a reservation.

 RESTAURANTS

● Louis' Lunch

263 Crown St., New Haven, (203) 562-5507, www.louislunch.com. Tues. and Wed., 11–4; Thurs.–Sat., noon–2 a.m.

Do your kids consider burgers one of the four major food groups? Take them to the place where America's first hamburger patty was slapped on a bun in 1898 (the original broilers are still in use). There's a children's menu, too. Located downtown, in the theater district.

● Frank Pepe Pizzeria Napoletana

157 Wooster St., New Haven, (203) 865-5762, www.pizzatherapy.com/pepes.htm. Mon., Wed., and Thurs., 4–10; Fri. and Sat., 11:30–11; Sun., 2:30–10. Closed Tues.

They've been making "tomato pies" here since 1925, so you can bet they're good at it. A must-stop—said to be where the original American pizza was born. Try the white cheese pizza with fresh clams and garlic or the classic tomato-parmesan pie. If the lines are long at Pepe's, head down the street to **Sally's Pizza** at 237 Wooster. In business since 1938, Sally's is New Haven's *other* famous pizza place. They, too, make fabulous sauces from scratch, topping a thin, chewy "Neapolitan" crust, cooked to crispy-edged perfection in a vintage brick oven.

● Glenwood Drive Inn

2538 Whitney Ave. (at the base of Sleeping Giant State Park), Hamden, (203) 281-0604. Apr.–Dec., daily, 11–10; Jan.–Mar., til 8.

This is a good, old-fashioned family restaurant, offering grilled hot dogs (with buttery, crunchy grilled buns!) and hamburgers and tasty seafood plates.

● Libby's Italian Pastry Shop

139 Wooster St., New Haven, (203) 772-0380. Call to confirm hours.

You'll swoon at the sight, and taste, of Libby's homemade Italian pastries. They also offer Italian ices, cappuccino, and espresso.

■ Southwest Connecticut

The southwest corner of Connecticut offers attractions aplenty for visiting families. State-of-the-art interactive museums and old-fashioned amusement parks wait to be explored; enticing natural attractions include beaches, woodland trails, and wildlife sanctuaries. You could bypass this area on the way to the Big Apple, but look what you'd miss: touring an 1868 lighthouse, taking a sleigh ride on a working farm, playing astronaut at the Challenger Learning Center, admiring the Siberian tigers at the Beardsley Zoo, and petting a shark (!) at Norwalk's Maritime Aquarium. Intrigued? Here are the details, and lots more to tempt you to meander a bit.

● Beardsley Zoological Gardens

1875 Noble Ave., exit 27A off I-95, Bridgeport, (203) 394-6555, www.beardsleyzoo.com. Daily, 9–4. New World Tropics Building, daily, 10:30–3:30. Closed Thanksgiving, Christmas, and New Year's Day. Adults, $6; 3–11, $4; under 3, free. Carousel rides, $1. Parking fee. **All ages.**

There are 300 reasons to like the Beardsley Zoo, Connecticut's largest— the 300 species that call this zoo home. Among the residents: toucans, ocelots, and timber wolves. Set on 36 acres, the zoo celebrates the wildlife of North and South America. Don't miss the New World Tropics Building, full of exotic rain forest animals and birds. Not all of the animals are real—a replica turn-of-the-century carousel features fanciful hand-carved creatures. If you're in the area, don't miss it.

● The Discovery Museum

4450 Park Ave., Rte. 15, exit 47, Bridgeport, (203) 372-3521, www.discoverymuseum.org. Tues.–Sat., 10–5; Sun., 12–5. Closed Mon. and major holidays. Adults, $7; 3–18, $5.50. **Ages 3 and up.**

Wow. This interactive art-and-science museum features 115 hands-on art and science exhibits, not to mention a planetarium, art galleries, and more. A major attraction is the Challenger Learning Center, where kids ages 10 and up can play astronaut with computer-simulated space missions.

● Captain's Cove Seaport

1 Bostwick Ave., exit 26 off I-95, Bridgeport, (203) 335-1433, www.captainscoveseaport.com. Mar. 1–Nov. 1. **All ages.**

This lively Victorian-style boardwalk on Black Rock Harbor is a fun place to stroll. From Memorial Day to Labor Day, you can take a harbor cruise and visit the 150-foot Nantucket, a floating lighthouse. You might also want to check out Dundon House, a restored 1893 Victorian mansion with a maritime exhibit and take a peek inside craft shops, eateries, and a fish market. On Sundays, from March through October, boardwalk band concerts provide a festive touch.

● The Barnum Museum

820 Main St., exit 27 off I-95, Bridgeport, (203) 331-1104, www.barnum-museum.org. Tues.–Sat., 10–4:30; Sun., 12–4:30. Adults, $5; 4–18, $3. **Ages 4 and up.**

Your kids may never have heard of tiny Tom Thumb, but they'll probably get a kick out of this circus history "lesson," dedicated to P.T. Barnum and "the Greatest Show on Earth." This century-old landmark building also houses exhibits on Bridgeport's industrial history and 19th-century Americana. The most child-pleasing space here is the third floor, with Tom Thumb's tiny carriage and furniture and a 20-by-40-foot, hand-carved miniature circus. The Clown Corner has clown props and costumes; put your nose to the clown's make-up mirror and see yourself in clown-face.

● Audubon Center in Greenwich

613 Riversville Rd., Greenwich, (203) 869-5272, www.greenwich.center.audubon.org. Year-round, daily, 9–5. Adults, $3; children, $1.50. **All ages.**

Families flock to the bird observation window here, and you're sure to find some new additions for your lifetime list—this 686-acre sanctuary offers an abundant variety of birds and is considered one of the premier hawk watching spots in New England. Guided walks for families are offered on weekends, along sections of the center's 15 miles of hiking trails. Hawk watches are held daily, 9–5, from mid-August to mid-November. Also check out the honeybee exhibit, visitors center, art gallery, and gift shop.

● Quassy Amusement Park

Rte. 64, exit 16E/17W off I-84, Middlebury, (203) 758-2913, (800)
FOR-PARK, www.quassy.com. Apr.–May and Sept.–Oct., Sat. and Sun.,
11–9; Memorial Day–Labor Day, daily, 11–9. Grounds: free. All day ride
pass, 45 in. tall and over, $13.95; under 44 in., $9.95. Parking fee. **All ages.**

Hot dogs, sno-cones, cotton candy, stomach-churning rides—what
more could any kid (or young-at-heart mommy or daddy) ask for? Well, how
about swimming and boating in Lake Quassapaug, a video arcade, a petting
zoo, and miniature golf? It's an old-fashioned, all-American good time,
complete with wandering minstrels, magic acts, and, on Friday nights, live
music (heavy on the oldies acts and country-and-western tunes).

● Stamford Museum and Nature Center

39 Scofieldtown Rd., Rte. 15, exit 35, Stamford, (203) 322-1646,
www.stamfordmuseum.org. Mon.–Sat. and holidays, 9–5; Sun., 1–5.
Planetarium shows: Sun., 3 p.m. Closed Thanksgiving, Christmas, and New
Year's Day. Adults, $6; 4–13, $4. Planetarium shows: adults, $2; children,
$1. **All ages.**

The showpiece of this 118-acre complex is a 19th-century working farm.
You'll enjoy poking around the country store and seven galleries (including
one highlighting Native American customs) and meandering the woodland
trails. Kids love the "natural playground," too. Be sure to visit the zoo and
catch a show at the planetarium. Seasonal activities, like maple-syrup-
making demonstrations, are a special delight here. If you're in town, don't
miss it.

● Boat Cruises

Soundwaters *Schooner, Brewers Yacht Haven Marina, exit 7 off I-95,*
Stamford, (203) 323-1978, www.soundwaters.org. Weekends, mid-Apr.–
mid-Nov. Call for schedule and reservations. Adults, $25; 12 and under,
$15. **Ages 5 and up.**

Stow away on this 80-foot, three-masted sharpie schooner. *Soundwaters*
is a replica of a 19th-century vessel, offering a delightful, interactive cruise
that's great for families. On a three-hour ecology cruise, you'll help hoist the
sails of this tall ship, haul in a trawl net filled with lobster and other creatures
of the deep, and learn about Connecticut marine life, firsthand. Five onboard
educators will answer your questions about Long Island Sound sea life, and
staff the plankton station, the salt marsh station, and the tank station, where
daring kids can handle some of the marine animals that are hauled in from
the deep.

● Bartlett Arboretum

151 Brookdale Rd., Stamford, (203) 322-0971. Daily, 8:30–sunset. Free.
All ages.

Let your little ones wiggle their waggles out in this natural woodlands area, while you peek at gardens of wildflowers and pines. There are marked ecology trails, a swamp walk, pond, and greenhouses, too. Guided tours and special workshops are offered throughout the year.

● Downtown Cabaret Theatre and Children's Theatre

263 Golden Hill St., exit 27A off I-95, Bridgeport, (203) 576-1636. Shows Sat., 12 and 2:30; Sun., 12. Children's Theater, Oct.–May; call for schedule. **Ages 2–12.**

Catch your favorite fairy tales and fables here, updated for contemporary kids and presented with original music. A recent double feature combined Little Red Riding Hood and the Three Little Pigs, with a scene-stealing, hip-hoppin' Big Bad Wolf. Performances are geared toward kids ages 2 to 12. It's a lovely way to spend an afternoon and a splendid rainy-day activity. BYO lunch or treats!

● Seaside Park

Exit 27 off I-95, Bridgeport, (203) 576-7233. **All ages.**

Open year-round, this pretty 370-acre park was donated to the city of Bridgeport by P.T. Barnum. Notable features include a beautiful beach and picnic areas.

● Maritime Aquarium at Norwalk

10 North Water St., exit 14N/15S off I-95, S. Norwalk, (203) 852-0700, www.maritimeaquarium.org. Daily, 10–5, July–Aug., 10–6. Closed Thanksgiving and Christmas. Adults, $8.75; 2–12, $7.25. IMAX Theater admission: adults, $6.75; children, $5; under 2, free. Discounted combination ticket available. **All ages.**

Sharks, seals, jellyfish, otters, and 125 other marine species are on view here, making the Maritime Aquarium one of the top family destinations in the area. Explore the marine life and maritime culture of Long Island Sound at this waterfront destination, where attractions include an IMAX theater, an aquarium, and a hall dedicated to maritime history with several interactive exhibits. Your kids will love the close-up glimpses of underwater inhabitants (they can even "pet" a shark through the glass); you may be inspired to build your own wooden boat after watching the craftspeople here demonstrate their techniques.

● Stepping Stones Museum for Children

303 West Ave., Matthews Park, Norwalk, (203) 899-0606. Memorial Day–Labor Day, Mon.–Sat., 10–5; Sun., 12–5; other times, Tues.–Sat., 10–5; Sun, 12–5. Admission, $6; under 1, free. **Ages 1–10.**

This hands-on learning center offers a variety of interactive exhibits focusing on the arts, science, technology, culture, and heritage.

● Sheffield Island Lighthouse

Ferry service from Hope Dock, corner of Washington and N. Water Sts., Norwalk, (203) 838-9444, www.seaport.org. Memorial Day–Labor Day; call for daily ferry schedule and rates. **Ages 3 and up.**

Could you handle living in a lighthouse? You wouldn't need a StairMaster. Take a scenic ferry boat ride on the *Island Girl* to this three-acre park with an 1868 lighthouse. Explore the lighthouse's four levels and 10 rooms; bring along a picnic. The lighthouse is adjacent to the Stewart B. McKinney U.S. Fish and Wildlife Sanctuary.

● Sherwood Island State Park

Exit 18 off I-95, Westport, (203) 226-6983, www.dep.state.ct.us/rec/ parks.htm. Daily, 8–sunset. Parking fee, Memorial Day–Sept.; off-season, free. **All ages.**

When you need a beach break, this one can't miss. It's a mile and a half of beachfront on Long Island Sound, suitable for swimming and saltwater fishing. Large, open fields are a great natural playscape—bring a ball and glove and a picnic. Services include a bathhouse and concessions. Two large picnic groves are situated near the water. Park rangers lead nature walks and interpretive programs; call for a schedule of events.

● Nature Center for Environmental Activities

10 Woodside Ln., exit 17 off I-95, Westport, (203) 227-7253, www.naturecenterwestport.org. Grounds: daily, 7 a.m.–dusk; building: Mon.–Sat., 9–5; Sun., 1–7. Adults, $2; children, $1. **All ages.**

Find out who's who-o-o in the animal kingdom at this 62-acre wildlife sanctuary. Nature trails, natural science exhibits, a live-animal hall, a discovery room, and an aquarium offer plenty to see, do, and explore.

● Concerts on the Green

First Presbyterian Church, 1101 Bedford St., Stamford, (203) 324-9522. July, Thurs., 7 P.M. Free. **All ages.**

If your idea of a classic New England outing includes an outdoor concert on a balmy evening, don't miss the carillon and band concerts here on Thursday nights in July.

● Silverman's Farm

451 Sport Hill Rd., Easton, (203) 261-3306, www.silvermansfarm.com. Daily, 8:30–5:30. Grounds: free; petting zoo: adults, $3; children, $2.
All ages.

This is a combination farmers market and petting zoo, with pick-your-own produce (in season) and a working cider mill.

● Blue Jay Orchards

125 Plumtrees Rd., Bethel, (203) 748-0119. July–Jan. Free. **All ages.**

Celebrate autumn here, as you stroll the farm market, meet resident barnyard animals at the petting zoo, see the cider mill at work, and pick your own apples and pumpkins (September through October).

● Railroad Museum of New England

176 Chase Rd., exit 36 off Rte. 8, Waterbury, (203) 575-1931. May–Oct., Sat., Sun., and holidays, 9:30–5:30. Adults, $8; children, $6. **All ages.**

Attention, Thomas the Tank Engine fans: Take a 10-mile ride on a restored historic railroad. Chug-a-lug your way from brass mills, through a state forest, along the Naugatuck River, and past a dam.

● The Nature Conservancy

33 Pent Rd., Rte. 15, Weston, (203) 226-4991. Year-round, daily, dawn–dusk. Free. **All ages.**

They call it Devil's Den, but this nature preserve is heaven to hikers, with more than 20 miles of trails on 1,746 acres. Nearby, the Katharine Ordway Preserve offers three miles of trails and an arboretum on 62 acres. No biking, camping, or dogs allowed. Guided nature walks, such as evening Owl Prowls, and interpretive programs are offered; call for information.

● New Canaan Nature Center

144 Oenoke Ridge, New Canaan, (203) 966-9577. Grounds: daily, dawn–dusk; buildings: Mon.–Sat., 9–4. Free. **All ages.**

Birds, butterflies, flowers, and live animals combine to make this a fun destination for outdoor-loving families. There are 40 acres to roam with walking trails, herb, wildflower, and butterfly gardens. At the on-site Discovery Center, you'll find hands-on exhibits, live animals, and horticultural exhibits. There's a maple sugarhouse, too, that's popular in the spring. Special workshops and programs are held throughout the year.

● Garbage Museum

1410 Honeyspot Rd., Stratford, (203) 381-9571. July–Aug., Tues.–Sat., 10–4; Sept.–June, Wed.–Fri., 12–4. Free. **Ages 3 and up.**

Want to help teach your children about recycling, reuse, and the environment? Head to this modest-size facility for a quick lesson in environmental education. Check out the "Trash-O-Saurus" and other hands-on exhibits and meander across the enclosed skywalk for a look at the on-site recycling plant.

 ## RESTAURANTS

● The Restaurant at Captain's Cove

1 Bostwick Ave., exit 26 off I-95, Bridgeport, (203) 335-7104, www.captainscoveseaport.com. March–Oct., Mon.–Thurs., 11–midnight; Sat., 11–1; Sun., 11–11.

Captain's Cove is a great place to knock around, with its boardwalk, charter boats to gawk at, and little Victorian shops. The restaurant here is a favorite among visitors and locals alike. Fare ranges from a boxed lunch to a lobster bake—and just about everything in between: hamburgers, fish platters, salads, pasta daily specials, and more. Grab your plate and head to a picnic table on the boardwalk, sit out on the deck, or snag a table inside next to a giant fish tank.

● Sycamore Drive-In

282 Greenwood Ave., Bethel, (203) 748-2716. Year-round, Mon.–Sat., 6:30–9:30.

Picky about your upholstery? Forget this place and skip ahead to the next listing. The Sycamore is one of the last authentic drive-ins on the planet. Yes, they offer carhop service; you flash your lights, they take your order, and eventually the carhop will attach a tray of food to your window. This isn't just a restaurant, it's a cultural experience. And the food's not bad; try the chicken-in-a-basket with a mug of the Sycamore's secret-recipe homemade root beer. Promise us you'll stop here when you're in the area; we can't let this place go the way of the T'bird.

● Bacco's

1230 Thomaston Ave., Waterbury, (203) 755-0635, www.baccosrestaurant.com. Lunch, Fri., noon–5. Dinner: Tues.–Thurs., 4–9:30; Fri.–Sat., 4–10; Sun., noon–8:30. July–Aug., dinner, Tues.–Sun., 4–9.

This is a homey, family-style Italian place, with an absolutely killer pizza. The sublime pie is covered with fresh clams and garlic and is baked to perfection in a brick oven. Not bad for a place that's been around for more than 60 years. Kids won't touch clams or garlic? Order a pizza for the grown-ups, and get the kids a nice order of lasagna. *Mangia!*

■ Litchfield Hills Area

The village of Litchfield could be a movie set entitled "Quaint New England Town." It has the requisite white clapboard homes, a town green, even pristine 18th-century mansions that could be museums but in fact are private homes. The area is, without question, one of New England's most richly blessed when it comes to natural beauty.

If your children consider the appeal of a picturesque colonial village on par with a trip to a plumbing supply store, not to worry. Litchfield County and the surrounding area offers more than just a pretty face. Northwestern Connecticut is studded with state parks where you can camp, fish, hike, swim, ride, and picnic. Beautiful country walks abound. For hardy hikers, Litchfield County offers a stretch of the Appalachian Trail featuring Connecticut's highest peak, Bear Mountain. Round out your visit with a museum, take in the action at Lime Rock racetrack, and stop at a local pick-your-own farm to load up on fresh produce. For more information about the area, visit www.litchfieldcty.com.

● Carousel Museum of New England

95 Riverside Ave., exit 31 off I-84, Bristol, (860) 585-5411, www.carouselmuseum.com. Apr.–Nov., Mon.–Sat., 10–5; Sun., 12–5. Dec.– Mar., Thurs.–Sat., 10–5; Sun., 12–5. Closed major holidays. Adults, $4; 4–14, $2.50. **Ages 4 and up.**

Remember the thrill of your first carousel ride? Probably not, but you'll have a real appreciation for those painted ponies after a visit here. Housed in a restored, turn-of-the-century factory are wonderful examples of antique carousel art, where painters and carvers work painstakingly to restore old pieces to their past glory. Tours run every half hour; "Kidstuff" programs offer classes in papier-mache. Call for a schedule.

● Lake Compounce Amusement Park

822 Lake Ave., exit 31 off I-84, Bristol, (860) 583-3300, www.lakecompounce.com. Mid-May–Oct., 11–8. Thurs.–Sun. only in May; weekends only, Sept.–Oct. All-day ride pass: adults, $28.95; under 5 ft. tall, $19.95; 3 and under, free. Parking fee, $5. **All ages.**

Only a true curmudgeon could resist the charms of this attraction. America's oldest continually open amusement park is an appealing blend of Victoriana (old-time shops, a carousel) and contemporary thrills, like the Thunder River white-water raft ride and the Boomerang roller coaster— fifteen new rides in all. Better eat that corn dog later—the Boomerang turns you upside down six times! Also new at Lake Compounce: a circus-themed Kiddie Land. Stop and catch your breath at one of the live stage shows.

● White Memorial Foundation and Conservation Center

Rte. 202, Litchfield, (860) 567-0857, www.whitememorialcc.org. Conserva-
tion Center and Museum: Mon.–Sat., 9–5; Sun., 12–5. Adults, $4; 6–12,
$2. Sanctuary open year-round, daily. Free. **All ages.**

This 4,000-acre wildlife sanctuary—including half the shoreline of
Bantam Lake and the Bantam River—offers 35 miles of hiking trails. Take
a guided tour or set your own pace, with time out for a picnic along the way.
Bantam Lake is great for swimming, or rent a rowboat or canoe, or make it
a real getaway and camp out at one of the family campgrounds on the
property. Be sure to stop by the Conservation Center and Nature Museum
near the entrance, for a quick lesson in local flora and fauna. Exhibits include
interesting things like a working beehive, an aquarium with turtles, snakes,
and fish; and stuffed hawks and owls on display.

● Mount Tom State Park

Rte. 202, Litchfield, (860) 567-8870, www.dep.state.ct.us/rec/parks/htm.
Daily, 8 a.m.–sunset. Parking fee in season: $4 weekdays, $5 weekends for
in-state (CT) vehicles; $5 weekdays, $8 weekends for out-of-state vehicles.
All ages.

Ready for a workout? The summit of this park is 1,325 feet above sea
level, crowned by a stone tower. Other features here include a hiking trail,
lake swimming, fishing, boating (non motors), even scuba diving. Go ice
skating here in winter.

● Topsmead State Forest

Buell Rd., Rte. 118, Litchfield, (860) 567-5694, www.dep.state.ct.us/rec/
parks/htm. Grounds: Open year-round, 8–sunset. Mansion: June–Oct., second
and fourth weekends, 12–5. Free. **All ages.**

The principal attraction here is a Tudor-style cottage, the summer
home of Edith Morton Chase. Miss Chase donated the 514-acre forest to the
state upon her death in 1972. The cottage is open to visitors during the
summer; call first to confirm the schedule. The grounds include a 40-acre
wildflower preserve and nature trail. Have a picnic at one of the tables, or
spread a blanket wherever you choose. Cross-country skiing and
snowshoeing in winter.

● Sandy Beach

Bantam Lake, E. Shore Rd. (Rte. 109), Morris, (860) 567-5387. Memo-
rial Day–June, weekends only, 9–7; July–Labor Day, daily, 9–7. $5 fee for
vehicles and boats; $1 fee for walkers and bicyclists. **All ages.**

This secluded cove is a welcome find on a balmy day, with lifeguards,
bathhouses, a snack bar, picnic area, and canoe launch.

● Action Wildlife Foundation

337 Torrington Rd., Rte. 4, Goshen, (860) 482-4485. Spring–fall, Mon.–Sun., 9:30–5. Admission: $3. **All ages.**

Small children will love the petting zoo at this 100-acre wildlife sanctuary. Roam the grounds and take a look at some of the foundation's gathering of exotic animals—the sanctuary is home to more than 100. There are hayrides on the weekends and special programs throughout the summer season.

● Horseback Riding

Lee's Riding Stable, in Litchfield, offers guided horseback rides (on easygoing mounts) and pony rides, on beautiful wooded trails. The stables are located at 57 E. Litchfield Rd.; call (860) 567-0785 for information. **HORSE of Connecticut,** at 43 Wilbur Road in Washington, is a nonprofit rescue organization, offering daily tours to view and feed the horses. Book in advance for a trail ride. Call (860) 868-1960 for details.

● Canoeing/Kayaking/Tubing

You'll catch glimpses of the Housatonic River as you drive and hike around the Litchfield Hills; if you'd like an on-river experience, a couple of local outfitters will be happy to comply. **Clarke Outdoors,** on Rte. 7 in West Cornwall, (860) 672-6365, www.clarkeoutdoors.com, offers 10-mile trips on the Housy by canoe, kayak, or raft. Trips run April through October, daily; call to see which sounds like a good match for your group. Reservations are recommended. **Main Stream Canoe,** based in New Hartford, offers flatwater and white-water canoe day trips, moonlight trips (in summer), and kayak "adventures." Trips run daily, Memorial Day through Labor Day, and weekends during shoulder seasons. Call (860) 693-6791 or visit www.mainstreamcanoe.com. for details. **Farmington River Tubing** offers thrilling river rapids rides for families with older kids (ages 10 and up) who know how to swim. One person rides on each tube, traveling stretches that are alternately calm and peaceful, and wild and woolly. Call (860) 693-6465 or log on to www.visitconnecticut.com/farmingtonrivertubing.com.

● Institute for American Indian Studies

38 Curtis Rd., off Rte. 199, Washington, (860) 868-0518. Mon.–Sat., 10–5; Sun. 12–5. Jan.–March, closed Mon.–Tues. Adults, $4; 6–16, $2. **Ages 4 and up.**

This museum is more child pleasing than its name implies. Exhibits highlight the Native American experience in New England, with artifacts spanning 10,000 years. Most kids are intrigued by the re-created Onandaga Indian longhouse filled with household objects and appearing as though the family will return home any minute. Dino-philes will delight in the mastodon skeleton, unearthed in nearby Farmington. Walk along an Indian trail, visit a 17th-century Algonkian Indian village, and view a simulated archaeological dig.

● Lime Rock Park

Rte. 112, Lakeville, (860) 435-5000 or 800-RACE-LRP, www.limerock.com. Racing on most weekends, Apr.–Nov. Call for schedule. Rates vary with event: $12–$75 for adults; 12 and under, free. **Ages 5 and up.**

If your kids love fast cars, lots of noise, and action, head to the track. Pro national and amateur road-racing events are held here, with car shows and auto festivals rounding out the calendar. If you're bringing a small child, consider a regional race (not to mention earplugs); they're shorter (30 minutes as opposed to 2.5 hours) and less crowded than other spectator events. Spectators are also welcome at Tuesday practice sessions. Your ticket entitles you to a walk around the paddock area, where drivers and crews are at work on their cars.

● Sharon Audubon Center

Rte. 4, Sharon, (860) 364-0520, www.audubon.org/local/sanctuary/sharon. Mon.–Sat., 9–5; Sun., 1–5. Closed major holidays. Trails open daily, dawn–dusk. Adults, $3; children, $1.50. **All ages.**

This 890-acre sanctuary is a hiker's paradise, with 11 miles of nature trails, and some beautiful wildflower and herb gardens. A standout among the trails: the Bog Meadow Trail, a short (1.25 miles), moderately challenging hike through some beautiful territory. Clearly marked, the trail is at its best in autumn, when the maples and aspens are in their fall colors. Walk along the boardwalk and beside a pond that's home to ducks, turtles, minks, and beavers. There's also a children's adventure center and a nature store.

● Lake McDonough

Rte. 219 off Rte. 44, Barkhamsted, (860) 379-3036. Boating, mid-Apr.– Labor Day; fishing from shore, mid-Apr.–Nov.; swimming, Memorial Day– Labor Day. Mon.–Fri., 10–8; Sat.–Sun. and holidays, 8–8. **All ages.**

Rent a rowboat or paddleboat and putter around this pretty, popular lake. You may also BYOB (bring your own boat) and pay a small fee ($4) to launch it. Or go swimming, fishing, hiking, picnicking—this place has it all.

● Macedonia Brook State Park

Macedonia Brook Rd., off Rte. 341, Kent, (860) 566-2304, www.dep.state.ct.us/rec/parks/htm. Daily, 8–sunset. **All ages.**

Beautiful and wild, this park is blessed with forests, mountainous terrain, a deep gorge, upper and lower falls, wildlife, and, of course, a brook. It offers great views of the Catskill and Taconic mountain ranges, too. Hiking trails here are plentiful and color coded, and some extend along the Appalachian Trail. There's fishing and cross-country skiing in winter.

● Peoples State Forest

East River Rd., Barkhamsted, (860) 379-2469, www.dep.state.ct.us/rec/ parks/htm. Grounds: open daily, 8–sunset. Museum: Memorial Day– Columbus Day, Sat.–Sun., 9–5. Free. Parking fee on weekends and holidays: $5, in-state (CT) vehicles; $8, out-of-state vehicles. **All ages.**

More great hiking, with trails leading past caves and springs. Look for beavers building dams in the marsh. Stop for a picnic among the 200-year-old white pines in Mathies Grove, and take a peek inside the small nature museum (summer only). Go cross-country skiing and snowmobiling here in winter.

● Burr Pond State Park

Burr Mountain Rd., Rte. 8, 5 mi. north of Torrington, (860) 482-1817, www.dep.state.ct.us/rec/parks/htm. Daily, 8–sunset. Parking fee in season: $5, in-state (CT) vehicles; $8, out-of-state vehicles. **All ages.**

Features here include trout-stocked Burr Pond, a sandy beach, streams, rivers, and interesting rock formations. Swimming, boating, and fishing are permitted. It's a great place to paddle a canoe; rent one here from Farmington River Tubing. A scenic path encircles the 88-acre pond. The cross-country skiing is easy, and there's also ice skating in winter.

● Haystack Mountain

Rte. 272, 1 mi. north of Norfolk, (860) 566-2304. Daily, 8–sunset. **All ages.**

Drive halfway up the mountain and enjoy the view, especially lovely during fall foliage season. From there, active types can hike the half-mile trail to the top of the mountain. At the summit, you'll see a 34-foot-high stone tower; climb it for dramatic vistas of Long Island Sound and the Berkshires.

● Housatonic Meadows State Park

Rte. 7, 1 mi. north of Cornwall Bridge, Sharon, (860) 672-6772, www.dep.state.ct.us/rec/parks/htm. Daily, 8–sunset. Camping: mid-Apr.– Dec. Park: free. Camping: $10 per night. **All ages.**

If your group enjoys fly fishing, the clear, cold Housatonic River is a great place to test your skills on trout and bass. A two-mile stretch of river is limited to fly fishing. Enjoy a picnic under the pines on the riverbank. You can even spend the night, if you wish; call ahead to reserve a space at a riverside campsite. Best hiking is on the Pine Knob Loop trail, which joins the Appalachian Trail.

● Kent Falls State Park

Rte. 7, 3 mi. north of Kent, (860) 927-3238, www.dep.state.ct.us/rec/parks/ htm. Daily, 8–sunset. Parking fee on weekends and holidays: $5, in-state (CT) vehicles; $8, out-of-state vehicles. **All ages.**

The cascading waterfalls at this state park are the main attractions drawing thousands of visitors each year. Climb the pathway adjacent to the falls for great views at all levels. This is a favorite scene for professional and amateur photographers. There are lots of great places for picnics and toe-dunking. Hiking and fishing, too.

● Mohawk Mountain State Park and Forest

Rte. 4, Cornwall, (860) 566-2304, www.dep.state.ct.us/rec/parks/htm. Daily, 8–sunset. **All ages.**

In summer or, even better, during peak fall color, drive to the mountaintop for enchanting views. An abandoned fire tower serves as a lookout. There are plenty of hiking opportunities throughout the forest, with several loop trails and a section of the Appalachian Trail. Don't miss Black Spruce Bog, near forest headquarters, home of a unique community of insect-eating plants. Cross-country ski on forest roads and trails or join the downhill skiers at Mohawk Mountain Ski Area.

● Mohawk Mountain Ski Area

46 Great Hollow Rd., off Rte. 4, Cornwall, (860) 672-6100, www.mohawkmtn.com. Lift tickets (anytime): adults, $35/day; 5–15, $29/ day; 4 and under, $12. Ski-Wee and Mini-Riders, ages 5–12, $80/day, including rental equipment and lunch. **Ages 3 and up.**

Family skiing is the name of the game at Mohawk Mountain. Run by a mother-daughter team, the resort does not serve alcohol, and it offers a friendly, low-key atmosphere. Noteworthy features include night skiing, snowmaking over 95 percent of the mountain's ski-able terrain, and a small, on-mountain resort area. Don't expect much vertical (the most is 650 feet) or a lot of tough runs (80 percent of the trails are easy beginner and intermediate). But you'll find easy cruising on 23 trails (14 have lights for nighttime skiing) and five lifts. For folks in the southern New England area, this manageable, family-friendly resort is a great place to introduce your kids to the sport.

● Cross-Country Skiing

Connecticut's numerous state parks and state forests are open to Nordic skiers, as are several nature centers and preserves. There are also a number of cross-country ski centers, offering groomed trails, equipment rentals, and snack bars. Recommended destinations include **Mohawk Mountain** ski resort with more than 40 miles of trails, in Cornwall, (860) 672-6100, www.mohawkmtn.com; the **Blackberry River Inn** in Norfolk, (860) 542-5100, with more than 10 miles of trails, and rentals and lessons; and **White Memorial Foundation** in Litchfield, (860) 567-0857, www.whitememorialcc.org, with 35 miles of trails through varied and beautiful conservation land.

 ## RESTAURANTS

● Deer Island Gate Restaurant

Rte. 209, on Bantam Lake, Morris, (860) 567-4622. Wed.–Sat., 5–10; Sun. buffet, 1–7. Closed for a few weeks each winter; call for reservations.

This is a large, casual restaurant with great views of Bantam Lake. The menu is ambitious, offering daily fish specials, steaks, pork, duck, chicken, lamb, and German dishes. There's no children's menu, but they're happy to offer half portions of most entrees for a reduced price. Local folks love the Sunday German buffet.

● Aspen Garden

51 West St., Litchfield, (860) 567-9477, www.aspengarden.com. Sun.– Thurs., 11–9; Fri.–Sat., 11–10.

This cozy and casual local favorite sits across the historic green in downtown Litchfield. The expansive menu offers dishes in all the main entrée categories: fish, pasta, poultry, steaks, pizza, burgers, sandwiches, and even an array of Greek specialties—and prices are reasonable, especially for upscale Litchfield. There's three-season alfresco dining on the heated porch.

● Wood's Pit BBQ and Mexican Café

123 Bantam Lake Rd., Bantam, (860) 567-9869. Sun.–Thurs., 11:30–9; Fri.–Sat., 11:30–10.

Craving for some smoky and BBQ-sauce-smothered baby backs? If you're in the Litchfield Hills area, you're in luck. Come hungry to this popular eatery, famous for its giant pork rib platters. They smoke their own meat and sausage, here, for mouth-watering, fall-off-the-bone results. The sauce is tangy with lots of vinegar. There are a number of Mexican choices on the menu, too. How can a family go wrong here? Tacos and ribs . . . mmmm.

■ Northeast Connecticut

"Off the beaten track." "Where the crowds aren't." These phrases describe Connecticut's quiet corner. If modern life-with-children has left you worn out, strung out, and in need of escape, this might be the perfect place to reconnect. Besides, how could you miss showing your kids the statue honoring General Israel Putnam, who said, "Don't fire until you see the white of their eyes?" And life is far too short to miss indulging in a homemade ice cream at the University of Connecticut's dairy bar—the perfect reward for hiking local hills and biking country roads.

Rolling countryside, working farms, and historic inns give a pastoral feel to this undiscovered corner of Connecticut; we'll provide suggestions for some pleasant diversions as you roam.

● Connecticut State Museum of Natural History

University of Connecticut, Rte. 195, exit 68 off I-84, Storrs, (860) 486-4460, www.mnh.uconn.edu. Mon.–Fri., 9–6; Sat.–Sun., 10–4. Free.
All ages.

Great white sharks, a life-size wigwam, mounted birds of prey—these totally cool exhibits will surely capture your child's attention, along with the minerals and fossils on display at the University of Connecticut's natural history museum. And did we mention the 20 life-size interactive video games? Awesome. Special children's workshops and family festivals are held periodically; call for a schedule of events.

● University of Connecticut Dairy Bar and Animal Barns

(See previous listing for address.) Animal barns located at Horsebarn Hill Rd.; dairy bar located at 3636 Horsebarn Rd. Ext. Dairy bar: Year-round, Mon.–Fri., 10–5; Sat. and Sun., 12–5. Animal barns: year-round, daily, 10–4. Closed July 4th, Easter, Thanksgiving, and Christmas. **All ages.**

The University of Connecticut was founded in 1881 as a land-grant school of agriculture; part of that heritage remains today. Visit the friendly dairy cattle, sheep, horses, and swine housed at U-Conn's barns (time your trip for early spring to see the newborns). Next, head to the dairy bar for the local delicacy—wonderfully sinful homemade ice cream.

● Nathan Hale Homestead

South St., off Rte. 44, Coventry, (860) 742-6917. Mid-May–mid-Oct., daily, 1–5. Adults, $4; children, $1. **Ages 3 and up.**

Explore the life and times of Connecticut hero Nathan Hale at his 1776 family farm. The best feature for kids is a walled-in, grassy field where they can try hoop-rolling and walking on stilts. (Many parents can't resist these stilts, either.) You can picnic on the grounds, keeping an eye out for resident animals. Plan your visit to coincide with one of the special events held here: "Hale to Spring," featuring baby animals; "Muster and Colonial Encampment," with tents and musket shooting, in July; and the "Lantern Tour," a house tour by candlelight, in October. Call for dates.

● Photomobile Model Museum

1728 Rte. 198, Woodstock, (860) 974-3910. Sat., 10–5; Sun., 12–5. Adults, $2; under 16, $1. **Ages 5 and up.**

Now here's something we'll bet you don't see every day—solar-powered model cars, boats, planes, and trains. See 'em demonstrated outdoors (on sunny days) or indoors, under the floodlights.

● River Bend Mining & Gemstone Panning

41 Pond St., Rte. 14A, Sterling, (860) 564-3440. Mid-Apr.–mid-Oct., Tues.–Thurs., 10–5; Fri., 10–8; Sat., 10–7; Sun., 9–5. Mine: adults, $6.50; children, $5.50. Sluice: $3.25. **Ages 5 and up.**

Guided by the lamp on your miner's helmet, enter an authentic mine. Mine for gems, fossils, minerals, and shells, or try panning "sluice" (a gravelly mixture that may contain gemstones) and see what sparkly treasures you uncover. This activity is fairly common in some states, like Montana and Tennessee, but out-of-the-ordinary here in New England. It's semieducational, and fun. Also see the wildlife exhibit, with 40 animal displays.

● Ballard Institute and Museum of Puppetry

Weaver Rd., off Rte. 44, Mansfield, (860) 486-4605. Mid-Apr.–mid-Nov., Thurs.–Fri., 10–3; Sat.–Sun., 12–5. **Ages 3 and up.**

Beyond Punch & Judy—see more puppets than you've ever imagined here, where changing exhibits highlight puppets from a collection of more than 2,000. Thus inspired, the kids will be ready to put on some whiz-bang puppet productions back home.

● Creamery Brook Bison Farm

19 Purvis Rd., Brooklyn, (860) 779-0837. Year-round, Mon.–Fri., 2–6; Sat., 9–2. Guided tours by reservation. Adults, $6; 3–11, $4.50. **All ages.**

Some people actually do have a home where the buffalo roam. Take a 40-minute ride through this 100-acre dairy farm where the buffalo (more accurately, American bison) roam. A fun way to see it—on a hayride.

● Wright's Mill Farm

63 Creasey Rd., Canterbury, (860) 774-1455. Year-round, daily, 9–5. **All ages.**

Hike and picnic amid the pastoral pleasures of this 250-acre farm complex. Horse-drawn carriage and wagon rides, pumpkin-hunt hayrides, and cut-your-own Christmas trees are offered (in season, of course). Guided tours of the historic mill village are led, by appointment.

● Quinebaug Valley Trout Hatchery

Trout Hatchery Rd., exit 89 off I-395, Central Village, (860) 564-7542. Daily, 10–4. Free. **All ages.**

Fish-o-rama! Nearly 600,000 pounds of brook, brown, and rainbow trout are produced here each year, making this one of the largest hatcheries in the East. Watch them in action through glass viewing walls.

● Roseland Cottage

Rte. 169, exit 72 off I-84, Woodstock, (860) 928-4074. June–mid-Oct., Wed.–Sun., July 4th, and Columbus Day, 11–5. Adults, $4; 5–12, $2; under 5, free. Teas: $12 per person. **Ages 3–14.**

This is one of those local landmarks that just can't be missed. This striking pink Gothic Revival home is now designated a National Historic Landmark. It was built by publisher Henry Bowen as a summer home. Kids will get a kick out of the indoor bowling alley, in the barn. Presidents Grant, Hayes, Harrison, and McKinley visited Roseland (wonder if Bowen made them wear those goofy bowling shoes?). A nice feature for families: Special teas are held for children throughout the summer, on various Sundays. Themes (these change from year to year) include a Children's Victorian Tea Party, Miss Tiggy Winkle (from Beatrix Potter stories) Tea, and a Tussy Mussy Tea. Each lasts about two hours. Children ages 3 to 14 take part; parents can join the tea party if they desire. A wonderful event happens here, on the first Saturday in August: an old-fashioned Children's Lawn Party, just as Henry Bowen would've done it, with period games and activities.

● Bigelow Hollow State Park

Rte. 197, Union, (860) 928-9200. Parking fee, weekends and holidays in season. **All ages.**

Explore this scenic woodland area—although, since it's 513 acres, you probably won't see it all—by foot or by boat. Parklands surround Mashapaug Lake. Recreation opportunities include fishing, hiking, boating, and, when the snow piles up, snowmobiling and cross-country skiing.

● Connecticut Audubon/Pomfret Farms

220 Day Rd., off Rte. 169, Pomfret, (860) 928-4041. **All ages.**

Enjoy the pastoral beauty of Connecticut's "Quiet Corner" at this 140-acre property, as you meander the hiking trails that loop around it. Guided bird walks and wildlife workshops are offered on a regular basis.

● Saddletown

281 Newport Rd., Oneco, (860) 564-1171. July–Aug., Sun., 11–6. $5.
Ages 2 and up.

What's an authentic replica of an old Western town doing in northeast Connecticut? We don't know, either, but if you're curious about their cowboy shows, pony rides, and petting animals, mosey on over.

● Mashamoquet Brook State Park

Rte. 44, Pomfret, (860) 928-6121. Fee, weekends and holidays in season.
All ages.

This 1,000-acre park is the home of the famous (well, around here, anyway) wolf den, where Reverend Gen. Israel Putnam is said to have slain the last wolf in Connecticut. Follow Wolf Den Trail to the site.

● Horseback Riding

Diamond A Ranch, in Dayville, is home of the "Pizza King ride." No, Pizza King is not a horse; you actually ride to a pizza parlor. Other rides are available, tailored to your interest and ability. Rides are offered year-round, weather permitting. Call the ranch at (860) 779-3000 for details.

 RESTAURANTS

● Willington's Pizza

25 River Rd., Rte. 32, Willington, (860) 429-7433. Daily, 11–11.

Not just any pizza—award-winning pizza is served here. So good, *Good Morning America* visited, chowed down, and did a story on them.

● Zip's Diner

Junction, Rtes. 12 and 101, Dayville, (860) 774-6335. Daily, 6–9.

This authentic 1954 diner serves home-cooked grub worthy of the "diner" name. Get your meat loaf and mashed or mac-and-cheese here. This is how Mom cooked before she went fat-free.

● We-Li-Kit Ice Cream

728 Hampton Rd., Rte. 97, Pomfret, (860) 974-1095. Summer, daily, 12–9:30.

Lu-Vit is more like it. This is real ice cream, made from the milk of real Connecticut cows. How do we know for sure? They're right here, on the property, about 150 of 'em. Bet Ben & Jerry can't say that.

● Stoggy Hollow General Store

Rte. 198, Woodstock Valley, (860) 974-3814. Daily, 7–8; Fri. and Sat. til 9.

Hard to find but worth it, this general store and eatery is cute as can be. The oversize sandwiches are messy and delicious, and the home-baked sweets are sheer heaven. But wait, there's more. An expanded menu features gourmet pizza, soon-to-be-world-famous hand-cut french fries, and "nostalgia drinks" like root beer floats and egg creams. Sit in the parlor of this 1836 colonial and enjoy the food and atmosphere. Or sit outside and watch the world go by. The general store, next door, has fun stuff like penny candies and classic small toys.

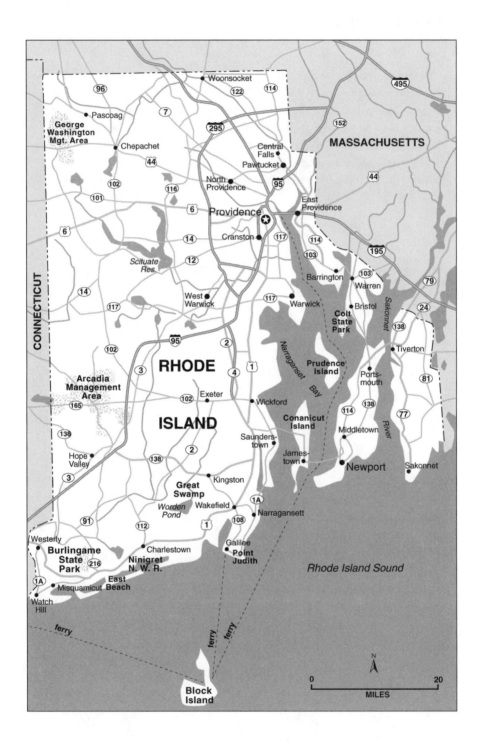

Rhode Island

■ Providence Area

If it's been awhile since you've visited, get ready for a surprise: This little city recently completed a multimillion-dollar revitalization program. The waterfront fairly sparkles, with landscaped river walks and Venetian-style footbridges for meandering pedestrians. Meanwhile, kayaks and canoes add color to the waterways that snake through the city. Some evenings, 100 "singing" bonfires—they call it "waterfire"—add a festive feel to the downtown waterfront. There's an IMAX theater and a skating rink that's *twice* the size of Rockefeller Center. The amphitheater at Waterplace Park, the city's four-acre urban park, is a lively scene when the free summer concerts are in swing. There's plenty of action along South Main Street, too, where historic colonial buildings have been authentically restored and now house boutiques, galleries, and restaurants.

As if that wasn't enough, Providence is now home to six-foot-tall statues of . . . potatoes! Or, rather, Mr. Potato Heads, part of a tourism campaign dubbed "Rhode Island—the Birthplace of Fun" featuring the homegrown spud created by Pawtucket-based toy maker, Hasbro. No word on what the state of Idaho thinks about this, but the artist-designed spuds are pretty goofy. The campaign is now over, and several taters have been auctioned off for charity, but some are still on location around town. There's one in the State House, another one at Caserta's Pizza. Keep your eyes peeled.

Need a souvenir? Pick up a jar of Mayor Buddy Cianci's own marinara sauce. (Proceeds sponsor scholarships for Providence schoolchildren.)

For information on events and lodgings, contact the Providence/ Warwick Convention and Visitors Bureau at (401) 274-1636 or (800) 233-1636 or visit www.providencecvb.com.

● Roger Williams Park Zoo

950 Elmwood Ave, off I-95, Providence, (401) 785-3510,
www.providencezoo.net. Open mid-May–mid-Oct., daily, 9–5; weekends and
holidays, 9–6. Open Oct.16–May 14, 9–4 every day. Adults, $7; 3–12,
$4.50. **All ages.**

It's easy to spend a pleasant, busy day exploring this wonderland of parks, ponds, lakes, and gardens that cover more than 430 acres. But Roger Williams Park is more than a nature tour; its centerpiece is an award-winning zoo. More than 160 species—nearly 1,000 animals—are housed here in expansive, naturalistic settings. Known for its conservation efforts, Roger Williams Zoo has been called "one of America's top ten zoos" by *Travel & Leisure Family.* Exhibits are grouped geographically, featuring Plains of Africa (home of elephants, giraffes, zebras, and more), Tropical Rainforest, Madagascar, and the Arctic (where polar bears Norton and Trixie frolic in their pool). One of the oldest zoos in the country, this one keeps getting better.

Don't go home yet—there's more to see and do. Walk the wetlands trail and try to identify native animals and plants. Visit the Museum of Natural History and the planetarium. Don't forget to take a ride on the carousel and the antique railroad train. Or—a must on muggy days—rent a paddleboat at the boathouse and explore the park's connecting waterways.

● WaterFire

101 Regent Ave., Providence, (401) 273-1155, www.waterfire.org. Apr.–Dec., weather permitting. Free. **All ages.**

What, exactly, is WaterFire? It's a fire sculpture, created by Providence artist Barnaby Evans, in which 100 bonfires blaze just above the surface of the three rivers that pass through the city's downtown. This fiery display is enhanced with music and ritual chants. From sunset to midnight or so, volunteers move up and down the river on a barge, rekindling burning torches as they burn during the evening's performance. Don't worry that your kids will have to get close to fire to see this spectacle; it's visible from several sites along the waterfront.

● Waterplace Park

Memorial Blvd., Providence, (401) 785-9450. Open year-round. Free.
All ages.

This four-acre urban park is a pleasant oasis in the heart of downtown. Surrounding a tidal basin, the park is edged by landscaped river walks and Venetian-style footbridges. An amphitheater is the site of free concerts throughout the summer.

● Fleet Skating Center

2 Kennedy Plaza, Providence, (401) 331-5544, www.ertp.com/fleetskating. Open daily, 10–10. Ice skating, Oct.–Mar.; alternates with roller skating during spring and summer months. Call for skating times. **Ages 3 and up.**

At 14,000 square feet, this outdoor rink is twice the size of Rockefeller Center's, and it offers both ice and roller skating, and skating lessons. Located in the heart of downtown, the skating center offers skate rentals, a pro shop, lockers, and a concession stand.

● Providence Children's Museum

100 South St., Providence, (401) 273-KIDS, www.childrenmuseum.org. Summer hours, open daily, 9:30–5; Fri. til 8; rest of year: open Tues.–Sun., 9:30–5 and Mon. holidays. Free first Sun. of each month. $4.50 per person.
Ages 1–10.

This terrific, interactive museum offers several fun activities, including a time-travel adventure and a wet-and-wild water exploration.

● Providence Performing Arts Center

220 Weybosset St., Providence, (401) 421-ARTS, (800) 455-TKTS, www.ppacri.org. Box office hours: Mon.–Fri., 10–6; Sat., noon–5. Ticket prices vary. **Ages 3 and up.**

This historic theater was built in 1928 as a Loew's Movie Palace. Now, live theater offerings include Broadway shows, revivals of classics like *Carousel* and *Grease* and productions for children such as *Magic School Bus Live!* Free organ concerts here in spring and fall.

● Feinstein IMAX Theatre

9 Providence Pl., Providence; (401) 453-IMAX, www.imax.com/providence. Films and showtimes vary. Ticket prices vary; generally about $11 for adults and $9 for kids 12 and under. **Ages 3 and up.**

Even though these mammoth screens are popping up everywhere, it's pretty thrilling to watch remarkable images on a six-story-high screen with wraparound digital sound. This 400-seat theater is located in the Providence Place Mall, directly across from Dave & Buster's, a giant entertainment complex with video games, billiards, and a restaurant. (Dave & Buster's may well be more enticing to older kids than the movies!)

● Museum of Art, Rhode Island School of Design

224 Benefit St., Providence, (401) 454-6534, www.risd.edu. Open Tues.–Sun., 10–5; third Thurs. of the month til 9 (free). Adults, $6; 5–18, $2. Free Sun., 10–1, Fri., 12–1:30, and on Free-for-All Saturdays (last Sat. of the month). **Ages 5 and up.**

Since RISD is one of the best art and design schools in the country, its art museum is worth a look. Collections include classical art from ancient Greece and Rome, 18th-century European porcelains (you might want to skip this if you've small children in tow), Chinese and Indian pieces, Egyptian objects, and, in Pendleton House, 19th-century American furniture and decorative arts. In all, collections feature 85,000 works of art, in all media, from all cultures. Perhaps the most interesting space for children is the Daphne Farago Wing, featuring contemporary art.

● Rhode Island State Capitol

82 Smith St., Providence, (401) 277-2357. Mon.–Fri., 8:30–4:30, except holidays. Self-guided tours during business hours; guided tours by appointment. **Ages 3 and up.**

Many believe that this impressive, white-domed Georgian marble structure is the most beautiful capitol building in America. Inside, see the full-length portrait of George Washington painted by Rhode Islander Gilbert Stuart.

● Crescent Park Carousel

At end of Bullock's Point Ave., E. Providence, (401) 435-7518, (401) 433-2828. Easter Sunday–Memorial Day, Sat. and Sun., 12–7. After Memorial Day, Fri.–Sun., 12–8. July–Labor Day, Wed.–Sun., 12–8; closed Mon.–Tues., except for summer holidays. Labor Day–Columbus Day, Sat. and Sun., 12–8. $.50 per ride or 5 rides for $2. **All ages.**

What a treasure! More than a century old, this carousel—once part of a large amusement park—is one of the few complete carousels of its type still in operation. Designed in 1895 by Charles I. D. Looff, it features 66 one-of-a-kind figures.

● Slater Memorial Park

Rte. 1A, Pawtucket, (401) 728-0500, ext. 252. Park: Memorial Day–Labor Day, 8 A.M.–9 P.M.; Labor Day–Memorial Day, 8–dusk. Carousel: Easter Sunday–June 30, Sat.–Sun., 11–5; July 1–Labor Day, daily, 11–5; Labor Day and Columbus Day weekends, 11–5. **All ages.**

Play some tennis, enjoy a picnic, and take a whirl on the restored 1894 Looff carousel, said to be the fastest Looff carousel ever made.

● Pawtucket Red Sox Baseball

McCoy Stadium, 1 Columbus Ave., Pawtucket, (401) 724-7300; www.pawsox.com. Tickets (general admission): adults, $5; 12 and under, $4. **All ages.**

This is the AAA baseball league farm team of the Boston Red Sox, so you never know if one of the young hotshots on the field will make it to the majors. Cheer 'em on from April through August.

● Slater Mill Historic Site

Roosevelt Ave., Pawtucket, (401) 725-8638; www.slatermill.org. Hours for general public: June–Nov. 1, Sat., 10–5; Sun., 1–5. Mar.–May and Nov.–third Sun. in Dec., Sat. and Sun., 1–5. Closed major holidays. Adults, $8; 12 and under, $6; under 6, free. **Ages 5 and up.**

This excursion is for older children who like the sounds of and are intrigued by the mechanisms of machinery. (You know who we're talking about: the kids who can't resist a construction site and adore dismantling small home appliances.) Billed as the birthplace of American industry, the site includes the Sylvanus Brown House (1758), an early skilled-worker's home; the Wilkinson Mill (1810), which houses an authentic 19th-century machine shop; and a working, 16,000-pound waterwheel. The 90-minute tour includes demonstrations of early textile machinery, hand spinning, and weaving.

● Canoeing and Kayaking

Take a guided kayak or canoe trip—we'd call it an urban river tour—with Paddle Providence and see the city from a different perspective. They're happy to tailor a trip to your interests (ecology, perhaps). They can also arrange paddling tours on nearby waterways. No paddling experience is necessary. Rentals and instruction are available. Canoes seat two to four people; kayaks seat up to two people; and "war canoes" seat eight to ten. For paddling in individual boats, kids should be 10 or older. A nonprofit program, Paddle Providence is based at Waterplace Park and operates on weekends in May, June, September, and October, and every day in July and August. For information, call (401) 453-1633.

● Fruit Picking

A number of Rhode Island farms offer fruit-picking possibilities—mostly raspberries, strawberries, blueberries, blackberries, and apples in season. Pick-your-own produce farms are located throughout the state, including several in Providence County. For listings, contact the Rhode Island Division of Agriculture, 22 Hayes St., Providence, RI 02908, (401) 277-2781.

 RESTAURANTS

● Caserta Pizzeria

121 Spruce St., Providence, (401) 272-3618. Open Sun.–Thurs. 9:30 A.M.– 10:30 p.m; Fri. and Sat. til 11:30.

The best pizza in Providence—no small feat in a college town with lots of competition! The atmosphere is strictly "middle-school cafeteria," but who cares when you're chowing down on a Wimpy Skippy (spinach, mozzarella, pepperoni) or an enormous, thick-crusted Sicilian pie with tangy sauce and cheese? The college crowd also swears by **Spikes,** at 273 Thayer St. (401) 454-1459, for awesome hot dogs, including good veggie dogs, the spicy "Angry Buffalo" dog, and super curly fries. Spikes' chicken sandwiches get high marks, too.

● Fire & Ice

48 Providence Pl., Providence, (401) 270-4040, www.fire-ice.com. Sun.– Thurs., 11:30–11; Fri. and Sat., 11:30–midnight.

Bright, bold Seuss-like decor is a feast for the eyes; for the tummy, it's build-your-own grill platters, piled as high as you dare. It's not cheap, and, yeah, you could make a comparable stir-fry at home, but it's kind of a fun experience. Kids choose which ingredients they want, so you can't miss. Since the crowd can be couple-y, it's best for (well-behaved) older kids.

● The Boathouse Restaurant

1 American Express Way at Waterplace Park, Providence, (401) 272-1040. Tues.–Fri., 11–10; Fri. and Sat., 11–11.

Sometimes, you just have to splurge on a waterfront restaurant. Here, the upstairs grill is upscale, while the lower level offers a casual atmosphere, appropriate for family dining. Seafood and steaks are specialties.

● Angelo's Civita Farnese

141 Atwells Ave., Providence, (401) 621-8171. Mon.–Thurs., 11–8:30; Fri. and Sat., 11:30–9; also open Sun. 12–6:30, Labor Day–Memorial Day.

This comfortable family restaurant is located in "Little Italy," and it's a true classic, known for megaportions and miniprices. All your favorite pasta dishes are on the menu, available in half-size portions for kids. (That may not be necessary if you have a small child—regular portions are huge enough to share.) *Mangia, bambini!*

■ Newport

America's First Resort. Millionaire's Playground. Queen of American Resorts. Yachting Capital of the World. Visit Newport, and you'll soon understand why this island seaport has earned such superlative titles. The city echoes its past, first as a 17th-century colonial town of merchants and traders, later as the summer resort of America's richest society members. You'll find the narrow streets surrounding its harbors lined with clapboard houses that were once home to sea captains and traders. You'll also see magnificent Gilded Age mansions, extravagant summer "cottages" for the wealthy American aristocracy during the Industrial Age, hugging the shoreline.

Newport remains a prestigious East Coast resort community; opulent sailboats and powerboats dot its harbors. The 17th-century mercantile harbor is now a contemporary center of fine restaurants, shops, and outdoor cafes. The beauty of the island, with its dramatic views of Narragansett Bay and the Atlantic Ocean, remains.

The summer season is crowded and congested, so you'll want to find time to venture out beyond Thames Street (the main drag) and the wharves. Tour a mansion or two, by all means, but take a drive to Fort Adams Park for a picnic. Take a harbor cruise, or walk the dunes at Second Beach for a pretty (and unhurried) view of this elegant coastal community. Your first stop might be the Gateway Visitor Information Center. You can park there, or at one of the other public garages, and plan to tour Newport on foot as much as possible. While it's possible to rent bicycles to cruise around town, we'd never recommend it with kids in tow—you'd be a nervous wreck in downtown traffic. Trust us—you'll be happiest if you travel by foot or by boat as much as possible.

For information, contact the Newport County Convention and Visitors Bureau at (401) 845-9123 or (800) 976-5122 or visit www.GoNewport.com.

● Newport Mansions

Plan on seeing only one or two mansions during your Newport visit, especially if your kids are very young. Children quickly tire of the hour-long tours and the inevitable summer crowds that flock to see how the Vanderbilts, Belmonts, and Berwinds lived. You'll enjoy the tours most with older kids (ages eight and up), but if you're taking an infant or toddler, be prepared to carry them—most mansions are not stroller accessible. Also, note that combination tickets are available for properties that are part of the Preservation Society of Newport County. These include The Breakers and Green Animals Topiary Gardens. Here are three mansions that families will enjoy the most:

● The Breakers

Ochre Point Ave., (401) 847-1000, www.newportmansions.org. Apr.–Oct., daily, 10–5; July–Labor Day, Fri. and Sat., 10–6. Decorated for Dec. holidays every other year; open 10–4. Adults, $15; 6–11, $4.50. **Ages 3 and up.**

The Breakers, built for Cornelius Vanderbilt, is the most palatial of Newport's mansions. You'll marvel at this 70-room castle of marble, mosaic, alabaster, and mahogany, resembling a 16th-century northern Italian palace. View the music room, library, bathrooms that deliver both salt and freshwater, a magnificent double loggia with commanding ocean views, and an opulent dining room. The "cottage" served as a children's playhouse.

● The Astors' Beechwood

580 Bellevue Ave., (401) 846-3772, www.astors-beechwood.com. Mid-May–Oct., daily, 10–5; Nov., daily, 10–4. Weekends, Feb.–mid-May, 10–4. Adults, $15; 6–13, $10; 5 and under, free. Family rate, $45. **Ages 8 and up.**

Kids enjoy The Beechwood; it's a living-history tour. Instead of roped-off displays and dry narration, you'll encounter the Astors' staff of servants, who will show you around the house. You are the Astors' guests—and members of high society, no less—for their anniversary ball. The Beechwood Theater Company reenacts life as it would have been at The Beechwood in the summer of 1891. The annual Children's Day features games, storytelling, and special activities.

● Cliff Walk

Put the baby in a backpack and grab the little ones' hands for this dramatic walk overlooking the Atlantic Ocean. On this steep, picturesque hike, you'll see the rocky coastline at its best and pass by some of Newport's mansions. The 3.5-mile trail runs from Memorial Blvd. and Eustis Ave. to Bailey's Beach. Walk all of it or just a part.

● Fort Adams State Park

Ocean Dr., (401) 847-2400. Year-round, sunrise–sunset. **All ages.**

Built in 1824, the fort was designed to accommodate 2,400 soldiers with 468 mounted cannons. It is not open for public viewing, but its park is a great place to picnic. Features include a small beach, fishing pier, boat launching ramps, barbecue grills, picnic tables, and plenty of room for the kids to run and play while you savor the oceanside setting.

● Newport Exploration Center

Easton's Beach, (401) 849-8430, neaq.org. Open Memorial Day–Labor Day, daily, 10–4. Admission, $4; under 3, free. **All ages.**

Get up close and personal with the fascinating undersea residents of Narragansett Bay here, at Rhode Island's only aquarium. Pet a real shark, find out if an ocean pout (a species of fish found in these waters) actually pouts, hold a living fossil, learn about tide pool treasures. Great summer camps, too.

● Rhode Island Fisherman and Whale Center

144 Spring St., (401) 849-1340. Daily, except Wed., 10–5. Adults, $2; 5–13, $1; under 5, free. **All ages.**

Ahoy, mate! Young salts will enjoy this interactive exploration of the sea. See—and touch—Rhode Island marine life (horseshoe crabs, starfish, sea urchins), and take a turn at the wheel of a fishing boat. Listen to recorded "fish stories," go on a (videotaped) whale watch, and try your hand at tying a bowline and other nautical knots. Test your skill as a quahogger. (Don't know what a quahog is? You'll find out.) You can even eavesdrop on real fishermen chatting over the marine radio.

● International Tennis Hall of Fame

194 Bellevue Ave., (401) 849-3990, (800) 457-1144, www.tennisfame.org. Year-round, daily, 9:30–5. Adults, $8; under 16, $4; family rate, $20. **Ages 6 and up.**

Tennis buffs will not want to miss this. Housed in the Newport Casino Building, it's billed as the birthplace of United States tennis tournaments. Some of the game's greatest players have played here, including Rod Laver,

Chris Evert, and Martina Navratilova. Old Davis Cup films are shown in a 450-seat theater. A simulated tennis gallery and interactive videos allow you to test your tennis savvy.

● Green Animals Topiary Gardens

Cory's Lane, off Rte. 114, Portsmouth, (401) 847-1000, www.newportmansions.org. Open May–Oct., daily, 10–5. Adults, $10; 6–11, $4. **All ages.**

This maze of charming sculptured geometric figures and animal shapes is sure to delight young children and amaze adults. The gardens contain nearly 80 plant sculptures that have been lovingly pruned and shaped; 21 pieces are animals or birds made of California privet and yew. The main house features Victorian toy collections.

● Old Colony and Newport Railway

19 America's Cup Ave. (across from the Gateway Visitor Information Center), (401) 849-0546, www.ocnrr.com. July–Labor Day, Tues.–Thurs. and Sat.; May–June, Sept. and Nov., Sun. only, 12:30 P.M. Adults, $6; under 14, $3.50. **Ages 3 and up.**

Board a vintage 1930 railway car for a 10-mile scenic round-trip along the eastern shore of Narragansett Bay. During the 80-minute trip, you'll enjoy views of Jamestown Island and Quonset Point. There's plenty to see, so kids don't get bored. Check out the power- and sailboats, tugs and barges, and ogle the naval warships as you cruise through the naval base.

● Sailing

Fort Adams State Park, Ocean Dr., (401) 849-8385. Memorial Day–Labor Day.

Visit the Yachting Capital of the World without getting out on the water? Unthinkable! Plus, you'd miss seeing Newport from the water side. If you're adept at handling a small sailboat, rent one from Sail Newport Sailing Center; they offer 6- to 24-foot vessels by the hour or half day, and (if you need a refresher course) private and group instruction for kids and adults. (A word of advice: This isn't for Nervous Nellies; Newport Harbor is incredibly busy. Keep an eye out for those party boats!) Call ahead to reserve on busy summer weekends. Rate information is available by phone.

● Viking Queen

Goat Island Dock, (401) 847-6921, www.captain-cook.net. Mid-May– mid-Oct., Mon.–Sat. Trip schedule: mid-May–June, 11:30, 1, 2:30; July 1–Labor Day, 10, 11:30, 1, 2:30, 4; Labor Day–Columbus Day, 11:30, 1, 2:30. Adults, $8; 5–11, $4. **All ages.**

If a ferry boat cruise is more your style, relax aboard the *Viking Queen*'s one-hour, narrated bay and harbor cruises. Take in Newport's famous sights, including Fort Adams, the Newport Bridge, Hammersmith Farm (summer White House of the Kennedys), the "House on the Rock," and more.

● Butterfly Zoo at Newport Butterfly Farm

1038 Aquidneck Ave., Middletown, (401) 849-9519, www.butterflyzoo@webtv.net. Open daily, May–Sept., 11–4. Weekend rates: adults, $5; under 12, $3; weekday rates: $4/$3. Under 3, free. **All ages.**

This 30-by-100-foot greenhouse structure is home to butterflies from all over the world. Mingle with these gorgeous insects (hint: they're most active on sunny days) and take pictures if you wish. You're inside *with* the butterflies, not just looking in, so you might have a butterfly perch on you. (They're looking for salt from perspiration, we're told.) You might even see a butterfly laying eggs. (Note: No rest rooms here; closest are at Dunkin' Donuts, down the street.)

● Newport on Foot

Tours leave from Gateway Visitor Information Center, (401) 846-5391. Mid-Apr.–Oct. One-hour tours; schedule varies. Kids, $6 (must be accompanied by an adult; no charge for adult). **Ages 5 and up.**

What's the story behind those splendid storefronts and stately homes? Who's buried in Newport's ancient graveyards? Find out on a guided, narrated walking tour designed for kids, departing from the Gateway Visitor Information Center. Themed tours include the intriguingly named "Ghosts and Graveyards" (you make grave rubbings) and "Skeletons and Angels." At tour's end, guests enjoy lemonade and cookies.

● Beavertail State Park and Lighthouse

Rte. 138, Beavertail Point, Jamestown, (401) 423-3270. Memorial Day–June, weekends only. June–Aug.; tours daily, Wed.–Sun., 10–4. **All ages.**

The centerpiece of this park is the lighthouse at Beavertail Point. Park naturalists give tours three times daily; you'll also enjoy panoramic views of the Atlantic coastline.

● Norman Bird Sanctuary and Museum

583 Third Beach Rd., Middletown, (401) 846-2577, www.normanbirdsanctuary.org. Memorial Day–Labor Day, daily, 9–5; Labor Day–Memorial Day, Tues.– Sun., 9–5. Open Wed. til dark in summer. Trail use: adults, $4; 3–12, $2. Museum is free. Free Sun. morning bird walks in spring and fall, 8 A.M. **All ages.**

This 450-acre refuge is a wonderful outdoors getaway for families, with seven miles of walking trails. Don't miss Hanging Rock Trail—this gently sloping hike (one mile each way) will take you to a dramatic rock formation overlooking the ocean. Before leaving the sanctuary, stop in at the trailside museum, housed on the second floor of the large barn. You'll see specimens of local birds and animals mounted on the walls, with explanations of their habitats and habits. Kids can crawl into the authentically reconstructed bark wigwam.

● Beaches

Kids might find that the best thing to do in Newport is to head for one of its beaches. Besides swimming at the small beach area at **Fort Adams State Park,** you can ride the waves (or just dunk your toes) at **First Beach** (Memorial Blvd., running from Cliff Walk to Middletown); the three-mile-long, sandy **Second Beach** (Sachuest Point area in Middletown); and **Third Beach** (Sachuest Point area on the Sakonnet River). **Easton's Beach** now has a wonderful feature for kids, the Newport Exploration Center. (See listing.)

 ## RESTAURANTS

● The Market on the Boulevard

43 Memorial Blvd., Newport, (401) 848-2600. Open Memorial Day– Labor, daily, 8–8; off-season, open Mon.–Sat., 8–7; Sun., 8–6.

Open for breakfast, lunch, and dinner, this "gourmet" deli/bakery offers carryout cuisine—perfect for those times when the kids can't handle a sit-down restaurant, but you'd like a tasty bite (hold the fast food, please). This is also a good bet for do-it-yourself grocery items for boating or beach feasts.

● Scales & Shells

527 Thames St., Newport, (401) 846-FISH, www.scalesandshells.com. Open Mon.–Thurs. 5–10; Fri. and Sat., 5–11, and Sun., 4–10. Reduced hours off-season.

We couldn't send you to a seaport town and not recommend a great fish place, now could we? This is our pick, thanks to the terrific fresh fish (we love whatever they've got sizzling on the mesquite grill), and kid-friendly fish-and-chips. If someone in your party won't eat anything with gills or a shell, get an order of pasta with red or white sauce. They don't offer a kids' menu, but the chef will make half orders on most items. Craving a burger? You won't do better than another Thames Street eatery, **Brick Alley Pub & Restaurant** (140 Thames St., 401-849-6334). This local fave/award winner features extra-lean, wondrous burgers, plus steaks, seafood, and southwestern-style cooking, even a kids' menu.

● Flo's Clam Shack

4 Wave Ave., Middleton, (401) 847-8141. Please call for current hours.

We know, the kids won't go within 10 feet of a squishy, yucky fried clam, so give 'em a PB&J and get yourself a delightfully briny, just-greasy-enough heap o' Flo's clams. They've been dipping clams into the Fryolator since 1936 and—dare we say it?—they turn out the best in the Ocean State. They've also got an amazing raw bar, with 90 sauces.

● Bannister's Wharf

In the heart of downtown Newport, you'll find lively Bannister's Wharf. Sit outside under a Cinzano umbrella and order oysters on the half shell, lobster rolls, or a bowl of chowder. Order sandwiches, salads, sweets— virtually anything—from outdoor cafés while you watch the harbor activity.

■ South County

Tiny Rhode Island offers an astonishing 400 miles of scenic coastline. Nowhere is this more evident than the South County region. From Narragansett Pier to Watch Hill, the southwestern edge of the state is nearly one continuous stretch of sand, offering beaches for every taste.

Perhaps the best family beach is in Narragansett—**Sand Hill Cove.** This one is inside the breakwall, so the surf is calm. This beach also has a brand-new pavilion and amenities such as lifeguards, bathhouses, and snack bars. **Narragansett Town Beach** is a fun scene for older kids who like wild waves and bodysurfing. This beach is popular with surfers, especially when storms threaten. (Some surfers do their thing here year-round, wearing heavy wet-suits.) This beach has facilities as well. Arrive early to find a parking space.

Charlestown Beach, at the edge of the Ninigret National Wildlife Refuge, is popular with residents and visitors alike. You'll find it clean and spacious, with changing rooms, showers, and a small store for refreshments. If you'd like to get away from the ocean beach crowd, pack a picnic basket, and head for the Ninigret National Wildlife Refuge. You'll find peaceful walking trails to the small pond beach.

You won't be alone at **East Beach,** but the crowd is a mellow one. Located at the eastern edge of the wildlife refuge, East Beach is considered one of the best around. You'll find nearly three miles of white sand and lots of dunes. Kids enjoy the walk to Ninigret Pond, where they can watch windsurfers sail the protected waters. There are no facilities here, and the small parking lot fills up early (before nine) on weekends, so arrive early. Right next to East Beach is **Blue Shutters Beach,** where many East Beach-goers trek for refreshments and rest rooms. Blue Shutters has nearly four miles of clean sand, plus amenities, concessions, and kids, kids, kids.

Like to be where the action is? Proceed to busy **Misquamicut Beach,** where the air is filled with the smell of suntan lotion and the sound of boom boxes, and the sand is a mosaic of colorful beach towels. Of course, kids love all this, especially the snack bars and beachside activities—including minigolf, kiddie rides, and a Ferris wheel. The total opposite experience is at Watch Hill, a quiet Victorian town on the western border of the state. **Watch Hill Beach** is small and rarely crowded, with showers, changing rooms, and a cluster of restaurants and shops nearby. Generations of kids have enjoyed the beach's Flying Horse Carousel.

For information, contact South County Tourism Council at (800) 548-4662; www.southcountyri.com.

Beyond the beaches, here's a look at some other favorite South County attractions.

● The Enchanted Forest

Rte. 3, exit 2 off I-95, Hope Valley; (401) 539-7711. May–mid-June, Wed.–Fri., 10–2; Sat. and Sun., 10–5. Mid-June–Labor Day, daily, 10–5; month of Sept., Sat. and Sun., 10–5. Per person, $12; under 2, free. Extra charge for go-carts. **All ages.**

Too, too cute, this fairyland-themed amusement park will tickle the small fry in your bunch. Fun features include storybook exhibits, a jump castle, a carousel, tame roller coasters, two Ferris wheels, favorite carnival rides such as "paratrooper" and "scrambler," a petting zoo, miniature golf, go-carts, and batting cages. There's a snack bar and picnic area, too.

● Adventureland

Point Judith Rd., Narragansett, (401) 789-0030. Weekends, mid-Apr.–mid-June and Labor Day–mid-Oct., 11–6. Daily, mid-June–Labor Day, 10–10. Activity prices vary. **Ages 7 and up.**

Junior sports fiends will be in heaven here. If yours are into minigolf, they'll find the course here a hoot, with waterfalls, caves, streams, and an island. Bumper boats, batting cages, and a go-cart track round out the offerings. This attraction is recommended for ages seven and up; go-carts require a height of 56 inches.

● Canonchet Farm and South County Museum

Off Boston Neck Rd., Scenic 1A, Narragansett, (401) 783-5400, www.southcountymuseum.com. Farm: open daily. Museum: May–Oct., Wed.–Sat., 11–4. Adults, $4; 12 and under, $2. **Ages 5 and up.**

Spread over this 174-acre park is a 19th-century working farm, a cemetery with graves dating to 1700, nature trails, picnic areas, and the South County Museum. The museum features articles of early Rhode Island life, including antique toys and dolls and a collection of carriages. At Canochet Farm, see demonstrations of farm activities, hear stories, and visit with barnyard animals. Special events are held frequently; call for a schedule.

● Water Wizz

330 Atlantic Ave., across from Misquamicut Beach, Westerly, (401) 322-0520, www.waterwizz.com. Memorial Day–mid-June, Sat. and Sun., 11–4. Mid-June–Labor Day, daily, 10–6:30. Call for current rates. **Ages 5 and up.**

If the kids are feeling hot, sticky, and crabby after a couple of hours at the beach, this will cool them down—and give grown-ups a chance to sip an iced tea in peace. Watch them squeal and splash down six giant water slides, four twisty serpentine slides (including a kiddie version), and two 50-foot-high speed slides. It's best for bigger kids, but little ones can ride with an adult.

● Flying Horse Carousel

Bay St., Watch Hill, (401) 596-7761. Mid-June–Labor Day, daily, 1–8. Children only. $1 per ride. **Ages 2–12.**

This 1867 merry-go-round is believed to be the oldest in America and is designated as a National Historic Landmark. Each hand-carved horse has a real tail and mane; horses are suspended from a center frame, swinging out or "flying" when in motion. Grab the brass ring and win a free ride.

● South County Bike Path

Off Rte. 139, Kingston train station, W. Kingston, (401) 789-4422. **All ages.**

This 3.7-mile multiuse path starts at Kingston train station and passes through Great Swamp and Ministerial Rd. to Peace Dale and Wakefield. Bikers, walkers, and in-line skaters share the paved pathway.

● Fisherville Brook Wildlife Refuge

Pardon Joslin Rd., Exeter, (401) 231-6444, www.asri.org. Open dawn–dusk. **All ages.**

This 937-acre preserve provides a cool, leafy escape on a sweltering day—and loads of natural beauty anytime. A walking trail meanders through 70 acres of property, snaking through pine forests, fields, streams, and past a waterfall. A historic cemetery is also on the property.

● Yawgoo Valley Ski Area & Sports Park

Off Rte. 2, Exeter, (401) 295-5366, www.yawgoo.com. Open during ski season and in summer months. **All ages.**

Rhode Island's only ski area offers 12 trails for day and night skiing and a snow-tubing area. In summer, the action turns wet, thanks to two water slides and a swimming pool.

● Boat and Whale-Watching Cruises

You'd expect that a sea-faring region like South County would have more than a couple of options for getting out on the water. You'd be right. A couple of the best bets for families are these: **The Frances Fleet** offers whale-watching cruises, sailing out of Peace Dale. Call (401) 783-4988 or (800) 863-5937 for information. For narrated sightseeing cruises of Point Judith Harbor and nearby islands, consider taking the **Southland Riverboat,** a double-decker, 145-passenger vessel, departing from State Pier 3, in Galilee. Trips last an hour and three-quarters; they also offer fall foliage trips. Call (401) 783-2954 or visit www.southlandcruises.com.

● Casey Farm

2325 Boston Neck Rd., Saunderstown, (401) 295-1030. Open June–mid-Oct., Tues., Thurs., Sat., 1–5. **Ages 3 and up.**

This 300-acre working farm is a rare example of the original plantation farms of the colonial era. The 1750 farmhouse, overlooking Narragansett Bay, was a site of Revolutionary War activity. Today, the farm is community supported and grows Rhode Island certified organic produce. Tour the house museum and family cemetery, stroll the hiking trails, and perhaps take home some organic seedlings and produce.

 RESTAURANTS

● W.B. Cody's

265 Post Rd., Westerly, (401) 322-4070, www.wbcodys@aol.com. Mon.–Thurs., 11:30–9; Fri., 11:30–10; Sat., noon–10; Sun., noon–9.

A little bit of the Wild West in Westerly, this is one of those places where they give the entrees annoyingly cute names. You'll have a serious chow-fest, though, especially if you order the Fred Flintstone-size rack o' ribs, or the "Mae West chicken dinner" (you guessed it—all white meat). The kids' menu features the usual lineup; we like the fact that kids (12 and under) eat free on Sunday. Saves some change when you're feeding a coupla lil cowpokes.

● George's of Galilee

250 Sand Hill Cove Rd., Port of Galilee, (401) 783-2306. Mid-Feb.–Memorial Day, 11:30–9; Memorial Day–mid-Oct., 11:30–10; mid-Oct.–mid-Feb., Thurs.–Sun., 11:30–9.

This is one of those big, bustling, shore dinner-with-view outposts. Ferries headed for Block Island depart here, so it gets busy; rather than wait in lines, we advise you to head upstairs to the deck for an inexpensive menu and great views of Long Island Sound. The menu leans toward local fresh fish, including fish-and-chips, seafood salads, fried clams, and, for those who prefer turf to surf, chicken and beef. They offer a kids' menu, and kids who finish their dinners can pick out a toy (to keep) from the toy chest. Now, there's an inducement to join the Clean Plate Club!

■ Other Rhode Island Highlights

These family-friendly attractions don't fit neatly into any of our geographic categories, but they merit inclusion anyway. And in Rhode Island, you're never too far from anyplace else!

● Coggeshall Farm Museum

Colt State Park, Rte. 114, Bristol, (401) 253-9062. Mar.–Sept, 10–6; Oct.–Feb., 10–5. Adults, $2.75; children, $1.50. Rates vary for special events. **All ages.**

What was it like to live and work on a New England farm in the 18th century? Find out here, at this 35-acre working coastal farm located near a salt marsh on Narragansett Bay. These days, rare breeds of livestock are raised here, including oxen, pigs, chicken, and sheep, who roam the property freely. Depending on the season, visiting kids can help shear a sheep, see maple sugaring demonstrated, watch a team of oxen till the soil, and see craftspeople at work. The best time to visit with kids is during the Days of Merriment, held in June. Activities include 18th-century children's games. Call for information.

● Easy Bay Bicycle Path

This paved path is open only to walkers and bicyclists, following 15 scenic miles between Providence and Bristol, through parks that line Narragansett Bay. Attractions along the way include a Looff carousel, several state parks, and Brickyard Pond. There are several places to stop for refreshment along the way, too. Rest rooms are available at Colt State Park and Haines State Park. Need to rent a bike? Try **Bay Path Cycles,** 13 State St., in Bristol.

● Environmental Education Center

1401 Hope St., Rte. 114, Bristol, (401) 245-7500, www.asri.org. Open May–Sept., daily, 9–5; Oct.–Apr., Mon.–Sat., 9–5; Sun., noon–5. Adults, $5; 4–12, $3. **All ages.**

This state-of-the-art living museum features a 40-foot, life-size model of a right whale, a tide pool touch tank, and several more intriguing indoor and outdoor exhibits.

● Emilie Ruecker Wildlife Refuge

Seapowet Ave., Tiverton, (401) 949-5454; www.asri.org. Open daily, dawn–dusk. **All ages.**

Managed by the Audubon Society of Rhode Island, this 48-acre wildlife sanctuary offers 1.5 miles of hiking trails, winding through woodland, meadow, and salt marsh. Look for feeding herons, egrets, and osprey as you wander; enjoy expansive views of the Sakonnet River.

■ Block Island

"This place is like Martha's Vineyard was, twenty years ago," some say, and they mean it in the best possible way. If your description of the perfect getaway features words like "serene" and "relaxing," and if your vision of the perfect place includes windswept dunes and pastoral vistas, consider Block Island.

There's plenty to do on Block Island. It's just that, once you arrive here, you won't feel compelled to rush around and do them. The pace is slow and the pleasures are simple: Building sandcastles on the beach, bicycling around the seven-mile island, kite-flying, kayaking, and fishing along the beach are popular pursuits.

The ferry ride to the island will put you in the mood, as you watch Block Island slowly appear on the horizon. Look closely to see if you can spot the buoys marking the harbor entrance as you get closer to port. Ferries depart to Block Island from Point Judith, Rhode Island, year-round, and from Newport and Providence, Rhode Island, and New London, Connecticut, and Montauk, New York, during the summer season. Even if your ferry accepts cars, don't bother to bring one. The only proper way to do Block Island is on a bicycle. (In bad weather, it's okay to take a taxi.)

Block Island is less pretentious than other New England resorts, and somewhat less expensive as well. It's "less" of a lot of things, which makes it more attractive to families who want a relaxing getaway.

For information, contact the Block Island Tourism Council at (401) 466-5200 or (800) 383-2474 or visit www.blockislandinfo.com.

Getting There: For ferry information, call Interstate Navigation Co./ Nelseco Navigation Co. at (401) 783-4613 (in Rhode Island) or (860) 442-7881 (in Connecticut). For Montauk ferry information, call (516) 668-2214. A quicker, pricier option: The Island Hi-Speed Ferry, a catamaran, sails from State Pier in Galilee, Rhode Island, arriving in New Harbor, Block Island, in about 30 minutes. Call (877) 733-9425 for information.

● Mohegan Bluffs

These rugged clay cliffs may be found at the southernmost tip of the island. Follow Spring St. to Mohegan Trail. Climb up a path to the 200-foot elevation and gaze out over the Atlantic. You'll also see Southeast Light, a beacon to seafarers since 1874. The lighthouse was moved back from the crumbling cliff face, amid much fanfare, in 1993 to ensure it wouldn't tumble into the sea. Wooden stairs will take you back down to Mohegan Bluffs beach, which is secluded but pebbly.

● Block Island Beaches

This island is practically surrounded by beaches. It's hard to tell where one beach ends and the next one begins! There's two-mile **Crescent Beach,** on the starboard side as you arrive by ferry; **Frederick J. Benson Beach** (closest to town) has amenities and rentals. To the north is **Scotch Beach** and, farther north, **Mansion Beach,** where only the stone walls of a vanished mansion remain. South of the ferry landing is **Ballard's Beach.** The best way to discover your favorite: Kick off your shoes, slather on the sunscreen, and start walking. You're sure to find an enticing little cove of sand and surf.

● Bicycling

Pedal around this 7-mile-long, 3.5-mile-wide island for views of rolling hills festooned with wildflowers, windswept dunes, and the Victorian architecture of Old Harbor. You may also see Great Salt Pond and the pleasure-boat basin, New Harbor. Old Harbor is the commercial wharf where the ferries dock. At the northern tip of the island, you'll see Settler's Rock and the North Light Lighthouse (open for tours) at Sandy Point. (Please don't swim at Sandy Point, due to dangerous currents.) You'll also see numerous freshwater ponds and wildlife refuge areas. Bicycles may be rented at several shops, including **Esta's** on Water St. at Old Harbor, (401) 466-2652. They offer child seats and Tag-alongs, those small-size add-ons that allow small fry to pedal along, much like a bicycle built for two. These are really great because, frankly, Block Island's hilly terrain can be challenging for little legs, and the curvy roadways make it difficult to keep everyone in sight as you roll along. Once you get the hang of pedaling in tandem, a Tag-along bike is a dandy way to tour Block Island.

● Fishing

Block Island is famous for fishing. Besides the deep-sea charter boat trips, you can surf-cast for blues, striped bass, or flounder, or get a license and try your luck with the freshwater ponds for bass, perch, and pickerel. To rent a fly rod or surf rod, try **Oceans & Ponds** on Ocean Ave.; they also offer guided fishing trips. Bait and tackle are available at **Twin Maples** at 22 Beach Ave., (401) 466-5547.

● Rustic Rides Farm

West Side Rd., (401) 466-5060. Summer and fall. **Ages 3 and up.**

A sunset horseback ride, on the beach, no less, may well be your most special Block Island memory. Try to overlook the rather chaotic appearance of the property (animals and equipment scattered about); soon, you'll be astride a gentle horse and be heading down the rugosa rose–lined pathway to the beach. The farm is owned by a family with children, so their guides are good with kids. Rides last about an hour.

● Hotel Manisses Animal Farm

One Spring Rd., (800) MANISSE, (401) 466-2421. **All ages.**

The Hotel Manisses is certainly lovely, but you don't have to stay there to enjoy its most child-friendly feature: a pasture full of animals, including exotics like llamas, a Scottish Highland steer, and fainting goats. Stroll around—nobody will mind—and take a peek. The hotel is a short walk from Old Harbor.

● Hiking—Clayhead Nature Trails and the Greenway

Entrance to Clayhead Nature Trails and parking off Corn Neck Rd. Guided walks, daily, mid-June–Labor Day. Donation suggested. Schedule printed in Block Island Times *newspaper, or call (401) 466-2129 for details. Greenway trails have several access points; pick up trail map at The Nature Conservancy office, near Deadeye Dick's.* **All ages.**

Hiking families love Block Island, where a quarter of the land is protected from development. Hiking trails offer plenty of variety. Don't miss the Greenway, a network of trails that wind through park, conservancy, and private lands from the center of the island to the southern shore, and Clayhead Nature Trails, on the north side of the island. The Nature Conservancy offers naturalist-led nature walks; guides point out Island birds and plant life, with (depending on your guide) a smattering of natural history and coastal ecology. Or go it alone, armed with a trail map. Pick up a map, with all Block Island trails diagramed, at The Nature Conservancy office. Clayhead Trails are hilly, but not too steep (stay on the trails to avoid poison ivy); follow side trails to the beach. On the way back, stop by Littlefield Bee Farm, across the street. See how honey is produced, and pick up a jar of Block Island honey at their farm stand for a sweet souvenir. The Greenway trails have several access points. Inspired by the Greenway system of trails in England, these consist of more than 25 miles of clear paths, winding through the southern half of Block Island. A highlight is the Enchanted Forest, a cool oasis of tall red pines, spruce, and maples.

● Rodman's Hollow

Off Cooneymus Rd. **All ages.**

Hop off your bikes and visit this cool, natural spot. Created by a deep glacial depression, a scoop of lush hills slope toward the ocean's edge. This is the only U.S. habitat of the Block Island meadow vole, a little mouselike creature; maybe your little sharp-eyed creature will spot one.

● Kayaking/Canoeing

Block Island's Great Salt Pond is a haven for paddlers. The folks at **Oceans & Ponds** on Ocean Street will direct you to the best places to go, based on your abilities. Most paddlers put in at Great Salt Pond for a leisurely paddle in protected water. After a short briefing from the folks at Oceans & Ponds, even neophytes can handle this serene inner pond or the inland tributaries of Trims and Harbor Ponds. Or perhaps Sachem Pond, to the north, great for swimming, picnicking, and bird-watching. Don't want "serene"? Rent an ocean kayak, and get a rousing workout, versus the ocean waves and currents. If you're looking for a real adrenalin rush, surf-ride the ocean waves in a sit-upon Kahuna, also available from this Orvis retailer. They also rent canoes. Call (800) ORVIS or (401) 466-5131.

● Shellfishing

A license is required for shellfishing. Obtain one at the Block Island Police Station on the corner of Beach and Ocean Aves.

● Block Island Farmers Market

In season, Wed., 9–11 A.M., near Rebecca's; and Sat., 9–11, at Negus Park on Ocean Ave. **All ages.**

Block Island's bounty is on display at the farmers market, where island farmers and artisans offer locally grown produce, baked goods, and homemade crafts. You'll find much more interesting souvenirs than the same old T-shirts, along with great goodies to pack for a picnic at the beach.

 RESTAURANTS

● Finn's

Water St., Old Harbor, (401) 466-2473. End of Apr.–Columbus Day, 11:30–9 or 10.

Eat indoors or outdoors at Finn's and watch the ferries docking at Old Harbor. They have their own fish market next door, so you know the catch is fresh. You can get an inexpensive sandwich or a lobster dinner or anything in between all day, so the kids can choose fun food while adults enjoy a leisurely meal. The number-one kids' choice here is the fish sandwich; adults rave about Finn's baked stuffed shrimp.

● Rebecca's

Water St., Old Harbor, (401) 466-5411. Memorial Day–Labor Day, 7–9.

Want to take a picnic to the bluffs or the beach? Sure you do. Many delis and restaurants on the island offer food to go. We like Rebecca's, where you can get child-pleasing dogs and super sandwiches (try the Southwest chicken), packed to go.

Annual Events

MASSACHUSETTS

January
Bright Lights at Forest Park, Springfield, (413) 748-6190

February
Washington's Birthday Celebration, Old Sturbridge Village, Sturbridge, (800) SEE-1830
Winter Week, Hancock Shaker Village, Pittsfield, (413) 443-0188

March
Boston St. Patrick's Day Parade, South Boston, (617) 536-4100

April
Boston Marathon, Boston, (617) 236-1652 or (508) 435-6905
Reenactment of the Battle of Lexington and Concord, Lexington Green, (781) 861-0928
Daffodil Festival, Nantucket Island, (508) 228-1700

May
Higgins Faire, Higgins Armory Museum, (508) 853-6015
Museum-Goers' Month, Greater Boston, (800) 888-5515
Seaport Festival, Salem, (978) 262-1414
Art Newbury Street, Boston, (617) 267-7961

June
Art in the Park Festival, DeCordova Museum, Lincoln, (781) 259-8355
St. Peter's Fiesta, St. Peter's Square, Gloucester, (978) 283-1601
Taunton Riverfront Festival, Taunton, (508) 821-9347

Blessing of the Fleet, MacMillan Wharf, Provincetown, (508) 487-3424

Cambridge River Festival, Cambridge, (617) 349-4380

St. Anthony's Festival, North End, Boston, (617) 536-4100

July

Boston Harborfest, Boston, (617) 227-1528

Boston Pops Fourth of July Concert, Charles River Esplanade, Boston, (617) 266-1492

Festival Americana 4th of July Parade, Pittsfield, (413) 443-6501

Yankee Homecoming Days, Newburyport, (978) 462-6680

Lowell Folk Festival, Market St., Lowell, (978) 970-5000

New Bedford Summerfest, New Bedford, (508) 999-5231

Barnstable County Fair, East Falmouth, (508) 563-3200

Independence Day Celebration and Parade (historical parade), Old Sturbridge Village, Sturbridge, (508) 347-3362

Green River Festival, Greenfield, (413) 773-5463

August

Gloucester Waterfront Festival, Gloucester, (978) 283-1601

Fall River Celebrates America, Fall River, (508) 676-8226

Plymouth Lobster Festival, Plymouth, (508) 746-8500

Sand Castle and Sculpture Day, Jetties Beach, Nantucket, (508) 228-1700

Taste of Northampton, Northampton, (413) 584-1900

Marshfield Fair, Marshfield, (781) 834-6629

September

Three Apples Storytelling Festival, Harvard, (617) 499-9529

Essex Clamfest, Memorial Park, Essex, (978) 283-1601

Bourne Scallop Fest, Buzzards Bay Park, Bourne, (508) 759-6000

The Big E (state fair), Eastern States Exposition fairgrounds, West Springfield, (413) 737-2443

Franklin County Fair, Wisdom Way, Greenfield, (413) 774-4282

October

Head of the Charles Regatta (rowing event), Charles River, Cambridge/ Boston, (617) 864-8415

Haunted Happenings, Salem, (978) 744-0013

Fall Foliage Festival, North Adams, (413) 663-3735

Cranberry Harvest Festival, South Carver, (508) 295-5799

Topsfield Fair, Topsfield Fair Grounds, Topsfield, (978) 887-5000

November

Plimoth Plantation Thanksgiving Celebration, Plymouth, (508) 746-1622
Old Sturbridge Village Thanksgiving Day Celebration, Sturbridge,
   (508) SEE-1830
A Plymouth Thanksgiving, Plymouth, (508) 746-2334

December

Christmas Tree Lighting and Carol Sing, Prudential Center, Boston,
   (617) 236-3744
Boston Common Tree Lighting, Boston Common, (617) 635-4505
Berkshire Museum Festival of Trees, (413) 443-7171
Nantucket Noel and Christmas Stroll, Nantucket Island, (508) 228-1700
First Night Boston (New Year's Eve celebration), Boston, (617) 542-1399

NEW HAMPSHIRE

January

Cross-Country Apres Ski Socials, Jackson Touring Center, (603) 383-9355
Winter Workshops, Appalachian Mountain Club, Gorham, (603) 466-2727
Family Discovery Weekends, Appalachian Mountain Club, Gorham,
   (603) 466-2727

February

Family Frolics Weeks, Cranmore Ski Resort, North Conway,
   (800) SUN-N-SKI
Winter Workshops, Appalachian Mountain Club, Gorham,
   (603) 466-2727
Winter Carnival, King Pine, East Madison, (603) 367-8896 or
   (800) FREE-SKI

March

Spring Carnival, Cranmore, North Conway, (603) 356-5544 or
   (800) SUN-N-SKI
Annual Coca-Cola Rites of Spring, Black Mountain, Jackson,
   (603) 383-4490
March Madness, King Pine, East Madison, (603) 367-8896 or
   (800) FREE-SKI
Telemark Skiing Camp, Appalachian Mountain Club, Gorham,
   (603) 466-2727

April

Annual Easter Egg Hunt at the Mill, Lincoln, (603) 745-2245
Annual Beach Party, Bretton Woods, (603) 278-3300

New Hampshire Spring Arts and Crafts Festival, Manchester, (603) 528-4014

Annual Spring Fest Weekend, Waterville Valley, (603) 236-8311

Festival of Flowers, Sunapee, (603) 763-4914

May

Annual Children's Fun Run, Portsmouth, (603) 436-3853

Annual Spring Fair, Concord, (603) 226-8016

Sheep and Wool Festival, New Boston, (603) 352-4550

Lilac Family Fun Festival, Rochester, (603) 332-8863

New Hampshire's Annual Lilac Time Festival, Lisbon, (603) 828-6336

Annual Chowder Festival, Portsmouth, (603) 436-2848

June

Fields of Lupine Festival, Franconia, (603) 823-5661

Market Square Day, Portsmouth, (603) 431-5388

Annual Snickers Fat Tire Festival, Lincoln, (603) 745-6281

Monadnock Valley Indian Festival & PowWow, (603) 647-5374

Annual Open Water Ski Tournament, Wolfeboro, (603) 569-3132

Colonial Follies, Keene, (603) 352-2033

Trout Tournament, Littleton, (603) 444-6561

International Children's Festival, Somersworth, (603) 692-5869

Mount Washington Road Race, Gorham, (603) 863-2537

Strawberry Moon Festival, Warner, (603) 456-2600

Seacoast Jazz Festival, Portsmouth, (603) 436-2848

Strawberry Festival, Laconia, (603) 524-8813

July

Fourth of July Celebration, Gorham, (603) 466-5538

Independence Day Gala Celebration, Bretton Woods, (603) 278-1000

Fourth of July Celebration, Littleton, (603) 444-6561

Parade and Celebration, Lebanon, (603) 448-5121

Annual Gunstock Crafts Festival, Gilford, (603) 293-4341

Fourth of July Celebration, Jackson, (603) 383-9356

Hebron Fair, Hebron, (603) 744-5584

Hanover Street Fest, Hanover, (603) 643-3115

Annual Native American Cultural Weekend, Twin Mountain, (603) 846-5058

Hillsborough Balloon Fest and Fair, Hillsborough, (603) 464-5858

Canterbury Fair, Canterbury, (603) 783-4349

Annual Lakes Region Open Waterski Tournament, Wolfeboro, (603) 569-6963

Celebration in Hampstead, Hampstead, (603) 329-5789
Stratham Fair, Stratham, (603) 772-4977

August
Annual Hot Air Balloon Rally, Pittsfield, (603) 435-6291
Attitash Bear Peak Blueberry Festival, Bartlett, (603) 374-2368
Annual League of New Hampshire Craftmen's Fair, Newbury,
    (603) 224-3375
Annual NH Waterski Championships, Wolfeboro, (603) 569-6263
Annual Up and Running Festival, North Conway, (603) 356-7031
Old Time Farm Day, Milton, (603) 652-7840
Children's Festival, Hampton Beach, (603) 926-8718
Annual Children's Fair, New Ipswich, (603) 878-1327
Festival of Fireworks, Jaffrey, (603) 532-4549
Annual Professional Lumberjack Festival, Lincoln, (603) 745-8111

September
Hopkinton State Fair, Contoocook, (603) 746-4191
World Championship Mud Bowl, North Conway, (603) 356-3171
Annual Riverfest Celebration, Manchester, (603) 623-2623
Annual Seafood Festival, Hampton Beach, (603) 926-8718
Annual Hew Hampshire Highland Games, Lincoln, (800) 358-SCOT
Francestown Labor Day Festival, Francestown, (603) 588-2540
Lincoln-Woodstock Chamber of Commerce Rubber Ducky Regatta,
    (603) 745-6621
Deerfield Fair, Deerfield, (603) 463-7421
Rochester Fair, Rochester, (603) 332-6585
Annual Frontier Days, Franklin, (603) 934-6909
Annual Fall Festival and Scarecrow Display, North Conway,
    (603) 356-7031
Lancaster Fair, Lancaster, (603) 788-4531

October
Annual Fall Foliage Festival, Barrington, (603) 332-8374
Annual River Market Gathering, Walpole, (603) 563-8801
Harvest Moon Festival, Warner, (603) 456-2600
Annual Bavarian Fall Foliage Festival, Lincoln, (603) 745-8111
Annual Gunstock Oktoberfest, Gilford, (603) 293-4311
Halloween Hauntings, Holderness, (603) 968-7194
Sandwich Fair, Sandwich, (603) 284-7062
Guinness Book of Records Pumpkin Festival, Keene, (603) 358-5344

November

Turkey Trotter at Conway Scenic Railroad, (603) 356-5251 or
(800) 232-5251

December

Santa Claus Express, Conway Scenic Railroad, (603) 356-5251 or
(800) 232-5251
First Night, Portsmouth, (603) 436-2848
Festival of Lights, Enfield, (603) 632-7087

MAINE

January

Annual Carter's Last Stand, Bethel, (207) 539-4848.
Ski Fest, Sunday River Cross Country Ski Center, (207) 824-2410
Snowmobile Snodeo, Rangeley, (207) 864-3368
White White World Week, Sugarloaf/USA, (207) 237-2000

February

Annual U.S. National Toboggan Championships, Camden Snow Bowl,
(207) 236-3438
International Snowmobilers Festival, various towns, (207) 728-7000
Mushers Bowl, West Bridgton, (207) 647-3472
Rangeley Classic Kid's Race, Rangeley, (207) 864-2122

March

Family Fling Week, Sugarloaf/USA, (207) 237-2000
Rangeley Lakes Sled Dog Races, Rangeley, (207) 864-5364
Northern Maine Trade Fair, Fort Fairfield, (207) 472-3802
Maine Maple Sunday, sugarhouses around the state, (207) 287-3491
Norlands Maple Days, Norlands Historical Living Center, (207) 897-4366
Annual Can Am Crown Sled Dog Races, Fort Kent, (800) 733-3563
Eat the Heat Chili Cook-off and Firefighters Race, Newry, (800) 543-2SKI

April

Spring Carnival, Newry, (800) 543-2SKI
Patriot's Day, Ogunquit, (207) 646-2939

May

Moose and Fun Run, Rangeley, (207) 864-5364
Bar Harbor Lobster Race, Bar Harbor, (207) 288-3511

June

Blessing of the Fleet, Kennebunk, (207) 967-0857
Carnival Weekend, Madawaska, (207) 728-7000
Old Port Festival, Portland, (207) 772-6828
Dixfield Summerfest, Dixfield, (207) 562-8151
Boothbay Harbor Windjammer Days, Boothbay Harbor, (207) 633-2353
Acadian Festival, Madawaska, (207) 728-7000
Norlands Annual Heritage Days, Norlands Historical Living Museum,
    Livermore, (207) 897-4366
Castine's Annual Summer Festival, Castine, (207) 326-4884
Ogunquit Strawberry Festival, Ogunquit, (207) 363-2749

July

Bath Heritage Days, Bath, (207) 443-9751
Houlton Agricultural State Fair, Houlton, (207) 532-3250
Boothbay Harbor Old-Fashioned Celebration, Boothbay Harbor,
    (207) 633-6201
Schooner Days, Rockland, (207) 794-3543
Kittery Seaside Festival, Kittery, (207) 439-3800
Annual Maine Potato Blossom Festival, Fort Fairfield, (207) 472-3802
Native American Festival, Bar Harbor, (207) 288-3519
Annual Yarmouth Clam Festival, Yarmouth, (207) 846-3984
Annual Camden Arts and Crafts Show, Camden, (207) 236-4404
Annual Central Maine Egg Festival, Pittsfield, (207) 487-5282
Friendship Sloop Days Annual Homecoming, Rockland, (207) 272-9658
Logging Museum Festival Days, Rangeley, (207) 864-5364
Annual Country Fair, Jefferson, (207) 549-5224
Annual Lobster Festival, Rockland, (207) 596-0376
Annual Maine Festival, Brunswick, (207) 772-9012

August

York Beach PowWow, York Beach, (207) 363-6724
York Days, York, (207) 363-1040
Skowhegan State Fair, Skowhegan, (207) 474-2947
Wilton Blueberry Festival, Wilton, (207) 645-2214
Annual Machias Wild Blueberry Festival, Machias Bay, (207) 255-4402
Rangeley Lakes Blueberry Festival, Rangeley, (207) 864-5364
Houlton Potato Feast Days, Houlton, (207) 532-4216

September

Camden Windjammer Days, Camden, (207) 236-4404
Island Adventure Week, Deer Isle, (207) 348-2508

International Seaplane Fly-in, Greenville, (207) 695-4571
Wooden Boat Sail-In, Brooklin, (800) 807-WIND
Oxford County Fair, Oxford, (207) 743-6723
Franklin County Fair, Farmington, (207) 778-4215
Common Ground County Fair, Windsor, (207) 623-5115
Fryeburg Fair, Fryeburg, (207) 935-3268
End of the Trail Festival, Millinocket, (207) 723-4443

October

Annual Scarecrow Festival, Fort Kent, (800) 733-3563
Chowdah Challenge, Freeport, (207) 865-3985
Apple Festival, Rangeley, (207) 864-5595
Annual Fall Festival, Camden, (207) 236-4404
Annual Fall Foliage Fair, Boothbay, (207) 633-4924
Harvestfest Celebration, York Village, (207) 363-4422

November

Lighting of Nubble Lighthouse, York, (207) 363-1040
Santa Claus Parade, Houlton, (207) 532-4216
Victorian Holiday Horse and Carriage Parade, Portland, (207) 772-6828

December

York Village Festival of Lights, York Village, (207) 363-4422
Christmas-at-Norlands, Norlands Historical Living Museum,
   (207) 897-4366
Harbor Lights Festival, Boothbay Harbor, (207) 633-2353
First Night, Bar Harbor, (207) 288-5103

VERMONT

January

Dairy Farmer's Appreciation Day, Jay Peak Ski Resort, (802) 988-2611 or
   (800) 451-4449
Stowe Winter Carnival, Stowe, (802) 253-7321
Brookfield Ice Harvest, Brookfield, (802) 276-3959
Sleigh Ride Weekends, Billings Farm and Museum, (802) 457-2355

February

New England Regional Sled Dog Championship, Waitsfield,
   (800) 517-4247
Tubbs Family Snowshoe Fest, Stratton, (802) 297-2200
Snowflake Festival, Lyndon and East Burke, (802) 626-5475
Winter Carnival, Brattleboro, (802) 254-4565

March

Ontario Week Celebration, Jay Peak Ski Resort, (802) 988-2611 or
(800) 451-4449

Vermont Maple Syrup Experience, Arlington, Dorset, and Manchester,
(802) 375-2269

April

Bear Mountain Mogul Challenge, Killington Ski Resort, (802) 422-6252

May

Annual Spring Farm Festival, Billings Farm and Museum, (802) 457-2355

Burlington Annual Kids Day, Burlington, (802) 864-0123

June

Lake Champlain Balloon and Craft Festival, Champlain Valley Expo,
(802) 899-2993

Annual Ben & Jerry's One World One Heart Festival, Sugarbush Resort,
(800) BJ-FESTS or (800) 53-SUGAR

Stowe Flower Festival, Stowe, (802) 253-7321

Quechee Hot Air Balloon Festival and Crafts Fair, Quechee,
(802) 295-7900 or (800) 295-5451

Rutland Region Ethnic Festival, Rutland, (802) 747-3950

Ethan Allen Days Festival, Arlington, (802) 375-9491 or (800) 375-2800

July

Grafton Annual Fair Day, Grafton, (802) 843-2230

Cracker Barrel Bazaar, Newbury Common, (802) 866-5518

Summerfest, Newport, (802) 334-6345

Swanton Summer Festival, Swanton Village Green, (802) 868-7200

August

French Heritage Gathering, Hardwick, (802) 434-3190

Castleton Colonial Day, Castleton, (802) 273-2122

Rutland Air Show, North Clarendon, (802) 273-2747

Dummerston Annual Fair, Dummerston, (802) 254-2249

September

Bennington Fair, Bennington, (802) 442-2911

Sugarbush Brewers Festival, Mad River Valley, (802) 583-2381

Woodstock Wool Day, Billings Farm and Museum, (802) 457-2355

Annual Harvest Festival, Shelburne Farms, (802) 985-8686

Festival of Traditional Crafts, Fairbanks Museum and Planetarium,
(802) 748-2372

October

Townshend Pumpkin Festival, Townshend, (802) 365-7793

Northeast Kingdom Annual Fall Foliage Festival, various towns, (802) 748-3678

Burlington Autumn Fair, Burlington, (802) 865-4556

Fall Foliage Fair, Chester on the Green, (802) 875-3267

Annual Vermont Apple Festival and Craft Show, Springfield, (802) 885-2779

Annual Foliage Craft Fair, Brattleboro, (802) 257-7145

November

Annual Holiday Craft Show, Burlington, (802) 223-2636

Festival of Lights, Essex Junction, (802) 878-5545

Festival of Trees, Bennington, (802) 447-3311

December

Prelude to Christmas, Manchester and the Mountains Region, (802) 362-2100

Holly Days Festival, Brattleboro, (802) 254-4565

Woodstock Wassail Celebration, Woodstock, (802) 457-3555

First Night Burlington, Burlington, (802) 863-6005

Annual Blessing of the Sleds, Wilmington, (802) 464-8092

Christmas at Billings Farm, Billings Farm and Museum, (802) 457-2355

Christmas Market, St. Johnsbury, (802) 626-5836

CONNECTICUT

January

Annual Eagle Watches on the Connecticut River, Madison, (203) 245-9056

Annual Eagle Watch Cruises, Essex, (860) 526-4954

February

Kids' Liberty Days, Mystic Seaport, Mystic, (860) 572-5315

May

Lobsterfest, Mystic Seaport, Mystic, (860) 572-5315

Lime Rock Grand Prix (largest race in North America), Lakeville, (800) RACE-LRP

June

Yale-Harvard Regatta on the Thames River, New London, (203) 432-4747

Taste of Hartford, downtown, Hartford, (860) 728-3089

July

Fourth of July Town Celebration, Enfield, (860) 749-1820
Riverfest, Hartford and East Hartford locales, (860) 293-0131
Guilford Handcrafts Exposition, Town Green, Guilford, (203) 453-5947

August

Connecticut Summer Dance Festival, various locales, Watertown,
    (860) 274-0004
SONO Arts Celebration, Washington and South Main Streets, South
    Norwalk, (203) 866-7916
Mark Twain Days, citywide, Hartford, (860) 247-0998
Brooklyn Fair, fairgrounds, Brooklyn, (860) 774-7568.
Woodstock Fair, South Woodstock, (860) 928-3246

September

Norwalk Oyster Festival, Veterans Memorial Park, East Norwalk,
    (203) 838-9444
Durham Fair (Connecticut's largest agricultural fair), Durham,
    (860) 349-9495
Family Nature Day, White Memorial Foundation, Litchfield,
    (860) 567-0857
Goshen Fair, Goshen, (860) 491-3655

October

Scottish Festival, Goshen, (203) 366-0777
Apple Festival, Orange, (203) 795-4514
Berlin Fair, Berlin, (860) 828-0063
Harvest Festival, Guilford, (203) 457-1669
Arrival of the Great Pumpkin, Canterbury, (860) 774-1455

November

Corn Odyssey corn maze; Middletown, (860) 346-3360
Winter Festival, Norwich, (860) 892-1813

December

Christmas at Mystic Seaport (holiday lantern light tours), Mystic,
    (860) 572-5315
Christmas Town Festival, Bethlehem, (203) 266-5557
First Night Hartford (New Year's Eve celebration), Hartford,
    (860) 728-3089
First Night Danbury, Danbury, (203) 792-5095

RHODE ISLAND

January

New Year's Plunges (ocean swims to benefit charities), Wickford Town
  Beach, North Kingstown; Newport Beach, Newport; Mackeral Cove,
  Jamestown

February

Newport Winter Festival (New England's largest winter festival),
  Newport, (401) 849-8048

March

Irish Heritage Month, citywide, Newport, (401) 849-8098

May

Gaspee Days, various locations in Cranston and Warwick, (401) 781-1772
Sail Newport Family Sailing Festival, Fort Adams State Park, Newport,
  (401) 846-1983

June

Great Chowder Cook Off, Newport, (401) 846-1600
Gaspee Days Parade, Warwick, (401) 781-1774
Rhode Island National Guard Open House & Air Show, Quonset State
  Airport, North Kingstown, (401) 886-1423

July

Bristol 4th of July Parade (the nation's oldest), Bristol, (401) 253-0445
Warren Art Festival/Quahog Festival, Warren, (401) 245-4583
Black Ships Festival (Japanese cultural events/kite competition), Newport,
  (401) 846-2720
South County Hot Air Balloon Festival, Kingston, (401) 783-1700

August

Narragansett Heritage Days, Narragansett, (401) 783-7121
Charlestown Chamber Seafood Festival, Ninigret Park, Charlestown,
  (401) 364-4031
Fools' Rules Regatta ("anything that floats" contest), Town Beach,
  Jamestown, (401) 423-1492
International Quahog Festival, Wickford, (401) 885-4118

September

Jonnycake Storytelling Festival, Peace Dale, (401) 789-9301

Rhythm & Roots Festival (family cultural event), Charlestown,
(401) 397-3725

Heritage Festival, State House Lawn, Providence, (401) 277-2678

Taste of Rhode Island, Newport Yachting Center, Newport,
(401) 846-1600

October

Newport Harvest-by-the-Sea Festival, citywide, Newport, (401) 849-8048
or (800) 326-6030

Octoberfest, Pawtucket, (401) 738-2000

Autumnfest, Woonsocket, (401) 762-9072

December

Christmas in Newport, citywide, Newport, (401) 849-6454 or
(800) 326-6030

Festival of Lights, Wickford Village, North Kingstown, (401) 295-5566

First Night Providence (New Year's Eve celebration), Providence,
(401) 521-1166

Opening Night (family festival), Newport, (401) 845-9123

Tourist Information

Massachusetts
Massachusetts Office of Tourism, State Transportation Building, 10 Park Plaza Ste. 4510, Boston, MA 02116, (617) 973-8500; fax, (617) 973-8525; www.massvacation.com

New Hampshire
New Hampshire Office of Travel and Tourism Development, P.O. Box 1856, Concord, NH 03302-1856, (603) 271-2343; fax, (603) 271-2629 or 6784; www.visitnh.gov

Maine
Maine Office of Tourism, 33 Stone St., Augusta, ME 04333, (207) 287-5710; out-of-state, (800) 533-9595; fax, (207) 287-8070; www.mainetourism.com

Vermont
Vermont Department of Tourism and Marketing, 134 State St., Montpelier, VT 05602, (802) 828-3236; fax, (802) 828-3233; (800) 833-9756 (automated fax service); www.vermontchamber.com

Connecticut
Connecticut Office of Tourism, 505 Hudson St., Hartford, CT 06106, (860) 270-8080; (800) CT-BOUND; www.ctbound.org

Rhode Island
Rhode Island Tourism Division, One West Exchange St., Providence, RI 02903, (401) 222-2601; www.VisitRhodeIsland.com

Index by Age Group

Alphabetical Index